Developments in German Politics 4

WITHDRAWN FROM STOCK

Developments titles available from Palgrave

Alistair Cole, Sophie Meunier and Vincent Tiberj (eds)
DEVELOPMENTS IN FRENCH POLITICS 5

Maria Green Cowles and Desmond Dinan (eds)
DEVELOPMENTS IN THE EUROPEAN UNION 2

Richard Heffernan, Philip Cowley and Colin Hay (eds)
DEVELOPMENTS IN BRITISH POLITICS 9

Erik Jones, Paul M. Heywood, Martin Rhodes and Ulrich Sedelmeier (eds)
DEVELOPMENTS IN EUROPEAN POLITICS 2

Stephen Padgett, William E. Paterson and Reimut Zohlnhöfer
DEVELOPMENTS IN GERMAN POLITICS 4*

Gillian Peele, Christopher J. Bailey, Bruce E. Cain and B. Guy Peters (eds)
DEVELOPMENTS IN AMERICAN POLITICS 7

Stephen White, Paul Lewis and Judy Batt (eds)
DEVELOPMENTS IN CENTRAL AND EAST EUROPEAN POLITICS 5*

Stephen White, Richard Sakwa and Henry E. Hale (eds)
DEVELOPMENTS IN RUSSIAN POLITICS 7*

If you have any comments or suggestions regarding the above or other possible *Developments* titles, please write to Steven Kennedy, Publishing Director, Palgrave, Houndmills, Basingstoke RG21 6XS, UK, or e-mail s.kennedy@palgrave.com.

Rights World excluding North America.

Developments in German Politics 4

Edited by
Stephen Padgett
William E. Paterson
and
Reimut Zohlnhöfer

Selection, editorial matter and Introduction © Stephen Padgett, William E. Paterson and Reimut Zohlnhöfer 2014

Individual chapters (in order) © Christian Stecker and Klaus H. Goetz; Charlie Jeffery and Carolyn Rowe; Russell J. Dalton; Margret Hornsteiner and Thomas Saalfeld; Ludger Helms; Dieter Rucht; Anke Hassel; Reimut Zohlnhöfer; William E. Paterson; Andreas Busch; Alister Miskimmon; Martin Seeleib-Kaiser; Stephen Padgett; Simon Green 2014

All rights reserved. No reproduction, copy or transmission of this publication may be made without written permission.

No portion of this publication may be reproduced, copied or transmitted save with written permission or in accordance with the provisions of the Copyright, Designs and Patents Act 1988, or under the terms of any licence permitting limited copying issued by the Copyright Licensing Agency, Saffron House, 6–10 Kirby Street, London EC1N 8TS.

Any person who does any unauthorized act in relation to this publication may be liable to criminal prosecution and civil claims for damages.

The authors have asserted their rights to be identified as the authors of this work in accordance with the Copyright, Designs and Patents Act 1988.

First published 2014 by
PALGRAVE MACMILLAN

Palgrave Macmillan in the UK is an imprint of Macmillan Publishers Limited, registered in England, company number 785998, of Houndmills, Basingstoke, Hampshire RG21 6XS.

Palgrave Macmillan in the US is a division of St Martin's Press LLC, 175 Fifth Avenue, New York, NY 10010.

Palgrave Macmillan is the global academic imprint of the above companies and has companies and representatives throughout the world.

Palgrave® and Macmillan® are registered trademarks in the United States, the United Kingdom, Europe and other countries

ISBN 978-1-137-30163-5   hardback
ISBN 978-1-137-30162-8   paperback

This book is printed on paper suitable for recycling and made from fully managed and sustained forest sources. Logging, pulping and manufacturing processes are expected to conform to the environmental regulations of the country of origin.

A catalogue record for this book is available from the British Library.

A catalog record for this book is available from the Library of Congress.

Typeset by Cambrian Typesetters, Camberley, Surrey, England, UK

Printed in China

This book is dedicated to the memory of Gordon Smith, founding editor of the *Developments in German Politics* series of books

Contents

List of Tables and Figures

Tables

Figures

Preface

Our purpose in *Developments in German Politics 4* is to provide an up-to-date assessment of current trends in the Federal Republic as it confronts the challenges of the twenty-first century. All chapters are entirely new and specifically written for this volume. Its three predecessors have focused on the repercussions for German politics and society of unification and globalization. *Developments in German Politics 3* (2003) focused on the pressures of globalization on the German economic model and the implications of the 'resource crunch' for the country's role in the European Union and the wider world. The problems and perspectives of this book are very different. In particular, most aspects of German politics are now overshadowed by the euro crisis. The 'reform miracle' of the late 2000s has restored the economy to health, and Germany has ridden the global economic crisis without the escalating unemployment and state debt experienced by many of its neighbours. Consequently, the wider world now looks to Germany to harness its economic strength to the task of fixing the euro, and to Angela Merkel to provide the necessary political leadership. But Germany's European vocation has weakened over the last decade or so, and it appears reluctant to assume this hegemonic role. Many of the chapters in this book touch upon this paradox of the 'reluctant hegemon'.

Chapters focus on the latest developments in domestic politics and political economy, and Germany's role in Europe and the world, drawing on current material that is available only in German language sources. At the same time, the discussion is combined with sufficient background information to make the book accessible to readers who do not have a detailed knowledge of German politics. It is designed, therefore, to be used either as a complement to a basic textbook or on its own, depending on course requirements. We also hope that it will be interesting to the general reader and to practitioners in politics and policy.

We wish to thank our contributors – German, American and British – for their willing cooperation, despite all their other commitments, and to our Palgrave Macmillan editors for their understanding and guidance.

STEPHEN PADGETT
WILLIAM E. PATERSON
REIMUT ZOHLNHÖFER

Notes on Contributors

Andreas Busch is Professor of Comparative Politics and Political Economy at the University of Göttingen. He has published widely on comparative public policy, regulatory policy and the German political economy. Currently his research interests focus on internet policy and on parties and Protestantism in the Federal Republic, 1945–90.

Russell J. Dalton is Professor of Political Science at the University of California, Irvine and was the founding director of the Center for the Study of Democracy at that institution. He has received a Fulbright Professorship at the University of Mannheim, a Barbra Streisand Center fellowship, a German Marshall Research Fellowship and a POSCO Fellowship at the East/West Center. He has written or edited over 20 books and 150 research articles that reflect his scholarly interests in comparative political behaviour, political parties, social movements and empirical democratic theory.

Klaus H. Goetz holds the Chair in Political Systems and European Integration at the Department of Political Science, University of Munich. He previously taught at the London School of Economics and the University of Potsdam. His recent research has focused on time rules, time budgets and time horizons in democratic politics. He is currently working on a research project, funded by the German Research Foundation, that investigates the effects of staggered membership renewal in second chambers, including the German *Bundesrat*. He has been co-editor of *West European Politics* since 2000.

Simon Green is Professor of Politics, Executive Dean of the School of Languages and Social Sciences and Co-Director of the Aston Centre for Europe at Aston University. He has written widely on the politics of migration in Germany, as well as more recently on the CDU. He is the author, together with Dan Hough and Alister Miskimmon, of *The Politics of the New Germany* (Routledge).

Anke Hassel is Professor of Public Policy at the Hertie School of Governance and member of the faculty of the Berlin Graduate School for Transnational Studies. Previously she was at the Max Planck Institute for the Study of Societies in Cologne, and the Jacobs

University, Bremen. She was also Senior Visiting Fellow at the European Institute of the London School of Economics, and a visiting scholar at the Social Science Research Center, Berlin and King's College, Cambridge, UK. In 2003/04, she worked for the Planning Department of the Federal Ministry of Economics and Labour (BMWA). She received Fellowships from the Alexander von Humboldt Stiftung, Volkswagen Stiftung, Friedrich Ebert Stiftung and Hans Böckler Stiftung. In 2012/13 she served as an Expert Member of the Enquete Commission of the German Federal Parliament on 'Growth, Wealth, Quality of Life'. Her research interest focuses on the interplay between modern business and social systems including the institutional foundations of business systems, labour rights and corporate social responsibility. She has written extensively about the transformation of the German political economy in a comparative perspective and the role of labour market institutions in the eurozone.

Ludger Helms is Professor of Political Science and Chair of Comparative Politics at the University of Innsbruck, Austria. He has previously held affiliations at the University of Heidelberg and Humboldt University, and visiting affiliations at, inter alia, Harvard, Berkeley and the London School of Economics. He has published widely in the fields of German and comparative politics and specializes in comparative political institutions, political leadership and democratic governance. He is an editor of the journal *Government and Opposition* and founding editor of the book series *Palgrave Studies in Political Leadership*.

Margret Hornsteiner is Lecturer in Political Science at the University of Bamberg. Her research focuses on decision-making within political parties. Her regional foci are Germany and the Nordic democracies. In particular, she works on the gestation of election manifestos in Germany and the role of intra-party policy conflicts in electoral competition and coalition governance.

Charlie Jeffery is Professor of Politics and Vice Principal for Public Policy at the University of Edinburgh. He is currently working with Carolyn Rowe on a project supported by the German Academic Exchange Service on 'New Perspectives on German Federalism'.

Alister Miskimmon is head of the Department of Politics and International Relations at Royal Holloway, University of London where he co-directs the Centre for European Politics. Alister is the author of a number of books including (with Ben O'Loughlin and Laura Roselle) *Forging the World: Strategic Narratives and International Relations*

(Michigan University Press, forthcoming) and *Strategic Narratives: Communication Power and the New World Order* (Routledge, 2013) Alister has also published the following in the field of German politics: (with Simon Green and Dan Hough) *The Politics of the New Germany* (Routledge, 2012); (with William E. Paterson and James Sloam) *Germany's Gathering Crisis: Germany and the Grand Coalition since 2005* (Palgrave Macmillan, 2013) and *Germany and the Common Foreign and Security Policy of the European Union* (Palgrave Macmillan). Alister's main research interests are German foreign policy and strategic narrative in International Relations.

Stephen Padgett was Professor of Politics at the University of Strathclyde. Previously he held the Chair in Politics at the University of Liverpool and was Reader in Politics at the University of Essex. He has published widely on political parties and public policy in Germany and Europe. His most recent work on European energy policy appeared in the *Journal of Common Market Studies* (2011) and the *Journal of Public Policy* (2012). He was a co-editor of *German Politics* during 1992–2012.

William E. Paterson is Honorary Professor of German and European Politics at Aston University. Previously he held chairs at Warwick, Edinburgh and Birmingham. Co-founder of the journal *German Politics*, he was also co-editor of the *Journal of Common Market Studies*. Shortly after German Unity he delivered the eulogies for Willy Brandt and Helmut Kohl at their honorary doctoral ceremonies at Warwick and Edinburgh respectively. He has authored, co-authored or co-edited 26 books and published over 160 articles. Professor Paterson is very active in German–UK relations.

Carolyn Rowe is Senior Lecturer in Politics at the Aston Centre for Europe, Aston University. Her research interests lie in the fields of European territorial politics, German politics and comparative federalism. She is the author of *Regional Representations in the EU: Between Diplomacy and Interest Mediation* (Palgrave Macmillan, 2011).

Dieter Rucht was Professor of Sociology at the Free University of Berlin and co-director of the research group Civil Society, Citizenship and Political Mobilization in Europe at the Social Science Research Center, Berlin. His research includes political participation, social movements, political protest and public discourse. Recent books include *The World Says No to War: Demonstrations against the War on Iraq* (University of Minnesota Press, 2010), *Meeting Democracy: Power and Deliberation in Global Justice Movements* (Cambridge University Press, 2013) and *Die*

Sozialen Bewegungen in Deutschland seit 1945: Ein Handbuch (Campus, 2008).

Thomas Saalfeld is Professor of Political Science at the University of Bamberg and Convenor of the Bamberg Graduate School of Social Sciences (BAGSS). His main research interests are in the field of comparative legislative studies with a particular focus on representation, legislative parties and cabinet stability. He is Managing Academic Editor of *German Politics*, the leading academic journal in this field in the English language. His recent publications include *The Oxford Handbook of Legislative Studies* (Oxford University Press 2014, joint editor with Shane Martin and Kaare Strøm) and *The Political Representation of Immigrants and Minorities* (Routledge 2011, joint editor with Karen Bird and Andreas M. Wüst). He has published articles in the *European Journal of Political Research*, *German Politics*, *International Studies Quarterly*, *The Journal of Legislative Studies*, *Parliamentary Affairs*, *Rivista Italiana di Scienza Politica* and *West European Politics*.

Martin Seeleib-Kaiser is Barnett Professor of Comparative Social Policy and Politics, and Head of the Department of Social Policy and Intervention at the Oxford Institute of Social Policy and a Professorial Fellow at St Cross College, University of Oxford. Before joining Oxford he held appointments at the Universities of Bremen and Bielefeld as well as Duke University and was a visiting scholar/guest professor at George Washington University, Shizuoka University, Japan and Aalborg University, Denmark. His research focuses on comparative welfare state analysis, and the relationship between globalization and welfare systems. He has published widely, including articles in the *American Sociological Review*, the *British Journal of Industrial Relations*, *Comparative Political Studies*, *German Politics*, the *Journal of European Social Policy*, *Social Policy and Administration*, *Social Politics* and *West European Politics*.

Christian Stecker is a researcher and lecturer at the Department of Political Science, University of Munich. His research on German politics includes studies on party unity, minority governments and the German *Bundesrat* published in *Party Politics*, the *Journal of Legislative Studies, German Politics* and *Zeitschrift für Parlamentsfragen*.

Reimut Zohlnhöfer is Professor of Political Science at the University of Heidelberg, Germany. Previously he was Professor of Comparative

Public Policy at Otto-Friedrich-University, Bamberg, and John F. Kennedy Memorial Fellow at the Center for European Studies, Harvard University. He has published in many leading political science journals including *Comparative Political Studies*, *German Politics*, *Governance*, the *Journal of European Public Policy*, the *Journal of European Social Policy*, the *Journal of Public Policy*, *Social Policy and Administration* and *West European Politics*. He is also the editor of numerous volumes and special issues, most recently 'The Validity Problem in Measuring Welfare State Generosity' in the *Journal of European Public Policy* (2013) with Georg Wenzelburger and Frieder Wolf.

List of Abbreviations

ACTA	Anti-Counterfeiting Trade Agreement
AfD	Alternative für Deutschland (Alternative for Germany)
BMU	Federal Ministry for the Environment, Nature Conservation and Nuclear Safety
BMWi	Federal Ministry of Economics and Technology
BRICS	Brazil, Russia, India, China and South Africa
CAP	Common Agricultural Policy
CDU	Christlich Demokratische Union (Christian Democratic Union)
CFSP	Common Foreign and Security Policy
CMEs	coordinated market economies
CSDP	Common Security and Defence Policy
CSU	Christlich–Soziale Union (Christian Social Union)
ECB	European Central Bank
ECJ	European Court of Justice
EFSF	European Financial Stability Facility
EMS	European Monetary System
EMU	Economic and Monetary Union
ERM	Exchange Rate Mechanism
ESCB	European System of Central Banks
ESDP	European Security and Defence Policy
ESM	European Stability Mechanism
ETS	Emissions Trading Scheme
EU	European Union
FAZ	Frankfurter Allgemeine Zeitung
FCC	Federal Constitutional Court
FDP	Freie Demokratische Partei (Free Democratic Party)
FT	*Financial Times*
FW	Independent Voters
GHG	greenhouse gas
GJMs	global justice movements
ISAF	International Security Assistance Force
LMEs	liberal market economies
NATO	North Atlantic Treaty Organization
NPD	Nationaldemokratische Partei Deutschlands (National Democratic Party of Germany)
NSMs	new social movements

NSU	Nationalsozialistischer Untergrund (National Socialist Underground)
OAF	Operation Allied Force
OECD	Organisation for Economic Co-operation and Development
OMT	Outright Monetary Transactions
PDS	Partei des Demokratischen Sozialismus (Party of Democratic Socialism)
RuSt AG	Reichs und Staatsangehörigkeitsgesetz (Imperial Citizenship Law)
SED	Socialist Unity Party
SPD	Sozialdemokratische Partei Deutschlands (Social Democratic Party of Germany
St AG	Staatsangehörigkeitsgesetz (Citizenship Law)
VET	Vocational Training System
VOC	Varieties of Capitalism
TFR	Total Fertility Rate
WASG	Wahlalternative Arbeit und Soziale Gerechtigkeit (Electoral Alternative for Labour and Social Justice)

Glossary

Alternative für Deutschland	Alternative for Germany (AfD)
Anwerbestopp	migration ban after oil shock
Ausländergesetz	Foreigner's Law
Bundesrat	Federal Council
Bundestag	Federal Parliament
Bundestagswahl	Election to German Parliament
Bundeswehr	German armed forces
Einbürgerungsrichtlinien	naturalization guidelines
Energiewende	energy transformation
Forschungsgruppe Wahlen	Research institute for election analysis
Grundgesetz	Basic Law
Grünen, Die	The Greens
Integrationsgipfel	integration summit
Länderfinanzausgleich	Fiscal Equalization System
Linke, Die	Left Party
Migrationshintergrund	migrant background
Modell Deutschland	Model Germany
Nationaler Integrationsplan	national action plan
Piratenpartei	Pirates Party
Politikverflechtung	interlocked decision-making
Reformstau	reform blockage
Reichsverfassung	Imperial Constitution
Schuldenbremse	debt brake
Spätaussiedler	late resettlers
Volksparteien	people's parties
Waldsterben	forest death
Wutbürger	angry citizen
Zukunftsdialog	future dialogue
Zuwanderungsgesetz	Immigration Law

Introduction

STEPHEN PADGETT, WILLIAM E. PATERSON AND
REIMUT ZOHLNHÖFER

This new fourth edition of *Developments in German Politics* coincides
with a critical juncture in the European economy and politics in which
Germany occupies centre stage. The eurozone crisis of 2010–11 was
stabilized by the pledge of the European Central Bank to do 'whatever it
takes' to save the euro and its actions in buying distressed eurozone
members' sovereign bonds. Many of the underlying problems, however,
remain unresolved. Growth in the southern periphery countries remains
low; public and private debt is still too high; and the disparity in competitiveness between north and south is undiminished. The eurozone is thus
at a crossroads. The problems are complex, and there are no straightforward solutions, but most are agreed that without decisive action the eurozone faces an uncertain future of muddling through from crisis to crisis as
distressed economies struggle with debt.

Germany's export-led economy benefits greatly from the euro, and
'fixing' the eurozone is its central foreign policy concern. One approach
would be to deepen financial integration between eurozone countries,
perhaps leading ultimately to a banking and fiscal union. The dilemma for
Germany is that sharing responsibility for eurozone banks and fiscal policies entails sharing the attendant risks. As Europe's largest and strongest
economy, it could find itself underwriting the insolvent banks and sovereign debt of its eurozone partners. For Germany, a European *fiscal* union
could mean a *transfer* union in which it was permanently responsible for
subsidizing the poorer eurozone periphery. The terms of European banking and fiscal policy integration, and its institutional architecture, are
therefore subject to deep differences between Germany and its partners,
and are becoming increasingly evident in domestic political discourse.

Differences of perspective over the management of the euro crisis and
the future of the euro have created political tensions across the eurozone
and in Germany. The southern periphery countries suffer from 'austerity
fatigue', engendering anti-European sentiment and political instability
that put pressure on beleaguered governments struggling to fulfil the
terms of bailouts. For its part, Germany suffers from an incipient 'bailout
fatigue'. Under Chancellor Angela Merkel's Christian–Liberal coalition

(2009–13) cross-party and public support for German participation in bailouts for Greece, Portugal and Spain was conditional on their being accompanied with tough austerity packages. In 2013 this consensus was breached by a new party, the *Alternative für Deutschland* (Alternative for Germany), which stood for respect of the 'no bailouts' clause in the European Union (EU) treaty and for new flexibility for countries to leave the euro. And whilst Merkel's 2013 election campaign emphasized solidarity with poorer EU partners, and Germany's economic interest in stabilizing the euro, it also defined a limit – in the form of 'no eurobonds' – beyond which she would not go in the interests of European financial integration. So the expectation of Germany's EU partners that a new Merkel government would be more amenable to the consolidation of the euro is unlikely to be fully realized. The new coalition partner, the SPD, basically accepted the position of the previous government on the eurozone.

From sick man of Europe to economic powerhouse

The German political economy is inextricably linked with the crisis of the euro. As Andreas Busch shows in Chapter 10, the current account deficits that lie at the heart of the sovereign debt crisis in the eurozone periphery countries has been fuelled in large part by the competitiveness of the German export economy. This crisis in turn will have important consequences not only for Germany's role in Europe but also for German economic policy. As Europe's largest and strongest economy Germany will have to carry the bulk of any financial burden of any bailouts that become necessary, and this will put severe strain on government finances.

This situation could hardly have been anticipated in 2003, when Germany languished as the 'sick man of Europe'. Its economic woes were reflected on almost every relevant indicator. Unemployment remained stubbornly high, growth was low and the budget deficit exceeded the limit of 3 per cent of GDP set by the EU's Stability and Growth Pact in four consecutive years between 2002 and 2005. Many observers doubted Germany's ability to recover its economic health. Two reasons were given for this pessimism. First, the German political system seemed unable to produce significant reform. The governing parties at the time, particularly the Social Democratic Party (SPD), were torn between rival factions that disagreed on most aspects of economic and social policy. What is more, electoral competition deterred parties from the kind of unpopular reforms that experts deemed necessary to revive the German economy.

And the *Bundesrat* (second chamber of parliament) was under the control of the opposition, giving it a veto over reforms. Given this state of affairs, many observers believed it to be extremely unlikely that major reforms would be forthcoming (König et al., 2003: 105).

Second, the German variety of 'organized capitalism' with its focus on centralized wage bargaining, patient capital (i.e. long-term financing of businesses via house banks) and cooperative interfirm relations was seen as doomed. The very foundation upon which the post-war German economic model rested was thus in danger. Wolfgang Streeck (2009a: 96) in particular argued that German capitalism was in a process of 'disorganization', understood as 'a decline in centralized control and authoritative coordination in favor of dispersed competition and spontaneous ... individualized decisions'. Streeck and Hassel (2003) spoke about 'the crumbling pillars of social partnership'; shareholder value gained in importance as capital became less patient; ties between companies loosened; and trade unions and employer organizations weakened. Thus, the viability of the German model was questioned by many authors (see Busch, 2005).

Yet, ten years later, things seem to have changed fundamentally. Germany has adopted a number of substantial reforms in all relevant areas of economic and social policy, as Reimut Zohlnhöfer and Martin Seeleib-Kaiser show in Chapters 8 and 12. Corporate tax rates have been reduced quite substantially, ending (for the time being) a 20-year-long debate. Although the business tax rate is still not below the EU average, it is at least not far above average any more, as it had been for a very long time. Pensions have been reduced and the pension age increased. Moreover, family policy has been reformed extensively with an earnings-related benefit for parents staying at home to take care of infants during the first year after birth, and a legal right for a child's place in day care from age one. These reforms aim at an increase of labour force participation of young mothers in particular and depart very clearly from the traditional German male-breadwinner/female-caregiver model. The comprehensive Hartz reforms of the labour market head in a similar direction. By substantially reducing benefits for the long-term employed, tightening the conditions under which unemployed persons can reject a job offer, and making low-wage employment more attractive the government has tried to boost labour market participation. Again this is a departure from the traditional path of coping with unemployment in Germany via early retirement and disincentives for female labour market participation. Finally, the German government responded to the financial crisis that started in 2007 in an unprecedented manner, as it adopted bank rescue measures and stimulus packages of volumes previously unheard of in the Federal Republic.

These reforms seem to have worked. Observers now refer to the German 'employment miracle' (OECD, 2012a: 10; Reisenbichler and Morgan, 2012). The German economy and the labour market in particular have weathered the multiple crises since 2007 remarkably well. Unemployment is lower and employment higher in 2013 than they were before the crisis. Thus, Germany has outperformed many of its peers in the last half-decade.

Explaining the reform miracle

How can this outcome be explained in the light of the allegedly institutionally induced reform gridlock and the disorganization of German capitalism? Institutional reform, more precisely the reform of federalism, could provide one answer to this question. As Charlie Jeffery and Carolyn Rowe discuss in much more detail in Chapter 2, the *Bundestag* and *Bundesrat* set up a commission in 2003 to work out proposals for a reform of the federal system. The main aim of this first reform commission was to reduce joint decision-making. This meant that on the one hand the *Länder* were to be given more competences for which they would be responsible on their own, while on the other hand the number of bills for which approval of the *Bundesrat* was necessary was to be reduced. After intricate negotiations the reform which turned out to be the most extensive reform of the federal constitution to date was finally adopted in 2006 (a second part dealing with financial issues was adopted in 2009).

Although the reform of federalism did reduce the number of bills needing *Bundesrat* approval, there are two reasons why it cannot explain economic policy and welfare reforms. First, most of these reforms, e.g. the Hartz labour market reforms, were adopted before the reform of federalism had come into effect. So for them, the old rules applied. Second, *Bundesrat* approval remained necessary for most key decisions in the area of economic policy and the welfare state. For example, almost two out of three of the most important economic and social policy reforms that were adopted under the 2005–09 grand coalition of the Christian Democratic Union/Christian Social Union (CDU/CSU) and the Social Democratic Party (SPD) needed the approval of the *Bundesrat* (Zohlnhöfer, 2011). Therefore, the reform of federalism can certainly not solve the puzzle of the German 'reform miracle' between 2003 and 2007.

So why were comprehensive reforms possible? Why did the constellation of a government led by the Social Democrats and a second chamber controlled by the bourgeois opposition not lead to deadlock as predicted? In Chapters 8 and 12, Zohlnhöfer and Seeleib-Kaiser point to two interrelated factors. First, the problems in the economy and the welfare state were so serious that it was impossible for policy-makers to deny or ignore them. Second, the two main parties' perceptions about the reasons for the dismal economic performance began to converge at the beginning of the new decade. The CDU and the liberal Free Democratic Party (FDP) had already argued in the mid-1990s that Germany's high statutory tax rates and the ever-growing burden of the welfare state impaired competitiveness. While still in government at the end of the 1990s, the CDU/CSU and FDP therefore tried to reform (business) tax and all relevant social security programmes. The SPD, however, did not (yet) agree with this diagnosis. Consequently they blocked those reforms that needed the approval of the Bundesrat, and revoked the rest of the reforms after the change of government in 1998. Only after the failure of their attempts to reduce unemployment through demand management (Zohlnhöfer, 2004) did Chancellor Schröder eventually initiate the Hartz labour market reforms. Given their programmatic convergence it was no surprise that the grand coalition of CDU/CSU and SPD (2005–09) essentially continued on that reform path.

Withstanding the global economic crisis

When the financial crisis hit Germany in the autumn of 2008, these two parties also managed to respond reasonably fast to what turned out to be the deepest recession in the history of the Federal Republic. Although the bank rescue packages and stimulus programmes were far from coherent – reflecting at least in part some remaining partisan differences – Germany recovered remarkably fast from the recession. The increase in the country's debt between 2007 and 2012 remained far below the OECD average. At the same time, unemployment actually fell from 8.7 per cent in 2007 to 6.0 per cent in 2011 – in sharp contrast to countries like the UK or the USA where there was a steep rise in joblessness.

This impressive employment performance has spurred talk about a German miracle. It's a miracle, however, that can be explained. The labour market reforms of the early 2000s as well as emergency responses to the great recession have clearly played their part in mitigating the employment effects of the crisis. But, as Anke Hassel shows in Chapter 7, firm-level cooperation was also important. Indeed, some would argue that this is the crucial factor in explaining recent German employment performance. Rather than undermining the viability of the German model, the process of disorganization has enabled firms to make use of 'internal flexibility instruments' (Reisenbichler and Morgan, 2012: 559). These instruments boosted firms' competitiveness prior to the crisis and allowed them to hoard labour rather than letting employees go when the crisis hit. Hoarding labour was a rational thing to do in the German variety of capitalism since it spared them the need to look for highly skilled workers once the crisis was over. Thus, as Hassel argues, the crisis has shown that the liberalization and disorganization of the German economy are shaped by the characteristics of the old German model, which is thus unlikely to converge on an Anglo-Saxon model of capitalism anytime soon.

Nonetheless, although labour market reforms may have boosted German employment performance, they have also caused new problems which need to be addressed. First, as Seeleib-Kaiser shows in Chapter 12, liberalizing reforms have led to a substantial increase of 'atypical' and low-paid work and consequently to a rise in inequality and poverty in Germany over the past 15 years – although poverty is still way below American levels. The grand coalition government which came to power after the 2013 election has agreed to introduce a general minimum wage and to take action to fight the poverty of certain groups, in particular pensioners. Second, the problem of demographic change needs to be addressed in the near future. The increase in the statutory pension age will be phased in until 2029 but is very likely not to be sufficient. Similarly, the remarkable changes in family policy have not (yet) resulted in increasing fertility rates. Although net immigration helps mitigate the situation it is likely that any future government will have to deal with the diverse problems of demographic change. If Germany is burdened with supporting the distressed countries of the eurozone, it will make it more difficult to solve the newly arising problems of inequality and to invest in infrastructure and education as the two most important assets of Germany's political economy.

The political context

The capacity of political parties and their leaders to meet the challenges of reforming the economy, regaining international competitiveness, containing the costs of the welfare state and managing the crisis in the eurozone depends in large part on the political context. In many ways the political landscape is becoming more difficult for policy-makers. As Russell Dalton shows in Chapter 3, the weakening of traditional ties between citizens and parties means that voting behaviour continues to become more fluid and volatile. This is reflected in an increasingly fragmented party system, with a decline in the two large catch-all parties and an increase in support for smaller parties mobilizing around particular issues. Political leaders are thus less able to shape the political agenda and have to be more attentive to public opinion on issues like the environment, nuclear power, social justice and European integration. Yet despite these trends, government has remained remarkably stable, due largely to the cartel-like behaviour of the main political parties, an elite consensus on the main lines of policy, and the leadership skills of Chancellor Merkel in reconciling elite consensus with public opinion.

Partisan de-alignment and electoral volatility

'Partisan de-alignment' refers to a weakening of the ties between political parties and their voters. Traditionally, social class and religion created enduring alliances between social milieu and parties that shared their political vision. Social status was thus central to political identity and electoral choice, with the Ruhr steelworker voting predominantly for the SPD and the middle-class Catholic supporting the CDU/CSU. Widespread affluence and social security, however, and the disengagement of large sections of society from church activity, has eroded these ties. Whilst religious activity remains a guide to political loyalty, fewer voters are church-going. And although social class is still a factor in electoral choice, class boundaries are less clearly defined, and there are fewer manual workers in the old industrial sectors. Consequently, more and more voters lack the sense of social group identity which structures electoral choice.

The decline of old electoral alignments is compounded by the emergence of new cultural conflicts surrounding globalization and cross-border migration. Global economic competition creates winners (skilled professionals able to compete in international markets) and losers (the unskilled in sectors that are vulnerable to competition). Whilst the former embrace liberal cosmopolitan values, the latter retain a strong sense of national identity, which shapes their attitudes towards issues like immigration and multiculturalism. Most mainstream party elites tend towards cosmopolitanism, which alienates more traditionally oriented voters.

The erosion of long-term party preferences engendered by social group belonging or individual party attachment has changed the basis of electoral choice. Although some people still vote for the same party at election after election, an increasing number of them now approach each election with an open mind. Choice depends on voters' perceptions of party competence in confronting the issues they regard as important, or their perceptions about chancellor candidates. Increasingly, these judgements are made during the election campaign. The last three elections (2005, 2009 and 2013) have seen a steady increase in the percentage of 'late deciders', some leaving it as late as the actual election day. There has also been an increase in the percentage of people switching votes between parties from one election to the next. In 2009 around 25 per cent of voters reported switching party. Moreover, an increasing percentage of people now split their vote between parties (Germans have two votes: one for a constituency candidate and one for a party list). These tendencies point towards a more sophisticated, informed electorate exercising choice rather than following habit.

Political protest and the 'angry citizen'

The weakening of links between voters and parties is reflected in the rise in the politics of protest, articulated outside the party arena through protest movements. As Dieter Rucht shows in Chapter 6, Germany is a very active 'movement society' with a high volume of protest mobilization (Berlin alone has around 4,000 protest events annually). Protest movements fill gaps in the party system, mobilizing the *Wutbürger* ('angry citizen') who demands a say on issue positions that are not represented by the political parties. Rucht identifies four types of protest. First, there are new social movements – left liberal groups promoting human rights; citizen participation; peace and disarmament; women's, gay and lesbian rights; environmental protection; and opposition to nuclear energy. A second type of social protest focuses on labour, welfare and social security. Traditionally mobilized by trade unions, this type of protest now embraces a wider range of activists in welfare organizations and the global justice movement, targeting welfare cuts, minimum wages, working conditions and unemployment. A third set of protest movements is located on the radical right, motivated by xenophobia and opposition to immigration. Fourth, there is a disparate category of ad hoc or 'pop-up' groups that form around specific issues, such as airport runway extensions (Frankfurt, Munich and Berlin) and the construction of a massive new railway station complex in Stuttgart.

Some of these protest movements have entered the party system, challenging the dominance of the old established parties. The Greens are a classic example of the 'challenger party', emerging from the peace and environmental movements in the 1980s, becoming established in the party system and entering government between 1998 and 2005. More recently, the *Linke* (Left Party) emerged in 2007 out of a merger between the Party of Democratic Socialism (PDS) – until then confined to eastern Germany – and a west German movement of opposition to welfare cuts and labour market reform. The *Piratenpartei* (Pirate Party) sprang from the movement for internet freedom and digital privacy in 2009. And in

2013, the *Alternative für Deutschland* (Alternative for Germany) was formed as a reaction against German participation in bailouts for distressed eurozone countries. Movements such as these that capture the attention of the media and have the potential to affect voting behaviour can put political leaders on the defensive. A dramatic example of this was Chancellor Merkel's U-turn over nuclear energy in 2012, reversing her previous decision to prolong the life of Germany's nuclear power plants in the face of massive protests fuelled by the Fukushima catastrophe.

Party system fragmentation

As a consequence of partisan de-alignment and the rise of protest parties, the German electorate – once the model of stability – is now subject to increasing volatility. In the 1980s and 1990s the party system consisted of two relatively stable blocs: first, the CDU and its Bavarian sister party the CSU along with the FDP on the Right; second, the SPD and the Greens on the Left. Within these blocs the two large *Volksparteien* (people's parties) – the CDU/CSU and SPD – were heavily dominant, acting as the pillars of the system. Despite a long-term decline from their high point in the 1970s, the *Volksparteien* together still accounted for around 75 per cent of the vote in the 1990s and early 2000s. Their decline has accelerated sharply since then, however, reaching an all-time low of 56 per cent in 2009 before recovering to 67 per cent in 2013.

Volkspartei decline has been notably asymmetrical. Whilst the CDU/CSU share of the vote has declined steadily over the last three decades, it retained about 35 per cent of the vote between 1998 and 2009. Its recovery to 41.5 per cent in 2013 shows that *Volkspartei* decline is not an immutable law, and that given favourable circumstances – a flourishing economy and a popular leader – a party can buck the trend. The SPD, on the other hand, has been unable to recover from the electoral haemorrhage it suffered in 2009, and it is now confined to an electoral ghetto at around 25 per cent. Its decline can be seen as the legacy of Chancellor Schröder's programme of welfare cuts and labour market reform in the early 2000s, the main losers from which were the party's core electorate of blue-collar workers. Subsequent attempts by the SPD to disassociate itself from Schröder's legacy have lacked credibility.

The corollary of this pattern of *Volkspartei* decline is the rise of small parties, and in particular the rise in support for 'outsider' parties like the Left Party, the Pirate Party and the Alternative for Germany. Of these, only the former has succeeded in attaining the 5 per cent of the vote required to enter the *Bundestag* (parliament), though this is sufficient to exert a debilitating effect on coalition-building, since it 'robs' the SPD and

Greens of seats required to build a coalition of the Left. And whilst the Alternative for Germany narrowly failed to win seats in the *Bundestag* in 2013, its votes were decisive in squeezing the FDP below 5 per cent, thereby depriving the centre right of a majority. In short, the decline of the *Volksparteien* along with increased support for small outsider parties has led to a weakening of the two-bloc party system. Two of the last three elections have seen both the centre-right and centre-left blocs falling short of a government majority, resulting in grand coalitions between the CDU/CSU and the SPD.

Yet despite the decline of the main political parties, and party system fragmentation, German government has remained relatively stable, compared to other European countries. In the last three decades, only one government (that of 2002–05) has ended prematurely. Moreover, the Grand Coalition of 2005–09 worked smoothly and effectively, and a majority of Germans (52 per cent) in 2013 saw a grand coalition as their preferred government outcome. Margret Hornsteiner and Thomas Saalfeld in Chapter 4 account for this paradox with the concept of a 'party cartel'. On critical political issues the mainstream parties tacitly agree not to disagree, and thus to maintain a consensus that supports governments formed across the left–right blocs.

Political leadership

Another explanation for government stability in the face of party system fragmentation may be found in the quality of political leadership. As Ludger Helms notes in Chapter 5, in turbulent times democratic regimes are in desperate need of leadership. Angela Merkel's leadership style does not conform to the usual model of a strong leader with charisma and a visionary policy agenda. On the other hand, it may be argued that her rather 'unheroic' policy style is well adapted to dealing with complex and difficult issues in a world of uncertainty. Eschewing the certainties of ideological policy agendas, she favours a pragmatic approach to policy-making, weighing all sides of an issue before coming to a decision. She is also adept at compromise, which is an asset in grand coalition governments. These qualities – along with her instinct for keeping in touch with public opinion – have enabled her to establish a personal popularity extending well beyond her own party. In the election of 2013, 60 per cent of Germans preferred her as chancellor over her SPD rival. Merkel's policy style is criticized by some as reactive and hesitant, citing her tardiness in committing Germany to measures to stabilize the euro. Her cautious incremental approach, however, may be the best way to persuade reluctant Germans to assume the burdens of eurozone hegemony.

Germany's shrinking European vocation

Germany's default preference of invariably adopting a 'more European' posture has been a defining feature of its European policy since the early days of the Federal Republic. This preference, normally expressed in a close alliance with France, provided the spine of European integration. Some doubts were expressed that a policy formed in a divided Germany would survive German unity and the regaining of full sovereignty in 1990. These doubts appeared to be confounded by the deepening of European integration under the leadership of Helmut Kohl and François Mitterrand in the early 1990s. In more recent years, as William Paterson shows in Chapter 9, a contradictory pattern has emerged in which Germany's European vocation has weakened just at the point when the country has become increasingly central to European integration.

The first cracks in Germany's European vision appeared at its apogee, the conclusion of the Maastricht Treaty providing for Economic and Monetary Union in 1992. Up until then German European policy had been supported by a positive public opinion. The Maastricht Treaty marked a turning point, since when public opinion has become increasingly less enthusiastic. German unity provides part of the explanation. East German citizens had not shared in the pro-European socialization of their West German counterparts. The EU enjoyed a short period of support after unity, though this weakened when the East Germans found that the EU did not provide the bulwark against post-unity adaptation they had mistakenly expected.

German elite support for European integration held up much better than mass opinion, with only The Left (Die Linke) adopting a hostile line. By the time of the 2009 federal election the European vision had visibly shrunk and occupied a much smaller place in political discourse. Chancellors of a post-war generation like Gerhard Schröder and Angela Merkel lack the emotional connection to European integration of their predecessors. In Chancellor Merkel's case this greater distance to the EU also reflects her upbringing in the German Democratic Republic.

German support for European integration was for long characterized by a 'virtuous circle' in which this policy seemed to have no downside. Support for integration allowed Germany access to export markets around which it built its amazingly successful political economy. It provided the context in which all its neighbours supported German Unity after the Wall fell in 1989. The shaming nature of the Third Reich and German division had left post-war West Germany with a damaged identity. European integration helped furnish a substitute identity which did much to integrate the Federal Republic both internally and externally, a result that could not have been achieved by economic progress alone.

Goetz wrote of support for multilateral integration having entered the German elites' genetic code (Goetz, 1996: 24). These positive results were, in the view of Peter Katzenstein, greatly facilitated by the congruence of German and European institutions. It was this familiarity which he thought would preserve the commitment of German elites to European integration. In a sense attachment to German institutions was simultaneously an attachment to European institutions.

This 'virtuous circle' has been under increasing strain in recent years, a process that began with the gradual weakening of mass support. The grand EU enlargement of 2004 brought in a large number of smaller and poorer members which placed a strain on the practice of side payments that Germany had hitherto employed to secure support for its European policy goals. Traditionally, Germany's European vision was carried out in tandem with France but that country's weakening economic power has severely constrained the traction of this alliance.

Germany and the eurozone crisis

The tipping point came with the eurozone crisis. This crisis challenged the view that European integration was a permanent 'win–win' for the Federal Republic by opening up the prospect of potentially huge losses. This prospect appalled German mass opinion and forced elites to think much more deeply about their European vision, which was in danger of becoming drained of content and carried out as mere lip service. Whilst the main political parties remained largely pro-European, Germany's very important para-public institutions – the Federal Constitutional Court and the *Bundesbank* – were increasingly seen as challenging the EU level, as Busch agues in Chapter 10. They acted as self-confident representatives of Europe's largest and most successful state, a far cry from the new institutions of the pre-sovereign Federal Republic of the early years. As defender of the Basic Law (German Constitution), the Federal Constitutional Court did not accept the jurisdiction of the European Court of Justice where in its view the judgements of the latter clashed with the Basic Law. Many thought that the *Bundesbank* had lost much of its relevance with the creation of the eurozone. However, the eurozone crisis raised the painful issue of sound money, leading the *Bundesbank* to recover much of its prominence since its views on the primacy of sound money are widely shared at both a popular and elite level, and are strongly backed by the *Frankfurter Allgemeine Zeitung* (FAZ).

Ironically, as Germany's European vision weakened, the country has come to play an increasingly central role. Paterson (2011) has coined the term 'reluctant hegemon' to characterize Germany's position in the eurozone, where its ever strengthening economy and principal creditor status has placed it in the driving seat in relation to crisis management. This was reinforced by the inability of France to take on a co-leadership role in the traditional manner. Finally, as the the first Merkel government's role in rescuing the Lisbon Treaty demonstrated, objections by other states to solo German leadership have faded, a position that has been adopted with great reluctance and which is not supported by German public opinion. This is complicated by persistent interventions from the Federal Constitutional Court and the *Bundesbank*, with the result that Germany has failed to provide the public goods necessary for a hegemon to play a stabilizing role. Unsurprisingly this has caused great resentment in southern Europe.

This contested role where 'Germany's ability to offer additional propulsion is compounded by domestic "gear box" problems and European resistance' (Bulmer and Paterson, 2013: 15) suggests a lack of stability concerning the role, thus potentially leaving EU politicians at the mercy of the financial markets. Eurozone problems suggest that deeper integration might be a solution, but there is very little consensus on this, and the prospect of a referendum in one or more member states is a huge disincentive. A smaller eurozone group of northern European states would push the currency upwards, as would also be the case if Germany left the eurozone. In his new book former Chancellor Schröder has identified avoiding a rise in currency value as the key aim of German European policy (Schröder, 2014).

Part of the uncertainty arises from the way Chancellor Merkel has played her hand. Traditionally, German Chancellors have been preoccupied with regaining and maintaining trust and have stressed predictability and dependability. Some, like Konrad Adenauer and Kohl, had a European vision designed to mobilize opinion internally and externally. Merkel has no European vision and has changed her position a number of times during the crisis as she tracks public opinion. This has left her with high poll ratings but led critics to suggest she is not addressing the deeper issues (Habermas, 2013). What is beyond doubt is that she has not revealed her future preferences apart from ruling out eurobonds. How far will she be prepared to accommodate the wishes of the United Kingdom for an even more detached position in the EU? Is she prepared to put more effort into the Franco–German relationship? How does she see the future of financial cooperation in the eurozone?

So far Germany has put huge emphasis on framing the rules for the eurozone and keeping up the pressure for reforms – but is this merely to make a more generous posture possible later? And is there a Plan B if things go wrong? None of these issues were resolved in the 2013 election, and no clear answers have emerged in the wake of the election. The watchword will continue to be caution until after the European Parliament election in 2014 and the replacement of EU Commission President José Manuel Barroso in 2014.

Stefan Kornelius, who is close to the Chancellor, has suggested that her preference is to bid goodbye to the Community method and to rely on the member states who will proceed at different speed (Kornelius, 2013a: 263–4). There is also talk of strengthening EU budgetary control over national finances and giving the Commission a much greater role in this process (*Spiegel Online*, 2013). These rumours raise a large number of questions. Would Germany really welcome budgetary control? What view would the Federal Constitutional Court take of any weakening of national control of budgetary policy? How does this policy square with the growing distrust of the European Commission?

Foreign and security policy

Participation in the Kosovo intervention led many to expect Germany to play a role internationally in line with its economic strength, which translated directly into power in the eurozone crisis. But as Alister Miskimmon shows in Chapter 11, Germany continues to punch below her weight in foreign and security terms. In part this reflects a quietist and deeply civilian public opinion. A failure to reform German armed forces, in a manner that would make them fit for purpose, and very low defence spending create further barriers to any active military role – France and Britain continue to provide the teeth if fighting is required. Germany remains multilateralist but its contribution does not measure up to its economic weight – it has emancipated itself from dependence on the United States and it decides on intervention issues on a case-by-case basis. This is new. Traditionally the Federal Republic was seen to exercise a defensive role, where fighting 'out of area' was excluded. That changed with Kosovo. Pre-unity German security policy was circumscribed by NATO, and dependence on the United States was total. Chancellor Schröder's decision in the Iraq crisis not to offer the United States support emancipated Germany and left her free to decide on a case-by-case basis.

In line with its European vocation Germany expended a lot of effort in the European Common Foreign and Security Policy and strove to catch up after the St Malo agreement on defence between the United Kingdom and France in 1998. In more recent years this has slowed; as Miskimmon writes in Chapter 11, there has been 'a noticeable loss of momentum since the coming into force of the Lisbon Treaty'. Germany is not going to become a serious military power in the way many feared, but it will remain, in Hans Kundnani's (2011) words, 'a geo-economic power'.

Foreign and security policy made no appearance whatsoever in the 2013 federal elections. In a series of speeches at the Munich Security Conference in January 2014 Federal President Gauck, Foreign Minister Steinmeier and Defence Minister Von der Leyen suggested that Germany needed to adopt a more ambitious defence policy (Leonard, 2014). Doubts remain about whether this will go beyond rhetoric. There is unlikely to be any increase in resources and public opinion remains very sensitive about body bags. Germany will remain a geo-economic power.

₋overnment at the Centre

CHRISTIAN STECKER AND KLAUS H. GOETZ

According to Article 65 of the German Constitution – the Basic Law – the federal government consists of the federal chancellor and the federal ministers: together they form the political apex of the federal executive. The provisions of the Constitution and political conventions as they have developed since the foundation of the Federal Republic in 1949 have placed the government firmly at the centre of the German political system. Konrad Adenauer's election as the first Chancellor of the Federal Republic on 15 September 1949 (with the narrowest of majorities) might, at the time, have seemed like a throwback to the Weimar Republic, the democratic state that had come into being in 1919 and which had been liquidated by the Nazi regime in 1933. Not only were there parallels between the Weimar Constitution and the Basic Law in respect of the definition of the powers and responsibilities of the chancellor, but the person of Adenauer himself – who, at the time of taking office, was already 73 – seemed to point to the past, for Adenauer's political career had begun during the Wilhelmine Empire.

Yet, in retrospect, it is clear that links with the Weimar past notwithstanding, the executive led by Adenauer heralded a new departure in the history of German government. The defining features of the new government included full accountability to parliament and an unambiguous concentration of executive authority in the government and its members. While the president had enjoyed far-reaching powers under the Weimar constitution, including the right to dissolve parliament and dismiss the government, the new Basic Law now restricted the president to a largely ceremonial role. Both the institutions and the key personnel of government were to exhibit remarkable stability and continuity in the decades to come. Executive authority, parliamentary accountability and stability have thus characterized the experience of government at the centre since 1949.

The following discussion defines the position of federal government in the wider context of the key political institutions and clarifies the relationships amongst the government as a collegiate body (the Cabinet), ministers and the chancellor. It concludes with a discussion of the likely future of power at the centre.

The federal government in context

Government at the centre implies parliamentary, party, coalition, federalized and Europeanized government. This fivefold characterization not only helps to locate the federal government in the wider political system, but also points to the nature of the key institutional relationships the government entertains and indicates the chief political constraints under which it operates.

Parliamentary government

The federal government bears the hallmarks of a classical parliamentary government in that it is dependent on the confidence of the majority in the federal parliament, the *Bundestag*. This confidence relationship is concentrated in the chancellor. The chancellor is elected by an absolute majority of *Bundestag* deputies and then formally appointed by the president. To date, each candidate for the office has been elected during the first round of voting. The chancellor may, at any time, be replaced through a constructive vote of no-confidence, through which a successor is elected by an absolute majority of deputies. This 'constructive' version of dismissal was one of the central lessons learnt from the Weimar Republic, during which many 'destructive' no-confidence motions fatally weakened government stability (Fromme, 1969). The constructive vote of confidence has only been invoked successfully once, in 1982, when Chancellor Helmut Schmidt was ousted by Helmut Kohl, who was to remain chancellor for 16 years. Federal ministers are formally appointed (and dismissed) by the federal president upon the binding proposal of the chancellor. Although not required by the Constitution, ministers are usually *Bundestag* deputies and are often leading party figures (Kaiser and Fischer, 2009).

The government's continuous accountability to parliament is secured through a variety of formal and informal mechanisms. Next to the exhaustive scrutiny, deliberation and amendment of government bills in the standing committees of the *Bundestag* (Ismayr, 2008), these mechanisms include, inter alia, the detailed monitoring of the implementation of the federal budget by the *Bundestag*'s powerful budget committee (Ismayr, 2012: 341–54) and parliamentary control of Germany's secret services (Gusy, 2011: 121–36). The opposition parties, in particular, make very intensive use of their right of information, notably through parliamentary questions and interpellations. Investigatory committees and the possibility of asking the Federal Constitutional Court to examine the constitutionality of bills add to the armoury of parliament. Importantly, these rights are explicitly granted to minorities in the *Bundestag* so that parliamentary control does not depend on the goodwill of the governing majority. By contrast, control within the parliamentary majority relies predominantly on informal mechanisms, such as regular meetings between ministerial officials and the corresponding policy experts of the majority party groups (Schüttemeyer, 1998; Kropp, 2010a).

In recent years, parliamentary accountability has come under growing pressure. First, under the grand coalitions of the CDU/CSU and the SPD of 2005–09 and since 2013, the government party groups make up more than two-thirds of the *Bundestag*'s seats. Under these circumstances, the opposition parties may fall short of the minimum number of deputies required to invoke important control mechanisms. Second, the financial and economic crisis has forced the Bundestag to take many complex and far-reaching decisions often under intense time constraints, so that scrutiny has suffered. Faced with urgent votes, most importantly on the permanent euro bailout fund (part of the European Stability Mechanism (ESM)), deputies from the government and opposition parties complain about how little time they have for scrutiny and deliberation (Bannas, 2012). The Federal Constitutional Court has reminded the federal government of its obligation to inform the *Bundestag* 'at the earliest possible time and continuously' about decisions under the ESM (Federal Constitutional Court, 2012) and, more generally, to respect the need for parliamentary time when it comes to making far-reaching decisions.

Party and coalition government

While parliamentary government is an expression of constitutional norms, party and coalition government has developed as a constitutional convention. Mair (2008: 225) has defined 'party government' as a situation in which 'a party or parties wins control of the executive as a result of competitive elections ... and when that executive is held accountable through parties'. Throughout the history of the Federal Republic, party government has also meant coalition government, as the proportional electoral system has prevented either of the two main political camps – the CDU/CSU and the SPD – from gaining an absolute majority of seats in the *Bundestag*. Only once, in 1957, did the CDU/CSU win an outright majority, but Chancellor Adenauer chose to invite two ministers from the small German Party (DP) to join the government (see Table 1.1). With the

Table 1.1 *Federal governments since 1949*

Legislative period	Cabinets/chancellors	Coalition partners
1949–1953	Adenauer I	CDU, CSU, FDP, DP
1953–1957	Adenauer II	CDU, CSU, FDP, DP, GB/BHE
1957–1961	Adenauer III	CDU, CSU, DP
1961–1965	Adenauer IV (until 1962)	CDU, CSU, FDP
	Adenauer V (1962–63)	
	Erhard I (from 1963)	
1965–1969	Erhard II (until 1966)	CDU, CSU, FDP
	Kiesinger I (from 1966)	CDU, CSU, SPD
1969–1972	Brandt I	SPD, FDP
1972–1976	Brandt II (until 1974)	SPD, FDP
	Schmidt I (from 1974)	
1976–1980	Schmidt II	SPD, FDP
1980–1983	Schmidt III (until 1982)	SPD, FDP
	Kohl I (from 1982)	CDU, CSU, FDP
1983–1987	Kohl II	CDU, CSU, FDP
1987–1990	Kohl III	CDU, CSU, FDP
1990–1994	Kohl IV	CDU, CSU, FDP
1994–1998	Kohl V	CDU, CSU, FDP
1998–2002	Schröder I	SPD, Greens
2002–2005	Schröder II	SPD, Greens
2005–2009	Merkel I	CDU, CSU, SPD
2009–2013	Merkel II	CDU, CSU, FDP
2013–	Merkel III	CDU, CSU, SPD

Notes: DP = *Deutsche Partei*; GB/BHE = *Gesamtdeutscher Block/Bund der Heimatvertriebenen und Entrechteten.*

exception of three brief interludes of minority caretaker governments in 1962, 1966 and 1982 – in each case after the breakdown of a coalition – the federal government has always been based on a coalition commanding a majority in the *Bundestag*.

Political parties, their parliamentary party groups and coalitions are hence the central actors in the process of government formation and in structuring the relationship between government and parliament. The election of the chancellor and the subsequent appointment of the federal ministers after the quadrennial *Bundestag* elections reflect the decisions of the main representatives of the national parties during lengthy coalition negotiations. During these talks, the future partners work out a coalition agreement, that is a detailed policy programme for the entire legislative term, and settle the distribution of ministerial portfolios (Saalfeld, 2003b; Proksch and Slapin, 2006; Gadinger et al., 2013). Parties and coalitions also structure the interaction between government and parliament. The majority parliamentary (coalition) parties and the government are said to constitute a 'composite actor' (Beyme, 1997: 358) that confronts the opposition in the *Bundestag*. Different behavioural patterns illustrate the dominance of this dualism. For example, most successful bills originate in the government and are passed into law by its cohesive party groups. By submitting mostly unsuccessful bills and amendments, opposition parties seek to signal alternative policy proposals (Bräuninger and Debus, 2009).

Coalitions have not only been compatible with stable government, but have underpinned stability in institutions and continuity in personnel. Chancellor Konrad Adenauer headed CDU/CSU-dominated coalitions between 1949 and 1963, and his last coalition, which included the Free Democrats, was continued by his successor, Ludwig Erhard, until 1966. After the brief experience of a grand coalition between the CDU/CSU and the SPD from 1966 to 1969, under Chancellor Kurt Georg Kiesinger (CDU), the Social–Liberal pact between the SPD and the FDP lasted from 1969 until 1982 (following the resignation of Willy Brandt in 1974, Helmut Schmidt was elected chancellor). Schmidt was succeeded by Helmut Kohl (CDU) who, together with the FDP, won four successive federal elections in 1983, 1987, 1990 and 1994 and governed until 1998.

After the general elections in 1998, for the first time in its history, the Federal Republic experienced a complete rather than partial change of government, since none of the three former coalition partners – the CDU, the CSU and the FDP – was represented in the new government. This brought to power an SPD–Green coalition headed by Gerhard Schröder (SPD). After a surprising re-election of the red–green coalition in September 2002, a string of lost *Länder* elections led Schröder to seek early elections in 2005. They resulted in the formation of the second grand coalition led by CDU's leader Angela Merkel. While the grand coalition was credited with dealing quite successfully with the first phase of the financial and economic crisis (Zohlnhöfer, 2011), the general elections in 2009 saw huge losses for the Social Democrats and a remarkable increase in the votes for the liberal FDP. The CDU/CSU would now govern with the FDP until September 2013. In the 2013 elections, the CDU/CSU won a stunning victory and only narrowly missed an outright majority in the *Bundestag*. The FDP failed to clear the 5 per cent threshold and lost parliamentary representation for the first time since 1949. In December 2013, the CDU/CSU and SPD formed the third grand coalition in German history.

Federalized government

Germany is a federal polity, and decentralization of policy influence, responsibilities and resources is one of its fundamental constitutional principles. The federal government is thus only one among 17 governments, as each of Germany's 16 *Länder* has its own fully fledged executive. Combined with a tradition of strong non-executive institutions, such as the independent *Bundesbank* or the Federal Constitutional Court, federalism gives Germany the character of a polycentric polity, in which the scope for unilateral action on the part of the federal government is closely circumscribed (Katzenstein, 1987). Yet the constitutional principle of a vertical division of powers is modified by strong unitary dynamics, not least propelled by voters who favour unified policy solutions for the entire country (Oberhofer et al., 2011: 183). Thus, the German version of federalism does not equal effective political decentralization.

The practice of 'cooperative federalism' requires close cooperation between the federal government and the *Länder*, most notably in legislation. The Basic Law grants the *Länder* the power to participate in the federal legislative process via the *Bundesrat*. The *Bundesrat*'s rights depend on the nature of the matter to be legislated. In the case of objection bills (*Einspruchsgesetze*), it may exercise a suspensory veto, which must then be overturned with an absolute majority in the *Bundestag*. In the case of consent bills (*Zustimmungsgesetze*), which cover important issues such as taxation, the *Bundesrat* possesses an absolute veto. Frequently, the majority of votes in the *Bundesrat* is controlled by parties that are in opposition; their veto leads to the need for broadly based compromises in legislation (Manow and Burkhart, 2007; Kropp, 2010b). As a consequence, Germany often functions as a 'grand coalition state' (Schmidt, 2008), even when smaller minimal winning coalitions form the federal government. Moreover, the federal governing parties cannot take for granted the support of *Länder* governments led by their own supporters. For example, during the 2009 to 2013 term, *Länder* governments led by CDU prime ministers showed an increasing determination to use their power in the *Bundesrat* to resist decisions of the CDU/CSU and FDP government that they considered inimical to their financial interests (Glaab, 2010: 141; Bannas, 2011b).

Its constrained scope for autonomous action notwithstanding, the federal government is the central target for popular demands and expectations. It tends to be held politically responsible, even where the Constitution envisages problem-solving by *Länder* or local governments, and *Länder* elections are often heavily influenced by the popularity of the federal government (Burkhart, 2005). The range of political matters with which the federal executive deals is scarcely less extensive and popular demands and expectations no less urgent than in unitary systems. Politically, the federal government can rarely afford to neglect a policy issue, although its relevant formal powers may be closely circumscribed.

Europeanized government in times of crisis

The federal government is part of a multilevel governance system that extends both 'downwards' to the *Länder* and local government, and 'upwards' to a host of international and transnational organizations in which Germany participates and which increasingly share in the governance of the country. Of these, the EU is the most important (in the field of defence and security policy, this distinction belongs to NATO); but there are many others, such as the Council of Europe, the United Nations with its many suborganizations, the OECD and cooperation in the form of the G-8 summits. The orientation towards European integration and the concomitant 'opening of the state' (Wessels, 2000) constitute defining features of the German polity. Partly as a result of the historical co-evolution of the Federal Republic and the European integration project, German statehood has become progressively Europeanized (Knodt and Kohler-Koch, 2000; Dyson and Goetz, 2003), so that there is a very intensive interaction between national policy-makers and EU actors, extending to virtually all fields of domestic public policy and also to foreign and security policy (Jacobs, 2012).

Policy impulses coming from the supranational level have to be synchronized with national preferences and priorities. For example, it is estimated that approximately one-fourth of all laws passed by the *Bundestag* are the result of EU-level initiatives, with much higher averages in some fields, such as agricultural policy (König and Mäder, 2008; Töller, 2008). This Europeanization of policy-making was forcefully illustrated during the coalition talks between the CDU/CSU and the SPD in November 2013. In the middle of their talks, the two chief negotiators of both parties in the area of energy policy – the acting Federal Minister of the Environment and the Minister-President of North-Rhine Westphalia respectively – travelled to Brussels to meet with the EU Commissioner responsible for competition policy. They wanted to explore whether the deal they sought to strike on exemptions to the cost of renewable energy would be considered compatible with EU law by the European Commission ('Altmaier und Kraft kämpfen um Industrierabatte', *Handelsblatt*, 7 November 2013).

Since 2008, the most pressing demands for policy solutions have resulted from the financial and economic crisis. The federal government has had to bail out German banks, launch stimulus packages to help the ailing economy and – in concert with other euro-countries – stabilize the common currency (Zohlnhöfer, 2011). The necessity for fast action under extreme stress has led to a concentration of decision-making in the hands of the government, most notably the Chancellery and the Ministry of Finance. In its judgement on the ratification of the ESM, the Federal

Constitutional Court sought to erect hurdles against the marginalization of the *Bundestag* on the grounds of urgent decision-making (Goetz, 2014). Nevertheless, the demands of crisis management appear to have increased the autonomy of central government relative to parliament (Fleischer, 2010: 362; 2011b) and political parties. At the same time, however, even more so than before the crisis, the national legislative and policy agenda is at best partly under the control of national law-makers, let alone the federal government.

What is the consequence of the political and institutional embeddedness of the federal government and the permeability of boundaries between the government, political and parliamentary parties, the *Länder* and the *Bundesrat*, and EU institutions? The autonomy of the federal government in the German political system is low. Unilateral action is rare; even when it might be legal, it is seldom politically feasible. Managing cooperative ties is, therefore, a preoccupation of both the political and the administrative parts of the federal executive. The need to cooperate should not, however, be confused with a lack of executive authority, for the government's power resides in its capacity to shape and drive the agenda, to negotiate, persuade, cajole and, if necessary, 'bribe' other decision-makers on whose cooperation, or at least acquiescence, it depends.

Inside the federal executive

Three principles shape the internal life of the government, as laid down in Article 65 of the Basic Law. First, the Cabinet principle states that 'the federal government resolves differences of opinion amongst ministers' and decides on matters of political importance. Second, the departmental principle gives ministers independent responsibility for conducting the affairs of their departments. Third, the chancellor principle means that the chancellor 'determines and is responsible for the general guidelines of policy'. These principles are open to political interpretation and their relative importance has varied over time, notably in response to coalition politics, and across policy areas.

Cabinet

After the formation of the new government in December 2013, the federal government consisted of the chancellor and 15 federal ministers, including the chief of the Chancellery (see Table 1.2). The government as a collegiate body is often referred to as the Cabinet. It holds weekly meetings, usually on Wednesdays. In addition to the chancellor and the ministers,

Table 1.2   *Composition of the federal government as of March 2014, Cabinet Merkel III*

Office title	Name of holder
Chancellor	Angela Merkel (CDU)
Minister of Economics and Energy	Sigmar Gabriel (SPD)
Minister for Foreign Affairs	Frank-Walter Steinmeier (SPD)
Minister of the Interior	Thomas de Maizière (CDU)
Minister of Justice and Consumer Protection	Heiko Maas (SPD)
Minister of Finance	Wolfgang Schäuble (CDU)
Minister of Labour and Social Affairs	Andrea Nahles (SPD)
Minister of Food and Agriculture	Christian Schmidt (CSU)
Minister of Defence	Ursula von der Leyen (CDU)
Minister of Family Affairs, Senior Citizens, Women and Youth	Manuela Schwesig (SPD)
Minister of Health	Hermann Gröhe (CDU)
Minister of Transport and Digital Infrastructure	Alexander Dobrindt (CSU)
Minister for the Environment, Nature Conservation, Building and Nuclear Safety	Barbara Hendricks (SPD)
Minister of Education and Research	Johanna Wanka (CDU)
Minister of Economic Cooperation and Development	Gerd Müller (CSU)
Minister for Special Tasks (Head of the Chancellery)	Peter Altmaier (CDU)

non-voting participants include the Chief of the Chancellery, the ministers of state in the Chancellery, the heads of the Federal President's Office, the Federal Press and Information Office, the Chancellor's Office (that is, the chancellor's personal office in the Chancellery), and a scribe (Busse and Hofmann, 2010). Others who are customarily in attendance are the minister of state in the Foreign Ministry dealing with EU affairs, the deputy press spokesman of the federal government, and the heads of division in the Chancellery. Still others attend more irregularly. For example, the head of the *Bundesbank* is usually present at the meeting at which the government adopts the federal draft budget; and key members of the coalition parliamentary parties might be invited to a Cabinet meeting to speak on a particular point.

Cabinet is pre-eminent in that it has wide-ranging prerogatives to consider and decide matters. By law or custom, many issues must formally be settled by federal government as a collegiate body rather than individual ministers or the chancellor. In addition to a number of specific matters reserved for Cabinet decision-taking on the basis of constitutional and statutory law, the Rules of Procedure of the Government stipulate that all matters of political importance must be referred to Cabinet for consideration and decision-taking, including, inter alia: all bills and government ordinances; major ordinances by individual ministries; comments by the *Bundesrat* on government-sponsored bills; and disagreements between ministers, including major ones on plans for the federal budget. Answers to major parliamentary interpellations and reports to the *Bundestag* must also pass through Cabinet, as do personnel matters in the case of top officials. Collective decision-taking is thus a fundamental feature of executive policy-making.

The meetings of the Cabinet are not the place for detailed substantive discussion or conflict resolution (Saalfeld, 2003a: 60; Rudzio, 2005). To the greatest possible extent, disagreements are resolved in advance. Conflicts amongst ministries and amongst coalition parties are typically intertwined. Interministerial disagreement is rooted in different perceptions of problems and solutions and diverging institutional interests. Traditionally, ministerial portfolios have been organized along the lines of specific clientelistic interests (Derlien, 1996), which have created 'natural' tensions within the federal government, particularly amongst the ministries responsible for farming, consumer protection, the economy and environmental protection (Döhler et al., 2007: 27). In order to resolve interministerial conflicts both formal procedures and custom show a bias towards 'more, rather than less consultation' (ibid.: 17). The 'co-signature' procedure stipulates that legislative drafts be circulated among all other affected ministries – starting at the lowest bureaucratic level – and serves to identify agreement and disagreement. As drafts move up the hierarchy, conflicts amongst ministries are expected to be resolved. Only if this horizontal coordination amongst officials fails are ministers brought in to seek conciliation at the highest level, if necessary together with the chancellor.

This way of organizing the preparation of bills in the federal bureaucracy was criticized in a seminal study by Mayntz and Scharpf (1975: 72–4, 147) nearly four decades ago as leading to 'negative coordination'. In drafting bills, small ministerial units with a parochial focus on particular policy problems would anticipate objections by other, equally blinkered units in other ministries, resulting in a fragmented policy output. While this general bottom-up approach to legislation has not changed fundamentally, we can see more integrative approaches to public policy-making today (Hustedt and Tiessen, 2006: 27). In particular, interministerial or coalition working groups, central coordination units in the ministries and task forces foster a more integrative approach to the development of federal public policy (Saalfeld, 2003b: 366; Goetz, 2007; 2011; Busse and Hofmann, 2010).

Conflicts also result from the diverging policy preferences of coalition parties that need to be aggregated into a common government policy

(Martin and Vanberg, 2011). Each coalition partner is granted a veto during this process; cooperation with the opposition against other coalition partners is explicitly ruled out in coalition agreements. The coalition of the CDU/CSU and the SPD between 2005 and 2009 was particularly plagued by conflicts in the area of social policy, which meant that coalition unity in parliamentary votes suffered (Delius et al., 2013). The likelihood of a smooth working of grand coalitions is generally considered low, as both sides are the main competitors in elections aiming for the chancellorship (Miller and Müller, 2010). Moreover, they compete intensely across the entire range of policy domains, unlike in a coalition with one catch-all party and a smaller party that appeals only to a narrower set of voters. Although the CDU/CSU and FDP coalition between 2009 and 2013 was seemingly more cohesive in terms of general policy outlook, it was also marred by constant conflicts over policy and, sometimes, personnel. In particular, the pro-market positions of the FDP and conservative social values of the CSU frequently clashed. To resolve coalition conflicts, the governing parties draw on a range of instruments, partly contained in the formal coalition agreements, including special coalition committees in which compromises are hammered out (Rudzio, 2005; Miller, 2011).

Ministries and ministers

The rules concerning the demarcation of ministerial portfolios allow for a great deal of flexibility. Departmental organization is a prerogative of the chancellor, who establishes and abolishes ministries through a simple administrative ordinance and determines the interministerial distribution of responsibilities. Only three ministries – Finance, Defence and Justice – are, in principle, exempt from this far-reaching organizational power, since they are explicitly mentioned in the Basic Law. Once more, however, the logic of coalition government is an important qualifier of the chancellor's prerogatives, as departmental organization is subject to agreement amongst coalition partners.

When it comes to ministerial organization, no more than 'small modifications of the status quo' have been the norm throughout the history of the Federal Republic (Derlien, 1996: 564). One central innovation was the creation of a Ministry of the Environment, Conservation and Nuclear Safety in 1986 during the Kohl chancellorship (Pehle, 1998), which has since developed into a high-profile federal department. Chancellor Schröder concentrated the dispersed responsibilities for federal cultural policy in the newly created office of the Federal Commissioner for Culture and Media, overseen by a minister of state and directly subordinated to the chancellor (a constitutionally sensitive development given the

Länder's prerogatives in this policy domain). Angela Merkel has continued this arrangement.

Under the Basic Law, the chancellor enjoys the exclusive right to form the government and select ministers. Yet, Chancellor Merkel's discretion is effectively restricted to her own party. The other coalition partners are free to nominate candidates for the ministerial posts they have been granted. For example, when worsening results in *Länder* elections led to ructions in the FDP, a cabinet reshuffle in May 2011, involving no less than three FDP positions, was carried out without substantive input from the chancellor. By contrast, in a rare show of the full use of her constitutional prerogatives, the chancellor, in May 2012, explicitly dismissed the minister of the environment, Norbert Röttgen, a member of her own party, when he refused to accept her request for a face-saving resignation.

Although it is not a constitutional requirement, most ministers are *Bundestag* deputies. In selecting ministers (Fleischer and Seyfried, 2013), political parties pay a good deal of attention to achieving a certain balance in terms of ministers' regional background, gender, religious denomination (especially in the case of the CDU/CSU) and general political outlook. With the formation of the first Schröder government in 1998, continuity in key political personnel, highlighted above as an important feature of post-war executives, was initially broken. Neither the chancellor nor any of his ministers had previous ministerial experience at the federal level. This contrasted with the formation of earlier governments, which had always included some members of the previous administration, allowing some ministers exceptionally long periods in office. The best-known example is Hans-Dietrich Genscher, former FDP leader, who headed the Foreign Ministry for 18 years. The first Schröder government also set new records in ministerial turnover in that its four years in office saw the resignation or dismissal of no fewer than seven ministers. The subsequent grand coalition exhibited remarkable continuity and stability in personnel: several SPD ministers from the Schröder government and Wolfgang Schäuble, who had already served under Kohl, now entered the Merkel-led government and turnover during the grand coalition was low. Similarly, in 2009, personnel continuity was ensured by CDU/CSU ministers, but the government experienced a string of resignations and dismissals between 2009 and 2013. The most notable casualty was Karl-Theodor zu Guttenberg (CSU), who became the media darling of the coalition, only to fall spectacularly in March 2011, when he was found to have committed plagiarism in his doctoral thesis. In the coalition that has been in power since the end of 2013, all the principal ministries are headed by politicians with extensive executive experience.

In running their departments, ministers rely on an organization that follows a common blueprint. In addition to the minister, the leadership of the ministry consists of between one and three administrative state secretaries and one or two parliamentary state secretaries. Administrative state secretaries, who are civil servants, occupy the highest grade in the federal administration, and are regularly amongst the key figures in the ministerial policy process. They deputize for the minister in running the department, and they operate directly at the interface between politics and administration. Their special position is recognized in their status as 'political civil servants' as defined by the Federal Civil Service Law. It is acknowledged that they need to be in permanent basic agreement with the government's views and objectives in order to perform their task of helping to transform the government's political will into administrative action. Political civil servants, who also include heads of division, need not be recruited from amongst career civil servants. Already by the early 1980s, some 40 per cent of political civil servants had been recruited to their position from outside the ministry in which they served (Mayntz and Derlien, 1989: 392); of these about half were genuine external recruits, not previously employed in the federal administration. As political civil servants, they can also at any time be sent into early retirement by the political leadership, and ministers use this possibility frequently (Goetz, 1997; 1999; 2011).

In 1967, the post of parliamentary state secretary was added to the organization of federal ministries. Parliamentary state secretaries must be members of the *Bundestag*, with the exception of those serving in the Chancellery. They do not formally belong to the federal government, yet in coalition negotiations these posts, too, are subject to intense bargaining. The Law on the Legal Status of Parliamentary State Secretaries defines their function only in the broadest of terms: to support the minister (or, in the case of parliamentary state secretaries in the Chancellery, the chancellor) in his governmental functions. According to the Rules of Procedure of the Federal Government, the parliamentary state secretary generally deputizes for the minister in making official statements to the Bundestag, the Bundesrat and in Cabinet meetings. Beyond these stipulations, the parliamentary state secretaries' tasks are, in principle, determined by the minister. In general, the nurturing of relations with the parliamentary parties, committees and working groups, and often also with *Länder* governments and the *Bundesrat*, constitute a major part of their work. As politicians, they tend to focus their attention on the external relations of their ministry rather than its internal processes.

There is no clear dividing line between politics and administration in the federal ministries, either in terms of formal organization or personnel (Bogumil and Jann, 2009). Below the top leadership level, the ministries are hierarchically organized into divisions, subdivisions and sections. In the words of the Joint Rules of Procedure for the Federal Ministries, the key unit in a ministry is the 'section, which is the initial decision-making authority in all matters assigned to it within its area of competence' (§7 (1)). Formally, the section has primary responsibility for policy development (Mayntz and Scharpf, 1975: 67ff.). Heads of section must possess detailed policy expertise and, once they have been appointed to a particular section, they are unlikely to move again, unless they are promoted (the exception to this rule are sections that belong to the political support units). It is not uncommon, therefore, to find the same official in charge of a particular policy issue for many years.

However, the traditional picture of a policy process 'from below', in which policy development is driven by the experts at the 'working level' of the ministry, is increasingly in need of revision. Political support and coordination units, which are directly attached to the ministerial leadership and operate outside the main departmental line organization, have greatly gained in importance. The core of the political support units is typically made up of the personal assistants to the minister, the parliamentary and administrative state secretaries, and at least three further offices: the Minister's Office; the Office for Cabinet and Parliamentary Affairs, which is sometimes split into two; and the Press and Information Office, which is often divided into a press office and an office for public relations (Goetz, 1997). Increasingly, these support units do not just monitor the work of the mainline administration and structure access to the ministry's leadership; rather, they direct the work of the line divisions and ensure that the latter 'stay on message'. Thus, the ministerial policy process has, over the years, become more 'top-down', in that political support and coordination units increasingly direct the activities of administrative line units.

Given the proximity of these units to the top ministerial leadership, it is not surprising that they should act as key informal training grounds for future top officials, for they cultivate expertise, access and 'political craft' (ibid.), i.e. the capacity to operate effectively in a politicized environment. Senior officials, including heads of subdivisions and many heads of section, need to be able to act in a way that maximizes the chances for the realization of the government's political objectives. This requires that they must be able to interact freely with, and enjoy the trust of, political actors, not just in their own ministries, but also in parliament, political parties and *Länder* governments. It is estimated that between 25 and 50 per cent of ministerial top officials are members of a political party (Ebinger and Jochheim, 2009: 333–6). Whereas some observers criticize this as evidence of 'illegitimate party patronage' (Arnim, 1980), it may also be seen as a way of ensuring that democratically selected ministers are able to keep political control over their departments (Manow, 2005). Government alternation regularly involves major change in top administrative personnel. The first Schröder government, in 1998, sent virtually all administrative state secretaries and around 60 per cent of the heads of division into early retirement. And even though, in 2005, the SPD remained in the new government formed by Chancellor Merkel, turnover in top officials exceeded 60 per cent (Ebinger and Jochheim, 2009: 332).

Chancellor, chancellery, party and coalition

The roles of the chancellor and the Chancellery have never been determinate (Müller-Rommel, 1997; Rüb, 2011: 88). During the first decade of Adenauer's chancellorship, many argued that the Federal Republic was developing into a 'chancellor democracy' (Niclauss, 1988), distinguished by the concentration of formal and, in particular, informal political powers in the chancellor (Ridley, 1966). Strong central coordination of government policy, chancellorial control over (and interference with) the activities of ministers, compliant coalition parties, an executive-dominated parliament and a marginalized opposition, it was suggested, made the chancellorship into the unrivalled centre of power. As the last years of Adenauer's tenure and the experiences of his successors have shown, this concentration of powers in the chancellor cannot be taken for granted (Mayntz, 1980). The actual strength of Chancellors Erhard, Kiesinger, Brandt, Schmidt, Kohl, Schröder and Merkel within the federal executive, and the political system more broadly, has depended on their – varying – capacity to mobilize constitutional, party political, coalitional, electoral and policy resources (Smith, 1991). Each chancellor's success (and failure) has been based on a distinct formula. For Kohl (1982–98), the degree of domination that he exercised over his own party by building close networks throughout the party organization was seen as key to his longevity in office (Clemens, 1994; 1998). Schröder often distanced himself from his party, drew his power from high personal approval ratings and relied on his ability to mobilize voters at election time. He also showed how constitutional resources can be used to discipline a quarrelling party and coalition. By requesting a vote of confidence attached to the question of going to war in Afghanistan in 2001, he successfully quelled dissent in the ranks of the Red–Green coalition (Döring and Hönnige, 2006).

Merkel's ascent to the chancellorship and her survival in office have followed a different logic. Raised in East Germany, she only entered politics after the fall of the Berlin Wall and did not have the chance to build networks within the party over many years, something hitherto seen as indispensable. Her pragmatic and flexible approach to politics – coordinating rather than leading (Glaab, 2010: 130) – has proven to be a 'winning formula' in the CDU, a catch-all party with many factions across the spectrum of economic left–right positions and, increasingly, in questions of morality policies and civil rights (Wiliarty, 2008; Clemens, 2011).

Coalition politics is central to explaining the relative strength of a chancellor (Helms, 2013: 243). In a grand coalition between partners determined to be seen as equal, the chancellor's power to define the 'guidelines of federal policy' is severely constrained. To some extent, therefore, between 2005 and 2009, Merkel was a 'coordination chancellor', similar to Kurt Georg Kiesinger, who led the first grand coalition (Olsen, 2011). Yet, coalitions with smaller partners enable the chancellor to take on a more overt leadership role. In such a coalition, the chancellor has greater scope to determine both the overall government approach and, when needed, policy detail. Chancellor Schröder quite often engaged in such 'spatial leadership' (Helms, 2005b) by declaring an issue a 'matter for the boss' (*Chefsache*). Most prominently, the far-reaching reform of the welfare state that came to be known as 'Agenda 2010' was centrally planned and coordinated within the Chancellery (Siefken, 2007; Tils, 2011).

Since the foundation of the Federal Republic, foreign policy and European integration policy have been domains in which chancellorial involvement and intervention have been especially pronounced and continuous (Paterson, 1994); this focus on foreign and European policy is seen as a defining feature of a chancellor democracy (Niclauss, 1999; 2001). Under Kohl, European policy was early on established as a pivotal chancellorial domain, and his intense engagement with European policy meant that he decisively shaped the course of European integration (Dyson and Featherstone, 1999). Schröder, too, chose to interpret his guideline competence very extensively in this field, to the dismay of his foreign minister, Joschka Fischer, from the Green Party. And while Schröder did not create a Ministry for European Affairs, as had been mooted, he did, for the first time, establish a division within the Chancellery devoted exclusively to EU matters, asserting his claims in this policy domain. Again, Merkel continued with this arrangement. The demands of the financial and economic crisis have further increased the central role of the chancellor across the range of EU policies (Fleischer and Parrado, 2010; Fleischer, 2011a).

The Chancellery is the most important institutional resource of the chancellor (Busse, 2006). It is at the heart of the core executive, that is, 'all those organizations and structures which primarily serve to pull together and integrate central government policies, or act as final arbiters within the executive of conflicts between different elements of the government machine' (Dunleavy and Rhodes, 1990: 4). Its principal tasks include administrative and political support and advice to: the chancellor in his or her capacity as chief executive, member of the *Bundestag* and party leader; the chief of the Chancellery and the parliamentary state secretaries

– with the title of ministers of state – working in the Chancellery; and the government as a collegiate body. The Chancellery is at the hub of inter-ministerial coordination and the management of executive–external relations, with a special emphasis on relations with the governing parties, parliament, interest groups and the media. Several supplementary responsibilities may be added, such as: policy planning and development, especially in domains that are of special interest to the chancellor; fire-fighting, that is, political crisis and ad hoc emergency management in the case of major natural catastrophes, terrorist threats or foreign policy emergencies; and special tasks that for political or administrative reasons are entrusted to the Chancellery rather than ministerial departments or non-ministerial agencies, e.g. the direct supervision of the intelligence services exercised by the Chancellery.

Some 500 staff work in the Chancellery, the most important function of which is to assist consensus-building between different centres of power – between the chancellor, the chancellor's party, the party groups, *Länder* parties and *Länder* governments, the coalition partners and, importantly, Germany's European and international partners (Saalfeld, 2003b: 53; Kaiser, 2007: 16; Glaab, 2007: 78; Sturm and Pehle, 2007). During the grand coalition from 2005 to 2009, the core executive became to some extent bifurcated (Fleischer, 2010). Before coordinating with the CDU/CSU, SPD-led ministries and other SPD actors were now coordinated, in the first instance, from the office of the Minister for Labour and Social Affairs, which was sometimes labelled the 'Vice Chancellery'. This procedure has been revived under the grand coalition formed in 2013, where SPD ministries are coordinated from the office of the Minister of Economics and Energy headed by SPD-leader and Vice-Chancellor Sigmar Gabriel.

Similar to ministries the Chancellery is divided into political and working levels. The chancellor's key aide is the chief of the chancellery, whose remit covers, in principle, the full breadth of federal policies. In contrast to the chief of the chancellery, the remaining top personnel occupy much more narrowly defined roles. They typically include a minister of state who is particularly closely involved in the coordination with the *Länder*, the *Bundestag* and the *Bundesrat*; and federal commissioners, such as the commissioner for culture and media. The working level's most important components are 'mirror sections' which closely monitor and coordinate the activities of the respective working units in the ministries.

What future for the centre?

It should have emerged from the preceding discussion that the federal executive is a complex institution. Complexity is not so much a matter of intricate organigrams of the Chancellery and ministries or the formal Rules of Procedure of the Federal Government and the more elaborate Joint Rules of Procedure of the Federal Ministries. Rather, it results from the intricate interplay of politics and bureaucracy, institutions and people, and formality and informality. Where power lies within the federal executive and what power shifts may be observed continues to be a topic of great fascination to both political scientists and political commentators. Some see signs of a 'dual concentration': power in the German political system is increasingly concentrated within the federal executive at the expense of parliament, political parties and the *Länder*; and, within the executive, the chancellor's powers have increased, whilst collegiate decision-making and departmental autonomy are progressively undermined. Indeed, some have spoken of a 'presidentalization' of the political system (Korte, 2000), in line with broader trends towards a strengthening of chief executives in Western democracies (Poguntke and Webb, 2005a). Others insist that Germany is not a chancellor democracy, let alone a presidentialized system, but rather a 'coordination democracy' or a 'negotiation democracy' (Holtmann, 2001).

Recent developments that affect power at the centre point in opposite directions. On the one hand, there can be little doubt that crisis policymaking privileges the executive at the expense of parliament, political parties and also societal actors. This was dramatically illustrated at the onset of the financial crisis when, in an impromptu joint press conference on 5 October 2008, Chancellor Merkel and the then finance minister, Peer Steinbrück, guaranteed that all savings in German bank accounts would be fully protected, an announcement designed to prevent the Hypo Real Estate crisis, which was thought to pose a 'systemic risk', from degenerating into a bank-run. Upon leaving office, Steinbrück (2010), in an interview with *Der Spiegel*, provided some insight into this decision:

> We knew that we were skating on thin ice. To be frank, we lacked the authority to make such a statement. There was no legal basis or parliamentary support. To this day, I'm surprised that the lawmakers never asked, after the fact: For God's sake, what exactly have you done?

Such crisis politics, associated with a concentration of decision-making powers in the executive, and justified on grounds of urgency and also confidentiality (Fleischer and Parrado, 2010), run the risk of becoming institutionalized, not least because of the hurdles to effective parliamentary involvement in decision-making under the European Stability Mechanism (ESM), established in 2012. Both its Board of Governors and its Board of Directors are made up of members of the national executives and, crucially, many of its procedures are subject to strict confidentiality, thus running the risk of marginalizing national parliaments.

On the other hand, developments in the German party system make it unlikely that the constraints on the core executive will lessen significantly. Unless the liberal FDP manages to stage a comeback in the 2017 federal elections, the CDU/CSU will, from now on, face the prospect of having to form a coalition with the Greens (or perhaps a new party entering the Bundestag) or enter a grand coalition. In both cases, programmatic cohesion will be low and rivalry intense. Equally, on the left, the prospect of a repetition of a Red–Green coalition now seems remote, as a majority for a government of the left is only likely with the inclusion of Die Linke in a Red–Red–Green coalition. In such a three-party government, an SPD chancellor would, by necessity, again be a 'coordination chancellor'. It is, then, ultimately still in the hands of the German voters how power at the centre is distributed.

Chapter 2

The Reform of German Federalism

CHARLIE JEFFERY AND CAROLYN ROWE

Since the founding of the Federal Republic in 1949, the highly consensual or 'cooperative' nature of the German federal system had widely been viewed as a central part of the country's political stability and economic success. However, widespread political malaise and pessimism in the 2000s was increasingly focused on the federal system, which was regarded as too inflexible to deal with the cumulative challenges of German unification, globalization, Europeanization and demographic change. As a result, over the past decade, Germany has undertaken the largest and most complex reform of its federal system. Changes made to the federal constitution in 2006 sought to reallocate political responsibilities within the federal system, strengthen policy autonomy at the *Land* level and streamline the decision-making process; further changes implemented in 2009 tightened budgetary controls, regulating public debt levels across both the Federal government and the *Länder*.

This chapter explores and explains these reforms in the context of the territorial diversity that has continued to shape German federalism in recent decades. It starts by considering the reform initiative and why a constitutional overhaul was felt to be necessary in the 2000s. It then moves on to consider the reform process itself, assesses the interests of the various actors involved in the decision-making process and sets out the conditions under which such a reform was ultimately made possible. Finally the chapter explores the two 'faces' the German federal system appears now to have: the (still) consensus-oriented politics at the national level; and a growing diversity of policy challenges and policy outcomes in the *Länder*. It assesses how these new dynamics of territorial politics are likely to put the federal system under continued pressure. New stages of reform appear, as a result, to be inevitable.

The evolution of Germany's federal system

The political system of the Federal Republic is founded on the *Länder*;

that is to say the *Länder* are fundamental building blocks in the architecture of German federalism and have a 'state-like' quality that imbues them with a significance not seen in other federations (Wehling, 2006). The existence of the *Länder* is one of the 'eternal', unchallengeable principles of the Basic Law. The reasons for this are historically rooted. The Basic Law, crafted in the wake of Germany's defeat in the Second World War, disperses political authority and enshrines consensus-seeking as a principle of governance. To do this, responsibility for policy-making was divided in the Basic Law in ways which require high degrees of cooperation between the *Länder* themselves and between them and the federal level of government. While the bulk of legislative powers were allocated to the federal level, the *Länder* were made responsible for the implementation and delivery of policy decisions in most fields. In addition, the second chamber of the national legislature, the *Bundesrat*, was constituted by *Länder* governments. As an absolute majority of votes in the *Bundesrat* was required for the passage of the majority of federal laws, the *Länder* were thus bound in as an integral part of national decision-making.

This situation of complex interdependency between levels of government also extended into the fiscal arena. The federal system of the West German state was engineered in such a way as to overcome the considerable diversity that existed between the 11 *Länder* in terms of population size, economic prosperity and administrative capacity. So while the *Länder* enjoyed considerable authority over both expenditure and borrowing decisions, they lacked significant tax-raising powers of their own, and were dependent on a system of revenue-sharing with the federal level (Moore et al., 2008). This system, together with a complex fiscal equalization process, sought to ensure the *Länder*, irrespective of their particular economic circumstances, were able to deliver a constitutionally mandated 'uniformity of living conditions'. (In 1994 this provision was revised to a mere 'equivalence' of living conditions.) This fiscal equalization system, known as the *Länderfinanzausgleich*, ultimately guarantees that every *Land* can rely on 99.5 per cent of the average per capita revenues raised across the *Länder* as a whole (Burkhart, 2009).

This drive for uniformity between the 11 diverse West German *Länder* was further extended in the late 1960s by the 'Joint Tasks' (*Gemeinschaftsaufgaben*), a highly elaborate system of policy programmes jointly financed and jointly planned by the federal government and the *Länder* in areas of key voter importance, such as higher education policy and policy on regional economic development (Scharpf et al., 1976). These changes further strengthened what became known as 'cooperative federalism' or – less positively – '*Politikverflechtung*' or 'interlocked decision-making' involving a constant negotiation process between the two levels of government.

A new dimension of 'interlocking' emerged as the competences of the EU grew following the Single European Act of 1986 and the Maastricht Treaty of 1991. The *Länder* successfully argued that they should have the right to participate in German EU policy-making in areas of European competence which had earlier been their responsibility. The result was what Hrbek (1986) dubbed a 'double *Politikverflechtung*' which evolved into an additional level of complex coordination machinery linking the *Länder*, the federal government and EU decision-making processes (Jeffery, 1996).

The result was, in comparative terms, a highly centralized form of federalism in which federal and *Länder* governments cooperated to produce policies with a uniform, nationwide reach. Legislative responsibilities became increasingly centralized at the federal level, with relatively modest powers held in the *Länder*, which were, however, compensated by the role of the Bundesrat which became a central veto player in German politics. This increasingly complex system of joint decision-making imposed very high consensus requirements but which tended towards policy immobilism and political stalemate, memorably described by Scharpf (1988) as a 'joint-decision trap' which favoured the status quo and often suboptimal policy solutions, and which impeded responses to new challenges.

Uniformity in diversity

Federal systems of government are often seen as a means of reconciling 'uniformity and diversity', of balancing nationwide and regional priorities. Germany's particular model of federalism has always tended to prioritize the notion of 'uniformity' over 'diversity', with its requirements for consensus-seeking and, in particular, the mechanism of the financial equalization system. Indeed, Germany has been described as a 'unitary federal state' (Wheare, 1953; Hesse, 1962). Yet the degree to which the federal system has actually delivered 'uniformity' has largely been overstated in scholarly interpretations. At the very least, since 1990 it has become abundantly clear that the constitutional debate around the 'uniformity of living conditions' is far removed from social reality.

Diversity is very apparent within German federalism, both in terms of the policy challenges to be met (in particular, dealing with rural populations or city states with their divergent infrastructure needs or caring for citizens living in remote communities) and the political weight which the *Länder* have at their disposal (see Table 2.1).

Recent analysis has shown that German federalism increasingly operates around territorial cleavages more familiar in other 'non-consensual'

Table 2.1   *The diversity of the* Länder

	Population size (millions)*	Size (sq. km)	Population density (per sq. km)*	Bundesrat votes
Baden-Württemberg	10.51	35,751	302	6
Bavaria	12.44	70,550	179	6
Berlin	3.32	887	3,945	4
Brandenburg	2.45	29,483	85	4
Bremen	0.65	419	1,577	3
Hamburg	1.71	755	2,382	3
Hesse	5.99	21,114	289	5
Lower Saxony	7.77	47,612	166	6
Mecklenburg-West Pomerania	1.60	23,190	70	3
North Rhine-Westphalia	17.54	34,092	523	6
Rhineland-Palatinate	3.99	19,854	201	4
Saarland	0.99	2,568	394	3
Saxony	4.05	18,419	225	4
Saxony-Anhalt	2.27	20,449	113	4
Schleswig-Holstein	2.80	15,799	180	4
Thuringia	2.18	16,172	137	4
Totals	**80.32**	**357,121**	**229**	**69**

* Data for December 2011.

Source: www.statistik-portal.de/Statistik-Portal/de_jb01_jahrtab1.asp.

type federal politics. This change has been underpinned by an increasingly sharp divergence of the socio-economic interests of the *Länder* in the wake of German unification, alongside tighter public finances, which have exacerbated distributional conflicts. The poorer *Länder* have tended to seek additional debt relief, whilst the richer ones have sought to challenge existing fiscal equalization mechanisms (Renzsch, 2010). Indeed, most economists argue, and a number of politicians agree, that the existing financial system is inefficient and counterproductive. The system of financial equalization offers little incentive for the *Länder* to govern efficiently since the weaker ones can rely on, and the richer need to give, equalization payments anyway. This gives neither the stronger nor the weaker *Länder* strong incentives to promote economic development (Burkhart, 2009).

It is clear that since German unification the economic disparities between the *Länder* have widened considerably on key measures such as GDP and unemployment (see Table 2.2). The highest unemployment in 2012 is still to be found in the territory of the former East (Berlin, Brandenburg, Mecklenburg-West Pomerania and Saxony-Anhalt),

Table 2.2   *Economic disparity across the 16* Länder

	GDP per head 2012 (€)	Unemployment 2012 (%)	Population change 2003–11 (%)
Baden-Württemberg	36,019	3.9	+0.9
Bavaria	36,865	3.7	+1.4
Berlin	29,455	12.3	+3.3
Brandenburg	23,179	10.2	−3.1
Bremen	41,897	11.2	−0.3
Hamburg	53,091	7.5	+3.7
Hesse	37,656	5.7	0.0
Lower Saxony	29,032	6.6	−1.0
Mecklenburg-West Pomerania	22,620	12.0	−5.6
North Rhine-Westphalia	32,631	8.1	−1.3
Rhineland-Palatinate	29,431	5.3	−1.5
Saarland	31,364	6.7	−4.5
Saxony	23,400	9.8	−4.3
Saxony-Anhalt	22,933	11.5	−8.3
Schleswig-Holstein	27,220	6.9	+0.5
Thuringia	22,241	8.5	−6.4
Totals	32,280	6.8	−0.8

Sources: Unemployment: www.statistik-portal.de/Statistik-Portal/de_jb02_jahrtab13.asp; GDP: www.statistik.baden-wuerttemberg.de/VolkswPreise/Indikatoren/VW_wirtschaftskraft.asp; migration: www.statistik-portal.de/Statistik-Portal/de_jb01_jahrtab1.asp.

though there are also some pockets of economic under-performance in the former Western territory, such as Bremen with an unemployment rate of 11.2 per cent. The lowest levels of GDP per capita are also to be found, even in 2012, in the territory of the former German Democratic Republic. It is perhaps no surprise, therefore, to see continued patterns of internal migration from East to West as people, particularly younger, more highly qualified workers, move to the economically prosperous *Länder* in search of employment.

This pattern of economic success concentrated into a few, largely southern *Länder* has been evident since the mid-1980s. This situation has underpinned the resolve amongst the 'big three' *Länder* – in particular Hesse, Bavaria and Baden-Württemberg – to utilize their political muscle in the Bundesrat to press for a reform of the system which, they argue, unjustly penalizes them for economic success and prudent fiscal management. Political elites in these three *Länder* have argued for a more competitive model of federalism, inspired by that to be found in North America and the notion of states acting as 'laboratories of democracy' (Osborne, 1988; Jeffery, 2002).

It is less clear what ordinary citizens think about the balance of uniformity and diversity in German federalism. Good quality research on public attitudes to this has been rare, with only isolated surveys over the decades dealing with questions to do with the federal system. These have typically been presented with limited data on sample sizes at the *Land* level and based on skewed questionnaire design that may direct the respondent to think more of uniformity than its alternatives (e.g. Grube, 2004; 2009; Wintermann et al., 2008). Other more recent work (Oberhofer et al., 2011), conducted as part of a systematic project comparing regional political attitudes in five EU states, presents a subtler analysis. Involving detailed survey work in Bavaria, Lower Saxony and Thuringia, Oberhofer et al. (2011: 104–6) found evidence of a 'multi-level citizenship' in which citizens view *both* federal and *Länder*-level politics as important, and combine a 'pronounced preference for a greater role of regional institutions in policy-making – that is *stronger Länder* – alongside clear preferences for state-wide uniformity of policy standards and fiscal equalization. There is a paradox here, however: citizens appear to trust the *Länder* more than the federal level and to want the former to do more, but not to do things differently (though in Bavaria there is a little more openness to policy variation and a less strong commitment to fiscal equalization, and in Thuringia there is less openness to variation and stronger support for fiscal equalization – echoing some of the themes noted above, where interests diverge in the east and the south). This, in comparative terms, is not unusual; as noted elsewhere (Henderson et al., 2013) this suggests an unresolved tension – and a capacity for change – around the balance of uniformity and diversity in decentralized states. We will return to this point below.

The need to reform German federalism

The Economist (3 June 1999) famously described Germany as 'the sick man of Europe'. On any number of economic indicators, such as unemployment rates, export rates and growth rates, Germany was lagging behind. The country's economy was stagnating, whilst most other European economies were growing at double the rate.

The worsening economic situation of the early 2000s coincided with a situation of deadlock within the German federal system, which had by now reached a crucial tipping point. Policy stagnation, seen against a negative economic climate, forced the idea of a streamlining of the federal system to the top of the political agenda. The federal structure of Germany's political architecture was no longer regarded as a positive system which had helped secure prosperity throughout the Cold War, but rather was seen as a block to modernization, flexible decision-making and meeting the demands of globalization which would ultimately lead to economic growth and long-term prosperity for its citizens. Germany needed to be freed from its own internal joint-decision trap (Lehmbruch, 2007).

The high number of legislative initiatives which were subject to a veto in the *Bundesrat* were regarded as a major blockage in the German decision-making machinery. Generally, when the governing parties held a majority in both the *Bundestag* and *Bundesrat* then there was little problem in passing bills through both chambers. However, in times of 'divided government', with different party constellations governing each of the houses of parliament, it was likely that different majorities would lead to a 'politics of gridlock' (Moore et al., 2008: 399); this situation of divided government had in fact come to be the norm. The result was a virtually permanent deadlock. By the early 2000s, around 60 per cent of all federal laws required the agreement of the *Bundesrat* (Burkhart, 2009). This high figure of course meant that the legislative process was slow and cumbersome, which had also never been the original intention of the founding fathers of Germany's federal system. However, there was now a perception that 'interlocking' politics had slowed down decision-making to a state of near paralysis. The overall conclusion was that Germany was unable to change.

By this point, Germany's federal system had come to be seen as being largely responsible for the country's numerous social and economic problems, both in the popular imagination as well as in elite circles. Its overly regulated architecture, its slow-moving decision-making machinery with the in-built need to achieve consensus across multiple political dimensions (between parties as well as between *Bundestag* and *Bundesrat*) meant that the country was widely held up in the media as being 'unfit' for purpose. Words such as 'reform log jam' (*Reformstau*), 'inertia' (*Stillstand*) and 'malaise' (*Verdrossenheit*) were commonplace in media reports and served to reinforce public sentiment that the federal system was largely to blame for the predicament. There emerged widespread agreement that the federal system was in need of re-engineering in at least four respects:

- The highly interlocked policy-making process demanded extreme levels of cooperation that proved virtually impossible to achieve, meaning ultimately that the status quo was favoured over new governing solutions.
- Election results tended to lead to 'divided government', with competing constellations of political party actors governing each of the parliamentary chambers (*Bundestag* and *Bundesrat*).

- The federal government was able to extract leverage in intergovernmental relations due to its dominant financial position.
- For the richer and more powerful *Länder*, a reform of the federal order would offer an opportunity to roll back the competence creep of the federal government and would look to streamline decision-making nationally by decentralizing greater functional capacity to the level of the *Länder*, which would extend their sphere of autonomous decision-making.

The first federal reform commission

The hurdles for changing Germany's federal system were very high, a consequence of the response to the ease with which democracy and the then federal system had been dismantled in the 1930s. The Basic Law established a high threshold of support necessary to make structural changes to the constitutional order – a two-thirds majority had to be secured in both *Bundestag* and *Bundesrat*. This threshold has subsequently underpinned the constitutional stability of the Federal Republic; but it also made it especially difficult for even widely supported changes to be approved and implemented.

For the purposes of constitutional review, the *Bundestag* and *Bundesrat* establish a joint committee, bringing together 16 members of each chamber (Benz, 2008). These cross-party forums are seen as a means by which to secure built-in support for any proposed amendments. In October 2003, a cross-party reform commission was formed, drawing together representatives of the governing coalition in the Bundestag, as well as the principal opposition parties, federal government representatives alongside representatives of the *Länder* themselves, and representatives of the *Länder* governments who also operated through the institution of the *Bundesrat*. This Joint Commission of the *Bundestag* and the *Bundesrat* for the Modernization of the Federal Constitutional Order (the Federal Reform Commission) was tasked with the overall brief of 'modernizing' the federal constitutional order and, in so doing, to improve the state's capacity both to operate and to take decisions (*Handlungs- und Entscheidungsfähigkeit*). In a reflection of negative public sentiment towards the federal system, the commission's particular aims were to consider:

- The allocation of legislative competence between the federal government (*Bund*) and the *Länder* themselves.
- The responsibilities and opportunities for co-decision-making that the *Länder* held in federal law-making (*Bundesgesetzgebung*).

- Financial relations between the *Bund* and the *Länder*. (Deutscher Bundestag, 2003)

The new territorial politics of German federalism was evident from the outset in this constitutional debate. Even in the prelude to the commission beginning its deliberations, divergences between the priorities of the *Länder* became apparent, and indeed shaped the ultimate scope of the commission's reform agenda. Clearly, the terms of reference for this exercise in constitutional redrafting offered enormous scope for the richer and more powerful *Länder* to secure greater policy autonomy in a range of areas which would allow them to compensate themselves to a degree for the perceived injustices of the financial equalization system, whereby their own economic success was effectively being penalized, or at least taxed, to shore up the economies of the less prosperous *Länder*. The smaller, and economically weaker, *Länder* themselves sought actively to insulate themselves from a potential retreat of the federal government (Bund) from a number of key areas of fundamental support. In order to do so, a coalition of East German and smaller, poorer West German *Länder* had, prior to the establishment of the reform commission, successfully lobbied the federal government in 2003 to exclude three significant areas from the debate in the commission itself:

- The territorial restructuring to redraw *Länder* boundaries and thereby to create a more homogeneous geographic and economic map.
- The existing financial equalization system (which was set to continue until 2019 in any case).
- The fiscal autonomy of the *Länder*, which the poorer ones feared would lead to potentially disastrous tax competition between them.

These exclusions effectively shelved the most divisive issues, improving prospects for agreement in other areas (Rowe and Turner, 2013) which might better recognize and accommodate the territorial diversity which had come to shape German politics over recent decades, whilst also modernizing, streamlining and improving the complexity of the decision-making process. As Edmund Stoiber, the prime minister of Bavaria at the time, anticipated, this was set to be a landmark moment for the development of a constitutional framework that would recognize the new territorial politics inherent in German federalism, delivering wide-reaching competence reallocation and 'the mother of all reforms' (Scharpf, 2007) (see Table 2.3).

Also with a nod towards the eventual accommodation of interests that would be required by this commission, there was a joint chairmanship,

Table 2.3　*Composition of the First Federal Reform Commission, 2003–04*

House	Representation	Number
Bundesrat	Each of the 16 *Land* premiers	16
Bundestag	SPD	8
	CDU	6
	Greens	1
	FDP	1
Total		32

Source: data from: http://www.bundesrat.de/cln_350/nn_8344/DE/ foederalismus/ foederalismus-node.html?__nnn=true&__nnn=true#doc23034bodyText4.

shared by Edmund Stoiber, at that time still the minister president of Bavaria and the leader of the CSU, representing the *Länder* level, and Franz Müntefering, leader of the SPD party group (Fraktion) in the *Bundestag*.

The commission met between 2003 and 2004, which was a window of opportunity between *Land* elections that would allow the business of reform discussions to be carried out away from the routine political competition of elections. The commission began its work in November 2003, with plenary sessions complemented by a network of working groups and hearings of official experts. Most of the meetings were held in public, but they received scant public or media attention (Benz, 2008: 446). The real conflicts were addressed in working groups held out of the public eye, or in informal meetings of representatives from the different groups. In practical terms, what this then led to was a set of debates about how the *Bundesrat* veto could be rolled back and thus speed up the decision-making process. In return, the more powerful *Länder* would be looking for a means to extend their own autonomous decision-making capacities. At the same time, the Joint Tasks (such as regional economic development where the federal and *Länder* levels jointly planned policy) would be reconsidered.

Given the tight window for decision-making within the commission, negotiations needed to be wrapped up in the late autumn of 2004. In fact, the real substantive debate was concluded even earlier than this; a prime ministerial working paper put forward to the commission in May by the *Länder* prime ministers rejected nearly all the proposals suggested by the federal level, excluded all the issues where conflict amongst the *Länder* themselves could not be resolved, and presented a long and comprehensive list detailing their own demands for the transfer of legislative functions and compensating fiscal transfers (Scharpf, 2005). To the minds of the *Bundesrat* negotiating side, therefore, this working paper was a final list of demands. Yet the working groups still carried on, even though this generated further splits between the *Länder* representatives in these forums, who were mandated to negotiate for further competence reallocation, and the specialists who were looking for the most appropriate solutions to problems of policy functions. A major critique of the commission was therefore that it did not itself facilitate enough bargaining across issue areas nor in the specialized working groups (ibid.). Package deals might have provided a solution, but time was running out.

The outcome of the First Federal Reform Commission

Ultimately, the Federal Reform Commission was unable to deliver on its original objective to bring forward proposals for constitutional reform which would likely secure the requisite cross-party support in both the *Bundestag* and *Bundesrat*. Ostensibly it was failure to agree compromise positions in the sensitive area of education policy that the commission fell apart. The *Land* negotiators were pushing for an extreme roll-back of the state on education policy; the federal government by contrast was seeking more control of federal frameworks for education than the *Länder* were willing to accept. Ultimately, the federal negotiators preferred the status quo to any of the options being put on the table. As a result, the negotiations ended without the commission submitting a proposal for constitutional amendments to the federal legislature, as it had been charged to do (Benz, 2008). To some observers, the *Länder* demands were simply mutually incompatible and were thus never likely to achieve a solution in this forum; greater autonomy would be impossible to align with an overarching commitment to an equivalence of living conditions, and certainly not within the confines of existing *Land* geographic boundaries (Scharpf, 2009).

However, in reality, it was disputes amongst the *Länder* themselves that led to the failure of the Reform Commission. The bigger and more prosperous *Länder* had already made quite significant concessions even before the commission took up its deliberations; in exchange, the eastern and smaller and/or economically weaker western *Länder* had gone along with demands for the abolition of joint tasks and for the transfer of autonomous legislative competence in the areas of regional economic policy, labour market policy, and social and environmental policy in return for the total elimination of federal competences in the field of education, a core area of *Land* sovereignty. But given that many of these weaker *Länder* were economically dependent on the federal level for financial support, coupled with their fears over their capacity to engage in a more competitive federalism, greater 'autonomy' often appeared to them as a threat, not an opportunity, and as a result they tended quite often to concede readily to the federal negotiators in the working groups. This meant that ultimately, when the final list of compromise agreements was reached, the stronger *Länder* felt that they had obtained very little from their willingness to compromise and ultimately from the deal that was struck (Scharpf, 2005). As the *Länder* had precommitted themselves to achieving consensus, the package deal fell apart and the two chairmen had to admit defeat (Benz, 2008: 448).

But whilst in the rawest terms the commission had ultimately failed to deliver what was demanded of it, there had been some notable progress made between the negotiators and compromise proposals had been reached in a number of important areas. For instance, in the final weeks of their deliberations, the commission members did achieve a minimal agreement on reducing the *Bundesrat*'s veto rights, although this fell far short of the federal government's original expectation. On the issue of autonomy and extending the exclusive legislative competences of the *Länder*, however, the compromise deals reached in the commission touched on only a number of relatively unimportant issues – the exceptions being universities and payment for civil servants (ibid.: 447).

Taking forward the reform agenda: the new grand coalition

National-level grand coalitions, such as that established after the 2005 federal election, are rare in German politics. The only previous grand coalition between two major political parties, the CDU/CSU and the SPD, was in office between 1966 and 1969. Grand coalitions do offer a different opportunity framework for taking forward large-scale political projects; indeed the 1960s grand coalition had produced the major reforms that introduced the Joint Tasks and strengthened the fiscal equalization processes which were now seen as so problematic. A grand coalition offers a unique window of opportunity for reform because a number of veto powers are rendered irrelevant (or 'absorbed') and electoral competition between both major parties is suspended. The objective is to deliver good governing solutions so as to secure a favourable result at the next election (Zohlnhöfer, 2011). With the issue of systemic malaise still unresolved, taking forward the agenda for a far-reaching reform of federalism was chief on the 'to do' list upon the CDU/CSU–SPD government taking office in 2005: it was listed as a key objective in the new government's coalition agreement and would be an important early marker of the new grand coalition's capacity to pass important legislation (Moore et al., 2008: 397).

Rather than reconvene a new reform commission, proposals for reform of the federal order were simply discussed in a series of specialist committees. These involved members of both the *Bundestag* and *Bundesrat* as well as members of the grand coalition government and the prime ministers of the *Länder*. Essentially, these committees cherry-picked several of the core ideas which had been negotiated in the 2003–04 commission, revising the final proposals which had been outlined, though never adopted, and putting forward clear proposals for constitutional amendments on this basis. Again, the more complex and controversial issues of public finance (fiscal federalism) as well as the fiscal equalization system and the contentious issue of boundary changes were left out of the negotiations. Discussions took place over three months, between March and May 2006, with votes on the proposals taken in both houses in June and July 2006. Only two *Länder* did not support the *Bundesrat* vote on the proposals: Mecklenburg-Western Pomerania rejected the full set of proposals, whilst neighbouring Schleswig-Holstein abstained in the vote. Nonetheless, the reform proposals were adopted and entered into force on 1 September 2006, representing the most extensive and far-reaching reforms to the Basic Law since the creation of the Federal Republic. In the *Bundesrat*, a qualified, or two-thirds, majority equates to 46 of the 69 votes available; even at the time of the vote, however, *Länder* governments led by parties in the grand coalition in the federal government (CDU/CSU and SPD) only totalled 44 votes, making engagement with the political demands of the FDP particularly crucial. One way of doing this was for the chancellor, Angela Merkel, to offer a personal commitment to the leadership of the FDP that the second stage of federal reform, that is to say, financial relationships, would be tackled relatively quickly in the new parliament. The FDP is a strong supporter of a more competitive form of federalism, especially around the incentive structures of the fiscal equalization process (Heinz, 2010).

The key component of the reform deal that was struck was to clarify and 'disentangle' legislative competencies with a view to unlocking the 'joint decision trap'. The Basic Law had set out three types of legislative powers:

1. *Exclusive powers at the federal level*, embracing important national strategic issue areas such as foreign policy and immigration.
2. *Concurrent powers*, areas where either the federation or the *Länder* can legislate, but over which federal law takes precedence, such as civil and criminal law, welfare policy or energy policy.
3. *Federal framework powers*, which are areas in which the federal level

can establish a legislative framework into which *Land* laws then have to fit, such as in higher education, regulation of the press or land-use planning.

In an effort to streamline the law-making process, the grand coalition made changes across the following areas:

- A series of new areas were added to the list of *exclusive* federal competences as set out in Article 73 of the Basic Law, including powers to fight international terrorism, to control gun ownership and on nuclear energy.
- In terms of *concurrent* powers, the role of the federal government was curtailed significantly, making it more difficult for the federal government to act as lead legislator. The federal level could henceforth only pass 'essential' legislation in ten specified areas, such as food security or welfare policy. A further set of areas would then be specified where the federal level did not have to meet the 'essential' criteria.
- Also in terms of *concurrent* powers, an innovation was put forward which would give the *Länder* the right to deviate from federal legislation in a list of specified policy fields, such as environmental protection or entry into higher education.
- *Federal framework powers* (Article 75 of the Basic Law) were abolished in a further bid to clarify legislative responsibilities in the federal system. It was the federal government's increasingly tight understanding of the areas where it could pass framework laws under Article 75, if it were 'essential' to promote equivalent living conditions, that had made for increased **Politikverflechtung** in these areas. The Constitutional Court was a significant actor here, ruling – in 2004 on junior professorships and in 2005 on student fees – that the federal government was interpreting 'essential' too broadly. (Benz, 2008)

From this point onwards, there were to be simply three types of legislative procedure: the exclusive law-making competence of the *Bund* (Articles 71 and 73), concurrent legislative powers shared between the *Bund* and the *Länder* (Articles 72 and 74), and the exclusive legislative authority of the *Länder* (Article 70).

The amendments put forward under the grand coalition also sought to limit blockages within the federal decision-making process, aiming to reduce the percentage of legislation that was subject to a *Bundesrat* veto from the then current levels of around 60 per cent to a lower level of 35–40 per cent. Achieving this compromise was complex, given that reducing the *Bundesrat*'s veto player capacity would necessarily entail a loss of power. The prime ministers of the *Länder* accepted proposals to reduce the *Bundesrat*'s veto capacity, both in the name of the greater good of reforming the federal system, as well as in return for the greater capacity to 'deviate' under areas of concurrent legislation, as set out above.

In addition, the *Länder* secured a number of new autonomous legislative powers in a set of core areas. These were not as extensive as the stronger, more powerful *Länder* had originally strived for, but they went some way towards offering a new capacity for independent policy-making at the *Land* level. Instead of full competence in regional economic policy, for instance, the *Länder* were now given the right to regulate shop closing hours and bars and restaurants. Rather than achieving full autonomy for social or health care policy decisions, the *Länder* were given the power to regulate one aspect of this area alone: care homes. Similarly, in the area of environmental policy, a full set of autonomous powers for the *Länder* was not achieved; instead they secured more narrowly circumscribed rights to legislate in the area of noise made by leisure activities. The power to adopt individual civil service regulations and pay scales was transferred wholesale to the *Länder*, though this was relatively undisputed.

The new reforms to the distribution of competences in the federal system in 2006 also addressed the 'double *Politikverflechtung*' of European policy-making in Germany. The previous stipulation that a *Bundesrat*-nominated representative of the *Länder* would exercise Germany's rights as a member state of the EU in any areas that fall under the exclusive competence of the *Länder* was restricted to exclusive competences in three areas alone: school education, culture and broadcasting. Other areas where the *Bundesrat* had previously been able to exercise those rights in the EU, such as leading for Germany on research policy or internal security, were now no longer open to it.

Initial assessments indicate that the reforms have indeed amended the scope of federalism in Germany. The reforms went some way towards redefining the scope for autonomous policy-making at the *Land* level and have opened up new scope for legislative diversity across the 16 *Länder*, which has started to be enacted. There has been a noticeable streamlining of the process of law-making. In the period between 1 September 2006 when the federal reforms came into force through to 27 October 2009, 39 per cent of laws passed required *Bundesrat* consent, considerably less than the 60 per cent average prior to the federal reforms, and in line with the objectives of the reformers. However, this number did rise slightly over the next 18 months to an average of 44 per cent, due largely to the *Landtag* elections in North Rhine-Westphalia in May 2010, where the election of an SPD–Green coalition removed the party political alignment between the *Bundestag* and *Bundesrat* (Schneider, 2012: 228). With regard to the new possibility for the *Länder* to 'deviate' from federal legislation, in the period from the entry into force of the federal reforms on 1 September 2006 and March 2012, this provision had been used only 14 times – contradicting the fears expressed by critics at the time that the deviation option would lead to an even stronger organizational splintering in the execution of federal legislation (Schneider, 2012).

Nonetheless, the 2006 reforms of federalism have widely been criticized for being minimal (e.g. Jeffery, 2008) and for not offering the root and branch reform of the federal system which is needed in the country. The key aims of 'disentanglement', less intergovernmental interdependence and fewer veto points would have allowed for more fleet-footed responses to new policy challenges but would also have allowed for a greater degree of transparency in German politics, allowing voters to assign responsibility for decisions to a particular level of governmental authority. Yet these aims have not been achieved to any significant extent. The constitutional amendments which were ushered in by this, the most comprehensive reform of the federal order in the history of the Federal Republic, remain marginal, or 'innocuous' as one prominent commentator has termed them (Scharpf, 2008). If anything, the aim of disentangling the complex interlocking of decision-making responsibility that these reforms have set out, simply create new opportunities for re-entanglements by other means. For instance, what the amended Articles 72–5 and 84 achieve in disentangling governmental responsibility, a new Article 104a on *Bund-Länder* financing takes away (Jeffery, 2008). In the area of EU policy coordination, the changes have ultimately resulted in increased complexity and further interlocking of responsibilities (Moore and Eppler, 2008).

The second set of federal reforms: tackling financial relations

Again under the unique 'window of opportunity' presented by a grand coalition government at the federal level, a Second Federal Reform Commission was established at the end of 2006, with an express remit to consider the thorny issue of fiscal federalism within the German system. This commission on 'the modernization of financial relations between the federal government and the *Länder*' took the same format as the first, failed reform commission in 2003–04, drawing together a cross-party selection of representatives from both chambers of parliament. However, this time there were representatives of the federal government taking part – the ministers of justice, the interior and the finance minister, as well as the head of the Chancellor's Office – and, on the other side, three of the smaller, less prosperous *Länder* – Rhineland Palatinate, Brandenburg and Thuringia – delegated their finance minister rather than their prime minister to attend the proceedings. This second commission was led by a joint CDU/CSU–SPD leadership, with Günther Oettinger (CDU prime minister of Baden-Württemberg) and Peter Struck (the leader of the SPD group in the *Bundestag*). The Second Federal Reform Commission was established in December 2006 and put forward its final recommendations in March 2009.

As with the First Federal Reform Commission, inter-*Länder* differences of interest came to shape the terms of the debate, most notably with regard to federal support for poor budgetary politics. The federal government in Germany has no control of the borrowing of the *Länder*; however, its dominant role in taxation makes it implicitly responsible for the debts which the *Länder* accrue (Rodden, 2006: 150). This then means that the federal government would find itself periodically having to 'bail out' the poorer, weaker *Länder* so as to avoid a fiscal crisis. This situation was unsatisfactory for the richer *Länder* in particular, who vehemently disagreed with making payments to their weaker counterparts, which would effectively penalize themselves for prudent household management/budgetary responsibility. Although this system was suboptimal, the two-thirds majority in both the *Bundestag* and *Bundesrat* required to reform this system made it especially resistant to change, because the weaker *Länder* would be able to form a blocking minority (Adelberger, 2001).

A further need to reform financial relations within Germany's federal system was indicated by a series of Federal Constitutional Court (FCC) rulings on *Land*-level debt. As far back as 1992, the FCC had ruled that two *Länder*, Saarland and Bremen, were effectively unable to solve their fiscal problems without support from the federal level. As a result, the *Bund* provided bailouts to both states between 1994 and 2004 (Feld and Baskaran, 2009). In the 2000s, Berlin, followed by Saarland and Bremen, all tried to convince the FCC of the need for additional bailout transfers. The Court, however, declined any claim to the constitutional right of a debt-ridden *Land* to be bailed out by the federal government; Berlin was deemed capable by the Court of solving its own fiscal problems. However, in its ruling, the FCC did demand that German politicians formulate effective borrowing restrictions in order to avoid the need for future bailouts (Rodden, 2006; Feld and Baskaran, 2009).

Negotiators on this reform commission were crucially aware of the growing public appetite for debt controls, particularly as the global economic climate worsened dramatically during their deliberations. This had two crucial impacts on the work of the commission. Firstly, it strengthened the resolve amongst those taking part to reform the German fiscal federalism system. Secondly, it led directly to an agreement on a new debt regulation formula, a mechanism that aimed to prevent the wide-scale debt issues which were widely perceived as underlying the financial crisis (Rowe and Turner, 2013).

However, once again the commission was narrowed in its scope before it even took up its deliberations. The key issues with the most potential to impact on disentanglement and accountability – that is, the fiscal equalization system and discussions on introducing a meaningful level of fiscal autonomy for the *Länder* – were again bracketed out of this discussion. Instead, the focus was placed on controlling debt. The aim was to make *Länder* governments more directly accountable for the debts they incur – yet this aim was then dropped in favour of introducing new techniques on debt management.

There was a general consensus that a deal could and should be brokered on the debt issue by the grand coalition, with powerful arguments being made by all parties that continued high levels of public debt would be not only financially unstable for the country as a whole, but could prove disastrous from the point of view of intergenerational justice.

The primary output of this reform commission was agreement on a so-called 'debt brake' (*Schuldenbremse*), which will come into effect fully in 2016 at the federal level, and in 2020 at the *Land* level. The debt brake replaces the previous constitutional restrictions on public borrowing (Articles 115 and 109 of the Basic Law). The debt brake aims to prevent future excessive fiscal indebtedness (Feld and Baskaran, 2009). Extra financial assistance was made available to five *Länder* with significant public debt issues (Berlin, Bremen, Saarland, Saxony Anhalt and Schleswig-Holstein) in a bid to ease the transition process through to 2020; from that point onwards, the *Länder* will not be allowed to incur any new public debt, apart from in very tightly regulated circumstances such as abnormal economic developments or natural catastrophes. Providing the enticement of additional side payments within the negotiations was seen as a further means by which a settlement could be agreed and which were ultimately regarded by the richer *Länder* as the only means by which their poorer counterparts would have any hope of setting balanced budgets in the future (Rowe and Turner, 2013). The territorial interests of the stronger *Länder* were also served by this reform, reducing the risk of future extraordinary bailouts of the poorer *Länder* and, significantly, enhancing the possibility of additional tax-setting autonomy in the future (Renzsch, 2010).

The ratification process of the commission's proposals also illustrated the increasing salience of territorial diversity in German politics. In the *Bundesrat* vote on the proposed measures, two *Länder* which were set to benefit from the transition payment scheme – Berlin and Schleswig-Holstein – both abstained, arguing that historic debts were not being adequately addressed (Rowe and Turner, 2013). The *Land* of Mecklenburg-West Pomerania also rejected the reforms, arguing that it had made significant cutbacks to balance its own books, was struggling with the highest unemployment rate amongst the German *Länder* and yet would still have to bear the burden of supporting this new budgetary 'consolidation assistance' for the other *Länder* as well (Pergande, 2009). *Länder* that had so far considered themselves as economically weak were now being forced to contribute to the reduction of public debt in other, potentially economically stronger though more indebted, *Länder* (Heinz, 2010).

This second set of federal reforms, which came into force on 1 August 2009, only concerned financial relations between the *Bund* and the *Länder*, whereas the 2006 reforms affected a broad range of policy areas. It is interesting to note that *Länder* in apparently similar economic positions voted differently on the reform measures, illustrating how policy preferences within them diverge, irrespective of objective economic indicators. We will return to this point below.

Understanding non-reform: the two faces of German federalism

Given the huge structural problems inherent within Germany's federal system, and the perception that federalism itself was to blame for so many of the country's problems, why then did the reformers ultimately fail in their ambitions to achieve comprehensive reform?

One primary argument focuses on the high institutional thresholds required within the system itself. It is very difficult to overcome the pathologies of joint decision-making through a process of joint decision-making itself, which is what both the commission-driven approach and the subsequent, albeit less formal, negotiations under the grand coalition ultimately did. Under these conditions, it is hard to change effectively the structures of a federal system (Behnke and Benz, 2009).

A second explanation put forward for non-reform is that Germany's unitary instincts prevent the kind of far-reaching reform which would allow for the political expression of divergent attitudes through policy choices (Jeffery, 2008). Political culture in Germany, it is argued, favours uniform, state-wide policies, rather than differences from *Land* to *Land* (Scharpf, 2008). This explanation is less convincing. It appears to discount – or ignore – the 'territorializing' pressures inherent within German federalism which have shaped innovation and difference in

Länder politics especially, but arguably not only since German unification. And it ignores the paradoxical structure of public opinion noted earlier which favours both *Land*-level decision-making and expects uniformity of outcomes.

The main drivers of all of the discussions on strengthening autonomy at the *Länder* level and disentangling responsibilities, after all, have been the bloc of rich, southern *Länder*: Bavaria, Baden-Württemberg and Hesse. It is these actors who have been in the vanguard leading calls for a more competitive version of federalism that allows for more inter-regional policy variation, alongside clear limitations on the scope of inter-regional solidarity that is provided for by the fiscal equalization mechanism. Successive leaderships in these *Länder* in the 1990s and 2000s have articulated forcefully a sense of territorial self-interest, based on a desire to use their economic muscle for their own ends, rather than in transfers to their less well-off counterparts. Where we have good data on Bavarian public attitudes, there are at least echoes of this territorial self-interest in public opinion.

Yet the consensual decision-making forums of German federalism, with their high thresholds for reform, have meant that this southern bloc is consistently outvoted on reformist agendas which would pave the way for greater independence and autonomous policy competence. The net effect has been to establish an asymmetric situation of dependence within German federalism, with the East German *Länder*, alongside some smaller West German *Länder*, economically dependent on the funding flows from the federal government. It is difficult in these circumstances to see Germany as straightforwardly unitarist. Instead it appears polarized between a pro-autonomy 'rich south' and a pro-federal 'poor east'. The remaining *Länder* oscillate between support for either agenda, depending on individual circumstances at the given time.

There is in other words a strong logic of territory at play within German federalism alongside the unitarist logic imposed by the institutional structures of the federal system. This logic has informed the competing positions which the *Länder* have brought into successive negotiations on reform of the federal constitutional order throughout the 2000s, and it is this logic which explains in large part also the failure within the Federal Reform Commission to put forward a position on reform proposals acceptable to all the *Länder* (Rowe and Turner, 2013). It is striking how much more attention has been given to this territorial logic by (especially younger) scholars of German federalism in recent years, where the focus has been on pinpointing *Land*-by-*Land* variations in parties and party systems (Jun et al., 2008; Bräuninger and Debus, 2012), coalition formation (Oberhofer and Sturm, 2010), voting behaviour (Hough and Jeffery, 2003; Völkl et al., 2008), parliamentarism

(Reutter, 2008), systems of government (Leunig, 2006), models of democracy (Freitag and Vatter, 2008), and public policy outcomes (Hildebrandt and Wolf, 2008; Turner, 2011).

This work challenges unitarist understandings of German federalism simply by taking the *Land* as a unit of analysis. The traditional unit of analysis has been a systemic one which explores the interlocked properties of the system as a whole, prioritizing a national view on the coordination processes between the *Länder* and federal governments and their nexus in the *Bundesrat*. These different units of analysis reveal different faces of German federalism: the one unitarist and focused on the politics of coordination, the other decentralized and focused on the politics of territorial difference. These two faces stand in tension, but not necessarily in contradiction. But their tensions suggest a political system that has not yet found a new balance of 'unity and diversity' as robust as the traditional one which favoured unity over diversity.

Conclusion

German federalism remains at a crossroads. In spite of the new settlements achieved under the grand coalition in 2006 and again in 2009, and under the significant amendments to the Basic Law which these introduced, unease over both policy-making autonomy and in particular financial relationships are likely to prompt further change in the near term. To start with, the analyses of the execution of the new policy competences which the *Länder* secured under the 2006 reforms show that these have as yet had minimal impact (Zohlnhöfer, 2008; Schneider, 2012); in order to execute these fully, it is likely that functional pressures will initiate a spillover effect, with the stronger *Länder* pushing for fuller competences at their level in order to enact properly the competences accorded to them under the 2006 reform programme. Secondly, whilst the impacts of the debt brake are likely to restrict *Land* government spending in the first instance, over the longer term, given different levels of economic activity in the *Länder* themselves, the brake could well serve to highlight that diversity even more, with the stronger *Länder* able to finance public projects which others are forced to shelve without recourse to public borrowing mechanisms. Finally, the implementation of the new federal equilibrium as it stands after the 2009 reforms is overshadowed by two impending financial negotiations which have significant implications for the long-term public finances of the *Länder*: the existing financial equalization system, the **Länderfinanzausgleich**, which is due to expire in 2019; and the second Solidarity Pact which offers legacy transition support to the poorer East German *Länder*, which is also due to end in

2019. Negotiations over future incarnations of both of these financial programmes sets up clear lines of conflict amongst the *Länder*, between the winners and the losers of each system, challenging further the very foundations of any notion of an 'equivalence' of living conditions in the Federal Republic.

It is clear that German federalism is not a static framework but rather a dynamic accommodation of competing pressures which is constantly under review. Yet the pressures inherent within it are increasingly centrifugal rather than centripetal: the relevance of the territorial dimension is in finding an increasing expression of federalism across the multiple facets of federal politics; and the new federal constitutional arrangements need to allow for – albeit modest – policy innovations to shift the delivery of *Land*-level policy even further away from a uniformity. To that end, Germany's newly established federal balance is simple a stepping stone in a long process of federal renewal.

Chapter 3

Partisan Dealignment and Voting Choice

RUSSELL J. DALTON

Herr and Frau Schneider had grown up in post-war Germany. They have very distinct images of the parties, and especially the two large *Volksparteien*. The Christian Democrats (CDU) had brought peace and prosperity to Germany, and they strongly agreed with the CDU on economic and religious issues as upper-middle-class Christians. In contrast, they see the Social Democrats (SPD) as untrustworthy and too close to the communists; they would never vote SPD. Thus both Schneiders have a strong political attachment to the CDU and vote consistently for the party.

Their son Christian has a different view of politics. Both large parties look a bit old-fashioned in terms of their issues and political style. He sees the Greens as more attuned to his tastes. The Greens caution about the excess materialism of Germany (as represented by his parents' two Mercedes in the garage and vacations abroad); the party is concerned about global warming and other environmental issues; and the Greens are more socially tolerant. If the Pirate Party looked to do well in the 2013 elections, Christian might also support this party.

This generation gap in the Schneider family is a microcosm of the German electorate. Although they live in the same house and share most of the same social characteristics in terms of class and religion, these family members have substantially different images of parties and elections. The elder Schneiders think of politics in terms of class and religious cleavages, and are sceptical of political change; Christian is interested in specific issues that don't always fit these frameworks. The elder Schneiders have strong party attachments; Christian isn't 100 per cent loyal to any political party.

These same patterns can be seen in the German electorate as a whole. Where once a stable basis of party competition seemed to determine electoral outcomes, fewer people today seem to have firm party ties. The traditional bonds to social groups, such as class and religion, have eroded over time. Certainly some voters remain connected to a social milieu or a habitual party tie, but the number of these voters has steadily decreased.

Instead of relying on such long-term party bonds, more Germans are entering each election without a certain party choice and are deciding their vote based on the issues and candidates of the campaign. This was clearly evident in recent *Bundestag* elections. All three minor parties – the FDP, the Greens and Linke – had record high vote shares in 2009 (while the SPD sank to a record low), and then the minor parties lost many of these votes in 2013 (while the Social Democrats rebounded only slightly). Recent elections give increasing attention to the personalities of the chancellor candidates and other party leaders, perhaps stimulated by the importance of televised political debates. Issues such as global warming, immigrant populations, the EU and foreign policy motivate many people to change their vote between elections – the inter-election volatility of voting results seems to be increasing.

While these examples of electoral change have steadily developed in the West, a different situation exists in the East. Since unification Easterners have celebrated their new democratic freedoms and have exercised their new voting rights. Easterners' relatively recent introduction to democratic elections precludes the type of long-term party ties that guide some Western voters like the elder Schneiders. Similarly, the social and economic dislocations of German unification blurred the social cleavages that historically provided a framework for electoral politics in the West. In short, Easterners are developing their party preferences in this dynamic political environment. Thus in comparisons to Westerners, Easterners are even more changeable in electoral terms.

This chapter focuses on the electoral behaviour of the German public and examines the political differences between Westerners and Easterners. Elections are a useful setting to study political attitudes and behaviours because they require that people think about contemporary issues and make voting choices. During elections, citizens express their judgements about the past accomplishments of political parties and make choices about the future course of the nation. Elections also mobilize and display the political cleavages existing within a society. Thus, a study of voting behaviour can tell us a great deal about how citizens think about politics and the political legacy of Germany's divided history.

The chapter begins by describing the weakening of party bonds that led to the present period of more fluid electoral politics. Social cleavages and party attachments are two main factors that provide the enduring basis of party competition, and the chapter discusses how these social cues have changed as well. I then examine the role of issues and candidate images in guiding electoral behaviour and in defining policy contrasts between Easterners and Westerners. The final section discusses the implications of these findings for the German party system and democratic process.

The erosion of traditional party loyalties

In the early history of the Federal Republic electoral research often viewed parties and elections in terms of relatively stable and enduring voting blocs. Parties normally build enduring alliances with social groups that share their political vision. Because of this, people use their social position or their judgements about the social group leanings of the parties as a guide to their voting choices. A Ruhr steelworker who votes for the Social Democrats, or a Bavarian Catholic who supports the Christian Social Union, is reflecting his or her own values as well as the political choices available at election time. Thus, social characteristics often provided a good way to describe differences in political values within a nation and the influence of alternative social networks on political behaviour.

Similarly, many people (like the elder Schneiders) develop long-term, affective attachments to a specific political party – often a party that represents their social milieu. Card-carrying SPD party members, for example, begin each election knowing who they will support, just as self-identified Christian Democrats habitually endorse the CDU/CSU. With continued support of their preferred party at successive elections, such affiliations strengthened during the early history of the Federal Republic. Each election typically pitted the same social groups and same partisan camps against one another, with most voters supporting the same party as in the previous electoral battle. Both of these factors – social group cleavages and party attachments – have weakened over the Republic's history.

The erosion of class influences

Social class differences were once central to the political identity and voter support of both the Christian Democrats and Social Democrats. Moreover, both parties were embedded in their own network of support groups (business associations and labour unions) and offered voters distinct political programmes catering to these group interests.

Despite the historical importance of the class cleavage, four decades of electoral results point to an unmistakable decline in class voting differences within the Federal Republic's party system (Knutsen, 2006; Elff and Roßteutscher, 2011; Dalton, 2013: ch. 8). At the height of class-based voting in 1957, the SPD received a majority of working-class votes (61 per cent) but only a small share (24 per cent) of middle-class votes. This produced a 37 percentage point gap in the class bases of party support, rivalling the level of class voting found in other class-polarized party systems such as Britain or Sweden. Over the next two decades, the level of class voting steadily decreased in Germany as in most other advanced industrial democracies. By the 1980s, the percentage point gap in class voting averaged in the teens and this has continued to the present. In the *Bundestag* elections of the 2000s, working-class support for the Social Democrats barely exceeds its vote share among the middle class.

Class differences in voting patterns have narrowed for several reasons. In the most general terms, the expanding affluence and social security of post-war Germany lessened these social divisions. It is not that economic issues are unimportant, but they are now more complex and less clearly linked to occupational status. Furthermore, a host of new issues have entered the political agenda and compete for voters' interests and shape their votes in non-class ways. In addition, the changing structure of the economy has blurred the traditional divisions between the working class and middle class. The dramatic growth of a new middle class (*Neue Mittelstand*) of salaried employees and government workers produced a strata that differs in social position and political behaviour from the traditional middle class (the self-employed and professionals) and the working class. The new middle class now represents the largest sector of the labour force, and in recent elections they have split their votes between left and right parties.

Voters still recognize these class cues; other evidence suggests that they are now better able to perceive the class ties of the parties. Economic and class issues are not less important: these issues still routinely dominate election campaigns. Rather, voters are not relying on social-class cues to make their choices as they once did.

The persisting impact of social class on voting choice is even more blurred for voters in the eastern *Länder*. In the first democratic elections in the early 1990s, it was difficult to apply Western notions of social class to a society that was in the midst of transition from socialism to capitalism. Moreover, the political ties between the parties and class-based interest groups in the East were equally unclear. Class voting patterns have thus fluctuated across elections since 1990. But the elections of the 2000s show a single digit gap in working/middle-class voting differences in the East.

In summary, while social class once was a potent cue in guiding the voting choices of many citizens, the impact of this cue has steadily eroded in the West. And the new voters in the East have not been integrated into this class voting structure, which further blurs the impact of social-class cues on contemporary German elections.

The erosion of religious influences

Historically, religion has also divided the political parties in the Federal Republic. Political debates on the separation of church and state, and persisting differences between Catholics and Protestants, had a formative influence on the party system. The CDU/CSU has tried to bridge the denominational divide. Still, Catholics and the religiously active of both denominations lean toward the CDU/CSU, while Protestants and the non-religious favour the SPD. Religion is often a silent issue in German politics, and occasionally becomes visible in conflicts over religious or moral issues, such as abortion, state support of church programmes and policies toward the family.

As a consequence of the communist era, religious ties are even weaker in the East. Although the German Democratic Republic accepted the existence of the Catholic and Protestant churches, they were under strict government control, which weakened religious ties. For instance, the 2006 World Values Survey found that 56 per cent of Westerners go to religious services at least once a year, compared to 32 per cent in the East; 60 per cent of Westerners consider themselves religious, but only 30 per cent of Easterners. In summary, the East is a much more secularized society, even though the West had experienced its own secularization trend. In addition, unification changed the religious balance of politics in the Federal Republic: Catholics and Protestants are roughly at parity in the West, while the East is heavily Protestant. Thus, unification significantly altered the religious composition of the new Germany.

This religious cleavage also follows a pattern of decline similar to the class cleavage. Changing lifestyles and religious beliefs have decreased involvement in church activities and diminished the church as a focus of social (and political) activities.

Those who are still centred in the class or religious milieus have distinct voting preferences (Elff and Roßteutscher, 2011). However, fewer people today fit the traditional bourgeois/proletariat class models and fewer are religious. Thus, as the number of individuals relying on class or religious cues decreases, the partisan significance of these social characteristics and their overall ability to explain voting also decreases.

The weakening of party attachments

In addition to class and religious ties that are relevant to voting preferences, electoral research finds that people develop direct personal attachments to their preferred political party, which guides their voting and other aspects of political behaviour (Dalton, 2013: ch. 9). Researchers call this a sense of 'party identification'. Party identification is generally socialized early in life, often as part of a family political inheritance or derived from social group cues, and then reinforced by adult voting patterns.

These party ties are important because they can structure a person's view of the political world, provide cues for judging political phenomena, influence patterns of political participation, and promote stability in individual voting behaviour. For instance, 80–90 per cent of partisans routinely support their preferred party at election time regardless of the candidates or the issues of the campaign. The concept of party identification has proven to be one of the most helpful ideas in understanding the political behaviour of contemporary electorates.

The Federal Republic has experienced two distinct phases in the development of party attachments. The stabilization and consolidation of the party system during the 1950s and 1960s strengthened popular attachments to the parties (Baker et al., 1981). In the late 1970s, however, this trend toward partisanship among Western voters slowed, and then reversed. Since 1972 surveys have asked a standard question: 'Many people in the Federal Republic lean toward a particular party for a long time, although they may occasionally vote for a different party. How about you: Do you in general lean toward a particular party? Which one?' Figure 3.1 documents a growing number of Germans who do not feel attached to any political party. In 1972 only 25 per cent of citizens in the West lacked a party attachment; this grew slightly during the 1980s and then accelerated in the 1990s. Today, 40 per cent of Westerners lack party ties. Among partisans the strength of their attachments is also weakening. In addition, other studies find declining membership in political parties and a growing antipathy toward parties and the party system (Mair and van Biezen, 2001; Dalton and Weldon, 2005). So there is broad evidence of declining party attachments and affect among the German public.

Several factors seem to account for this decline in partisanship. The weakening of the social bases of the parties – as represented by changes in class and religious voting – has also eroded voters' bonds to the parties. These social milieus once provided the foot soldiers for party politics, and there are now fewer recruits than in the past. In addition, social modernization has produced an increasingly diverse and fluid social structure, where hereditary party bonds seem anachronistic. People have become less loyal and deferential to political parties and other social and political institutions. One might claim this represents a performance deficit by German parties, the struggles of unification, or scandals over party and candidate finances which have tarnished party images. Many journalists and political experts criticize party politics for its shortcomings, which sends a negative message to the public. In addition, the growing sophistication of the Western electorate may contribute to the weakening of indi-

Figure 3.1   *The growing number of non-partisans*

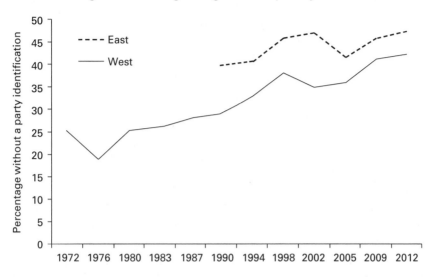

Note: Several pre-election and a post-election survey are included for most timepoints; the 2012 statistics are based on the September/October surveys.

Source: Surveys conducted by the *Forschungsgruppe Wahlen*.

vidual party ties. Similar to the decline of partisanship in the United States, a significant share of younger, politically sophisticated and better educated Germans lack party ties (Dalton, 2012a; 2014). These same individuals are developing self-expressive and post-material values that foster doubts of institutions such as parties. Furthermore, as voters begin to focus on issues as a basis of electoral choice, they are more likely to defect from their normal party predispositions, which erodes these predis-positions in general and makes further defections even more likely.

Party politics in the eastern *Länder* obviously followed a different course. Easterners began their democratic experiences in 1990, so few of them should (or could) display the deep affective partisan loyalties that constitute a sense of 'party identification' (Kaase and Klingemann, 1994). Although some research suggests that many Easterners had latent affini-ties for specific parties in the Federal Republic, these were not long-term attachments born of early life experiences that we normally equate with party identification. The tribulations of unification then strained many Easterners' opinions of the Federal Republic parties and politicians.

Regular measurement of partisan attachments did not begin in Eastern surveys until early 1991. By then, most voters had participated in two national elections (the March 1990 *Volkskammer* and the December

Bundestag elections) as well as regional and local contests. Still, in 1991 two-fifths lacked a party tie. And instead of increasing as people gained experience with the parties, Eastern partisanship remains weak. In 2009 and 2012 there are slightly more non-partisans than in 1991. In short, the first decades of democratic experience with the Federal Republic's party system has not developed partisan ties in the East.

So these trends describe a *dealignment* of the long-term attachments to political parties by a growing proportion of the German public. However, we can interpret these findings differently for the two regions. The decrease in partisanship among Westerners is similar to several other advanced industrial democracies, which suggests that Germany's special problems of unification may simply reinforce a general cross-national dealignment pattern.

In contrast, we might describe Easterners as a pre-aligned electorate. Democratic politics is still a learning experience for many Eastern voters. Party attachments normally strengthen through repeated electoral experiences, especially in newly formed party systems. Thus, the current situation in the East might be closer to the Federal Republic in the immediate post-war period. The partisan attachments of Easterners should strengthen over time, but the dealigning forces of contemporary politics seem to be countering the learning process.

From habituation to voter choice

Although many voters continue to support the same party from election to election, social and partisan dealignment is increasing the fluidity of electoral choice. One sign is the expansion of the party system. In the 1960s and early 1970s, the party system was characterized by a fairly stable pattern of party competition between the CDU/CSU, the SPD and the FDP (see Chapter 4). In the 1980s, the Greens and the issues they espoused introduced new political choices and new volatility in the electoral process. Unification has continued this process, with the introduction of the PDS and its evolution into Die Linke. In the 2013 *Bundestagswahl* the new Alliance for Germany fell only 0.3 per cent below the threshold for winning seats in parliament; the Pirate Party won seats in four state legislatures during the 2009–13 period. These are signs that the electorate is placing less reliance on the stable social and partisan cues that once guided their behaviour.

Evidence of this shift from habituation to voter choice is apparent in a variety of statistics (Schoen, 2004; Wessels, 2009). For instance, in the early 1970s barely 10 per cent of voters reported switching their party choice between elections (see Figure 3.2). This pattern of electoral stabil-

Figure 3.2   *Indications of increasing fluidity of voting choice*

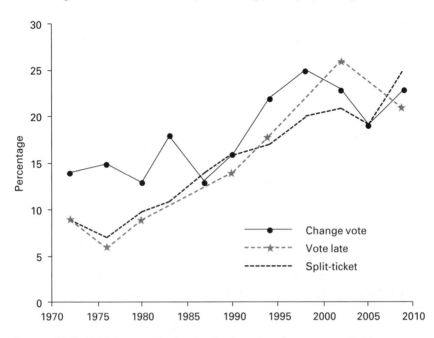

Source: 1972–2009 German Election Studies from *Forschungsgruppe Wahlen*.

ity changed in the 1980s, during which elections were characterized by intense political and personal rivalries between the parties. By the end of the 1990s, nearly a quarter of the Western electorate reported they switched votes. The recent *Bundestag* elections highlighted this volatility, with virtually all the parties experiencing large shifts in their vote shares. According to the 2009 German Longitudinal Election Study, 23 per cent of Westerners and 26 per cent of Easterners reported shifting their votes since the 2005 election. This is relatively high for a parliamentary electoral system. Moreover, because these figures are based on recollection of previous voting, these statistics probably underestimate the actual amount of vote switching.

Split-ticket voting is another possible indicator of the rigidity of party commitments. When Germans go to the polls they cast two votes. The first vote (*Erststimme*) is for a candidate to represent the electoral district; the second vote (*Zweitstimme*) is for a party list that provides the basis for a proportional allocation of parliamentary seats. A voter may therefore split his or her ballot by selecting a district candidate of one party with the first vote and another party with the party-list vote.

The amount of split-ticket voting has also inched upward over time (Schoen, 2000). At the start of the 1970s, less than 10 per cent of all voters split their ballots (see Figure 3.2). The proportion of splitters increased in the 1980s, and by the 1990s a sixth of voters claimed to cast a split ballot. In 2009 this reached 25 per cent among Westerners, and 18 per cent in the East. The growth of split-ticket voting partially reflects the increased strength of minor parties that siphon off second votes from the major parties. In addition, split-ticket voting exemplifies the increasing fluidity of contemporary voting choices.

Another sign of the changing pattern of electoral choice is the timing of voting decisions (Dalton and Wattenberg, 2000: ch. 3). Most Germans once began election campaigns with strong predispositions to support their preferred party, based on enduring social cues and affective party attachments. But as these predispositions weaken, more voters should be making their decisions on the issues and candidates of the campaign, and thus making their decisions later in the election cycle. If this is correct, fewer voters will say that they decided how to vote before the campaign, and more will claim that they decided during the campaign or even on election day itself.

Figure 3.2 indicates that an increasing percentage of Western voters say they are making their decision during the last few weeks of the campaign. The percentage of self-defined late deciders has doubled over time, from less than a tenth of the electorate in the 1960s to nearly a fifth in the 1990s. In the 2009 election, 24 per cent of Westerners said they decided during the last few weeks of the campaign, as did 24 per cent of Easterners. Three days before the 2013 election, the *Forschungsgruppe Wahlen* reported that 32 per cent of Germans were unsure of which party they would support.

In summary, fewer Germans are approaching each election with their decision already made. This volatility is even more clearly apparent among those who lack a party attachment. Instead of habitual or inherited party preferences, or those directed by external group cues, more voters are apparently making their decisions based on the content of the campaign and the offerings of the parties. In analysing those who switched their vote in 2002 and 2005, Bernard Wessels (2009: 413–14) concludes that voter shifts are motivated by legitimate political evaluations, rather than random fluctuations. Electoral politics is shifting from habituation to voter choice.

The changing basis of electoral choice

If the long-term sources of voting choice are weakening in influence, this raises the question of what factors people now use to make their choices. Inevitably, the erosion of social group and partisanship cues must lead to increased reliance on shorter-term factors, such as the issues and candidates of each campaign. Moreover, the evidence of increased party switching between elections suggests that such short-term factors are having an increasing weight on voter choice.

I will focus on the 2005 and 2009 Bundestag elections because the necessary public opinion surveys are available for analysis. These elections also illustrate the current state of the German party system. In 2005 the economy was stagnating despite the economic reforms of the Schröder government (Langenbacher, 2007; Clemens and Saalfeld, 2008; Gabriel et al., 2009). Schröder called for early elections as a mandate for his administration, and Angela Merkel led the challenge from a reinvigorated CDU/CSU. The election ended as a dead heat between the CDU/CSU and SPD – and both Merkel and Schröder declared victory. After weeks of negotiation and the exploration of potential coalitions, the CDU/CSU and a Schröder-less SPD agreed to form a 'grand coalition'.

The 2009 election reflected the tensions produced by four years of the grand coalition (Langenbacher, 2010; Rohrschneider, 2012). The CDU/CSU and SPD struggled to agree on reform policies to continue the upward economic trends, but little significant legislation was produced. When the global recession struck in late 2008, the parties struggled even more over how to react to the declines. This odd political marriage provided the backdrop for the 2009 elections, with the chancellor (CDU) and vice chancellor (SPD) now running against each other. The Social Democrats seemed to suffer most from the government's mixed policy record. Their traditional voters held them accountable for the government's failures, but gave them little credit for its successes. Conversely, Merkel and the CDU/CSU seemed to benefit more from the government's successes than its failures. Merkel emerged from the election as the head of a new coalition government of Christian Democrats and Free Democrats. The Social Democrats suffered their worst electoral showing in the history of the Federal Republic, as leftist voters deserted them for the Linke Party or the Greens. Indeed, all three minor parties – the Free Democrats, Die Linke and the Greens – recorded their highest vote shares ever, another rebuke of the grand coalition of Christian Democrats and Social Democrats.

The 2013 election saw a reversal of this trend towards minor party voting. The CDU/CSU benefited from voter confidence about the performance of the German economy, as well as Merkel's personal popularity, polling its highest vote in almost 20 years. Their success squeezed the minor parties, especially the FDP which failed to achieve the 5 per cent required to enter the *Bundestag*. The end result was an indecisive election, with prolonged negotiations eventually leading to a grand coalition of CDU/CSU and SPD.

In this section I examine various potential causes of citizen voting decisions. I begin by describing variations in social group support of the parties, then expand to describe the impact of political criteria, such as left–right attitudes, as correlates of the vote, before I summarize the weight of the various factors that affect how Germans make their party choices.

The social bases of the vote

Democratic elections are about making policy choices about a future government, and Germans have a rich set of parties and policy programmes from which to choose. As discussed above, factors such as class and religion have historically provided an organizational base for German parties and are a key source of party members and voters. In addition, other social characteristics – such as gender, region and generation – can influence how voters make their choices (Forschungsgruppe Wahlen, 2013a). The voting patterns of social groups also reflect the ideological and policy differences among the parties.

Using reports published right after the September 2013 election, we can describe social differences in voting in 2013 before shifting to more detailed analyses of the 2005 and 2009 elections. Table 3.1 shows that party support still somewhat reflects the traditional social divisions in German society. The CDU/CSU primarily draws its voters from the conservative sectors of society, with greater support from older people, retirees and the middle class. For example, 48 per cent of the self-employed voted CDU/CSU, compared to only 38 per cent among blue-collar workers. Other studies show that Catholics and those who attend church disproportionately support the party.

The SPD's voter base contrasts with that of the CDU/CSU: a disproportionate share of SPD votes comes from blue-collar workers, although middle-class citizens provide most of the party's voters. In some ways, the SPD has suffered because its traditional working-class-voter base has declined in size and it has not established a new political identity that draws a distinct voter clientele.

The Greens' electoral base is heavily drawn from groups that support 'new politics' movements: the middle class, the better educated, and urban voters. Despite the party turning 30 years old in 2010, it still appeals to the young, especially university-educated youth. In 2013 they garnered 11 per cent of the vote from those under 30, but only 5 per cent of the vote from senior citizens.

Die Linke also has a distinct voter base. This is first an East-oriented party, with about a third of its total vote in 2013 coming from there. The party's leftist roots also appear in its appeal to blue-collar workers and the

Table 3.1   *Voting by social characteristics in 2013 (%)*

	CDU/CSU	SPD	Greens	Linke	FDP	AfD	Other
Election result	41.5	25.7	8.4	8.6	4.8	4.7	6.1
Region							
West	42	27	9	6	5	4	6
East	39	17	5	23	3	6	7
Employment status							
Employed	40	26	10	8	5	5	7
Unemployed	22	25	10	21	2	7	13
Retired	48	29	5	9	4	4	1
Occupation							
Self-employed	48	15	10	7	10	6	4
Salaried employees	41	26	10	8	5	5	5
Civil servants	44	25	13	5	6	5	2
Blue-collar worker	38	30	5	11	3	5	8
Education							
Primary education	46	30	4	7	3	3	7
Secondary schooling	43	25	6	10	4	6	6
Abitur	39	24	12	8	5	5	7
University degree	37	23	15	9	7	5	4
Age							
Under 30	34	24	11	8	5	6	12
30–44	41	22	10	8	5	5	9
45–59	39	27	10	9	5	5	5
60 and older	49	28	5	8	5	4	1
Gender							
Men	39	27	8	8	4	6	7
Women	44	24	10	8	5	4	6

Notes: N = 1,572; some percentages may not total 100 because of rounding.

Source: September 2013 Politibarometer Survey, *Forschungsgruppe Wahlen*.

unemployed. It is a party for those frustrated with the economic and political path Germany has followed since unification.

The FDP voters include a high percentage of the middle class, both
white-collar employees and the self-employed. While the Greens attract
liberal, educated youth, the FDP attracts a disproportionate share of
young, better-educated conservatives. But squeezed on the left and right
by other parties, the FDP's lack of a clear identity contributed to their failings in 2013.

The new contender in 2013 was the Alliance for Democracy. The
party's criticism of the EU's policies and the costs of Germany's contribution to the EU were the basis of its appeal to voters. This position

resonated among retirees on fixed income, Easterners, and among some youth. The AfD voter base suggests it drew support away from parties on both the left and the right.

As noted above, these social group differences have generally narrowed over time, as fewer voters make their decisions based on class, religion or other cues. Yet, the ideology and clientele networks of the parties still reflect these traditional group bases, so they have a persisting but modest influence on voting choices.

Ideology and the vote

Issue positions are the currency of politics, and the choice of parties or the choice of governments is closely linked to the policies they will enact. Each campaign, however, has its own set of issues that reflect the political controversies of the day and the parties' choices about what themes to stress in their campaigns. Economics, unemployment and finance domi-nated the 2005 election; by 2009 unemployment, the global recession and the international financial system framed the campaign debate, and these issues continued to dominate the agenda in 2013. At the same time, other voters were motivated by issues such as environmental quality, minority rights and EU relations.

This shift in issue agendas makes it difficult to compare issue voting over time, because the issues themselves are changing as well as party positions. Moreover, we are more interested in the total impact of issues, rather than the specific set of issues that have affected each Bundestagswahl because issues inevitably change between elections.

Therefore I will illustrate the general influence of issue preferences on voting by examining the relationship between left–right attitudes and how people vote (Fuchs and Klingemann, 1989; Dalton, 2013: ch. 10). Left–right attitudes are a sort of 'super issue', summarizing positions on the issues that are currently most important to each voter. For some voters, their left–right position may be derived from views on traditional economic conflicts; for others, their position may reflect their stance on issues such immigrant rights or gender issues. The concerns of German unification or responses to the 2008 crisis of the monetary system can also be translated into a left–right framework. Specific issues might vary across individuals or across elections, but left–right attitudes can summa-rize each citizen's overall policy views.

Table 3.2 displays the relationship between left–right attitudes and party choice in the 2013 election for voters in both the West and East. In both regions there was a very close fit between left–right position and vote. Die Linke, for example, received disproportionate support from leftist voters, especially in the East where it was 63 per cent. In

Table 3.2 *Left–right attitudes and party support (in per cent)*

	Left	Center-Left	Center	Center-Right	Right
Western voters					
Linke	36	15	2	0	0
Greens	18	26	12	1	0
SPD	33	40	32	6	17
FDP	0	1	8	7	17
CDU/CSU	3	9	40	83	61
Other parties	9	9	5	3	6
Total	99%	100%	99%	100%	101%
(Percent of voters)	(4)	(20)	(60)	(14)	(2)
Eastern voters					
Linke	63	35	6	0	–
Greens	11	11	7	0	–
SPD	17	30	20	5	–
FDP	0	1	13	10	–
CDU/CSU	6	21	60	71	
Other parties	3	3	3	14	–
Total	100%	101%	99%	100%	
(Percent of voters)	(8)	(32)	(54)	(5)	(1)

Source: 2013 German Longitudinal Election Study: pre-election survey (not including Berlin). Missing data for far right in East is because of too few respondents.

contrast, few people on the right side of the political spectrum support Die Linke in either region. The Greens are also a predominantly leftist party, with a cultural and social appeal that is noticeably stronger in the West.

The ideological basis of support for the two large established parties is also clearly apparent in Table 3.2. The SPD again had a relatively poor showing in 2013, and this is apparent in its second place showing for far-left voters in both regions. In both regions the Social Democrats vote also erodes as one moves right. The CDU/CSU's voting base presents a mirror image: more than two-thirds of conservative voters support the Union parties, and this steadily declines as one moves left. In both regions there is more than a 60 per cent gap in CDU/CSU support between the most left-wing and most right-wing voters. Finally, as a party standing between the two large established parties, the Free Democrats garner most of their support from people who are just right of centre.

Table 3.2 thus indicates that left–right attitudes, and thereby the specific policy issues that define 'left' and 'right', have a very strong relationship to party preferences as they have in other recent elections. The relationship between left and right and who is voted for is noticeably stronger than the social differences in voting reported in Table 3.1. Research points to the increasing impact of issues and to left–right attitudes over time as voters focus more on what candidates and parties are emphasizing in each election (Roßteutscher and Scherer, 2012). This is one consequence of the shift from stable voting dispositions to more fluid party choice.

Candidate voting

In addition to issue voting, candidate preferences also affect citizens' voting choices. Since the German ballot is divided between a district candidate vote and a party vote, one might assume that candidate voting was always part of the electoral calculus. However, early voting studies found that many people were unaware of the candidates running in their district, and cast their candidate vote as a simple extension of their party preference. Moreover, since the Chancellor was selected by the parties in the *Bundestagswahl*, the image of the Chancellor candidates played a smaller role in *Bundestag* elections than in the candidate-centred direct elections of US or French presidents.

As voting choice has become more fluid, there is some evidence that the importance of candidate image has increased. First, party and candidate preferences are not as closely related as they were in the past (Dalton and Wattenberg, 2000: 53). Second, images of the Chancellor candidates appear to be increasingly related to party choice (Ohr, 2000; Brettschneider, 2001). German Chancellor candidates have turned to television to personalize the campaigns, arranging events for their video appeal and using televised town hall meetings to connect directly with citizens. The growing reliance on private television broadcasting has further accelerated these trends. In the 2002 contest, all the party leaders played a prominent role in party campaign advertising – the Schröder/Stoiber TV duel focused attention on the two Chancellor candidates. Because of the centrality of these candidates one leading political analyst called 2002 the first 'presidential election' in Germany. The Schröder/Merkel debate was also a critical point in the 2005 election; and candidate debates figured prominently in 2009. However, there was only one debate between Merkel and Steinbrück in 2013.

Electoral researchers debate the content of candidate images and thus their implications in predicting voting choices. In addition, there are complex methodological issues involved in measuring the impact of candidate images and separating their effects from party loyalties. Still, as fewer people enter elections with a predetermined party commitment, it seems inevitable that candidate images will gradually become more important in voting choices.

Combining explanations

When all of these potential causal factors – long-term and short-term – come together, they structure the voting choice of Germans. Some people take party cues from social groups, others vote out of habitual party loyalty, and some weigh the candidates and issues of the campaign. Many voters take all these factors into account. The weight of each factor may change from election to election, depending on the salience of issues or the characteristics of the party leaders in each campaign. No single factor solely determines the vote, which rather comes from a mix of factors.

The composition of the mix is illustrated in Figures 3.3 and 3.4 that display the impact of party sympathy, Chancellor candidate preferences, and left–right attitudes on voting choice in the West and East for the 2005 and 2009 elections. This is a simple model compared to the current state

Figure 3.3 *Factors affecting voting preferences in 2005*

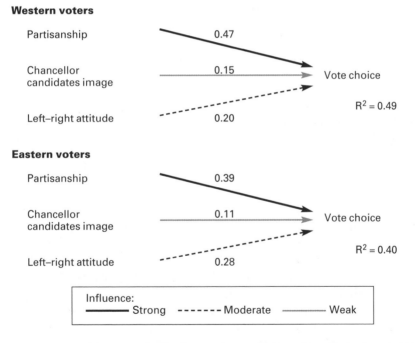

Notes: Figure entries are standardized regression coefficients. Vote choice is coded (1) PDS/*Die Linke*, (2) Greens, (3) SPD, (4) FDP, (5) CDU/CSU. Partisanship is measured by the difference between SPD and CDU/CSU sympathy ratings; candidate image is the difference between Merkl and Schröder sympathy ratings; and left–right attitudes are the respondents' position on an 11-point scale.

Source: 2005 German Election Study, Wissenschaftszentrum Berlin.

Figure 3.4   *Factors affecting voting preferences in 2009*

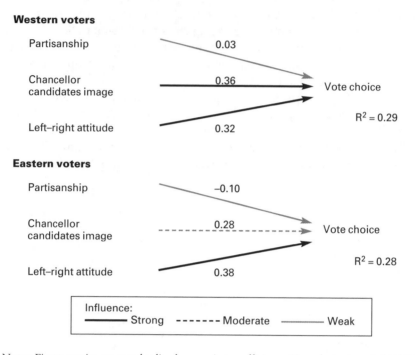

Western voters

Partisanship   0.03

Chancellor   0.36   Vote choice
candidates image

                                                                                                    $R^2 = 0.29$

Left–right attitude   0.32

Eastern voters

Partisanship   –0.10

Chancellor   0.28   Vote choice
candidates image

                                                                                                    $R^2 = 0.28$

Left–right attitude   0.38

Influence:
——————— Strong   - - - - - - Moderate   ————— Weak

Notes: Figure entries are standardized regression coefficients. Vote choice is coded (1) *Die Linke*, (2) Greens, (3) SPD, (4) FDP, (5) CDU/CSU. Partisanship is measured by the difference between SPD and CDU/CSU sympathy ratings; candidate image is the difference between Merkl and Steinmaier sympathy ratings; and left–right attitudes are the respondents' position on an 11-point scale.

Source: 2009 German Longitudinal Election Study.

of electoral research (Gabriel et al., 2009; Wessels et al., 2013), but it reflects some broad patterns that are generally seen in voting studies. The coefficients in the figure represent the influence of each factor while statistically controlling for the effect of the other factors.

Despite the dealignment trend described above, images of the major parties still weigh heavily on the vote choice in 2005, with slightly stronger effects in the West where party ties are stronger (see Figure 3.3). Sympathy towards the CDU/CSU versus the SPD is the strongest single correlate of vote choice in both West and East, and we should expect that those with partisan ties generally follow them at election time. Candidate image – the difference is the affective ratings of Merkel and Schröder – also had a significant impact as the two candidates represented sharply different policies and leadership styles. We expect that the role of candidate image will vary across elections, depending on the popularity of both candidates and the polarization in public opinion toward them. Left–right attitudes, and the issue positions represented by this super issue, also have a significant role in both regions, but with somewhat stronger effects in the East. In replicating this model over several elections in earlier editions of this book, we find there is a general tendency for the Eastern electorate to place more weight on left–right positions in making their voting choices, perhaps because their life conditions are more dependent on post-unification policies and they are less likely to have firm party attachments.

The electoral calculus changed significantly in 2009. The grand coalition blurred public images of the SPD and CDU/CSU that shared control of the government, and placed all the minor parties (both liberal and conservative) in opposition together. So the marked difference in 2009 was the virtual absence of differences in affect towards the SPD and CDU/CSU for predicting voting preferences. Instead, voters place more weight on both candidate images and left–right attitudes in making their voting choices. And again, Easterners place slightly more weight on left–right attitudes than Westerners. The 2009 election was exceptional because of the grand coalition, and one would expect the correlates of vote choice in 2013 to look more similar to the 2005 contest.

The two German electorates

This chapter has highlighted two broad characteristics of electoral politics in contemporary Germany. First, the country has been experiencing a gradual process of party dealignment. For the past three decades, long-term sources of voting choice have diminished in influence among voters in the West. Social class, religion, residence and other social characteristics have a declining impact on voting behaviour. Similarly, a dealignment trend signals a decreasing influence of party loyalties on voting decisions. Fewer Westerners now approach elections with fixed party ties based either on social characteristics or early learned partisan ties. It is not that voters lack partisan leanings, but that the nature of these predispositions are shifting from *strong ties* (group and party attachments) to *weak ties* (issues, candidate images and perceptions of party performance). Much like the findings of American or British electorate research, this erosion in the traditional bases of partisan support has occurred without producing new, enduring bases of support that might revitalize the party system (e.g. Rose and McAllister, 1989; Wattenberg, 1996). Indeed, the lack of a new stable alignment appears to be one of the distinctive features of contemporary party systems.

Citizens in the five new *Länder*, of course, have a much different electoral history. Rather than an erosion of previous social and partisan ties, the Eastern electorate is still learning about democratic politics and the rough-and-tumble life of partisan campaigns. They understandably began this experience with weaker party ties and less certainty about the general structure of political competition. It was uncertain whether they would quickly adapt to the political structures of the West, or remain weakly tied to the party system. Party bonds have not strengthened in the two decades since unification.

The modest impact of long-term determinants of party choice is likely to strengthen the role that policy preferences play in electoral choices. Although most people still habitually support a preferred party, the tentativeness of these bonds will increase the potential that a particular issue or election campaign may sway their voting choice, at least temporarily. More and more, the specific issues of an election will influence voter choice, as a large group of floating voters react to the political stimuli of the election campaign. There is even some evidence that candidate images are a growing factor in voters' decision-making, especially among Easterners. This shift toward issue-based voting is likely to make policy considerations a more important aspect of elections while injecting considerable fluidity into electoral politics – at least until (if ever) a new stable group basis of party support forms.

A second implication of our findings concerns the contrasts between Western and Eastern Germans. There are two distinct electorates within the one German nation, the most distinctive evidence being the sharply different religious preferences. The Western electorate is relatively religious, as well as conservative on economic and social welfare issues; the Eastern electorate is secular and liberal on social issues. In addition, Easterners are more likely to describe themselves as left wing on the left–right scale to a greater extent than Westerners. If the 2009 election had occurred only in the East, for example, the SPD and Die Linke would have won a majority; if we look only at the electorate of the West, the CDU/CSU and FDP majority would have been even larger.

The specific concerns of Easterners and frustrations with the two large governing parties undoubtedly contributed to Die Linke's (formerly the PDS's) success as spokesperson for the disenfranchised East. In 2009 and 2013 Die Linke even displaced the SPD as the largest party in the Eastern states. In contrast, the Social Democrats are the main leftist party in the West. The other minor parties are also developing distinct regional clienteles. The Greens split the leftist vote with the SPD and Die Linke in the West, but have limited appeal to Eastern voters. The Free Democrats appear distinctly more attractive to Westerners. And while the CDU/CSU now seem to draw roughly equivalent support in West and East, the social bases of this support differs.

Regional differences in the patterns of party support can create intra-party tensions. For instance, because CDU voters in the new *Länder* are significantly less religious and less Catholic than their Western counterparts, their attitudes toward abortion and other social issues conflict with the policy programme of the Western CDU. If CDU politicians from the East represent these views, it creates a tension with the party's official policies. If Eastern CDU deputies do not reflect these views, then this produces a representation deficit for Easterners. The SPD and the other parties face similar problems in representing contrasting constituencies in West and East. Thus, the complex relationship amongst horizontal integrations with the national party elite, and the vertical integration between party elites and their social constituencies, has been unbalanced by German unification.

Taken together, these patterns of partisan fluidity and contrasting political alignments across regions do not lend themselves to a simple prediction of the future of the party system. An already complex situation in the 1980s has become even more complex since unification. And dealignment opens the door to new political challengers, such as the AfD or Pirate Party. It appears that electoral politics will be characterized by continued diversity in voting patterns. A system of frozen social cleavages and stable party alignments is less likely to develop in a society where voters are sophisticated, political interests are diverse, and individual choice is given greater latitude. Even the new political conflicts that are competing for the public's attention seem destined to create additional sources of partisan change rather than recreate the stable electoral structure of the past. This diversity and fluidity may, in fact, be the enduring new characteristic of the electoral politics of Germany and other advanced industrial societies.

Note

The survey data utilized in this chapter were made available by the Inter-University Consortium for Political and Social Research in Ann Arbor, the GESIS archive in Cologne, and the *Forschungsgruppe Wahlen* in Mannheim. Neither the archives nor the original collectors of the data bear responsibility for the analyses presented here.

Chapter 4

Parties and the Party System

MARGRET HORNSTEINER AND THOMAS SAALFELD

Political parties could be defined as 'any group, however loosely organized, seeking to elect governmental officeholders under a given label' (Epstein, 1979: 9). Building on Key's (1964) fundamental distinction, Katz and Mair (1993) propose to observe party organizations at three organizational levels: the 'party on the ground', 'in central office' and 'in public office'. One further dimension of our subject, 'parties in the electorate', has already been covered in Chapter 3. Our focus will be the most important organizational features of political parties and their role in the German party system. A party system is more than the sum of the parties in a country or a legislature. It is 'the *system of interactions* resulting from inter-party competition. That is, the system in question bears on the relatedness of parties to each other, on how each party is a function ... of the other parties and reacts, competitively or otherwise, to the other parties' (Sartori, 1976: 44).

The present chapter will track continuities in, and changes to, the German parties and party system, with a focus on the period since unification in 1990 (for earlier periods see Smith 1992; 1996; 2003). This perspective requires, first and foremost, an appropriate theory of party (and, consequently, party system) change. The chapter draws on a number of theoretical approaches, including work on party organization. The organizational history of political parties in Europe resulted in a gradual democratization including a (limited) emancipation of the party on the ground vis-à-vis the party leadership in parliaments and governments. This development occurred between the nineteenth century and the end of the Second World War. Since 1945, modern 'catch-all parties' (Kirchheimer, 1966) and, somewhat later, 'cartel parties' (Katz and Mair, 1995) and 'electoral-professional parties' (Panebianco, 1988) reversed this development in Europe, and now involved a growing mutual independence of the party on the ground and the party in public office. The chapter then examines whether there is evidence for this reversal to have taken place in Germany's party organizations. Drawing on literature that seeks to explain the dynamics of organizational change it addresses the question of when and why parties are changing important features of their organization. Harmel and Janda (1994: 259) argue that change 'results from leadership change, a change of dominant faction within the party, and/or an external stimulus for change'.

The argument will be developed as follows. After a description of the transformation of Germany's party system from a two-block system to a 'fluid five-party system' (Niedermayer, 2013a) and the shrinking organizational base of German political parties in terms of their membership, the chapter examines how parties responded to these developments. Overall, the observations and arguments fit Katz and Mair's (2002) claim of a rise of the party in public office at the expense of the party on the ground. It will be demonstrated that party reform often involves programmatic rather than organizational changes. However, these programmatic moves do not seem to have credibility vis-à-vis voters, if they are not accompanied by a leadership change that reflects those shifts.

The party system: an overview

Between 1965 and 1983, the Federal Republic's party system in the Bundestag consisted of three parties: the Christian Democrats (CDU/CSU – these are two separate parties but have always formed a joint parliamentary party at the national level); the Social Democrats (SPD); and the Liberals (FDP). Many other parties also ran for elections, but from the late 1960s to the early 1980s none of them had sufficient electoral support to achieve representation in parliament. Pappi (1984) identified a triangular relationship amongst the three legislative parties:

1. The CDU/CSU and FDP favoured the social market economy as the key mechanism of economic allocation. The SPD, by contrast, advocated a stronger role for the government in managing the business cycle and addressing questions of social inequality in a market economy.
2. Despite their differences over economic policy, the CDU/CSU and SPD agreed that the involvement and support of major interest groups would be beneficial when important policy changes are made, especially in economic and welfare policies. This neo-corporatist approach was opposed by the more pluralist FDP.
3. The FDP and SPD, in turn, shared a commitment to liberal social values, which distinguished both parties from the CDU/CSU.

This triangular pattern, which allowed for coalitions between all three parties, effectively ended in 1982 with the painful dissolution of the

SPD–FDP coalition (1969–82) and the ascendance of the Greens. From 1983 onwards, the predominant pattern of political contestation at the national level and in the regions was a bipolar party system with the CDU/CSU and the FDP on the centre-right and the SPD and Greens on the centre-left (Saalfeld, 2005b). While German unification added a further party to the system (the Party of Democratic Socialism, PDS), it did not immediately alter this situation. The PDS was a successor organization of the former East German ruling party, the Socialist Unity Party (SED), and clearly promoted a socialist programme. The slight centre-right majority that had characterized Germany's national party system until 1989 was replaced by a slight preponderance for the parties left of the centre in 1990, with the PDS not considered 'coalitionable' at the national level.

Although this bipolar system has remained intact in ideological terms, it has eroded in electoral terms since the early 2000s. Niedermayer (2013a) thus characterized the party system that emerged in the early 2000s as a 'fluid five-party system'. On the one hand, fluidity refers to the growing volatility and uncertainty in the parties' electoral environment. For example, the SPD's vote in the election of 2009 dropped by over 11 per cent compared to the previous election in 2005. The FDP suffered a similar loss in the 2013 election when its share of the vote dropped to 4.8 from the 14.6 per cent the party achieved in 2009. In the same election, the CDU/CSU improved its vote from 33.8 to 41.5 per cent, and the Alternative for Germany (AfD), founded only a few months before the election, polled 4.7 per cent. Changes of that magnitude had been rare in previous decades. On the other hand, these changes have had implications for government formation. The bipolar alternation of centre-right and centre-left coalitions was no longer possible. As at the regional level, coalitions across the old left–right divide have become inevitable (for example the 2005–09 coalition of the CDU/CSU and SPD, and the coalition formed after the 2013 election).

Parties of the centre-right and right

The leading parties on the centre-right are the Christian Democrats, the CDU and CSU (for brief surveys in English, see Green, 2013b; Lees, 2013; Turner, 2013; Zolleis and Wertheimer, 2013). Both parties have been consistent advocates of the German social market economy and Germany's membership of NATO, and have showed a commitment to the process of European integration. Business-friendly in their economic policies, they have always had an organized trades-union wing amongst their membership. The ideological differences between the two parties are small – although the Bavarian CSU has always tended to be slightly more conservative on law and order and issues of social morality (Bräuninger and Debus, 2012). Both parties draw their electoral support from across the entire spectrum of the citizenry with a certain overrepresentation amongst practising Christians and middle-class voters. With the exception of the Bundestag elections of 1972 and 1998, the union of CDU and CSU has always been the leading competitor in national elections. Its national vote varied between a minimum of 29.5 per cent in 1949 and a maximum of 50.2 per cent in 1957. They led national governments between 1949 and 1969, 1982 and 1998, and from 2005 to the present day.

For much of the time between 1949 and 2013, the liberal FDP was the CDU/CSU's 'natural' partner in government coalitions (for brief reviews, see Steltemeier, 2009; Hough, 2011). Only between 1969 and 1982 did the Liberals form a coalition with the SPD and position themselves as a pivotal party between the two major ones in the triangular party system identified by Pappi (see p. 79). Ideologically, the party has always been a strong advocate of free enterprise and small government. From the late 1960s and early 1970s, it also became a party strongly associated with the process of détente and reconciliation with Germany's Central and East European neighbours. Its share of the vote ranged from a minimum of 5.8 per cent of the national vote in 1969 to a maximum of 14.6 per cent in 2009. Between 1949 and 2013, the FDP was in government for approximately 58 out of 64 years with both the Christian Democrats (1949–61, 1963–66, 1982–98 and 2009–13) and the Social Democrats (1969–82). With 4.8 per cent in the 2013 election, it failed to reach the statutory minimum of 5.0 per cent of the national vote necessary to be represented in the Bundestag. This shock triggered a reform of the party, both in its leadership and its policies, in the sense of Harmel and Janda's (1994) model.

The Christian Democrats' hegemony on the right, established during the 1950s, has begun to look more fragile since the early 2000s. This development led to discussions of a more 'fluid' party system, which became visible first in regional elections and later at the national level. There have been two main challengers to the Christian Democrats.

First, the competition of the Independent Voters (FW) has largely been confined to local and regional elections (for a brief survey, see Welsh, 2012). They were founded as a national party in 2009, but have been rooted deeply in local politics since the 1950s, especially in Baden-Württemberg and Bavaria. The FW advocate conservative policies similar to the CDU/CSU's with a stronger emphasis on local autonomy and direct democracy. Originally a loose federation of independent local groups, the party succeeded in gaining representation in the Bavarian state parliament following the elections of 2008 and 2013 (with 10.2 and 9.8 per cent of the vote, respectively). However, their result in the 2013 Bundestag election (1.0 per cent) demonstrated their limited national attractiveness.

Second, on the national level, the AfD emerged as a more dangerous competitor to the centre-right parties. It was founded in February 2013 by a group of CDU members critical of the party leadership's policy during the eurozone crisis, a policy that was broadly supported by all Bundestag parties except the Left Party. The core demand in the AfD's 2013 manifesto was Germany's withdrawal from the euro and a return to national currencies. Other policy areas were less developed. In the 2013 national elections, the AfD attracted voters from all political parties, including the extreme right. Concerned to position itself inside the spectrum of democratic parties, its leaders faced difficult questions concerning the membership of former activists joining from more extreme right-wing parties such as the *Republikaner*. In the election of 2013, it narrowly failed to straddle the 5 per cent threshold, winning 4.7 per cent of the national vote. This was a remarkable result only months after its establishment. The party's support was particularly strong in the Eastern states where it gained support from around 5.8 per cent of the voters. The fact that it drew voters from all parties demonstrates its character as a protest party.

The extreme right

A number of small extreme right-wing parties have been part of the German party system since 1949, although they never developed a stable voter or membership base and tended to suffer from internal fragmentation (for a discussion of the NPD's performance and prospects, see Decker and Miliopoulos, 2009). The first *Bundestag* elections in 1949 returned the German Right-Wing Party (DRP) with five seats. This conservative party was partially subverted by former National Socialists. After the Federal Constitutional Court banned the Socialist Reich Party (SRP) in 1952, it took a decade for the extreme right to establish a new party able to attract a significant amount of voters. Founded in 1964, the German National Democratic Party (NPD) has survived to the present day. The electoral fortunes of the NPD and various other small and extreme right-wing parties have varied over time (Saalfeld, 1997), yet they have never mustered enough votes to enter the *Bundestag*. Nationally, the NPD's vote ranged from a minimum of 0.2 per cent in 1980 to a maximum of 4.3 per cent in 1969. Nevertheless, the party has been represented sporadically in seven regional parliaments during the second half of the 1960s and, more recently, in the Eastern German states of Mecklenburg Upper Pomerania (2006 to the present) and Saxony (2004 to the present) for about a decade. The party's leadership has frequently been in severe disagreement over strategy, with some favouring a parliamentary strategy and others promoting more militant and confrontational extra-parliamentary tactics, including the use of illegal means. In December 2012 the federal state governments agreed to apply for the banning of the party by the Federal Constitutional Court.

Parties of the centre-left and left

The SPD, the oldest German party, has been the largest party left of the political centre (for recent reviews, see Egle, 2009a; Jun, 2011). In the first *Bundestag* election in 1949 its support was just under 30 per cent of the national vote, similar to the Christian Democrats. In the late 1950s and 1960s, the party responded to the growing electoral gap between itself and the soaring vote of the CDU/CSU by shedding some of its socialist policies. It developed a modern social democratic programme accepting the social market economy and Germany's incorporation into the Western defence alliance during the Cold War. This move to the political centre was rewarded with steady electoral gains, peaking in 1972 when the party was returned as the strongest parliamentary party for the first time in its history. The party's electoral support at national elections ranged from a minimum of 23.0 per cent in 2009 to a maximum of 45.8 per cent in 1972. It governed in coalitions with the CDU/CSU in 1966–69 and 2005–09; with the FDP in 1969–82; and with the Greens in 1998–2005. The 1998–2005 SPD–Green coalition under Chancellor Gerhard Schröder initiated major reforms to labour-market policy, social benefits and pensions, which were deeply unpopular with some of the party's activists and core voters and which severely depressed its electoral support after 2005.

The Green Party was founded in the 1970s as a broad and relatively disparate coalition of pacifists, environmentalists, feminists, left-libertarians and other groups (for short surveys in English with further references, see Blühdorn, 2009a; 2009b; Hough, 2011). Initially, it was critical of representative democracy and favoured direct action, rejected professional politicians and was committed to grassroots democracy. Over time, the party's more orthodox and left-wing factions were marginalized. The party developed into a modern democratic centre-left one with a strong focus on questions of environmental policy. In the 1983 *Bundestag* election, it polled more than 5 per cent of the vote for the first time and has been represented in the *Bundestag* ever since. Its national vote has ranged from a minimum of 1.5 per cent in 1980 and a maximum of 10.7 per cent in 2009. Its strongest electoral performance at the regional level was in the state election of Baden-Württemberg in 2011 when it achieved 24.2 per cent of the vote and formed a government coalition with the SPD under the first Green state minister-president. At the national level, it governed in a coalition with the SPD between 1998 and 2005. Very much an outsider during the 1980s and much of the 1990s, the party is now seen as a potential coalition partner for both the SPD and CDU/CSU at the national as well as the regional and municipal levels.

The Left Party was established in 2007 in a merger of the Party of Democratic Socialism (PDS) and the Electoral Alternative for Labour and Social Justice (WASG). The former had been the successor organization of the SED, the ruling party of the German Democratic Republic, which was disbanded in 1990. The latter was a party founded by trades unionists and former Social Democrats in January 2005 in opposition to the then SPD federal Chancellor Gerhard Schröder's reforms to labour-market policy, unemployment benefit, social insurance and pensions known as Hartz IV reforms (for recent surveys, see Olsen, 2007; Coffé and Plassa, 2009; Hough and Koß, 2009; Hough, 2011; Patton, 2013). Nevertheless, the merger to form the Left Party could not resolve intraparty tensions between pragmatic factions (mostly from the East) and more radical factions (mostly from the West). With its strongholds remaining in Eastern Germany and the Eastern districts of Berlin, the Left Party polled 11.9 per cent of the national vote in the 2009 election and 8.6 per cent in the 2013 election.

The Pirate Party was founded in 2006, following the example of a similar Swedish party. Substantively, it has focused on issues around internet policy (including copyright laws, data storage and internet censorship), as well as transparency, democracy and participation. It also aspired to a new political style of intraparty participation, exercised through a web-based tool called 'liquid feedback'. In the absence of a distinctive programme and partly due to the lack of political experience of its leaders, the party's initial spectacular success in several state elections (Berlin, Schleswig-Holstein, North Rhine-Westphalia and Saarland) could not be repeated at the national level in 2013. The party's organization was caught up between its own participatory aspirations and the realities and demands of professional politics and modern representative democracy (Niedermayer, 2012b: 58–9). Continuing leadership struggles and the lack of programmatic distinctiveness beyond its core issue of internet policy resulted in only 2.2 per cent of the vote in the 2013 election, a level far below the support the party had in opinion polls and regional elections in 2011–12. The party's rise and fall underlines the fluidity in Germany's new party system, highlighted by Niedermayer (2013a) and others. Nevertheless, the 2013 election demonstrates that the party retained its popularity amongst young voters.

Growing fragmentation and less reliable voters

These short portraits provide important contextual information but do

Figure 4.1 *Party system concentration: cumulated share of the two largest parties in national elections, 1949–2013 (%)*

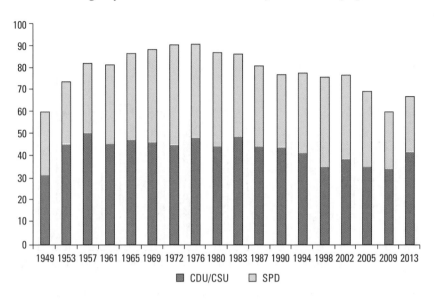

Note: Share of second votes (*Zweitstimmen*).

Source: *Bundeswahlleiter* (www.election.de) and own calculations.

not adequately describe the overall development of Germany's party system, which went through a sequence of distinctive episodes: (a) a phase of concentration (1949 until approximately 1961), followed by (b) a phase of relative stability (around 1961 until 1983), followed by (c) a phase of refragmentation and accelerating fluidity (since 1983).

These developments are summarized in Figures 4.1 and 4.2. The bar chart in Figure 4.1 plots the combined share of the total vote obtained by the two major parties, the CDU/CSU and SPD, between 1949 and 2013. The graph illustrates how the combined share rose from just below 60 per cent in 1949 to over 80 per cent in the 1957 and 1961 elections. In that period, the growing aggregate share of the votes for the two major parties was first and foremost a result of the improving performance of the CDU/CSU. The further increases in the combined share between 1965 and 1972, by contrast, were largely due to the SPD's growing attractiveness during that period. In the 1972 and 1976 elections, the combined share of the two major parties peaked at over 90 per cent of the vote. From 1976 onwards, it started to decline. The combined share of the two main parties in the past three elections (2005, 2009 and 2013) varied between 56.8 and 69.4 per cent of the national vote, which is even

Figure 4.2   *Party system fragmentation: effective number of parties in parliament, 1972–2013*

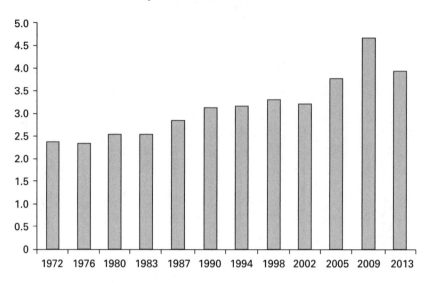

Notes: Laakso-Taagepera index calculated on the basis of vote shares in national elections (second votes); includes only parties represented in the *Bundestag*. The CDU/CSU are treated as one party.

Source: *Bundeswahlleiter* (www.election.de) and own calculations.

more severe if we consider the overall decline in electoral turnout from over 90 per cent in 1972 and 1976 to levels around 70 per cent in 2009 and 2013.

The declining aggregate strength of the major parties is also reflected in standard indicators of party system fragmentation. Figure 4.2 reports the 'effective number of parties' in the national parliament between 1972 and 2013, an indicator which accounts for the relative size of parties in parliament as well as their number. The index was invented by Laakso and Taagepera (1979) and is calculated here on the basis of shares of the second vote for party lists (for an explanation of the German electoral system, see Saalfeld 2005a). Larger parties contribute more to the index values than smaller parties. Between the 1970s and 1990s, the effective number of parties rose moderately from 2.5 to about 3.1. Throughout the 1990s and early 2000s, when there were already five parties in parliament, this figure remained relatively stable at around 3.2, due to the relatively small size of the FDP, Greens and PDS, which the index takes into consideration. However, recent years have witnessed a sharp increase in the effective number of parties to 3.8 in 2005, 4.7 in 2009 and just below 4.0 in 2013.

Figure 4.3 *Aggregate electoral volatility, 1972–2013*

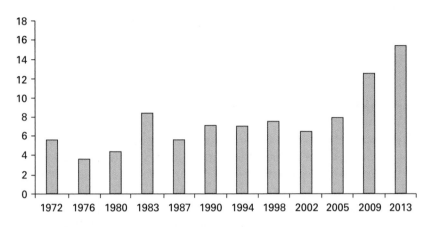

Note: Pedersen index uses net changes of aggregated electoral support for parties represented in the *Bundestag*.

Source: Faas (2010: 901) and own calculations.

The growing fragmentation of the party system since the late 1990s and early 2000s has been accompanied by a growing aggregate volatility. In other words, the parties' strength in an election at time t_0 has become a less meaningful predictor of their strength in the following election at time t_1. This is captured by the so-called 'Pedersen index' whose values are displayed as bars in Figure 4.3. This index is defined as the sum of all net changes of the parliamentary parties' electoral support (second votes) from one election to the next. While aggregate volatility had remained relatively constant between the early 1970s and the early 2000s, it jumped to a much higher value in the 2009 election (12.6) and reached a new historic peak in 2013 (15.4). This demonstrates that the electoral environment the political parties operate in has become far more uncertain. Unsuccessful government participation or poor leadership performance carry a much higher risk of severe electoral penalties than one or two decades earlier. This is illustrated by the dramatic losses of the SPD after 2005 and the fate of the FDP in 2013 (see p. 81).

In short, these changes provide some reasons to infer the beginning of a new period of the German party system. While the tenor of restricted change and overall stability (Smith, 2003) still held true for the party system of the early 2000s, the elections since 2005 have led to marked changes. The current party system, a 'fluid five-party system' (Niedermayer 2013a), is characterized by levels of fragmentation that are as high as in the early years of the Federal Republic: levels of aggregate volatility in 2013 were higher than at any time since the 1960s, the dominance of the two major parties has faded (some episodes of intermittent recovery notwithstanding) and coalition formation has become far more complicated than in the 1990s and early 2000s since stable government majorities have to be sought across the traditional divide between centre-right and centre-left.

A shrinking party on the ground

The party membership and organization 'on the ground' is an important resource for political parties. For traditional mass integration parties of the nineteenth and early twentieth centuries, membership dues were a vital component of parties' income. Vibrant links with 'collateral organizations' and associations in civil society (such as the trades unions in the case of the SPD) have created the societal roots that have stabilized the parties' positions in electoral terms. Although modern party organizations are less dependent on their membership base in Germany as well as in other European democracies (Katz and Mair, 2002), large membership organizations are still valued as providing recruitment and training grounds for the parties' leadership personnel (Klein et al., 2011).

Membership decline

In the mid-1970s, all three major German parties – the Christian Democratic parties of the CDU and CSU, as well as the Social Democrats – maintained a highly organized 'party on the ground'. In the years 1976 and 1977, the SPD had over one million members on the territory of the 'old' Federal Republic. The decline in its membership accelerated from the late 1990s and by the end of 2012 SPD membership had dropped to approximately 477,000. The Christian Democrats' membership continued to grow until the early 1980s but began to decline from 1984. Unlike the SPD, the CDU had had an organization in the former East German state (the German Democratic Republic). As a result, its membership received a certain boost through unification, but it has also declined since. At the end of 2012, the CDU had approximately 476,000 members. In the same year the CSU's count was at almost 148,000. The rate of decline experienced by the Christian Democrats was lower than for the SPD, however. Whereas in 1976, the combined membership of CDU and CSU amounted to just over 78 per of the SPD's, the two Christian Democratic parties' membership was over 130 per cent of the SPD's in 2012. Figure 4.4 illustrates the aggregate decline of party membership from its high point of around 2.4 million persons in 1990 (the year of unification) to just below 1.4 million in 2012. The 'peak' in 1990 was a result of unification and turned out to be a blip.

Figure 4.4   *Membership of the main German parties, 1968–2012*

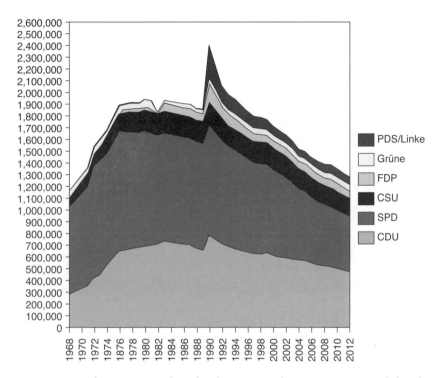

Notes: Figures refer to 31 December of each year. Data for 1968–87 are rounded to the nearest 1,000. Data for 1990 may not be entirely reliable.

Sources: 1968–89 Mintzel and Oberreuter (1992: 568); 1991–2012 Niedermayer (2013b: 2).

Figure 4.5 demonstrates that this decline is not primarily a result of demographic change. Even when the parties' membership is expressed as a percentage of the eligible population of all residents of 16 years of age and over, party membership nearly halved between 1990 and the end of 2011. In 1990 3.65 per cent of all German residents were members of a mainstream party (the CDU, SPD, CSU, FDP, Greens or the PDS). By the end of 2011, this percentage had dropped to 1.86 (with the Left Party replacing the PDS as its successor).

This has important practical consequences. The smaller parties, in particular, cannot rely on their activists as strongly as the larger parties when it comes to electoral campaigns, especially in the larger, less densely populated area of the north-east. The SPD and CDU/CSU still draw on a relatively dense network of activists in the larger Western states (especially Baden-Württemberg, Bavaria, Hesse and North Rhine-Westphalia) and the city states of Berlin, Hamburg and Bremen (Niedermayer, 2012a).

Figure 4.5   *Membership of the German mainstream parties as a percentage of eligible persons over the age of 16, 1990–2011*

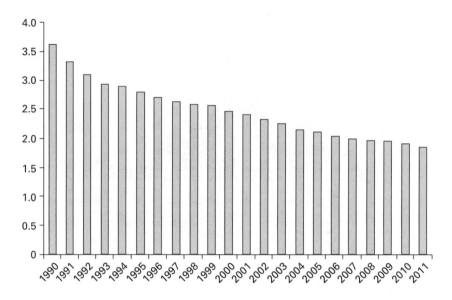

Note: Parties included are the CDU, SPD, CSU, FDP, Greens and the Left Party.

Source: Compiled by authors from data in Niedermayer (2013b: 3).

In some regions, especially in the Eastern parts, even the larger parties (except the Left Party with its regional strongholds) cannot rely on their local associations to fight campaigns and show their presence. They depend to a greater extent on the mass media, social media, their local members of parliament and their national and regional leaders to promote the party. As a result, the Eastern organizations look even more like 'modern' electoral-professional parties than some of their Western counterparts.

There are two main consequences of these patterns of membership decline. Firstly, the regional disparities in party membership have implications for the distribution of power within the political parties. When it comes to intraparty bargaining for leadership positions (including ministerial posts), large regional associations wield considerable power, generally in proportion to their share of the membership. In other words, regional considerations constrain the party leaders in their powers to take key decisions such as Cabinet appointments. For decisions of this type they need to have the elites of the major regional party associations on their side. Secondly, the decline in the importance of membership dues has led to a stronger reliance on public subsidies and donations, shifting the centre of gravity further away from the membership and activists and towards the party in public office.

Organizational reform

Political parties have sought to respond to the challenges of increasing electoral volatility and shrinking memberships by modernizing their organizations. In the main, these reforms were intended to increase the attractiveness of party membership by strengthening the powers of grass-roots members within the parties. In some cases, parties sought to enhance their attractiveness by opening up policy debates to non-members, or encouraging looser forms of association below the level of formal membership. Such reforms have taken place in all parties, albeit to varying degrees. In the case of the CDU, Turner (2013: 127) finds that slow organizational changes in the early 2000s led to an increasing involvement of party members in candidate selection, and to a lesser extent in leadership selection. The CDU's grassroots members, however, still have relatively little say in policy decisions, which remain the prerogative of formal party associations and representative party organs. The influence of non-members in ad hoc discussion forums and regional conferences is considered very limited in the CDU (Jun, 2009).

Other parties have gone further. Three examples of manifesto formation prior to the election of 2013 may suffice to further illustrate the developments in other parties. First, the FDP, which has used web-based platforms for programme discussion since 2002, introduced a new web-tool called '*Meine Freiheit*', in which it made its manifesto draft available for public discussion. Registered users (members and non-members alike) were invited to suggest amendments. Altogether, over 1,000 proposals were submitted via this platform; 700 of them were discussed at the party conference, which finally adopted the manifesto in May 2013 (see www.fdp.de). Also, the FDP is an example where intraparty groups have become more likely to force membership ballots on substantive policy issues on the agenda. Its 2011 membership ballot on a proposal rejecting the European Stability Mechanism (ESM) ended with a victory for the party leadership who opposed the proposal. Nevertheless, this is one example of growing membership involvement.

Second, the SPD also strengthened the voice of non-members as well as members in its procedures. In its organizational reform of 2011, the party lowered the threshold for groups who demanded ballots of the entire membership for leadership elections and important policy decisions. In the run-up to the 2013 election it launched a 'citizens' dialogue' (*Bürgerdialog*), in which the party called for proposals on 'how to improve Germany' (see www.spd.de/buergerdialog). In six months of local conferences and events, the party received over 40,000 proposals. A final 'citizens' convention' (*Bürgerkonvent*) resulted in 11 proposals that were eventually included in the 2013 manifesto. Although the manifesto was ultimately adopted by a conference of party delegates in April 2013, the strategy of increasing participation was designed to reach out beyond the group of traditional party members. These organizational changes seem to lend some support to the theoretical notion of 'cartel parties' (Katz and Mair, 1995), where the distinction between party members and non-members becomes increasingly blurred. A further example for the increased emphasis on meaningful membership participation is the SPD leadership's promise to its grassroots members to subject any coalition agreement negotiated with the Christian Democrats in 2013 to a vote of the entire membership.

Third, for the Green Party direct grassroots participation and a high level of leadership accountability have traditionally been characteristic organizational features. The rise of the Pirate Party as a potential competitor for members and votes may have encouraged the party to reaffirm its culture of rank-and-file participation. This was reflected in the process of candidate nomination and manifesto production. The most important membership ballot concerned the choice of the candidates (one male, one female) to head the party during the election campaign. In a highly competitive election, party members chose two candidates from a pool of 15 contenders. In the process of writing the manifesto, the party's executive committee discussed the draft directly with its members in several programme forums, which were held throughout the country. At the party conference in April 2013, more than 2,600 proposals for amendment had to be dealt with. After the manifesto had been adopted, the party started the next membership ballot on key projects and policy priorities, accompanied by an online debate and local events. This time, party members could vote for nine out of 59 key projects within three categories (energy policy, justice and modern society). It is significant to note that the results reflected the policy agenda of the leading candidates only very partially. The party grassroots unmistakably asserted themselves both in manifesto formulation and in leadership elections.

These examples illustrate that German parties have been adaptable in Harmel and Janda's terms as far as their organizational structures are concerned. External developments in the parties' environment (including social change and changes in political behaviour) have contributed to a loss of members and triggered responses by the parties on the ground. If assessed against Harmel and Janda's framework, some parties carried out organizational reforms in response to changes in the parties' environment, but not necessarily subsequent to changes in their leadership or the dominant faction. On the whole, the reforms undertaken aim at making it more attractive for citizens to get involved in the work of political parties. The reforms generally recognize that there is a demand for opportunities to participate, but that younger citizens, in particular, may not wish to access parties via a traditional membership model – at least in the first instance. The fact that these reforms occurred at all suggests that the rise of the modern 'electoral-professional party' (Panebianco, 1988) has not eliminated the need to cultivate a large membership base in the eyes of party leaders, who recognize the value of parties in electoral campaigns and see a growing membership as an indication of growing legitimacy in the electorate at large.

Leadership change and policy reforms

Reforms and adaptation have gone beyond the realm of organizational politics within the parties. The CDU/CSU and SPD provide strong evidence that, in line with Janda and Harmel's predictions, they have responded to serious external challenges with policy reforms, especially after any changes in leadership or dominant intraparty coalition. We will provide some evidence to corroborate this point in this section.

Most accounts of electoral competition are based on the idea that political candidates (whether individual leaders or parties) select the policies in their programmes and manifestos with a view to attracting an optimum of voters under the circumstances (see for example Hinich and Munger, 1997). These 'circumstances' depend on the party's own resources (for example, its reputation in terms of policy or past record in government; the size of its membership; its finance; its control of government positions), on important institutions (for example the electoral system) and on the positioning of its competitors. Depending on the circumstances, the optimum may be the overall majority of seats in a legislature, or the dominance in a particular 'niche' in the electorate (for example Green parties seeking to attract environmentalists).

Political scientists tend to understand the competition between parties as strategic moves in an ideological 'space'. Party leaders anticipate competitors' moves in this space and seek to protect their own position from 'intruders'. In its simplest form, this space may consist of a single dimension (usually on a line from 'left' to 'right' such as the one used in Figure 4.10). In the German case, however, there is little disagreement that competition between the parties is structured by at least two dimensions with 'socio-economic' policy issues clearly dominating all other dimensions. On the left end of this socio-economic continuum (the x-axis in Figures 4.6 and 4.7), voters and parties would favour a strong state

Figure 4.6   *Economy and social liberalism as main dimensions of party competition, 2002*

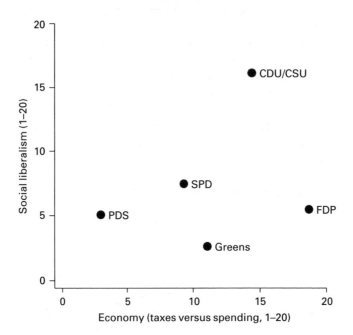

Source: Compiled by authors from data in Benoit and Laver (2006: Appendix B).

using taxation to redistribute income from the rich to the poor and to expand the welfare state with a view to protect those in need. On the right, there would be voters and parties advocating free enterprise, low taxation and a minimal welfare state functioning as a safety net. Figures 4.6 and 4.7 are based on the expert survey carried out by Benoit and Laver (2006) in 2002 to measure the parties' positions on a scale from 1 to 20. The data on the parties' locations on the socio-economic policy dimension suggest that the Left Party (or, rather, its predecessor at the time of the survey, the Party of Democratic Socialism, PDS) was closest to the welfarist pole, whereas the FDP was the most pronounced pro-market party.

The second important dimension in Germany is disputed and may have changed over time. Some researchers have found a cross-cutting dimension with individualist, libertarian, socially liberal values at one end of the spectrum and political views favouring law and order, religion and conservative family values on the other. This is represented by the y-axis in Figure 4.6. Here the smaller parties (FDP, Greens, PDS) are clustered together near the liberal and libertarian end of the spectrum; the CDU/CSU lean towards the traditionalist pole; and the SPD holds an intermediate position. A further contender for the second most important

Figure 4.7 *Economy and internationalization as main dimensions of party competition, 2002*

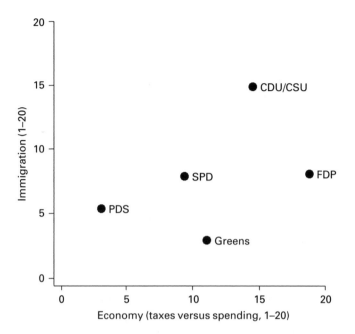

Source: Compiled by authors from data in Benoit and Laver (2006: Appendix B).

dimension of party competition concerns the role of Germany as a state in international politics, ranging from a cosmopolitan internationalist position at one end of the spectrum to a position emphasizing the protective role of the nation state in the processes of Europeanization and globalization at the other end (the y-axis in Figure 4.7). Specific issues dividing the parties along this dimension are European integration and immigration. The data on which Figure 4.7 is based do not support the frequent claim of the PDS and its successor, the Left party, to be a party of welfare protectionism. If attitudes towards immigration are taken as an indicator, the party is as internationalist as the Greens and the Social Democrats. The AfD (which is not yet included in such surveys), however, may have captured a niche in the electoral market, at the top-right end of the spectrum, combining neo-liberal economic policies and a deep scepticism towards European integration, especially towards the euro. This niche had been partially occupied by the national wings of all three governing parties in the 2009–13 *Bundestag* – the CDU, CSU and FDP – which were steered towards an accommodating position concerning the ESM by their more moderate party leaders in the Cabinet.

Figure 4.8   *Parties' right–left positions on macro-economic and welfare policies, 1994–2013*

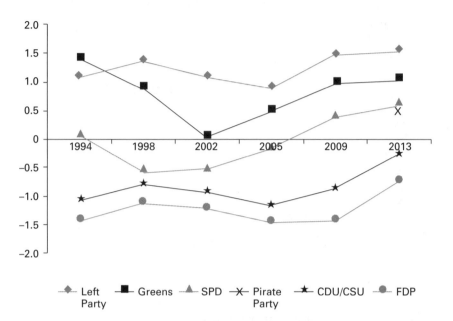

Notes: Parties' positions are estimated on the basis of word frequencies on a single dimension. For a detailed description of the method, see Slapin and Proksch (2008). Absolute values are not comparable across dimensions.

Source: Authors' own estimates based on the parties' election manifestos using the Wordfish method.

Figures 4.6 and 4.7 provide snapshots of the parties' locations based on the perceptions of experts shortly after the turn of the millennium. Nevertheless, the instrument of expert surveys tends to emphasize stable, longer-term positions in the policy space. Figures 4.8 and 4.9, by contrast, are based on a different technique, which is more sensitive to shorter-term changes. We used the Wordfish scaling model (Slapin and Proksch, 2008) to derive estimates of the parties' policy positions from their manifestos between 1994 and 2013. The analysis includes the manifestos of the CDU/CSU, the SPD, the FDP, the Greens and the Left Party. For 2013, the Pirate Party was included. The AfD's manifesto was too short to allow for reliable estimates. Figures 4.8 and 4.9 provide us with a shortcut to the parties' programmatic responses to electoral defeats (one of the external shocks Harmel and Janda assumed to cause party reforms).

Figure 4.8 provides estimates on the parties' positions on the dominant dimension of partisan conflict and social and economic policies. Low

Figure 4.9   *Parties' right–left positions on home affairs and justice,*
1994–2013

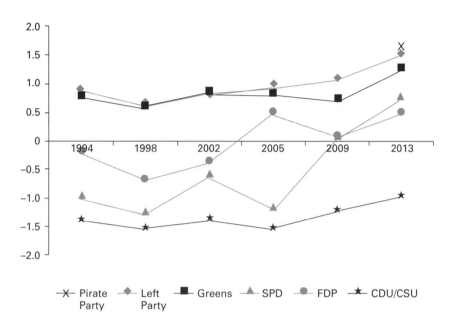

Notes: Parties' positions are estimated on the basis of word frequencies on a single dimension. For a detailed description of the method see Slapin and Proksch (2008). Absolute values are not comparable across dimensions.

Source: Authors' own estimates based on the parties' election manifestos using the Wordfish method.

values indicate a programme leaning towards the free-market end of the spectrum; high values indicate a welfarist position. The Left Party is clearly the most left wing in terms of economic and welfare policies. The analysis of FDP manifestos suggests that it has consistently been the party with the strongest emphasis on economic liberalism.

The most noticeable changes over time can be observed for the SPD. A narrow defeat in the election of 1994 in the dying years of the Kohl chancellorship (1982–98) paved the way for Gerhard Schröder's leadership and his commitment to a reform of labour-market policy. This policy shift is clearly reflected in the data in Figure 4.8, which shows the SPD's turn to the centre between 1994 and 1998. The party's 1998 manifesto shows a move towards the CDU/CSU's position in these policy areas. After its significant electoral losses of 2002 and 2005, the SPD's manifestos reveal a return to more traditional Social Democratic policies, which accelerated in 2005 after Schröder stepped down as Federal chancellor. Subsequently the party suffered from a credibility gap with a more left-wing programme on the one hand and the party's centrist candidates for the chancellorship, Frank-Walter Steinmeier (in 2009) and Peer Steinbrück (in 2013), on the other as both leaders had been key architects of the Schröder government's centrist reforms.

The Christian Democrats' gradual modernization under Angela Merkel's leadership after the defeat in the Bundestag election of 2002 is reflected more strongly here, which covers the areas of home affairs and justice and includes many issues relating to social liberalism such as legislation to tackle the discrimination of women, immigrants and disabled or gay persons. These changes from 2005 were moderate but are clearly reflected in in Figure 4.9. Nevertheless, the CDU/CSU remains the most traditional party in the system as far as home affairs, civil liberties and justice are concerned. The Pirate Party marks the most 'liberal' party on this dimension. It is also noteworthy that the SPD's move back to a more left-wing position in economic policies has been accompanied by a similar move towards more liberal positions in the areas of home affairs and justice, where its 2013 manifesto is much closer to the FDP's than to any other party.

Figure 4.8 also shows the dilemma of the Greens in economic policy. The party moved sharply to the centre in its 2002 manifesto and has since returned – equally sharply – to more pronounced left-wing positions. The latter development has led to criticism of the party leadership by the more conservative regional branches of the party, for example in the state of Baden-Württemberg. Figure 4.9 shows that the FDP's manifestos did respond to the party's growing struggle to distinguish itself from the Christian Democrats. In the areas of home affairs and justice, the party moved back to the liberal end of the spectrum between 1998 and 2005 and in its 2013 manifesto. Nevertheless, given the dominance of economic policy in the party's image, these changes were not reflected in the voters' responses. The FDP's strong programmatic commitment to civil liberties was not recognized by the vast majority of voters, partly because the party did not have charismatic leaders associated with this dimension. Taken together, electoral defeats and leadership changes explain some of the changing ideological positions of the main parties along the important dimensions of partisan conflict in Germany.

The stability of the party in government

Despite considerable changes in the electoral environment and membership of political parties, the 'party in government' at the parliamentary level has remained largely unaffected: Cabinet stability has remained remarkably high since the early 1970s. The refragmentation of the party system in the country and in parliament has not jeopardized stability. All Cabinets since 1983 save one (the second Schröder Cabinet of 2002–05) served their full four-year terms. This is in stark contrast to the considerable Cabinet instability in other European multiparty systems (Saalfeld, 2013: 65).

How might this discrepancy between growing fluidity at the electoral and membership level and continuing stability at the parliamentary and governmental level be explained? Katz and Mair (1995) offer an influential explanation by arguing that European parties have often compensated for their weakening ties with voters and civil society by partially suspending competition and jointly appropriating more and more state funds such as public subsidies in a 'cartel' of established parties. Despite some differences in emphasis, this answer is partly compatible with Panebianco's (1988) claim of a rise of the 'electoral-professional party' as a model of party organization where political life within the party is strongly dominated by a professional leadership in the governmental sphere, which is supported by professional agencies rather than rank-and-file members.

There is considerable support for Katz and Mair's argument if we look at the public funding of parliamentary parties. In January 2010, the *Bundestag*'s then five parliamentary parties were able to employ a total of 870 staff from public funds, 397 of whom occupied qualified degree-level positions. The total amount of funding available to the legislative parties in that year was over €78.7 million, in addition to the 4,209 publicly funded staff members employed by the members individually. This has allowed the parliamentary leadership and the 'party in public office' to claim more autonomy from the extra-parliamentary activists and collateral interest groups such as trades unions or church-based organizations. It remains to be seen whether the reforms summarized above will suffice to reverse this trend of a growing autonomy of the 'party in public office' from the 'party on the ground'.

In addition to organizational and institutional arguments, the so-called 'median-voter theorem' points to a further, strategic reason for the continued strength of the major parties as long as they maintain their position at the centre of the political spectrum in ideological terms. In an abstract way, the logic of this argument can be seen in Figure 4.10. In the simplest form of a coalition situation, there would be three parties in a party system (P_1, P_2 and P_3), none of which has an overall majority of votes or seats. In most simple spatial theories of voting and coalition formation, researchers will seek to rank these three parties on a single left–right continuum between extremely left wing (1) to extremely right wing (10). The Wordfish method referred to above (see Figures 4.8 and 4.9) or expert

Figure 4.10   *The median voter in one policy dimension*

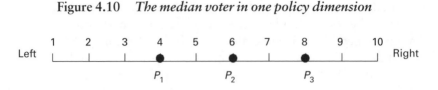

surveys are two methods of determining such rankings empirically. If each coalition of two parties has a majority in parliament, the median-voter theorem would predict that the ideological centre party, P_2, is in a privileged position. The reason is simple: a compromise between P_2 on the one hand and either P_1 or P_3 on the other would be politically less 'costly' than a coalition of P_1 and P_3.

The differential costs of coalitions are approximated by the ideological distances between the parties. Intuitively, larger distances would indicate higher costs than smaller distances. This can be seen easily in Figure 4.10. The difference between P_2 and P_1 is $6 - 4 = 2$. Thus if the two parties are rational and choose a policy somewhere between 4 and 6, the aggregate 'cost' of a coalition would be 2. Similarly, the difference between P_2 and P_3 is $6 - 8 = -2$. Again, if the two parties are rational and cannot agree on a policy that either of them prefers (for example point 1 on the scale) then the cost of this coalition would be 2 (the negative sign tends to be disregarded in such models). A coalition of P_1 and P_3, by contrast, would face a distance of $8 - 4 = 4$. This would be interpreted as a higher cost – although the median party may exploit its position.

Let us briefly return to the notion that the cost of '2' is an aggregate cost shared by both parties. P_2, the 'privileged median party', has in fact *two* credible coalition alternatives and could play P_1 and P_3 off against each other in coalition negotiations. For example, it could offer P_1 a policy at, say, scale point 5.9. If P_1 rejects, it could make an offer at scale point 6.1 to P_3. If P_1 knows that P_2 would not hesitate to make such an offer of 6.1 to P_3, it will accept the offer of 5.9 – despite the fact that the joint costs of the deal (2 scale points) are 'unfairly' distributed in P_2's favour: the compromise entails that P_2 moves 0.1 scale points away from its ideal point, 6, whereas P_1 is forced to concede 1.9 scale points, which is not the fair split of the joint cost at scale point 5.0. Thus, the middle party P_2 is in a strong position. Because all alternatives will be more costly in political terms, coalitions including the middle party tend to be 'in equilibrium' and, hence, relatively stable.

Since new contenders in the Bundestag have appeared at the ideological extremes (the Greens in 1983, the PDS in 1990 and the Left Party in 2009), one of the established centrist parties has always remained in the strong bargaining position of median party. In German parliamentary history since 1949, the position of the median party in a single ideological left–right space was occupied by the CDU/CSU between 1949 and 1957, by the FDP between 1957 and 1998, by the SPD from 1998 to 2009, by the FDP between 2009 and 2013 (Saalfeld 2009) and, again, by the SPD since 2013. Thus, despite the changes in the party system, despite growing fluidity, one of the established parties has thus far always controlled the parliamentary median, and the role of the main parties in government has remained a strong one. Hence, although electoral support for the main parties has eroded, although they have become more vulnerable to electoral shocks, they may have as much power over policy as in the times when they had in excess of 45 per cent of the vote (see e.g. Lees, 2013).

Conclusion

The German party system has experienced considerable change since the 1990s. It has become more fragmented; electoral volatility has increased; and the parties' organizational base has been eroded as far as grassroots membership is concerned. These developments in the 'party in the electorate' and the 'party on the ground' have largely resulted from economic and social changes in the environment of political parties in Germany and elsewhere (see Inglehart, 1997; Dalton and Wattenberg, 2000). Crucially for this chapter, political parties have responded to these trends in at least three ways. Firstly, they have reformed their organizations, making them more attractive organizations for (potential or existing) members and, to an extent, for non-members. Secondly, they have improved their access to state funds in line with the arguments made by Katz and Mair (1995). This has effectively strengthened the 'party in public office' within the parties, at the expense of the 'party on the ground' and the 'party in head office'. Thirdly, they have become more sophisticated strategic players in the policy space that constitutes the battle ground for party competition in German politics.

From a normative perspective, greater volatility may be attractive: voters are willing to effect a change in government and call government parties to account. The voters' decision to throw out the Kohl government in 1998, the electoral losses suffered by the SPD in 2005 and 2009, or the elimination of the FDP from the Bundestag in 2013 demonstrate this increased level of electoral accountability for (perceived or real) poor performance. Very long episodes of stable government (e.g. Adenauer's various coalitions dominated by the CDU/CSU between 1949 and 1963, or Kohl's reign at the helm of a CDU/CSU–FDP coalition in 1982–98) are less likely to occur as a result. However, this new fluidity not only amongst voters but also with regard to the parties' positioning does not come without risks. And, importantly, coalition formation between the parties has become more complicated and frequently requires deals across the traditional divide between centre-right and centre-left. As our brief explanations of the median-voter theorem suggest, the costs and benefits of such deals may be distributed unfairly, thus further alienating core voters of one or both of the coalition partners. This, in turn, may lead to severe electoral penalties in a situation where parties find it harder to fall back on their decimated 'parties on the ground'.

Chapter 5

Political Leadership

LUDGER HELMS

Recent developments in the discipline of comparative politics have included a notable rise in political leadership studies (see Helms, 2012). This trend is particularly pronounced in the academic study of German politics, with a remarkable number of contributions focusing on political leadership in Germany or even more often on German leadership in Europe (see, for example, Paterson, 2008; Chandler, 2010; Jones, 2010; Schild, 2012). These developments in academia echo the widespread realization by political actors and the wider public alike that, given the turbulent times that the world has been experiencing since the close of the first decade of the twenty-first century, democratic regimes are in desperate need of leadership. This is not to say that leadership is necessarily about sticking to one's guns at any price. Many recent conceptions of political leadership emphasize 'power-sharing' and 'post-heroism' as defining features of a type of leadership considered appropriate to democratically advanced regimes (Kane and Patapan, 2012: 171). To students of German politics this sounds familiar. Domestic political leadership in the Federal Republic has virtually always been marked by strong elements of consensus-seeking and attempts to accommodate a wealth of different interests.

While political leadership is not confined to the holders of any particular office, in representative democracies most people focus on the political chief executive – presidents, prime ministers or, in the German case, chancellors. This understanding of political leadership defines the framework of this chapter which centres on the chancellorship of Angela Merkel in the context of previous experiences. I begin by outlining the institutional setting of the German chancellorship, which often imposes on the incumbent the need to seek consensus across a range of institutional power-centres. I then focus more specifically on the recent developments in the later years of the Schröder chancellorship, and more particularly on the chancellorship of Angela Merkel. The main part of the chapter addresses the widespread view that political chief executives in democratic regimes are becoming increasingly important and powerful, resulting in a 'presidentialization' of politics and leadership.

The institutional parameters of executive leadership

Many contributions to the field of comparative political leadership high-light the structurally exposed position of the chancellor within the German executive branch (see, for example, King, 1994). Other things being equal, the holders of the German chancellorship have been more powerful figures than their counterparts in most other West European parliamentary democracies, and at least some of their strength seems to flow from their constitutional resources. For an adequate assessment of the institutional opportunity structure of German chancellors, a histori-cal perspective is perhaps even more revealing than any international comparison: one of the most important institutional innovations of the Basic Law, in comparison with the *Reichsverfassung*, was the structural weakening of the president. Whereas the Weimar Republic was a semi-presidential system with a marked predominance of the president (a 'pres-ident-parliamentary regime' in the parlance of the more recent literature on governmental systems – see Elgie, 2011), the founders of the Federal Republic established a different regime with just one largely unchallenged political chief executive, the chancellor. At the same time, a historical comparison points to the limits of purely constitutional explanations of the chancellor's power within (and beyond) the executive branch. The famous set of rules in Article 65 of the Basic Law, which contains the orga-nizational principles of the German executive branch including the chan-cellor's policy guidelines competence, was a direct import from the *Reichsverfassung* – which proved of conspicuously little help to the numerous German chancellors of the interwar period in their desperate attempts to lead their respective governments effectively.

Given this historical experience, it is surprising how much attention many present-day political observers, and political actors, continue to devote to the chancellor's policy guidelines competence. Even where the strategic aim of a public comment has been to warn chancellors against trying to lead too much from the front, many politicians have specifically pointed to the policy guidelines competence or, more precisely, to their effective suspension by the unwritten laws of coalition governance. Various recent examples were provided at the start of the first Merkel government, formed in late 2005 (see Glaab, 2010: 127–8). The curious fixation of many observers on this particular element of Article 65 of the Basic Law is all the more astonishing when one realizes that, originally, at the end of the First World War, the policy guidelines competence and its important specification ('within these limits every minister shall conduct the affairs of his department independently') was designed to strengthen Cabinet ministers against a, until then, largely unconstrained chancellor (see Gusy, 1997: 135–6). This notwithstanding, the overall distribution of constitutional and other institutional resources among the various players within the German core executive clearly makes the chancellor a strong rather than a weak head of government. The key challenges to his or her authority – including in particular the existence of governing coalitions and the dynamic requirements of coalition governance – all arise from the political game.

Beyond the executive branch, the chancellor's power, and that of his or her government, is more circumscribed (see Helms, 2005a: ch. 7). Apart from the sizeable control resources of the German *Bundestag*, both the institutions of the federal system and the Constitutional Court tend to constrain severely the room for manoeuvre of the federal government. The constraining effects of constitutional review are not doubted by any seasoned observer of German politics. While the Karlsruhe-based Court has lost some power to the European Constitutional Court in the course of European integration, it has remained a powerful counter-force that any federal government has to reckon with, and the experiences of the Schröder and Merkel governments (1998–2005, and since 2005 respectively) mark no exception to the rule (see Rath, 2013). Constraints relating to the federal system have held an even more prominent status in the Federal Republic's history, and the classic writings on the nature of political decision-making in post-war Germany (see in particular Lehmbruch, 1976; Schmidt, 1996). There have been several more recent changes, though. After the major reform of the federal system in 2006, the share of bills that cannot be passed without the explicit approval of the *Bundesrat* (*Zustimmungsgesetze*) dropped significantly, with the average share in the two most recent legislative periods (2005–09 and 2009–13) being more than 25 per cent lower than in the two preceding ones (2002–05 and 1998–2002). In constitutional practice, the more relevant aspect in terms of constraining the leverage of chancellors and their governments has of course been the pattern of party control of the *Bundesrat*. Whereas the grand coalition under Angela Merkel (2005–09) met a *Bundesrat* controlled by state governments that shared the federal government's colours, both the Schröder government (1998–2005) and the Merkel II government (2009–13) experienced long spells of a Bundesrat effectively governed by the opposition parties. As with the power of other veto players, many constraints flowing from the federal system develop powerful anticipatory effects with governments trying to keep their powder dry in the run-up to critical state elections which may change the patterns of party control in the *Bundesrat*. As the spheres of domestic and foreign policy have become ever more interdependent, it does not come as a surprise that observers have found chancellors occasionally delaying even important decisions in European policy until beyond the date of an important state election, as Angela Merkel apparently did in the context of the European debt crisis and the 2010 state election in North-Rhine Westphalia (see Jones, 2010; Schild, 2012: 28).

Patterns of leadership selection

As Gordon Smith once noted, 'throughout the life of the Federal Republic the ability of the political system to produce competent leaders has been of critical importance' (Smith, 1989: 60). This is obviously true of most other countries too, but given the historical experience of mediocre leadership in the Weimar Republic and of the evil leadership in the Third Reich, and the structurally elevated position of the chancellor in the Federal Republic, leadership recruitment has indeed been of particular importance to the overall performance of German post-war democracy.

Looking at Germany's two most recent chancellors, Gerhard Schröder and Angela Merkel, the rise of the latter has been by far the more spectacular one. While Gerhard Schröder has been described by many as a 'media chancellor', conspicuously detached from his own party and the Bundestag, his way to the top was pretty much in line with the patterns set by previous chancellors. His political experience included both several years as a member of the *Bundestag* and, more importantly, as minister-president of Lower-Saxony. Both his lack of experience as a government minister and party leader at the federal level are worth noting, but they do not constitute anything unique among the holders of the post-war chancellorship.

By contrast, Angela Merkel – similar to Margaret Thatcher – deserves to be described as an 'outsider' (see King, 2002; Murswieck, 2009: 26–7). One of the major distinguishing features of Merkel's background was her East German socialization. Among the CDU elite not being a Catholic represented another distinctive feature. There are several minor exceptions in her political background, such as the fact that – unlike all her predecessors in the chancellery since the late 1960s, except Helmut Schmidt – she had no previous experience as minister-president. However, the single most remarkable personal feature of Angela Merkel was of course her 'womanhood'. With a female head of government who has demonstrated remarkable resilience in office, Germany has become a prominent case study of female political leadership within the family of major advanced democracies. Even within the small group of female executive leaders, Merkel's case is special as her rise to power defies established institutional explanations of female leadership recruitment which hold that it is particularly difficult for women to secure the office of head of government if this represents the most powerful executive office within a given political system (Jalalzai, 2011). The bulk of substantive contributions, however, refrain from seeking to explain Merkel's performance as a political leader by her biological sex and gender alone and rather point to the distinctive combination of her life experience as a woman and that of an East German or a trained scientist (see Davidson-Schmich, 2011; Yoder, 2011).

Assessing leadership performance

Chief executives around the world tend to be compared in particular with their immediate predecessor in office, and many office-holders go out of their way to break away from their predecessor's legacy. The legacies that newly incoming leaders have to deal with are not confined to the policies of the previous administration but also include the expectations that the public has towards leaders and leadership that were shaped by the more recent experience, as Britain's Gordon Brown had to learn painfully when succeeding Tony Blair as prime minister (see Langer, 2010). Assessing the performance of German chancellors has followed slightly different patterns. At least the Federal Republic's second and third chancellor, Ludwig Erhard and Kurt Georg Kiesinger, were clearly judged against the performance of the 'founding chancellor', Konrad Adenauer. The concept of 'chancellor democracy', construed on the Adenauer experience, survived well into the later chapters of the Federal Republic's history (see Niclauss, 2004). However, both in politics and political science Adenauer has lost his status as the natural yardstick for assessing German chancellors of the twenty-first century. A more common, and arguably more reasonable, criterion is the type of coalition, and the party composition of the government, that chancellors face. Given the genuine novelty of the Red–Green project (1998–2005), Chancellor Schröder was largely considered a maverick for whom no natural criteria for comparison seemed to offer themselves. The differences in appearance and style between Angela Merkel and Gerhard Schröder were too obvious to attract much attention among observers. Merkel left no doubt that she was committed to replacing Schröder's flamboyance with a more reserved, less outgoing style. The formation of a grand coalition at the start of Merkel's first term led observers to develop in particular comparative perspectives focusing on Merkel and Kiesinger, the head of the Federal Republic's first grand coalition (1966–69), rather than on Schröder or any other earlier chancellor (Helms, 2006; Niclauss, 2008; Olsen, 2011). With the formation of a Christian–Liberal coalition after the 2009 Bundestag election, Merkel became the Federal Republic's first chancellor to perform under two different coalition formats. This not only bred widespread expectations of a more assertive leadership style that were largely disappointed during the first part of Merkel's second term (Helms, 2011), but the altered domestic context and the international challenges that the Merkel II government came to face also invited comparisons between Merkel and Kohl as 'coalition managers' and in particular as European leaders (Mayhew et al., 2011). If Kohl was in retrospect recognized as one of the chief protagonists of a 'Germany within Europe', even by several unlikely supporters, such as political philosopher Jürgen Habermas, Merkel faced widespread allegations of putting Germany before Europe (Gammelin, 2013).

The presidentialization of political leadership

One of the most interesting and rewarding ways of studying politics is to put developments in one country in comparative perspective. Even when there is little room for comparison, the use of concepts designed for such inquiry is rewarding as they provide focus and allow us to put subjects and findings in perspective (see Lees, 2006). This chapter is not the place for an extensive comparative inquiry into the changing dynamics of political leadership; however, it is still possible to relate the analysis of the German case to the major conceptual debates in the field. Recent research on political leadership in contemporary democracies has devoted much attention to notions of 'presidentialization'. While it is the evolution of the British premiership that has prompted most contributions in this field, there have also been a handful of contributions that characterize the performance of recent chancellors as *präsidial* or *präsidentiell* (see Lütjen and Walter, 2000; Korte, 2010). There are several competing understandings and conceptualizations of 'presidentialization', yet no single contribution has been more influential than the major volume edited by Thomas Poguntke and Paul Webb (2005a).

The concept of presidentialization

The main thrust of Poguntke and Webb's argument is that political chief executives in different democratic regimes have become ever more important and powerful – in the electoral arena, towards their parties and within the executive. A number of different factors have been identified as shaping the process. First, the internationalization of politics has given rise to an expansive system of international summitry whose main actors are the heads of governments. A second factor is the growth of the state, which has led to ever more complex policy agendas that have favoured a concentration of power with the political chief executive. The third factor is a changing structure of mass communication driven by a structurally altered media environment which is increasingly dominated by new electronic and commercial media. Fourth, the erosion of traditional social cleavages (see Chapter 3) has weakened the links between parties and voters, so it is increasingly important for political leaders to be able to project a personal appeal to citizens.

These 'underlying structural causes' are thought to combine with particular 'contingent causes', including the personality of leaders and their leadership style, in creating particular manifestations of presidentialization. As Poguntke and Webb hypothesize, there is also a strong amount of interdependence between the developments in the different arenas distinguished. For example, presidentialized electoral campaigns are not only expected to lead to voting decisions strongly shaped by voters' perceptions of the top candidates of the competing parties, but electorally successful 'personal candidates' are also thought to enjoy considerably greater leeway towards their party and within the government (Poguntke and Webb, 2005b: 19).

Other indicators of presidentialization that Poguntke and Webb suggest include: a growth of resources at the disposal of the chief executive; a trend towards increasingly centralized control and coordination of policy-making by the chief executive; a growing tendency of chief executives to appoint non-party technocrats as Cabinet ministers and an increase in Cabinet reshuffles while the head of government remains in office; the capacity of leaders to forge programmes autonomously of their parties; and the use of plebiscitary modes of political communication and mobilization (ibid.: 19–20).

The presidentialization of German elections

To what extent then can the developments of the past decade be characterized as a trend towards a presidentialization of leadership? As to what Poguntke and Webb refer to as the 'electoral face of presidentialization', the picture is mixed. As chancellors seeking re-election, both Schröder and Merkel pursued a campaign strategy that strongly focused on their personal popularity that well exceeded both the public support for their respective parties and that of the opposition party's chancellor candidate. Since 2002 live televised debates between the two main challengers – strongly reminiscent of US presidential campaigns – have been widely perceived as the top event of the campaign. However, there have been no signs of further expanding these practices. Whereas in 2002 two such debates were organized, there has been only one in all consecutive election years. In all three elections since 2002, it was Merkel, as challenger in 2005 and as incumbent chancellor in 2009 and 2013, who insisted on holding just one such event. The strongly personalized, or presidentialized, electoral campaigns left their mark on the electorate, but they have not as yet fundamentally altered the established voting patterns in terms of the preference assigned to parties over candidates. The trend is nevertheless obvious and remarkable. After 19 per cent in 2005 and 28 per cent in 2009, no less than 34 per cent of all respondents interviewed in the run-up to the 2013 *Bundestag* election declared that they considered the 'candidate question' to be more important than the party composition of the government (*Forschungsgruppe Wahlen*, 2013b: 2).

While in those elections they fought as incumbent chancellors, both Schröder (in 2002) and Merkel (in 2009 and 2013) were clearly the main assets of their parties. However, it would still seem difficult to establish as to what extent they were actually fitted with strong personal mandates to provide leadership in government. One of the most remarkable features of the 2009 election related to the conspicuously limited coat-tail effects that Merkel's popularity had on the CDU/CSU which experienced their second worst electoral result since 1949. This changed in 2013, when 68 per cent of the electorate identified Merkel as the main reason for the strong showing of the CDU/CSU at the polls, compared with only 21 per cent that considered the political and policy performance of the party to be the main reason for its impressive electoral result (ibid.). However, this amounts to less than a fully convincing proof of a strong personal mandate. Indeed, there are obvious limits concerning the push that chancellors can get from the electoral arena when it comes to dominating their government – a contention originally put forward in the British debate over presidentialization. At the helm of a coalition government, no chancellor (or prime minister for that matter) can hope to be granted special leeway by the junior governing party in exchange for his or her personal popularity with the electorate. The natural sphere of dominance of Christian Democratic chancellors is not only circumscribed by the other coalition party but also by the possibly competing agendas of the CSU, the CDU's Bavarian sister party. Compared with the CDU/CSU relationship under the leadership of Helmut Kohl and Theo Waigel, Merkel's relations with all three CSU party leaders of her first two terms (Edmund Stoiber, Erwin Huber and Horst Seehofer) have been difficult and prone to conflict. Moreover, in terms of Cabinet seats held by CDU ministers, Merkel's party-related power base in her first Cabinet was notably small. There were just five CDU ministers, alongside two CSU ministers and eight SPD ministers.

The presidentialization of the executive

What about the 'executive face of presidentialization'? One thing that stands in the way of making Germany a show case of dramatic intra-executive presidentialization is the fact the Federal Chancellery has nearly always provided the holder of the chancellorship with generous and effective support. It is the exceptions – such as during the short-lived chancellorships of Ludwig Erhard and Kurt Georg Kiesinger, and the second term of Chancellor Willy Brandt – that prove the rule. With an overall staff of about 450, which has remained fairly stable over the past decades, the personnel-related resources of the Chancellery have long been impressive by almost any standard. At the same time, a transatlantic comparative perspective easily identifies major differences between the German Chancellery and the Executive Office of the President which are not confined to numbers but include dramatically different patronage resources of German chancellors and American presidents.

Much of the Chancellery's effectiveness, and its strategic value for the chancellor, depend on the personal skills of the man at the top, the chief of the Chancellor's Office whose key tasks include the provision of information and interministerial coordination as well as the formulation and supervision of selected areas of government policy. The chief of office can be either appointed as a civil servant or as a federal minister with special responsibilities. Whereas until the early 1980s virtually all chiefs of office were appointed as civil servants, it is now more common to make the head of the Chancellery a federal minister. Among the more recent incumbents, Chancellor Schröder's second chief of office, Frank-Walter Steinmeier, marked the only exception. However, there is no apparent correlation between the formal status and the political performance of the head of the Chancellery. At least when looked at from the outside, the Chancellery under Frank-Walter Steinmeier (1999–2005) and Thomas de Mazière (2005–09) was more effective than under Bodo Hombach (1998–99) and Ronald Pofalla (2009–13). Since the Adenauer–Globke era (1953–63) an effective head of the Chancellor's Office has been widely considered both a prerequisite for and a reliable indicator of a strong chancellor and a successful chancellorship. However, the patterns are more diversified and complex than this early experience would appear to suggest. To some observers even and perhaps in particular the hapless Ronald Pofalla, who evinced the particular qualities of a political scapegoat, contributed much to letting Chancellor Merkel appear genuinely 'presidential' (see van Ackeren, 2011; Alexander, 2013).

All chancellors since Adenauer had 'kitchen cabinets' that included key players from beyond the pool of Cabinet ministers and civil servants (Müller and Walter, 2004). Today's mass media have become much more assertive in identifying the individual members of a chancellor's group of formal and informal advisers, and in assessing the informal power configurations amongst the chancellor's entourage. There was no secret about the changing teams of advisers during the chancellorships of Gerhard

Schröder and Angela Merkel. In any case, it would seem questionable to speak of a constant growth of advisers surrounding German chancellors that could in any meaningful way be considered to be reminiscent of the established patterns of presidential advice and leadership in the USA. In fact, halfway into Merkel's second term, the chancellor's depleted team of policy advisers was ridiculed as a 'one-leaf clover' (Bannas, 2011a).

There has also been no significant increase of non-party technocrat ministers under Schröder and Merkel. While the Basic Law assigns the right to select candidates for ministerial posts to the chancellor, the firmly established constitutional practice of party government has meant that the chancellor's room for manoeuvre in the government-building process has remained considerably more circumscribed than the constitution suggests. This includes in particular limited room for chancellors, even if they so wished, to appoint external technocrats to ministerial posts at the expense of senior party fellows or candidates nominated by the coalition party from within its own ranks. Indeed, Schröder's economics minister Werner Müller (1998–2002) was only the second clear-cut case of a non-party federal minister since 1949, and thus marked the exception that proved the rule.

Moreover, Cabinet turnovers, another key indicator of presidentialization with Poguntke and Webb, have not increased significantly. With six replacements, the Schröder I government (1998–2002) was marked by a low degree of ministerial stability, whereas there was not a single real replacement in the two and a half years of the Schröder II government (with Jürgen Trittin acting as caretaker of Renate Künast in the Ministry of Food, Agriculture and Consumer Protection from early to mid-October 2005, marking the only case coming close to an exception). In particular the history of ministerial replacements under Merkel serves as a reminder that it is necessary to distinguish between resignations and dismissals. Only the latter could meaningfully be considered to mark a feature of 'presidentialized leadership'.

Franz Müntefering, Horst Seehofer and Michael Glos, ministers in the Merkel I government, all resigned completely voluntarily. Also, it was mounting public pressure, rather than pressure from within the chancellery, that led to the resignations of Franz-Josef Jung, Karl-Theodor zu Guttenberg and Annette Schavan at various stages of the Merkel II government. The two changes in the FDP-led departments (involving Philipp Rösler, Daniel Bahr and Rainer Brüderle) were largely beyond Merkel's immediate control for reasons of 'coalitional restraint'. Merkel's role in the resignation of Hans-Peter Friedrich in February 2014 over his involvement in the 'Edathy Affair' was less obvious. While the chancellor was apparently happy to accept his resignation, she seemed not to have directly triggered Friedrich's stepping down. Thus, the case of Norbert

Röttgen, departing in May 2012, stands out as the only clear-cut case of a minister being bluntly dismissed by the chancellor, and at least temporarily it seemed as though this episode had severely damaged Merkel's reputation rather than boosting her authority within and beyond her party (see Fleischhauer et al., 2012).

With the important exception of the grand coalition years (2005–09, and post-2013) both Schröder and Merkel profited from the lack of any credible exit option of their party's junior coalition partner. In particular the Greens as the junior partner within a Red–Green coalition government (1998–2005) could not credibly threaten to leave the coalition and thus had to tolerate the concentration of much executive power in the Chancellery. For most of the time, it seemed that the FDP's position within the Christian–Liberal coalition forged in 2009 was even worse than that of the Greens under Chancellor Schröder. While in the beginning the Liberals could, just as much as the Greens did in 2002, claim to have made the formation of this particular coalition government possible by their exceptional strong electoral performance in the preceding *Bundestag* election, the FDP's electoral performance in many state elections, and its showing in public surveys, were so disastrous that even the most reserved observers considered the party to be threatened with destruction. There were of course moments in the lifetime of the Merkel II government when it seemed that the FDP would be able to triumph in future coalition-formation games, such as for example in the aftermath of the nomination of Joachim Gauck for the position of federal president. The Liberals had declared their support for Gauck who was known to be the SPD's and the Green's preferred candidate, and without first seeking any consensus within the coalition (von Hammerstein et al., 2012). However, whereas the CDU/CSU was widely considered able and possibly willing to form a viable coalition with any party in the Bundestag, apart from the Left, the FDP suffered from its own coalition statement given in the 2009 election that explicitly ruled out any participation in any SPD-led federal government. Even more important for the internal life of the Christian–Liberal coalition during the first two or so years of its existence, the FDP found its room for manoeuvre in most domestic policy areas severely circumscribed by having centred its 2009 election campaign almost exclusively on substantive tax cuts and by the unfavourable portfolio distribution within the Merkel II government (Saalfeld, 2010).

With the Foreign Office, the FDP initially seemed to have secured at least some independent power resources within the federal government. However, this impression was not to last for very long. Foreign Minister Guido Westerwelle was soon identified by many as perhaps the Federal Republic's weakest holder of that office. While his performance somewhat improved after his forced resignation from the position of FDP party leader early in 2011, the Foreign Office witnessed one of the most spectacular power drains in its history. Not only were most important foreign and European policy issues dealt with by the chancellor, there was also a remarkable institutional downgrading of the Foreign Office in the internal hierarchy of the federal government (see Neukirch, 2012). All this marked a major contrast both to the intra-executive distribution of power in the Merkel I government and the Schröder governments where, as in most previous governments, foreign policy was to some extent a reserved domain of the junior coalition party. Very much like Helmut Kohl during the 'Genscher era', but in stark contrast to Merkel within her Christian–Liberal coalition, Schröder also had to cope with a foreign minister from the coalition partner, Joschka Fischer, who enjoyed tremendous personal popularity that effectively limited the chancellor's influence in foreign affairs.

As Thomas Poguntke (2009) has observed, both Merkel and Schröder did indeed establish several expert advisory bodies that were superficially reminiscent of presidential commissions in the USA, though their impact on the administration's key decisions remained uncertain. To many observers, the impact of the Hartz Commission (2002) on welfare state reform is difficult to overestimate. Recent scholarship has shown that an expert forum organized by the Bertelsmann Foundation played an even more decisive role in developing the policy ideas that eventually led to the heavily contested Hartz IV legislation (Fleckenstein, 2008), which obviously does not run counter to the widespread perception that the Schröder years were marked by a notable degree of 'governing with experts'. Most expert commissions set up under Merkel had no similar clout. The 'ethics commission', established in the aftermath of the Fukushima incident, played little, if any, role in the government's spectacular U-turn on its energy policy, and – given the towering public opposition to nuclear energy – rather seemed designed to distract from Merkel's anxiety about her party's electoral fortunes at several upcoming state elections. Also, Merkel's initiative *Zukunftsdialog*, launched in 2011, which involved 120 handpicked experts, academics and practitioners from different backgrounds, organized into ten different working groups, was mainly located at the level of symbolic leadership.

A presidential leadership style

There is mixed evidence in support of the presidentialization thesis at the level of public leadership. Both Merkel and Schröder sought to professionalize government communication. However, neither of them pursued a communication strategy 'as a means of defining policy alternatives' (Poguntke and Webb, 2005b: 19). More often than not, Merkel waited as long as she possibly could for a consensus to emerge before she eventually joined the winning coalition, presenting the solution found as *alternativlos*. Alongside a wealth of major differences, this 'there is no alternative' rhetoric, if used very differently, marked one of the few shared features of Merkel's and Margaret Thatcher's leadership performance. If the relevant cases for comparison are to be drawn from the group of recent US presidents, Merkel's public leadership performance appeared for most of the time as rather unpresidential. There have been recent attempts by the Merkel team to establish new modes of public relationship – such as 'town hall meetings' – that could be said to be somewhat reminiscent of the public relations efforts of American presidents (see Nelles and Wittrock, 2012), but the more important element of successful presidential leadership – a compelling and mobilizing leadership rhetoric – never became a key feature of the Merkel chancellorship. If anything, Merkel's performance in terms of rhetorical leadership prompted accusations of a 'silent paternalism', understood as a form of leadership characterized by the leader's firm belief that his or her actions are in the best interest of society and in no need of being publicly explained and justified (Kurbjuweit, 2011). That this did not damage Merkel's nearly constantly high public popularity scores is fascinating in itself, and comes as a major blow to the popular thesis in leadership and communication research which holds that in the twenty-first century only leaders who manage to communicate effectively their decisions to the public stand a chance of being considered legitimate and worthy of being supported.

The presidentialization of the chancellor: party relations

Some of the most impressive evidence in support of the presidentialization thesis relates to the developments at the level of chancellor/party relations or, in Poguntke and Webb's terms, the 'party face of presidentialization'. While Schröder was not the first post-war chancellor to win the chancellorship without being the official leader of his party, he was the first to resign his party's leadership in a spectacular move in 2004 (see Gast, 2008). This was, however, only the final chapter in a relationship between the chancellor and his party that was from the beginning marked by a strong element of 'detachment' and mutual distrust. As an unenthusiastic successor to SPD party leader Lafontaine, Schröder provided little, if any, party leadership and showed a limited willingness to take much guidance from the SPD party manifesto for his decision-making in the Chancellery. His public launching of the *Agenda 2010* in a government declaration before the German *Bundestag* on 14 March 2003 was widely considered an exceptional move that seriously challenged both the SPD and its parliamentary party group in the *Bundestag* (see Braunthal, 2003).

For all the differences that marked Merkel's and Schröder's leadership style, and the political cultures of the CDU/CSU and the SPD, there has been much continuity in terms of the 'party face of presidentialization' since 2005. While Merkel belonged to the group of chancellors that combined the office of chancellor with that of party leader, it seemed unlikely from the beginning that she would establish a particularly impressive example of party government. As Clay Clemens has noted (2010: 34), 'never have expectations of a chancellor's hopes for party support been lower than they were for Angela Merkel'. While most actors in politics at some point in time need some luck, Merkel's rise to the CDU party leadership in 2000 as well as her becoming the party's chancellor candidate in 2005 certainly included a sizeable amount of luck, which is not to deny her determination and cleverness in exploiting her opportunities. Especially during the first years at the top of the CDU, there were many sceptics that speculated about an early end of the 'Merkel experiment'. Given this background, the successive disappearance of virtually all of Merkel's potential intraparty challengers (such as Friedrich Merz, Günther Öttinger, Roland Koch or for some time even Christian Wulff) is most remarkable. In terms of the 'party face of presidentialization' the extent to which the CDU allowed Merkel to shape its programmatic profile, and how much autonomy from her party Merkel enjoyed as chancellor, is even more noteworthy. While up to 2003 it seemed as if Merkel was committed to, and successful in, strengthening the neo-liberal edge of the party (a popular contention that has been challenged by recent empirical research; see Debus and Müller, 2013: 167), later moves were widely perceived as exercises of programmatic back-pedalling which earned Merkel allegations of seeking silently to 'socialdemocratize' the Christian Democrats. By any standard, there was an extensive list of decisions – stretching from family policy and immigration policy to energy policy and defence policy – made by the first two Merkel governments that were in apparent tension with longstanding policy positions of the Christian Democrats (see Green, 2013b; Clemens, 2013). The conspicuously late publication of the CDU/CSU election manifesto for the Bundestag election of 2013, just three months ahead of the polls, and the swift and smooth approval of the document by the two parties' executive boards, suggested that the Christian Democrats had eventually given in and accepted that Merkel was by far their greatest asset.

Conclusion

The past decade has seen important developments at the level of political leadership in Germany. If, and to what extent, these developments are perceived as presidentialization depends very much on the conceptualization of this much-debated phenomenon. As the observations above suggest, it is well possible to identify individual aspects that are in line with Poguntke and Webb's prominent notions of 'presidentialized' politics and leadership. However, even without a detailed conceptual critique it is easy to see that the authors' framework is rather selective. There are whole areas and features of presidential politics and leadership that are not covered, such as in particular the important field of executive–legislative relations. In the wider literature, both concepts of 'presidentialization' and its possible empirical manifestations in different contexts remain contested. It is not even clear that 'presidentialization', however defined, necessarily marks a continuous trend. Indeed, some scholars, such as Peter Lösche, have argued that, altogether, present-day party leaders face considerably less favourable conditions for acting 'presidentially' than party leaders of the early post-war age (Lösche, 2005).

It is even more difficult than in most other areas of German politics to forecast future directions and developments in political leadership. Since leadership, even when closely tied to a particular office, is essentially about the behaviour of individual leaders (and their followers), there is less stability, and less predictability, at the level of leadership than at the level of institutions. For example, the editors of the previous edition of this book concluded in their Introduction that 'the weak start to Schröder's second term in office suggests that his government lacks a clearly defined reform agenda' (Padgett et al., 2003: 16). What was to follow under the label *Agenda 2010* only shortly afterwards came as a strong reminder that, for all the heavy institutional and political constraints on German chancellors and their governments, sometimes even wide-ranging reforms can be launched successfully and virtually overnight. That said, there is room for debate about the exact relationship amongst leadership, change and reform. Many leadership scholars would contend that only leadership that produces substantive change through large-scale reforms fully deserves to be characterized as 'leadership' (see Burns, 1978: 414). But does this mean that even radical change is always a reliable indicator of leadership? There is reason to be sceptical. Whereas the Merkel government's unexpected farewell to nuclear energy – announced as a spectacular U-turn to one of its not too many core pledges of the 2009 Bundestag election campaign in the close aftermath of the Fukushima incident in 2011– certainly marked the start of a possible large-scale reform in energy policy, it takes exceptionally generous criteria to classify this episode as a convincing act of genuine democratic political leadership.

Chapter 6

The Politics of Social Protest

DIETER RUCHT

Views on the development of social and political protest movements in Germany during the last ten years differ widely. Some observers argue that protest has declined significantly and, as a consequence, lost much of its former capacity for shaping society and politics. Others take the opposite view, stressing the continuing or even increasing vitality and impact of protest movements, especially when considering the period from 2010 onwards. In the absence of systematic and reliable data, proponents of these diverging views each point to some empirical examples to undergird their position. The sceptics tend to take the huge mass demonstrations of the new social movements in the 1970s and 1980s as a yardstick for their diagnosis of a relative demobilization in more recent years. Their counterparts highlight the political awakening of a politicized citizenry as epitomized by the so-called *Wutbürger* (angry citizen) – a term that was introduced with a clearly derogative slant (Kurbjuweit, 2010). Allegedly, the rise of the *Wutbürger* has characterized the bulk of recent conflicts, most notably the massive and enduring resistance against 'Stuttgart 21', the project to build a new railway station in Stuttgart (Ohmke-Reinicke, 2012; Brettschneider and Schuster, 2013). In the wake of the debate around the *Wutbürger*, a series of journalistic and scholarly books were published, mostly sympathizing with the politicized citizenry (see Leggewie, 2011; Roth, 2011; Rudolf et al., 2011; Kessler, 2013).

Whereas the view that protest has decreased is predominantly influenced by the collective memory of now grey-haired (former) activists, the opposite perception is largely promoted by sensational journalistic accounts and their reception by younger or only newly activated people who are very optimistic about the prospects of their campaigns.

Regardless of whether one leans more towards the sceptical or the opposite perspective, it is clear that a number of protest movements were or are still active from the early 2000s (see Roth, 2011; Kessler, 2013; Walter et al., 2013). Beyond the widely known and intensively discussed case of Stuttgart 21, examples include the struggles around airport extensions in Frankfurt, Munich and Berlin, nuclear power and other energy infrastructures across the country, cuts to welfare provisions, speculative financial transfer, tax evasion, the widening gap between the rich and the poor, and – more generally – neo-liberal capitalism. Last but not least, one should also mention the continuation of right-wing extremist and xeno-phobic activities as well as a strong counter-mobilization by left-wing, liberal and moderate conservative groups. Taken together, these protest activities are far from being insignificant.

While, in principle, it is possible to assess and even measure the volume, composition and structures of protest in Germany in the last ten years in comparison with earlier periods, it is a much more difficult, and probably impossible, task to measure, in a cross-time perspective, the impact of these activities on politics and society (Giugni, 1998; Kolb, 2007). In this respect, hardly more than informed speculation can be offered, especially because many factors and actors come into play. Moreover, the long-term impacts of recent protests still have to be awaited.

In the following I will try to answer two key questions. First, what is the extent, thematic composition and structure of protest mobilization in Germany in the last ten years against the backdrop of earlier periods? Second, what is the impact of protest mobilization in terms of public agenda-setting, policy-making and the overall constellation of power?

Patterns and trends in the social movement sector

Most protest movements are not spontaneous outbursts in reaction to sudden grievances. Rather, they have undergone a previous phase of – widely unnoticed – infancy. In quite a number of cases, they have roots in past decades and, sometimes, even in past centuries. This also applies to the contemporary social movement sector in Germany with regard to the range of themes and issues, organizational forms, and action repertoires. Only when comparing the most recent period with earlier periods, can we become aware of both continuities and discontinuities (see Karapin, 2007; Roth and Rucht, 2008).

Themes and issues

By and large, today's social movement sector in Germany is comprised of three major components, each of which involves a set of ideologically similar groups and movements. In addition, one can identify a residual category composed of dispersed and mostly disconnected single-issue movements. As a rule, these have a minor and/or only short-lived mobi-lization capacity.

A first strong component of the social movement sector is largely based on the so-called 'new social movements' (NSMs). These stand in the tradition of left-liberal groups and networks, especially the New Left of 1960s, though not identical with the latter. Compared to the NSMs, the New Left of the 1960s was much more theory-driven, more attracted by revolutionary concepts and struggles (especially in developing countries), more provocative in their action repertoires (with regard to the prevailing ideas and values of their time), less structured, less diversified in their thematic range, and more narrow in their recruitment base (mainly intellectuals and students). Moreover, in countries such as Italy and France, but not so in Germany, the New Left sought, and partially succeeded, in creating a link to the labour movement.

The thematic range of the NSMs is variegated, covering issues such as: human rights; citizen participation; women's, gay and lesbian rights; peace and disarmament; environmental protection; nuclear energy; urban restructuring; and misery and poverty in developing countries.

A study on protest events from 1975 to 1989 showed that almost three-quarters of all protests in Germany, as reported in the nationwide newspaper *Frankfurter Rundschau*, could be attributed to the NSMs. This was the highest percentage among the group of four countries investigated (which also included France, the Netherlands and Switzerland – see Kriesi et al., 1995: 20). Contrary to some observers' perception, the NSMs have not disappeared, though their relative weight, when compared with other segments of the movement sector, has diminished. According to this database that has been updated by Swen Hutter for more recent periods up to 2005, the share of NSMs' protests has fallen in France to 25.7 per cent in the 1990s and to 27.9 per cent in the period from 2000 to 2005. In Germany, the respective figures are 54.1 and 56.5 per cent. Nevertheless, the role of today's NSMs should not be underestimated. Some of these movements, especially those centred around issues of environmental protection and nuclear power, have proven their ongoing vitality and extraordinary capacity for mobilization. It is safe to say that the German anti-nuclear movement, at least until the governmental decision in 2011 to phase out nuclear power, was the strongest in the world. One should also recall that the peace movement, being notorious for its short-lived campaigns which are mainly driven by external events, had its largest single demonstration in German history on 15 February 2003. This occurred on an international day of protest against the imminent war in Iraq (Walgrave and Rucht, 2010). On the other hand, some movements attributed to the NSMs, among them the women's movement, have already lost their momentum and many of their adherents since the 1990s. In terms of street protest, the movement has become almost invisible.

While it is still a matter of debate as to whether more recent groupings such as the global justice movements (GJMs) and the very recent Occupy movement should be treated as separate from NSMs, I consider them as a new generation or a kind of outgrowth from this older strand. After all, GJMs and Occupy have essentially the same value base and worldview as NSMs. They all converge in their claims for a participatory democracy, social justice and solidarity with people who are deprived and/or marginalized. Some small differences, however, can be identified. More than NSMs, GJMs and the Occupy movement focus on the structure of the global economy and define themselves in opposition to neo-liberalism. Also, spurred on by the availability of the internet, they cooperate much more across national and continental borders than the older NSMs. However, these are differences in degree rather than in principle.

But even when we include these younger movements in the broader category of NSMs, I would maintain that, relative to this inclusive category, two other types of movements have increased their proportion in all protest activities in Germany. It seems also that GJMs have lost some of their public appeal and quantitative support – an impression that applies to almost all such groups in Western democracies (Banse and Habermann, 2012). A telling indicator for this is the declining interest and participation in the European Social Forum meetings (Mosca et al., 2009), a process that is also mirrored in the Social Forum process in Germany.

A second important segment comprises movements and groupings focusing on labour, welfare and social security. While the German trade unions still follow their long-term trend of losing members (the total membership of the *Deutsche Gewerkschaftsbund* plummeted from 11.016 million in 1991, the high point due to the integration of the East German unions, to 6.152 million in 2012) and exhibiting a very low level of strike activity in international comparison, the struggle around specific issues such as equal pay for women, precarious working conditions, minimum wages, unemployment and social security has intensified since the early 2000s, though not consistently resulting in high numbers of protests. However, the trade unions, together with a range of other groups such as welfare organizations, religious groups and some GJMs, were active carriers of protests directed against the abolishment or reduction of welfare provisions. For example, large demonstrations were staged in autumn 2003 and even more so in the spring of the following year, attracting on one single day (3 April) around 500,000 protesters in the cities of Berlin, Cologne and Stuttgart. An impressive wave of nationwide protests against the so-called Hartz IV regulations culminated in the summer of 2004. These measures reduced the provisions of the unemployed and submitted these people to crossing bureaucratic hurdles to get access to these provisions. Interestingly, the protests received no or little support from the national and regional leadership of the trade unions and the big welfare organizations. In some places, protest activity, usually taking place every Monday, continues today, though attracting rarely more than a few dozen activists and so no longer covered by the mass media.

The third set of highly active and public visible movements is comprised by right-wing radical and xenophobic groups. These exhibited a stark rise in the early 1990s and continue to mobilize at a high level today. While they stage an impressive number of protest actions, many of these including acts of aggression and violence, the turnout is relatively low. Usually, right-wing protests attract a dozen or perhaps a few hundred followers. Only in a few cases are they able to mobilize more than say 5,000 participants. As a rule, these groups' activities trigger strong counter-mobilizations by radical and moderate left-wingers as well as liberal groups, which mostly outnumber the right-radicals by far. To a significant extent, this counter-mobilization comes from the ranks of the two major strands of 'progressive' movements mentioned above. It also includes so-called 'anti-fascist groups' whose very existence is a reaction to the rise of such extreme right and xenophobic movements. Like their counterparts, most notably the so-called *Kameradschaften* (comrade-ships), a sizeable proportion of the anti-fascists do not shy away from the use of violence by directly engaging in confrontations that the police, with varying degrees of success, desperately try to prevent.

Fourth, there is a residual category of disparate and mostly uncon-nected protest groups that tend to focus on very specific issues, often acting on behalf of a very distinct membership or clientele. In part, they defend their economically or otherwise privileged positions (e.g. dentists, well-off local residents); in part, they embrace the Nimby ('Not In My Backyard') outlook; in part they start in the Nimby spirit but eventually abandon it as the result of a learning process. Other groups, from their very beginnings, are fighting for the common good or, more specifically, for marginalized and needy people; for example fighting for the rights of asylum seekers and other immigrants. One example is the campaign against the Lufthansa airline (which had introduced the 'Lufthansa deportation class'). This included a computer server attack against the corporation on 20 June 2001 and a number of subsequent activities. Another manifestation of pro-immigrant mobilization are the annual 'No Border Camps'. These are organized by radical left-wing groups to strengthen the bonds between immigrants and their German supporters but also to make the public aware of the issue through acts of protest.

During the last ten years numerous groups with one or more of these different orientations have staged protest events and campaigns, such as in the fields of transport, energy, banking, communication/regulation of the internet, surveillance in public and semi-public spaces, nursing, schools and universities, hospitals, agriculture, homeless people, and asylum seekers. Sometimes such campaigns emerge at short notice and, at least to outsiders, seem to come out of the blue. As a rule, however, they are preceded by a mobilization process that, nowadays, includes both online and offline activities. This was true, for example, for the only loosely coordinated resistance against the intended Anti-Counterfeiting Trade Agreement (ACTA) regulations. At other times, protest campaigns are the result of a carefully planned and orchestrated mobilization process that may rest on considerable financial and personnel resources. It is noteworthy that some of these protests create new and unexpected divisions. For example, with regard to the installation of wind turbines, environmentalists can be found on both sides of the conflict line. While the majority tends to favour the deployment of wind turbines, and even large parks of them, as part of the so-called *Energiewende* (energy transformation) preference for non-fossil energy sources, a minority of environmentalists opposes these plans because the turbines can be noisy, kill birds or are aesthetically unwanted.

Overall, the size of this fourth category of protest groups has very likely increased, following a long-term trend of the diversification and specification of protest themes and issues, the inclusion of more social groups and different strata, and the increasing use of protest as a fairly rational means of defending and promoting both private and public interests in the public arena.

Data drawn from the left-alternative daily newspaper *Die Tageszeitung*, currently available for the period from 1993 to 2009, indicate shifts in the relative weight of different themes of protest from the 1990s to the 2000s. The issue areas of labour, regulation of the economy, farming, European politics, nuclear power and peace have attracted more protest events in the 2000s than in the period from 1993 to 1999 (when calculated for the yearly average in each of the two periods), while the opposite is true for the issues of democracy/citizen rights, social security/ welfare, environmental protection, women, and ethnic minorities/immigration.

Organizational and tactical forms

Parallel to shifts in the kind and relevance of major themes, organizational forms and tactical repertoires also change over time, though usually slower and less spectacularly than media reports suggest.

While most protests in the 1950s and the first half of the 1960s were staged by large and usually hierarchically structured organizations such as trade unions, churches and associations of war refugees (*Vertriebenenverbände*), in later periods smaller and more informal groups, among them mostly local citizen initiatives, have become more important. Both single protest events as well as large campaigns are often organized by broad and loosely coupled networks and alliances, some-times comprising hundreds of groups. This trend has continued and prob-ably even intensified up to the present. Large membership-based organizations, among them political parties, trade unions and churches, were and still are shrinking. The bulk of young activists in particular clearly prefer to engage in more informal groups with low thresholds of entrance and exit, therefore allowing for quick changes in the content, form and level of activity, a trend that has been coined 'situative engage-ment' (Paris, 1989). However, not all formal organizations involved in protest activities have experienced a decline in membership. Some large environmental associations such as Bund für Umwelt und Naturschutz Deutschland (German Association for Environmental and Nature Protection) and Greenpeace Germany continue to grow.

Almost across the board of all protest groups, a trend towards the profes-sionalization of public relations work can be observed. While large organi-zations have followed this track for many years by employing press speakers or even creating a department for media relations, small groups also increasingly design their activities to maximize media coverage. Movement-related groups that specialize in media work, for example Indymedia, have been set up in Germany as elsewhere. Internet-based, but not thematically specialized, campaign organizations have come into exis-tence, such as Campact!de, which bears the slogan 'Democracy in action' (see www.campact.de). Campact is a strategically oriented group inspired by the US-based MoveOn.org. Today, seven years after is inception, Campact has an annual budget of €2 million, a staff of more than 20 people, and a list of more than 900,000 subscribers (October 2013) of whom, depending on the issue, some tens of thousands or even more than 100,000 can be mobilized within a few days to sign electronically a declaration of protest. Only a small fraction of them, however, are ready and able to join a street protest that may accompany the collection of signatures.

The trend towards professionalization can be seen not only in genuine acts of protest activities but also in related activities such as: fund-raising; the production of fact sheets and scientific studies; organizing confer-ences; and lobbying. Some organizations have become big players. Greenpeace Germany, for instance, in 2012 had a budget of €52 million and some 150 full-time staff employed in its national headquarters in Hamburg. Noteworthy also is the creation of Die Bewegungsstiftung (see www.bewegungsstiftung.de), a tax-exempted foundation established in 2002. It not only funds and advises groups engaged in protest campaigns but also supports, via calls for donations, up to ten so-called *Bewegungsarbeiter* (movement workers). These are experienced activists who are committed full-time to political and social causes that, by and large, are on the agenda of NSMs and GJMs.

Partly due to the nature of the problems at stake, partly due to better and cheaper means of transport and communication, transnational protest campaigns have both absolutely and relatively increased in numbers and public visibility. By their very nature, topics such as peace, arms control, asylum, pollution of the seas, and whaling are prone to mobilization across borders, thereby resulting in the establishment of issue-oriented transnational organizations and networks. With the rise of GJMs in the 1990s and their global and continental social forums, a thematically broader infrastructure for protest mobilization has taken shape (Rucht, 2011) and may well serve as a vehicle for future transnational campaigns. On the other hand, the Occupy movement (Kraushaar, 2012) as well as the resistance against the planned ACTA regulations showed that transnational protest does not necessarily have to rely on strong organizations, especially when ample and sympathetic media coverage comes into play. But the example of Occupy also demonstrates that without an organizational structure (a feature that most of the Occupy activists rejected) it is almost impossible to maintain momentum. No wonder that the movement faded away almost as quickly as it had emerged (Rucht, 2013).

During the last ten years, the action repertoire of protest groups in Germany has not fundamentally changed. Depending on the issues and the context, most groups tend to apply a broad range of protest techniques, for the most part staying within legal boundaries. In quite a number of cases, ranging from protest against Stuttgart 21, to resistance against the transport of nuclear material, to anti-racist mobilization, protesters have resorted to tactics of civil disobedience and direct action. It appears that these forms of protest have gained some recognition even among the strata of 'ordinary' and 'decent' citizens. By contrast, protest violence is basically restricted to extreme right-wing and left-wing groups. A comprehensive dataset spanning the period from 1950 to – currently – 2002 shows that violent protests as a proportion of all protest activity per decade has increased from 2.9 per cent in the 1950s to 18.2 per cent in the 1990s, with a remarkable shift from prevailing left-wing violence up to the 1980s to prevailing right-wing violence starting from the 1990s. (For an overview on the methodology of the so-called Prodat project, see Rucht, 2001: 315–19.)

Figures available for the period from 2000 to 2002 drawn from the same source indicate an overall decline of protest violence when compared to the previous decade. This reduced level of violence seems to have stabilized, and probably even lowered, in the most recent years. It is important to note that the significant proportion of violent events are only accompanied by a very low number of participants. Throughout the whole period of observation, their number was always below 1 per cent.

Table 6.1   *Distribution of types of protest action in the 1990s and 2000s (%)*

	Moderate	Demonstrative	Confrontational	Violent
1993–99	17.4	54.9	11.3	16.4
2000–09	16.2	64.6	8.6	10.6

Source: compiled by the author from *Die Tageszeitung* newspaper reports.

Based on a different source, the daily newspaper *Die Tageszeitung*, we can also identify shifts in the relative weight of different types of protests from the early 1990s until 2009. When the specific forms of protest actions are grouped into four broader categories (moderate, demonstrative, confrontational, violent), it becomes clear that the proportion of violent protests has decreased significantly and that of confrontational protests slightly, while the proportion of demonstrative protests has increased (see Table 6.1).

Volume of protest

Regarding the volume of protest as measured in numbers of protest events and numbers of participants, detailed figures covering the full period from 2003 to 2012 are not yet available. Data derived from a systematic content analysis of two nationwide newspapers (*Süddeutsche Zeitung* and *Frankfurter Rundschau*) for the period from 1950 to 2002 indicate, apart from short-lived fluctuations, a general increase of the number of protest events until the mid-1990s, followed by a decline in subsequent years. More recent data based on a different source (the left-alternative daily *Die Tageszeitung*) but covering the period from 1993 to 2009 confirm the downward trend from the 1990s to the 2000s (see Figure 6.1). The average yearly number of protest events dropped from 780 in the period 1993–99 to 540 in the period 2000–09. In a similar vein, the average number of participants per protest dropped from 9,801 in the first period to 7,610 in the second period.

It is still unclear whether or not there was a new surge of protest after 2010, when the public debate on the *Wutbürger* started and protest, in general, was widely reported by the mass media. Preliminary results of a still incomplete database show that in the three-month period from September to November 2010, the numbers of protests as well as participants were higher than the respective period in the preceding years, though not reaching the peak years in the 1980s and 1990s. As for the officially registered announcement of protests in Berlin, they were higher in 2010 and still more so in 2011 (with more than 4,000 events).

Figure 6.1   *Number of protests and participants, 1993–2009*

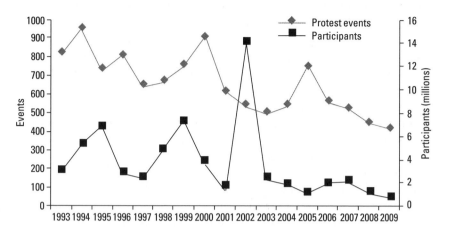

Source: compiled by the author from *Die Tageszeitung* newspaper reports.

The decline of protest activity after the 1990s suggest that there was hardly a strong positive effect of internet-based communication and the related new social media on the overall volume of protest. While internet communication increased and intensified in this period, protest did not, at least as far as Germany is concerned. This runs counter to the perception of many young activists and journalists who tend to claim that, thanks to the new media, we are witnessing a surge of protest. What can definitely be said, however, is that the dynamics of protest, both mobilization and demobilization, has accelerated as a result of the new media. For both organizers and policy-makers, this lowers the predictability of the course and size of protests.

Reactions to and impacts of protest politics

Protest, after all, is rarely an end in itself but rather a means to reach certain ends, most notably influencing specific policies, though sometimes also targeting a political regime as a whole or aiming to change society in fundamental ways. As already stated above, assessing the impact of protest politics, apart from a few clear-cut cases, is a difficult task so that arbitrary judgements and speculation come into play.

In general, it seems that protest as a rational and legitimate way of publicly presenting and pursuing political and social interests is, in principle, widely acknowledged among the German population. As a consequence, protest is also used by well-established groups and even by unionized police – a group that would not have considered employing such a means in earlier periods. This receptive trend of acknowledging protest is also reflected in the mass media that, with remarkable exceptions, do not question protest politics as such. Depending on the issues and actors, the mass media may even express explicit support for some campaigns. This, for example, could be observed in the case of the G8 meeting in Heiligendamm in summer 2007 when a broad alliance of protest groups managed to attract more media coverage than the official summit. Moreover, they were met, at least by some of the major media, with positive reactions (Rucht and Teune, 2008). A similar pattern could also be observed with regard to some other issues, among these anti-nuclear protests, protests against certain infrastructures, and protests against right-radical groupings.

While it is safe to say that some movements and some campaigns are very successful in influencing the public agenda and putting power-holders on the defence, we should not forget that protest only becomes visible to a large audience to the extent that it is covered by the mass media, which, simply due to the sheer number of protests and their own news value agenda, are very selective. So it is no wonder that out of the roughly 4,000 protest events taking place every year in Berlin probably only one-third or fourth are reported in the ensemble of local newspapers, and probably no more than 3 to 7 per cent make it into the nationwide newspapers. Hence the great bulk of protest activities, usually those which are small, peaceful, repetitive and relate to relatively small constituencies, remain unreported and thus unnoticed.

In other circumstances, protest not only gets ample media coverage but may also impress, or even alarm, the power-holders. Such a likelihood increases when protests attract masses, turn violent, are perceived as new or creative, refer to hot issues (especially when dividing political elites within and across political parties), have an impact on the overall constellation of political parties (e.g. bringing a new party such as *Die Piratenpartei* to the fore), are supported by key political figures or other celebrities, or are perceived to have an ultimate impact on voting behaviour.

However, whether political elites in general become more responsive to protest politics is hard to determine. On the one hand, the trend towards the 'normalization' and sometimes inflation of protest politics continues, thereby resulting in a more relaxed attitude on all sides (including the police). On the other hand, with the new communicative and organizational tools, including internet-based social media, protest becomes more unpredictable, as it can be organized in a very short period (as exemplified by the so-called 'flash mobs') and, under certain circumstances, reach surprisingly high turnouts, even without the support of traditional mass organizations and the mass media.

Attracting attention and influencing the public agenda is usually a necessary but by no means sufficient condition to make a policy impact which, after all, is the explicit aim of almost all contemporary protest groups. With regard to policy impacts of protest in Germany in the last ten years, a mixed pattern can be identified. On the one hand, there are a few stunning success stories that can be attributed, at least to some extent, to protest activities. The most spectacular case was the revival of the anti-nuclear power movement. Already on the rise in 2010, then fuelled by the incident in Fukushima, the movement prompted the government to shut down eight nuclear reactors, to reaffirm and accelerate the complete exit from nuclear power, and to promote an ambitious integrated energy policy with an emphasis on reducing energy consumption and replacing fossil fuel sources with renewable ones. Other (partial) successes of recent protest campaigns can be seen in areas such as the gradual acceptance of minimum wages, further moves towards gender equality and the rights of homosexual couples, the regulation of internet communication, the modification or prevention of some infrastructural projects, the abolition of student fees, and restrictions to produce and distribute genetically modified food.

In many other respects, however, recent mobilization has not, or not yet, yielded the intended results. This applies, for example, to the most recent Blockupy movement. Whereas the short-lived Occupy movement in Germany was largely spontaneous and excluded pre-existing protest organizations, the subsequent Blockupy movement, though symbolically referring to Occupy, was essentially a coalition of the usual – leftists and organized – players, including Attac, left youth organizations, parts of the trade unions, and sections of the political parties *Die Linke* and *Die Grünen*. In 2012 and 2013, Blockupy organized a series of protests in Frankfurt, targeting mainly the big banks that were involved in dubious financial transactions. These campaigns were met by relatively severe administrative, juridical and police restrictions that, in turn, provoked further protests. Though getting extensive media coverage, so far no policy outcomes have resulted from these activities. The same is true for protests against taxes on aeroplane flights and the widening gap between the rich and the poor. Many other groups, whether animal rights activists, milk farmers, students, the unemployed or asylum seekers, must conclude that in spite of all their efforts hardly any progress has been made.

There are indications that the combined effect of various progressive movements and the emergence or consolidation of political parties close to these kinds of movements (the Greens, the Party of Democratic Socialism and the Pirates) has increased the weight of the political Left in Germany since the early 2000s, though not (yet) showing a significant effect on the conservative-led government at the federal level. However, the trend towards a cultural liberalization which had begun already by the second half of the 1960s seems to continue today, as exemplified by the gradual changes of attitudes towards gender roles, non-conventional family patterns and the like – changes that can be found even within the conservative parties and the two major churches.

Comparative aspects and outlook

Focusing on Western democracies in a cross-national perspective, the question arises of whether protest politics in Germany is or is not exceptional. While certainly each national protest sector has certain characteristics that are outstanding or even unique, on a more general level we have little reason to assume that protest politics in Germany is an unusual case. Rather, German protest politics can be located somewhere in the middle ground, though probably closer to the pole of a high rather than a low-profile 'movement society' (on this concept, see Neidhardt and Rucht, 1993). This applies to the aggregate volume of protest as measured in terms of the number of events and participants, the overall range and diversity of protest themes, the distribution of action forms, and the social carriers of protest. When looking, for example, specifically at the turnout in protest events, it was found that among six Western European countries, the number of protesters per million inhabitants in the period from 1975 to 2005 was highest in France and lowest in Austria and the United Kingdom. Switzerland came second (close to France) and before Germany, followed by the Netherlands. When, however, collections of signatures (including referenda) are excluded, Germany ranks second after France in the group of six countries (Hutter and Teune, 2012: 13).

However, regarding some dimensions of protest, specific features of the German protest movement can be identified when compared with a distinct set of countries, either at the lower or higher end of the spectrum. For example, there is: generally less street protest in Scandinavian countries; more labour protests but less environmental protests in Italy, France and Spain; more animal rights protests in Britain when compared to Germany; a greater proportion of disruptive and violent protests in France than in Germany.

In terms of policy impacts, a similar overall assessment seems to hold. By and large, the movements in Germany, when compared to other Western democracies, are not really exceptional with regard to their failures and successes. With its relatively densely populated and professionally organized social movement sector, one might expect more substantial policy impacts in Germany than in many other countries. However, the groups in this sector are also fiercely competing for scarce attention, and personal and material resources, so that, in the end, they are partially neutralizing each other unless they join forces. But with the ongoing differentiation and specialization of the thematic spectrum in protest politics, the forging of broad and lasting alliances becomes more unlikely, especially in times when a pragmatic attitude prevails over grand anti-establishment concepts or utopian dreams. Accordingly, the impact of protest groups in Germany has been fairly limited during the last ten years, especially with regard to changes in basic political and economic institutions, the distribution of income and property, and other key features of society. To date, the debates about the need for the curbing of capitalism have had few tangible consequences. In a similar vein, in spite of the many claims for introducing more elements of direct democracy and more participatory planning procedures, little progress has been made.

Yet in some specific areas, the outcome of protest politics is rather exceptional, either tending towards the lower or the higher end in a cross-national perspective. For instance, the policy impact of environmental and anti-nuclear protest in Germany is quite impressive. On the other hand, it appears that protest movements in France, especially when resorting to disruptive means, are often able to achieve significant concessions from the government, whereas disruptive protest in Germany rarely makes a difference in terms of policy change.

Speculating about the near future, we have little reason to assume profound changes with regard to both the scope and patterns of protest mobilization and the impact of protest on politics and society at large. However, one caveat to such a scenario has to be made. During the last decade or so, the estrangement between the so-called political class and the ordinary citizenry has increased. Widespread public debate means that this popular dissatisfaction with the political class is now acknowledged and probably even strengthened. To date, it is little more than a diffuse feeling of discontent; and it is unlikely to make much impact as long as the great majority of the population have the impression that economic conditions are better in Germany than in most other countries. If, however, this perception of well-being weakens or if people get the impression that the 'system' is beyond control or is being steered in the wrong direction, then a polarization between those defending the status quo and those demanding fundamental change is likely to occur. Under these conditions, the mobilization potential of protest groups could turn into the sort of social and political conflict not seen in Germany since the Weimar Republic. However, compared to this dark experience of the past, a political crisis in contemporary Germany would differ sharply. After all, the vast majority of those taking to the streets do so to defend rather than to question the idea and basic institutions of democracy.

Chapter 7

The German Model in Transition

ANKE HASSEL

Over the last decade, the German model has seen a remarkable transformation and comeback. At the turn of the century, calls for a radical reform of the German market economy were heard everywhere. The change of government in 1998 was followed by the short boom and bust of the new economy, leaving the country in a most miserable situation. Unemployment reached five million in 2005 and Germany violated the deficit threshold of the European Stability and Growth Pact for several years in the early 2000s. The need for reform was ubiquitous in newspaper headlines, expert commissions and the international press. The country was constantly criticized for its failure to meet the challenges of reunification, globalization and demographic changes. 'Citizen' campaigns put newspaper adverts in German papers to call for reforms. Federal President Roman Herzog lamented, in a well-received speech in 1997, the mental depression that had befallen Germany and called for a *Ruck* (a sudden jerk) to liberalize the country. Germany had become the sick man of Europe (Hassel and Williamson, 2004).

By 2014 the situation could not be more different. The 'sick man' has become the unchallenged economic powerhouse of Europe. Not only did Germany survive the great financial crisis of 2008–09 in much better shape than almost any other OECD country, it is the only one where unemployment levels today are substantially lower than before the crisis. The German economy was hit hard by the recession in 2009 when GDP contracted by more than 5 per cent. However, growth bounced back swiftly after that and its performance has been solid compared with other OECD countries but particularly within the eurozone. In the midst of the financial crisis, the economy showed a remarkable recovery of the competitive position of German firms, higher than average growth and the highest employment levels ever (Möller, 2010). The country's economic institutions and economic policy are almost unchallenged in the way they work for the economy. Today no major reform calls can be heard in the country. Within the eurozone this is a different matter as German exports have out-competed all other trading partners, putting them into a permanent trade deficit.

133

Between 2003 and 2013 Germany witnessed a decade of fundamental change. The calls for reforms in the early 2000s did not go unheard. In March 2003 the then Chancellor Schröder outlined his Reform Agenda 2010 in an address to parliament. He announced far-reaching welfare and labour market reforms. Based on reports by several expert committees radical reforms were implemented, altering the German welfare state as it had developed over the years. Unemployment insurance, pension systems and social assistance schemes were all restructured, while capital market regulation was relaxed and corporate taxation lowered.

These developments beg two questions: how far did the changes of the German model go? Can we still talk about a German model? These questions are not new. Wolfgang Streeck already posed the question in 1995: 'German Capitalism. Does it exist? Can it survive?' (Streeck, 1995). Were the changes of the 2000s the precondition for its current success? This chapter will address both of these questions and put the policy reforms in the context of wider institutional changes. It starts by characterizing the trajectories of continuity and change in the German model during the last decade and then discusses them with regard to the two major challenges of our time: the financial crisis and the crisis of the eurozone.

Fundamental features of the German model

The German political economy has long been identified as being distinct from other market economies. In German political discourse, 'social market economy' is used to denote a concept that explicitly recognizes the limits of the market and thus defines the relationship between the market and the state by emphasizing that all liberal markets are embedded in a fundamental social order. As we know, neither the term nor the concept have much to do with the social dimension of a market economy, but it was a term coined by German economists to win political legitimacy and justification for the establishment of liberal markets in the climate of post-war Germany that was critical of capitalism. The general assumption of ordoliberal thinkers was that while the economy is based on markets organized by private businesses and consumers, the state is responsible for regulating those markets and for shaping the underlying social order. Defined in this way, the term 'social market economy' receives widespread approval from both the entire spectrum of political parties and the general public, since it provides legitimacy for the welfare state.

In the academic literature, the distinct features of the German political economy have been recognized in a similar way by terms such as 'German capitalism' (Streeck, 1995), 'Rhenish capitalism' (Albert, 1993) and the 'coordinated market economy' (Hall and Soskice, 2001). These conceptualizations emphasize the special features of the non-market relationships of German capitalism, which is characterized primarily by a strongly organized civil society, regulated corporate governance and labour markets as well as an extensive welfare state. This is in contrast to liberal Anglo-Saxon countries where the organization of civil society is decentralized and takes the form of local welfare associations; the welfare state is minimalistic and organized along liberal principles. In Germany, trade unions and employers as well as other economic and political players, such as welfare and industrial federations, are highly organized and deeply institutionalized in public policy. In the past, strong civil society has replaced market mechanisms with other forms of coordination, as evidenced, for example, by the regulation of wages via collective bargaining. The Bismarckian welfare state brings together conservative, status-oriented principles and a far-reaching responsibility of the state for its citizens in the form of a social safety net.

Among the wide range of perspectives taken to analyse and categorize the German political economy, the 'Varieties of Capitalism' literature based on Hall and Soskice (2001) is the most theoretically advanced. In contrast to other institutionalist-based perspectives, they put the firm at the centre of their comparative framework and distinguish between two different regimes based on five different spheres of firms' interactions: liberal market economies (LMEs) and coordinated market economies (CMEs). According to Hall and Soskice, these five spheres of interaction determine the institutional framework within a regime:

- In the first sphere of *industrial relations*, firms negotiate and coordinate with labour unions as well as other employers regarding applicable working conditions and wage levels. CMEs are traditionally characterized by a high level of organization, coordination and centralization of industrial relations, whereas industrial relations in LMEs are decentralized.
- In the second sphere of *vocational training and education*, capitalist regimes differ with regard to the contribution and involvement of companies within the process of developing the skills of their workers. Whereas CME firms rely heavily on the availability and formation of firm or industry-specific skills that cannot be easily transferred across firms, LMEs prefer the formation of general transferable skills.
- In the third sphere of *corporate governance*, firms choose their strategies and preferences in order to access finance and cope with shareholders.
- In the fourth sphere of *interfirm relations*, firms distinguish amongst various kinds of supplier and client relations, as well as amongst different strategies to access technologies.

- In the fifth sphere of *relationship with employees*, the coordination and communication between firms and their workers are analysed by referring to the latter's commitments and internalization of their firm's goals and interests, as well as their motivation. (Ibid.: 6)

In the Varieties of Capitalism literature, LMEs are contrasted with CMEs according to their differences in coordination of the relevant economic actors. The authors classify Anglo-Saxon countries as typical examples of LMEs, whereas Nordic and Continental European countries are classified as CMEs. The latter are predominantly characterized by non-market mechanisms which are present throughout the different spheres. The relationship between different spheres is characterized by institutional complementarities; institutional configurations are complementary to each other when one supports the other and reinforces the differences between regimes (ibid.: 17). For instance, the availability of specific skills is a core characteristic of firms' product market strategies in CMEs. As a consequence, these firms support vocational-training systems ensuring professional formation in line with their interests. This in turn feeds the demand for an industrial relations system that ensures job security for employees in order to protect these investments in specific skills. In addition, complementarities are supported by public policy in the welfare state. Social insurance-based welfare maintains: status and profession, employment protection legislation, job-specific unemployment insurance and earnings-related pension systems – all of which are geared towards the initial skill investment.

Firms in these institutional surroundings will take advantage of the high investment in skills. They will pursue strategies involving so-called 'diversified quality production' (Streeck, 1991) due to the variety of specific skills in their firms. Product development based on innovation and skills-specific knowledge on the firms' side will be strengthened by the employees' side in their demand for social protection and training policies that maintain this skill level. Institutional complementarities evolve within the context of skill formation and employment protection, the latter being dismissal protection or welfare provisions for this group of (skilled) employees. The higher the level of skill specification within a firm or industry, the lower the level of transferability of these skills and the higher the need for protection and stability for workers (Estevez-Abe et al., 2001).

Concomitantly, the interest of firms to protect workers' rights increases with their skill value for the firm. In Germany the strong focus on the formation and protection of specific-skilled workers has paved the way for systems with strong employment legislation and life-long earning-related unemployment benefits while maintaining a specific set of skills. The need to alter one's occupation or acquire new skills in the case of unemployment or market changes, as in the Nordic countries, was not part of the evolving German institutional framework.

Continuity and change in the German model

For more than two decades now, advanced political economies have started to display rather strong evidence of institutional change, particularly in continental European non-liberal market economies. Governments have implemented reforms of labour market policies (Bonoli, 2010), unemployment insurance (Clegg, 2007) and pensions (Häusermann, 2010), as well as corporate governance and financial market regulation (Deeg, 2005). Capital markets and corporate governance regulations have been the subject of intense reform pressure. Beginning in the mid-1990s, many governments liberalized capital markets towards LMEs (Culpepper, 2011). In some cases, reform was radical and far-reaching, while in others it was more incremental. Corporate finance shifted towards equity finance and some large national champions defined themselves as value firms similar to their Anglo-American counterparts.

In the following, a brief summary of the most important changes of the German model over the last decade will be provided. I will focus particularly on the key institutions as identified in the Varieties of Capitalism literature and subsequently assess to what extent these changes have altered the underlying model.

Collective bargaining institutions

Given the high levels of unemployment, low growth rates and strong criticism of economic performance, collective bargaining institutions were under a lot of pressure in the early 2000s. However, no policy changes were initiated, even though a reform of collective bargaining was mentioned in the Agenda 2010 proposal and was heavily discussed. The government announced its expectation that collective bargaining was to become more flexible if legal intervention was to be avoided. Such an intervention would have meant that plant-level bargaining would have been given priority over industry-wide bargaining. This would have led to a massive decentralization of pay setting.

The threat of legal intervention took place in the context of an ongoing process of bargaining decentralization, which had already been set in motion throughout the 1990s as a response to the shock of reunification and the recession in 1992–93 (Hassel, 2012). Big manufacturing plants negotiated plant-level agreements with works councils in order to cut costs and to increase flexibility and productivity (Hassel and Rehder, 2001). This in turn increased flexibility at the level of regional collective agreements. At the same time the institutional structure of industry-wide agreements setting standards for an entire industry and region did not change. Pressures on employers' confederations, and in particular their membership losses that were prominent during the 1990s, came to a halt during the 2000s as collective bargaining became more flexible. However, on both sides of industry, membership in associations continued to decline. Employers' membership rates declined from 63 to 60 per cent between 2000 and 2010. Particularly at the beginning of the decade, these associations experimented with new forms of membership which would not bind firms to collective agreements in order to pre-empt their increasing dissatisfaction. Union density rates, which had been in free-fall ever since reunification, declined from 24.6 to 18.6 per cent during the same period (Visser, 2013). Employers' associations and unions thereby tended to consolidate in core industries and not expand into new areas of the service economy. At the end of the decade, institutional and regulatory stability was combined with a far higher degree of flexibility of working practices at the firm level and an increasing weakness of employers' associations and unions.

Labour market and social policy

Changes to labour market and social policies were at the heart of the government's agenda in 2003. The Hartz reforms I–IV changed not only the institutional structure of the Federal Labour Agency and the interplay between local level poverty relief and national unemployment insurance, but also the general policy approach towards mobilizing the long-term unemployed. While in the past skilled workers were largely protected from the expectation to retrain, and instead encouraged to keep their primary skills in a particular trade during spells of unemployment, the emphasis shifted to retraining and getting back to work quickly (Hassel and Schiller, 2010). In particular, the focus was on the activation of the (long-term) unemployed through a cut in benefits and an increase of pressure to search for a job. The reform of the unemployment insurance system was comprehensive and involved a drastic cut to benefits for the long-term unemployed, who moved to social assistance levels after a period of 12 to 18 months of unemployment. Previous measures to protect skills by not forcing skilled workers to take on unskilled positions were removed. At the same time, a kind of negative income tax was introduced by enabling workers with low-paying part-time jobs to draw benefits so as to make ends meet. Different schemes encouraging early retirement were phased out and government subsidies for making elderly workers redundant were stopped.

As there is still no minimum wage, wages at the low end of the labour market declined and unskilled workers maximized their income by combining low-paid, part-time employment with benefits. The rate of the working poor shot up and moved Germany to be among those countries with the highest proportion of the low-paid within the EU. While in the old German model, the labour market position of skilled workers was highly protected and wages were comparatively egalitarian, today a process of segmentation of the labour market is occurring. An increasing share of labour market outsiders work on fixed-term contracts for temping agencies or positions in marginal employment. Dualization of the labour market has emerged as a major trend of the transformation of the German model (Eichhorst and Marx, 2009a; Palier and Thelen, 2010; Hassel, 2012).

Training

The Vocational Training System (VET) 'appears to be undergoing a period of subtle but significant change' (Busemeyer and Thelen, 2012: 89). Vocational training is still the dominant form of training after secondary education with more than 50 per cent taking up some form of apprenticeship. It is a highly structured approach towards training in which firms employ apprentices to train them on the job; they then attend school for part of the time. The licensing of training and the content and the examination of apprentices are organized and supervised by the local chambers of commerce. German-style vocational training has always been seen as a highly successful way of training young school leavers below the level of tertiary education. It has consistently produced low levels of youth unemployment and high levels of specialized training.

During the 1990s and 2000s three main developments created pressures within the vocational training system (ibid.: 76–8). First, the amount of firms that engage in it declined from 35 to 25 per cent, which reflected the downswing of business between the mid-1990s and the mid-2000s. Second – and related to the decline of firm participation – the demand for training by school leavers could not be met. Those at the lower end of school qualifications found it increasingly difficult to find training places. As the German government is committed to provide training until the age of 18, many of those ended up in a kind of 'transition system' (Baethge et al., 2007) of state-sponsored training. Third, the attitude of large firms towards the training needs of school leavers has changed. While in the past, firms increased training capacities beyond their business needs in order to meet demand, this form of corporate social responsibility has significantly declined over the last decade. Firms are more reluctant to train just to fill the demand for it. Outsourcing, restructuring and fierce competitive pressure have introduced a new emphasis on cost-cutting that does not allow for voluntary training.

With regards to policy change, some incremental adjustments were made. In particular, shorter training courses (two-year apprenticeships) were introduced and some of the content was removed. The government also introduced short courses for school leavers with low skills. As school leavers increasingly either drop out of low-quality training or cannot meet the expectations of high-quality training, a school-based training regime has evolved alongside the firm-based VET. The content of apprenticeships has also become more modular and flexible. Some of these developments took place in the context of the increasing Europeanization of training standards. Even though training is not part of core EU competencies, the European Qualifications Framework has introduced a credit system which should make VET in Germany more compatible with other countries.

While on the whole we can see institutional stability, many features and much of the content of training is markedly different today compared to the beginning of the period. However, given the current rapid demographic changes and rapidly declining numbers of school leavers, there is an expectation among policy-makers and firms that remaining school children will increasingly be pushed towards higher levels of training (Busemeyer and Thelen, 2012).

Corporate governance

Changes to corporate taxes at the beginning of the 2000s gave incentives to firms to abandon the previous tight network of corporate cross-shareholding. Since 1998 a series of laws has liberalized Germany's capital markets and the corporate sector as a whole. Four laws for the Promotion of the German Financial Market aim to provide a more transparent framework for stock trading. They have led to the establishment of a supervisory agency for stock trading at a federal level and to the setting up of rules of conduct for the participants (Hassel and Williamson, 2004). The Eichel Tax Reform in 2000–01 changed the laws on capital gains tax, enabling companies to more easily shed stakes in other firms. German companies were also enabled to apply international accounting standards (or US Generally Accepted Accounting Principles – GAAP) rather than German accounting standards (*Handelsgesetzbuch* – HGB). The system of interlocking directorships was loosened up. The Corporate Governance Codex, adopted in 2002, encouraged executives to hold no more than five supervisory board seats. However, while the Vodafone–

Mannesmann takeover did shake up the German corporate sector, the move towards a liberal market of corporate control has not developed further. There is still no active market for corporate control and corporate finance is still less stock based than in LMEs. Compared to the 1990s when the trend towards an Anglo-Saxon corporate governance structure took off, the 2000s saw a backlash. Among the 100 largest firms in Germany, the share of firms that were owned by large blockholders increased, while firms with a majority in dispersed shareholders declined. At the same time, the ownership of firms has become more international. According to a recent study by Ernst and Young, about 55 per cent of the stock of DAX companies is held by foreign investors, as opposed to only about 37 per cent by Germans (Wirtschaftswoche, 2013). Among the 100 largest firms in 2006, 28 per cent were owned by foreign investors compared to 18 per cent in 1996 (Hassel, forthcoming).

The German model and the great recession

Despite the changes over the last decade, there is evidence that the German model was a major factor as to why the German economy survived the great recession of 2009 in reasonably good shape. When the recession hit and GDP was in free-fall, firms, unions and the government resorted to the established policy instruments that were inherent in the 'old' German model to combat the crisis (Hassel and Schelkle, 2012).

In comparison to its European neighbours, the financial crisis hit Germany relatively late. Until the autumn of 2008, economic outlooks were comparatively optimistic, with a 1.8 per cent growth forecast by the Council of Economic Advisors supporting the government's initial position that the crisis would affect the USA, as well as other financial centres, but would bypass Germany (SVR, 2008). The first economic consequences became visible in late 2008, leading to a collapse in what had been the country's economic main pillar: exports and manufacturing.

By the second quarter of 2009 Germany experienced a drop of more than 6 per cent in comparison to the previous year, resulting in a worse situation than in those countries considered to be responsible for the crisis (Bodegan et al., 2009).

However, the collapse was followed by a rapid recovery in relation to other OECD countries. The economy was supported by two closely spaced stimulus packages on 5 November 2008 of €11.8 billion and on 27 January 2009 of c. €50 billion, combined with the welfare system's automatic stabilizer initiatives. The German equivalent of the 'Cash for Clunkers' programme which gave subsidies towards the acquisition of new cars of c. €5 billion aimed to subsidize car manufacturers on a global scale with particular focus on the protection of skilled workers in export-oriented industries. Overall, Germany's total contribution to global demand was above the OECD average (Hussel and Lütz, 2010).

In addition, another instrument helped not only to countervail unemployment in the short run during the crisis, but also to reduce it to below pre-crisis levels. According to the European Commission, the elasticity of employment relative to Germany's GDP was the second lowest among the EU member state countries (European Commission, 2010a). The main factor for this development was the initiative to reduce working hours (Lehndorff, 2010). This helped to disconnect business slumps from layoffs by adapting measures to reduce overtime, to implement working time accounts, to reduce the general working time and to use public short-time provisions. Being used by approximately 20 per cent of all firms, this package of initiatives was the most valuable tool to countervail the economic and social consequences of the crisis. With a total usage of *c.* 30 per cent of all firms, the implementation of working time accounts was the most important mechanism, followed by job rotation (14 per cent), extra holidays (13 per cent) and pay cuts (11 per cent) (Bodegan et al., 2009).

Through this strategy, German firms were able to keep their skilled labour and react quicker than liberal market regimes once the world markets showed the first signs of recovery. Referring back to Hall and Soskice's concept of institutional complementarities, the enabling force for labour hoarding and the initiatives taken with regard to reductions in working time were enabled by plant-level agreements between firms and their core employees during the late 1980s. From the employees' perspective, these measures helped to protect the skills of the workers. From the firms' perspective, it has had a long-term positive effect on unit labour costs. Whereas the latter increased first in 2009 as a consequence of the hoarding initiatives taken, they decreased in 2010.

Subsequently, the German economy experienced the highest employment levels ever, combined with a recovery of the positioning of its firms on a global scale (Möller, 2010). The combination of public policies, such as the implementation of 'short-term working models' with adjustment tools developed in dialogue between firms and labour during the post-unification crisis, fostered Germany's economic stabilization in the financial crisis.

Still, it remains to be shown how far the country's comparatively successful recovery refers to all sectors. In the absence of a national minimum wage and an increasing low-skilled service economy, the continuous focus on export-oriented, high-skill industry might lead to economic and social effects in the long run, on bargaining institutions as well as on the sphere of vocational training and skill formation.

The German model and the crisis of the eurozone

The German model plays an important role not only in the unfolding of the crisis of the eurozone but also in the attempts to overcome it. The model contributed to the crisis but is also seen as a benchmark for policy recommendations to combat it. In the following a short interpretation of the underlying mechanisms will be presented. The solution of the eurozone crisis will – among other things – depend on changes in the German model, which has itself been transformed by the eurozone.

European Economic and Monetary Union (EMU) imposed a unitary monetary policy to an economic area which is made up of different business systems. The German model is one specific business model in which wage setting is controlled by large wage-bargaining actors in which training is extensive and social policy has been reformed with the aim of lowering labour costs and improving competitiveness. Other Northern European countries such as the Netherlands and Austria, but also the Nordic countries, have similar wage setting and training institutions. Other members of the eurozone have very different economic models. In the literature, Southern European eurozone members have been described as 'mixed market economies', which have similar elements of coordination but which are more heavily dependent on the state to sponsor coordination (Molina and Rhodes, 2007). In the course of the first decade of monetary union northern eurozone countries have developed very differently from southern countries.

The incomplete and asymmetric currency area in which monetary policy is centralized but fiscal policy and wage setting is regionalized has systematically produced different trajectories of inflation and labour costs. Inflation differentials in a regime of standard interest rates have led to negative real interest rates in countries with higher inflation and to high real interest rates in those countries with low inflation. For the German model, which was particularly specialized in delivering long-term wage restraint, the harsh monetary environment during the first decade of the eurozone gave even further incentive to restructure and to keep labour costs low. The set-up of the eurozone therefore pushed the German political economy even further towards reducing labour costs and improving competitiveness.

On the other hand, the drive towards restoring the competitiveness of German business put an enormous burden on the southern countries which were institutionally not capable of using bargaining institutions to keep wages low. In addition, a whole range of structural factors increased the vulnerability of these countries significantly. First, southern countries benefited from low to negative real interest rates; second, they also benefited from the credit ratings of the eurozone as a whole; third, the emerging credit bubbles led to a deterioration of competitiveness; and fourth, once the crisis had struck, these countries did not have the instruments to deal with it.

Undoubtedly, the overarching challenge to the eurozone today is the diverging development of competitiveness amongst different regions which has led to major imbalances (Scharpf, 2011; Hancké, 2012). The one-size-fits-all monetary policy put a strain on economies with low inflation rates, such as in Germany, and did not balance overheated economies such as in Ireland. In both cases, monetary policy that was oriented towards an average target for the eurozone as a whole had a pro-cyclical effect. Governments did not use the cheap credit they accessed for economic development but rather for consumption. Over time current account deficits and surpluses accumulated and competitiveness diverged. These problems with the EMU were known from the beginning and did not come as a surprise to policy-makers or analysts.

For most of the 2000s, the standard macroeconomic indicators gave little concern for most countries of the eurozone. This is true even for those that had problems meeting the convergence criteria. Both nominal wages as well as inflation differentials diminished over the first decade of the euro. Nominal wages rose faster in Southern Europe than in Germany but the differences declined. The same is true for inflation differentials, which during the first half of the 2000s have remained unchanged (Scharpf, 2011). Greece, Ireland, the Netherlands and Spain all had significantly higher inflation than the eurozone average. Germany, on the other hand, had the lowest inflation and highest real interest rates and therefore was held back in growth. At the same time, lower prices in Germany in the long run benefited the competitiveness of its firms.

However, higher nominal wages and higher inflation in peripheral countries led to a loss in competitiveness in Southern Europe and eventually expressed themselves in current account deficits/surplus and diverging unit labour costs. These came into full view after the financial crisis in 2008 and forced governments to bail out banks. The subsequent recession and lack of access to capital markets revealed the reduced competitiveness of Southern Europe vis-à-vis Northern Europe.

During that time, Germany had persistently the lowest nominal wage increases in the eurozone and the OECD. The institutional basis for long-term wage restraint consists of the capacity to coordinate wage setting through pattern bargaining or centralized control over wages (Hassel, 2006: 165; Johnston, 2009). Pattern bargaining describes the process in which unions and employers in export-oriented industries set the upper limit for wage negotiations. They then serve as an orientation point for non-traded and public sectors. The fact that in Northern

Europe wage increases in the non-traded sector are generally not higher than in the export sectors is not a standard phenomenon – rather the opposite. In Southern Europe, the non-traded sector – fuelled by cheap credit – saw the highest pay increases in the 2000s. Private sector unions and firms were not able to hold down wage developments in the sheltered sector. This is a key factor in explaining the pay differentials within the eurozone and in turn the imbalances that emerged over the last decade.

The differences in wage setting institutions go directly to the core of the German model. Here, manufacturing firms have to stand the pressure of international competition, and labour costs are not only a major concern for these firms but also for the unions. Pay increases have been exchanged with job security in leading manufacturing firms through rounds of plant-level concession bargaining.

The response of the Troika to the troubled countries of Southern Europe has been to request structural reforms in exchange for financial help. Structural reforms often attack those elements which are part of the German model: centralized wage bargaining, organized civil society, highly regulated labour markets. At the same time, the debate within the EU has also recognized that there are two sides to imbalances: the German trade surplus mirrors the deficit of the southern countries. Therefore, the German government has frequently been targeted by those seeking reforms to increase domestic demand and reduce the reliance on an export-based growth model. For instance, the European Council published its country-specific recommendations at the end of May 2013 urging Germany to increase wages and lower high taxation for low-paid employment:

> Policy action to reduce the high tax wedge for low-wage earners and improve the integration of the long-term unemployed into the labour market has been limited so far. Germany should do more to reduce the high taxes and social security contributions that they levy on low wages. Further efforts are needed to improve transition from certain types of contracts, like mini-jobs, into more sustainable forms of contracts, thus avoiding labour market segmentation. (European Council, 2013)

In other words: the German model as it is today poses a major threat to the internal balance of the eurozone as it has developed a model of economic restructuring in which competitiveness of industries is boosted by driving down wages and conditions for peripheral labour. It is very much in doubt as to how the eurozone can develop a sustainable growth model without major changes to the German model.

Conclusion

The assessment of how far the transformation of the German model has gone is hotly debated. Some authors, in particular Wolfgang Streeck (2009a), maintain that the distinctiveness of the model compared to other political economies has become largely irrelevant as the process of liberalization and deregulation has introduced market mechanisms in all advanced political economies to an extent that the peculiarities of the training system, wage setting and corporate governance are not much more than decorative features. Others – Iversen and Soskice (2009) and Carlin and Soskice (2008) – argue that the core features of a coordinated market economy based on non-market coordination has remained intact and continues to dominate the central features of the political economy.

In-between these two main positions a third has emerged that recognizes the trends towards liberalization and deregulation but argues that these trajectories fundamentally differ in different kinds of political economies. 'Liberalization' – a vague term in itself – takes place in different forms in different institutional settings (Hall and Thelen, 2009; Palier and Thelen, 2010). The transformation of the German model towards a more liberal one therefore is undeniable, but in essence it remains 'German' in the sense that many of its institutional characteristics define the process of liberalization. For instance, the dualization of the labour market is not the same as a straightforward liberalization towards a liberal labour market as in the UK or USA. Compared to liberal countries, labour market regulation in Germany for labour market insiders is still strict. However, strong protection for some workers co-exists with very loose protection and low conditions for labour market outsiders. Dualization is a feature in liberalization of CMEs. Continued coordination at the core and increasing liberalization and dualization at the periphery are two sides of the same coin (Hassel, 2012). The transformation of the German model is therefore not primarily a process of converging on a liberal, Anglo-Saxon, model. It is a transformation in its own right.

The two main challenges to the German economic model during the 2000s – the financial crisis and the crisis of the eurozone – have shown the ongoing importance of its distinctive features. The growth stimulus in 2009 based on short-term working and stimulating the crucial car industry fed into the core institutions, as has been outlined. The crisis of the eurozone can only be understood when taking into account the role of the institutions of the German model, which cannot easily be replicated elsewhere. The competitiveness of German industries that combines strict cost control and high-quality production is a major source for economic imbalances in the eurozone. Therefore, to dismiss the German model as just one version of universal capitalist market economies (Streeck, 2009a), means to give up a conceptual understanding of market economies which has given observers so far the most powerful theoretical explanation of different business systems.

However, there is a dynamic process of change taking place. The German model is moving into a new era which combines coordination in the core features of the manufacturing sector with new liberal elements. It is a combination of continuity and change, which is the key to understanding current reform processes: institutions are hollowed out while their formal structures remain intact. As with the modernization of a house, the walls remain standing but the wiring and plumbing is replaced. In that sense, many formal institutions of the German model are still the same as they were in the post-war period: centralized collective bargaining, legal works councils, a dual corporate board structure, insurance-based social policy and the vocational training system are all based on the same institutional structure. Very little formal change has taken place.

The second key element of change consists of the underlying expectations, attitudes and values in business, politics and society (Hassel and Williamson, 2004). While the protagonists of the liberalization literature assume that it is mainly driven by a coalition of ill-advised policy-makers and international investors who insist on high returns at the expense of the wider population, incremental change within formal institutions is often driven by a new and different understanding of the role of work. For instance, while the 'old' German model gave a high premium to job tenure and life-long employment in major manufacturing firms, this model is not compatible with a workforce that is female and in the service economy and has a substantial share of migrant workers. Both women and migrant workers are more likely to change employers more frequently and therefore have less specific skills. The lower attachment to a particular employer makes it harder for them to attain and protect specific skills. The premium of skill specificity is therefore much harder to maintain when the workforce is more mixed.

Modernization of German society, higher employment rates of women, increasing competitive pressure on firms, the rise of global investors as well as the continuing deindustrialization of the economy have all impacted on the effectiveness of the traditional institutions of the German model. The initial reform policies in the area of the welfare state at the beginning of the 2000s had an important effect on the structure of the labour market. The decline of protected jobs in contrast to precarious jobs and the increasing dualization were major changes of the model.

On the other hand, traditional policy tools were used to combat the crisis using labour hoarding and short-term working. In the context of the eurozone crisis, it is the traditional feature of highly competitive wage setting and micro-corporatist cooperation between unions and firms that have led to strong export performance and contributed to the imbalances.

On the whole, the picture is therefore decidedly mixed. The old model has been revamped and appears in new clothes. The process of change is moreover far from complete and remains problematic as it has not even started to deal with imminent challenges. These are the commencement of rapid demographic change as the amount of young school leavers will decline rapidly over the next couple of years. The issue of migration and the role of immigrant communities, while highly important, have not been included in the German model which tends to treat migrant workers as labour market outsiders. The same is true for the role of women in the labour market and in society as a whole. Compared to many other countries in Europe, Germany still has a highly traditional male breadwinner model which assigns women the role of secondary earners. Low fertility is related to this as many qualified women are not prepared to play this role. There are many challenges ahead and it is very likely that during the next decade the transformation of the German model will continue.

Chapter 8

Economic Policy

REIMUT ZOHLNHÖFER

Germany has weathered the storm of recent crises comparatively well: the financial crisis that began in 2007/08, the economic crisis that followed it, and the current euro crisis. The OECD (2012a: 10) as well as academic observers (e.g. Reisenbichler and Morgan, 2012) have even talked about a 'miracle' with regard to the recent German labour market performance. Indeed, the German economic performance has been quite impressive since around 2007: unemployment has fallen substantially in the past half-decade while it increased in most other countries; and the public finances seem to be in a much better shape than in most other developed democracies, too (see Tables 8.1 and 8.2).

What is more, the German government under chancellor Merkel (as the government that will have to carry the largest burden of any bailout of a euro country should it become necessary) has insisted on the implementation of structural reforms and strict budgetary discipline as the only sustainable cure for the crisis in the countries of the euro periphery – a position the Merkel government could only take due to the comparatively good recent performance of the German economy. Ironically, maybe, Germany was called the 'sick man of the euro' not too long ago in an article in *The Economist* (5 June 1999). Although even at that time

Table 8.1   *Unemployment rates, 1998–2011*

	1998	2002	2005	2007	2009	2011
Germany	9.4	8.7	11.3	8.7	7.8	6.0
UK	6.1	5.1	4.8	5.3	7.6	8.0
United States	4.5	5.8	5.1	4.6	9.3	9.0
EU 15	8.2	6.6	7.3	6.3	8.5	9.5
EU 27	9.6	8.9	9.0	7.2	9.0	9.7
OECD total	6.9	7.2	6.9	5.8	8.4	8.2

Source: OECD (2013) General Statistics, Country Statistical Profiles, in OECD, Stat Extracts, http://stats.oecd.org (22.05.2013).

Table 8.2   *General government financial balance as a percentage of GDP, 2002–12*

	2002	*2005*	*2007*	*2009*	*2012*
Germany	−3.8	−3.3	0.2	−3.1	−0.2
UK	−2.0	−3.3	−2.8	−10.9	−6.6
United States	−4.0	−3.3	−2.9	−11.9	−8.5
EU 15	−1.3	−1.2	0.1	−6.7	−4.0
OECD total	−3.3	−2.4	−1.3	−8.2	−5.5

Source: OECD (2013) Economic Projections, OECD Economic Outlook No. 92, December 2012, in OECD, Stat Extracts, http://stats.oecd.org (22.05.2013).

Germany's export position was strong and inflation below the EU average, the country was among those EU countries with the lowest growth rates at the turn of the century and unemployment remained stubbornly high at over four million (at around 9 per cent) and even surpassed the five million threshold in 2005. Moreover, Wolfgang Streeck (2009b: 38–9) diagnosed a 'fiscal crisis of the German state': 'the structure of government revenue and spending commitments may over time turn from a response to social problems into a problem in its own right, confronting policymakers with a complex syndrome of dilemmatic choices, contradictory demands and irreconcilable imperatives from which there is no ready escape'.

Many observers saw the main problem of the German economy in the inability of the various governments to enact the reforms necessary to adapt the welfare state, the labour market and the tax system to the changes in the international economy often referred to under the labels of 'globalization' and 'Europeanization'. Commentators complained about a reform logjam (*Reformstau*) as governments were either unwilling or unable to adopt the much-needed reforms in the country's veto-ridden political system. In 2003, however, government and opposition were able to break the gridlock and to agree on a large-scale labour market reform that was complemented by welfare and tax reforms in the following years. In what follows, I will try to explain why it finally became possible to adopt these reforms at that time (and why not earlier) and how the German governments managed to get through the current crises so comparatively smoothly. I will start by outlining the pre-2003 situation and the reasons why various governments were unable to enact comprehensive reforms. I will then discuss the various economic and social policy reforms that were adopted, essentially between 2003 and 2007, before I present the country's reaction to the financial crisis and the economic policy reforms of the coalition of Christian Democrats and Liberals under Angela Merkel.

Germany's economic problems at the turn of the century

Germany's main economic problems at the turn of the century clearly were low levels of economic growth and the stubbornly high level of unemployment – with regard to both indicators, the country fared worse than the United States or the United Kingdom, but also worse than the average of the OECD or EU member states (see Tables 8.1 and 8.3). Low growth and high unemployment in turn had a detrimental effect on public finances. As a consequence, the German budget deficit exceeded the 3 per cent Maastricht deficit criterion for four consecutive years between 2002 and 2005 (see Table 8.2).

One reason for the dismal growth and labour market performance probably was the European Central Bank's (ECB) monetary policy. As the ECB could set interest rates only for the eurozone as a whole, it had to take care of the then booming economies on the periphery that were in danger of overheating as well as the stagnating German economy with its low inflationary pressures. Thus, interest rates were too high for the German economy after 1999 (Busch, 2005: 134). This situation certainly changed, however, as the ECB lowered interest rates in the course of the financial crisis.

Nonetheless, monetary policy was not the only impediment to economic growth. The tax system, and the statutory business tax rate in particular, were especially hotly discussed (see Ganghof, 2004; Zohlnhöfer, 2009: 295–379). A comprehensive tax reform of the Christian–Liberal coalition of Helmut Kohl had been blocked by the

Table 8.3   *Growth of real GDP, 1998–2011*

	1998	2002	2005	2007	2009	2011
Germany	1.9	1.0	0.7	3.3	−5.1	3.0
UK	3.5	2.4	2.8	3.6	−4.0	0.8
United States	4.4	1.8	3.1	1.9	−3.5	1.7
EU 15	3.9	1.9	2.6	3.5	−4.6	0.9
EU 27	3.0	1.3	2.0	3.2	−4.4	1.5
OECD total	2.7	1.7	2.7	2.8	−3.8	1.8

Source: OECD (2013) General Statistics, Country Statistical Profiles, in OECD, Stat Extracts, http://stats.oecd.org (22.05.2013).

Table 8.4   *Combined corporate income tax rates, 2002–12*

	2002	2005	2007	2009	2012
Germany	38.9	38.9	38.9	30.2	30.2
UK	30.0	30.0	30.0	28.0	24.0
United States	39.3	39.3	39.3	39.1	39.1
EU 15	32.3	29.8	28.1	27.0	26.6
OECD total	30.6	28.2	27.0	25.7	25.5

Source: OECD (2013) Taxation of Corporate and Capital Income, in OECD Tax Database, http://www.oecd.org/tax/tax-policy/tax-database.htm#C_Corporate Capital (22.05.2013).

SPD-dominated Bundesrat in 1997 and the tax reform of the Social Democratic government adopted in 2000, even though far-reaching in many respects, left the statutory business tax rate at a level far above the EU average (see Table 8.4), in part because the overall business tax rate in Germany is significantly higher than the corporate tax rate alone, as German companies not only have to pay corporate taxes, but also local business taxes (*Gewerbesteuer*) and the solidarity surcharge on the corporate tax. This high level of statutory business tax rates was seen as keeping enterprises from investing in Germany and inciting them to move abroad.

Moreover, and with regard to unemployment in particular, it was argued that the German labour market was too highly regulated and that non-wage labour costs were too high. The latter problem has to do with the way the German welfare state in general and reunification in particular were funded (Czada, 1995; Zohlnhöfer, 2009: 331–7). The most important way to raise the enormous amount of money necessary was an increase in social security contributions which, however, made hiring labour more expensive for employers. Therefore, the government of Christian Democrats and Liberals under Helmut Kohl had tried to reduce non-wage labour costs in the second half of the 1990s. Among other things the generosity of many welfare programmes was curtailed, including health care, unemployment insurance and the pension system (Egle, 2009b: 235–41). These cuts, together with a moderate liberalization of the labour market, turned out to be very unpopular and were one relevant factor that led to the electoral defeat of the Kohl government (Feist and Hoffmann, 1999).

The following coalition led by the Social Democrats under chancellor Gerhard Schröder revoked most of the reforms of the previous government in the first few months after taking over government and tried to reduce non-wage labour costs by increasing the revenues of the social insurance system (via an increase of tax funding and by making more people pay social insurance contributions; see Egle, 2009b: 262–77).

Nonetheless, these reforms turned out to have hardly any effect on the level of social security contributions, which did not fall significantly. The only structural reform the Schröder government enacted in its first term was a pension reform that introduced a voluntary state-subsidized private pillar to the pension system – but this reform failed to have any short-term effects on the level of social security contributions. Furthermore, the Social Democratic government regulated the labour market even further, e.g. by revoking the relaxation of dismissal protection introduced by the Kohl government, by restraining the renewability of fixed-term work contracts or by giving employees a legal right to change from full-time to part-time employment unilaterally (Zohlnhöfer, 2004).

In summary, both post-unification governments were unable to reduce significantly business tax rates and non-wage labour costs and to introduce flexibility on the labour market up until 2002. Three factors can account for this outcome. First, programmatic differences between the main parties were relevant. Diverging economic policy positions of the main parties either led to outright policy gridlock as the second chamber of parliament that was controlled by opposition parties for most of the time vetoed some reforms (most notably the 1997 tax reform) and substantially influenced others; or partisan differences induced stop-and-go policies where the government of the day revoked the reforms its predecessor had adopted. Second, a lack of internal party cohesion on the part of the SPD prevented the social democratic government from adopting comprehensive reforms as some factions of the party argued for more far-reaching changes, while others wanted to preserve the status quo. Third, electoral competition played an important role. Parties felt that voters were reluctant to accept economic policy reforms. For example, the SPD experienced spectacular electoral defeats in autumn 1999, at least partly as a result of the announcement of an austerity programme which included a number of welfare cuts (Broughton, 2000). At the same time, some election at the *Länder* level, which is important for the federal government because of the composition of the Bundesrat, is almost always forthcoming. Thus, governments were again and again heavily penalized for unpopular reforms at the ballot boxes which made them avoid these unpopular reforms as long as possible. Nonetheless, after 2002, the reform gridlock was broken. How was that?

The German 'economic policy reform miracle': adopting Agenda 2010 and beyond

From 2002 onwards, successive governments (all of which, however, included the Social Democrats) have adopted somewhat more far-reaching reforms with regard to the labour market, the tax system and most programmes of the welfare state. The SPD-led government that had been narrowly re-elected in 2002 introduced more flexibility on the labour market as dismissal protection was moderately liberalized and low-paid jobs were made more attractive. Moreover, benefits for the long-term unemployed were reduced substantially and the conditions under which the unemployed can reject a job offer have been tightened (Hassel and Schiller, 2010). Reforms of the health care system and a pension reform reduced entitlements in order to cut expenditure which in turn would allow keeping social security contributions under control (Egle, 2009b: 277–80).

The so-called grand coalition of Christian Democrats and Social Democrats under Angela Merkel that was in office between 2005 and 2009 essentially carried these policies further (for an overview, see Zohlnhöfer, 2010) by yet another pension reform which increased the statutory pension age (Schmidt, 2010). More importantly, the Merkel government implemented tax hikes; most notably value added tax was increased by 3 percentage points (from 16 to 19 per cent) in order to lower significantly social security contributions, particularly contributions to unemployment insurance which were reduced from 6.5 per cent of gross wages to 2.8 per cent (Dümig, 2010: 283). A business tax reform was finally passed in 2007. This reform aimed at improving Germany's competitive position in regard to business taxation (see SVR, 2007: para. 394 ff. for more details). The centrepiece was the reduction of the corporate tax rate from 25 to 15 per cent which also translated into a substantial cut to the overall business tax rate which fell from around 40 to around 30 per cent – still above the average rate within the EU-15 members, but at least no longer among the highest tax rates in the EU (see Table 8.4). At the same time, the government put a lot of emphasis on budget consolidation and was somewhat successful even in this respect – at least until the financial crisis hit Germany (see Table 8.2).

Why could these reforms be adopted after 2002 while partisan differences, the high number of veto players, a lack of internal cohesion and electoral competition had made them impossible before? One of the more intriguing observations in this respect is that the 'reform miracle' was not a result of a change of government. Rather, the same government of Social Democrats and Greens under the same chancellor, Gerhard Schröder, that had proved to be rather reform-resistant in its first term (Merkel, 2003; Zohlnhöfer, 2004) adopted the most far-reaching labour market reforms in living memory together with substantial welfare and economic policy reforms in its second term. How can this pattern be explained?

At the heart of the answer to this puzzle are the power relations inside the Social Democratic Party. The so-called traditionalist wing of the SPD that was close to the trade unions, and the trade unions themselves, had substantial leverage over labour market and social policy up until 2002. To some extent the unions were integrated into economic policy-making via the so-called 'Alliance for Jobs, Training and Competitiveness', set up in 1998 by the incoming SPD-led government as an institution where the chancellor and some key ministers met with the leaders of the most important trade unions and employer organizations on a regular basis to develop a joint strategy to tackle Germany's economic and above all employment problems (see Streeck, 2003). While this macro-corporatist institution neither served as a forum for coordinating policy nor as an institution where legislation concerning the labour market, the welfare state or economic policy was discussed and prepared, it allowed the trade unions to block or at least delay any reform attempts that the modernizer wing of the government might have put forward. Moreover, the traditionalist wing of the SPD and the trade unions had a remarkable influence on the Ministry of Labour and Social Affairs and could thus secure a number of policies in their favour without having to make concessions with regard to wage policy.

At least partly as a result of the government's reluctance to adopt economic reforms, the level of unemployment did not develop in the way the government had hoped for. On the contrary, unemployment that had fallen somewhat due to the economic recovery in the late 1990s started to rise again from 2001 onwards. This development was alarming for the government of SPD and Greens as Chancellor Schröder had promised in 1998 that unemployment would be reduced substantially (namely to 3.5 million) by the next election (to be held in 2002) – a promise the government was increasingly unlikely to keep. Thus, rising unemployment put the government's re-election at risk. Therefore, the chancellor used a scandal about wrong placement statistics of the Federal Labour Office to appoint an expert commission that was asked to work out proposals for labour market reforms (see Hassel and Schiller, 2010). This commission (which is colloquially referred to as the Hartz Commission) allowed the chancellor to kill two birds with one stone. On the one hand, the government needed to document its will and ability to fight unemployment if it still wanted to win the next election. The proposals of the Hartz Commission which were presented only a few weeks before the general election were of particular importance in this respect because the Commission itself claimed that the adoption of its proposals would reduce the number of unemployed by two million within three years (Hartz Commission, 2002: 5). On the other hand, the Commission allowed the chancellor to circumvent Germany's sectoral corporatism. Of its 15 members only two were union representatives and one came from an employer association. Two further members were social scientists, two were SPD politicians from the regional and *Land* level, one came from the Federal Labour Office and the rest came from management consultancies and large companies (see Siefken, 2007: 190 for details). Thus, the trade unions and the SPD's traditionalist wing did not possess a veto position in the Commission which allowed it to put a proposal on the agenda that would probably not have been tabled had sectoral corporatism and the Ministry of Labour not been circumvented.

Schröder promised to implement the Commission's proposals 'one-to-one' even before they were officially presented. Somewhat surprisingly maybe, the traditionalist wing of the SPD and the trade unions rallied behind these 'expert recommendations', too, although many of the Commission's proposals were at odds with these actors' positions. Nonetheless, as the Hartz proposals provided the Social Democrats with a chance to regain their competence with regard to labour market policy, and as they were presented to the public shortly before the election in the summer of 2002, SPD dissidents and trade unions did not have much of a choice. Internal conflicts about labour market policy would have had a devastating effect on the party's competence rating and thus also on its election result which was not in the interest of either SPD politicians or trade union leaders (Blancke and Schmid, 2003: 229–30). Thus, Schröder was able to commit his party and the unions to activating labour market reforms.

Once the election was over, the internal dissent over economic policy became apparent again – the chancellor himself complained about the 'cacophony' of opinions on economic policy in his own party, which led to a drop in the government's economic competence rating and dramatic electoral defeats in important *Land* elections (Zohlnhöfer and Egle, 2007: 12–13). As a consequence, a paper was prepared in the Chancellery in the winter of 2002/03 that outlined far-reaching economic-policy reforms. With next to no consultation of the parliamentary parties of the government coalition (let alone the parties on the ground) (Niclauss, 2011) these far-reaching reform proposals that were named 'Agenda 2010' were presented to the public in a government declaration of the chancellor on 14 March 2003.

The opposition against these proposals was widespread but it was particularly fierce among the traditionalist wing of the SPD and the trade unions. The opponents in the SPD even started an inner party referendum against Agenda 2010 and forced the SPD leadership to concede an emergency party conference where the reform proposals were discussed controversially. In the end, however, up to 90 per cent of the delegates approved of the government's proposals (*Frankfurter Allgemeine Zeitung*, 2 June 2003). This result does not necessarily indicate near unanimous consent for the reform in the party, however. Rather, Schröder had put pressure on the delegates by threatening to resign as chancellor and party leader should the party conference vote against the reform.

Despite the party conference's approval, the reform's adoption in the *Bundestag* proved difficult. The chancellor browbeat possible dissenters by again threatening to resign should the coalition not obtain a majority of its own in the imminent roll-call votes in the *Bundestag*. At the same time, some minor concessions were made to the dissenters (*Süddeutsche Zeitung*, 13 October 2003). Hence, the coalition secured own majorities in the roll-call votes on the major elements of the labour market reforms in the Bundestag with only one Green MP abstaining.

As the Social Democrats thus had (been) moved to the right in economic policy, partisan differences grew smaller. Therefore, the Christian Democrats who controlled the second chamber of parliament and who had advocated a more flexible labour market for quite some time did not object to these reforms. On the contrary, they were eager to push through more far-reaching changes as they were happy to see rather unpopular reforms being implemented for which they would not need to take full responsibility (Zohlnhöfer, 2009: 369). Electoral considerations on the part of the two large parties did not figure very prominently, either, as both parties were interested in getting the reforms passed. The Social Democrats needed to prove their ability to reform the labour market while the Christian Democrats wanted to get a reform off the agenda they believed was necessary but electorally risky.

When CDU/CSU and SPD formed a coalition in 2005, reform activities lost momentum. Nonetheless, even this so-called grand coalition was able to adopt further important economic policy reforms up until 2007 – now as formal coalition partners. The business tax reform, budget consolidation and the reduction of social security contributions are cases in point. What these reforms have in common is that they were perceived as essential in order to tackle some of Germany's most urgent economic policy problems. Both parties agreed that in all of these instances it was necessary to act. The fact that the nominal business tax rates were higher than almost anywhere else in the EU was seen as problematic by tax experts in all parties. In March 2005, the SPD-led government came to an understanding with the then opposition of Christian Democrats to lower business taxation substantially and a cross-party bill was introduced to the *Bundestag* (*Bundestag* printed matters 15/5554; 15/5555). Although this bill did not make it to the statute books due to the early elections in 2005, this episode shows that both coalition partners were aware of the urgency of a reduction in business taxes in order to solve the country's pressing economic problems.

The budget situation was similar: Germany had breached the European Stability and Growth Pact's deficit criterion for years, and the grand coalition would have been unable to present a budget adequate to the requirements of the Basic Law (i.e. the German Constitution) and the EU without measures aiming at a consolidation of the budget. Finally, both parties had agreed for a long time that social security contributions had to be reduced in order to boost employment. As a significant reduction of non-wage labour costs could not be attained with structural reforms alone (as both parties had experienced in the past), an increase in tax-financing of the welfare state was uncontroversial, at least in principle (even though the parties initially did not agree on which taxes were to be increased).

Once both large parties were in agreement about the necessity of a reform, the Bundesrat as second chamber of parliament did not play a significant role any more. Similarly, electoral competition was remarkably muted under these circumstances.

Nonetheless, as the next election (to be held in 2009) drew nearer and unemployment as well as the budget deficit decreased continuously, the reform momentum more or less came to a halt. As the economic situation had improved remarkably, more risky reforms would have been difficult to communicate to the voters (and the trade union wings in both parties grew increasingly unwilling to support them). Moreover, the emergence and relative success of the new Left Party, led by former Social Democratic Party leader Oskar Lafontaine, moved the party system's centre of gravity substantially to the left (Egle, 2010). This development resulted in what can be labelled a 'resocialdemocratization' of economic and social policy (Zohlnhöfer, 2010); examples include the minimum wage legislation for a number of sectors, the extension of the period that unemployed people over 50 can claim unemployment benefits, and extraordinary pension increases in 2008 and 2009. Because it suffered most from the success of the Left Party, the SPD embraced these provisions in order to make its mark as a party promoting social justice (Batt, 2008). The Christian Democrats accepted those changes because they, too, feared losing votes should they veto these reforms, and some reforms (such as the extension of the period that the elderly can draw unemployment benefits) were actually initiated by the Christian Democrats in order to attract more voters. This behaviour on the part of the CDU/CSU can be regarded as the 'lesson of 2005'. The Christian Democrats had fought the 2005 Bundestag election campaign with a remarkably liberal reform agenda. This agenda in turn was perceived as the main reason for the disappointing result of that election which did not allow the CDU/CSU to form a coalition with the liberal FDP despite huge leads in opinion polls until very close before the election (Zolleis and Bartz, 2010: 55–60).

So at the end of 2007 the period of more far-reaching reforms came to an end. It was only briefly followed by politics as usual, however, before the politics of crisis management became dominant again, as the government was confronted with the most severe economic crisis in German post-war history in the following years.

The German response to the financial crisis

The financial crisis that started in 2007 and which has exerted a dominant impact on the development of most Western economies since 2008 also hit Germany very hard. Already in 2007, a private bank (IKB Deutsche Industriebank) and two *Landesbanken*, owned by the *Land* governments of Saxony and North Rhine-Westphalia respectively, faced massive problems due to their involvement in the US subprime mortgage market. All of them had to be bailed out at least partly with public money. In the course of the crisis, even more banks got into trouble, among them further *Landesbanken* (Bayern LB and HSH Nordbank), but also two members of the DAX stock index, namely Commerzbank and above all Hypo Real Estate. The latter was even dropped from the DAX due to the crisis.

But the financial crisis also spilled over to the real economy. The significant weakening of household balance sheets which resulted from falling asset prices in the wake of the crisis, the tightening credit market conditions and declining consumer confidence led to a substantial contraction of world private demand. This in turn resulted in an unprecedented decline in international trade within months, from which countries with a strong export sector like Germany and Japan suffered particularly hard. German exports for example declined by close to 18 per cent in 2009, which in turn had a devastating effect on investment in plants and machinery which fell by 21.8 per cent in the first six months of 2009 alone (Zohlnhöfer, 2011: 227). Therefore, in terms of GDP decline, Germany was one of the countries affected most severely by the crisis, with a negative GDP growth rate of about 5 per cent in 2009. Thus, the financial crisis triggered by far the deepest recession of the German economy since the foundation of the Federal Republic in 1949.

The federal government's response was equally unique in post-Second World War German history (for a critical overview, see Enderlein, 2010; Zohlnhöfer, 2011). As long as the crisis was mainly a financial market crisis, the government primarily tried to restore public confidence in the banking system – by protecting people's savings accounts and supporting financial institutions through a package worth up to €480 billion. The Bundestag also adopted a law which allowed for a possible expropriation of banks whose activities were crucial for the proper performance of the financial system (although only for a short period of time and only as a last resort). Even though such an option was never actually used, the government proceeded to nationalize fully or partly some banks (Herweg and Zohlnhöfer, 2010).

However, the bank rescue package could not prevent the financial market crisis from spilling over to the real economy where it caused a deep recession. The federal government initially was highly reluctant to adopt a stimulus package and only responded in December 2008 with a €23 billion package, including investments in infrastructure, improved conditions for write-offs, and a special programme supposedly able to facilitate credit access for small and medium-sized enterprises. Two months later, a second package followed, this time worth €50 billion – the largest ever economic stimulus programme in the Federal Republic's history. Investment expenditure received a further boost, the income tax was slightly reduced, a one-off payment for families with children was granted, and a so-called 'scrapping bonus' (*Abwrackprämie*) for old cars was temporarily introduced to help the automobile industry that had been hit particularly hard by the crisis. According to this provision, buyers purchasing a new car received €2,500 if they scrapped their current one – provided it was at least nine years old. In addition, the increase in unemployment was fought by extensive active labour market measures, particularly short-time jobs (Dümig, 2010: 291–2). A final package worth €8 billion was adopted shortly after the change of government in December 2009 (Moog and Raffelhüschen, 2011: 248–50). It seems fair to conclude that such programmes as a whole were able to mitigate the crisis in a substantial way.

Nonetheless, it seems unlikely that the rather interventionist and at least to some extent counter-cyclical response to the financial crisis marks a longer-lasting reorientation of German economic policy (see Zohlnhöfer, 2011). In contrast, policy-makers made it entirely clear that these were extraordinary emergency measures and that they intended to return to the supply-side path of budget consolidation and privatization as soon as the crisis was over. Thus, they introduced a constitutional debt brake and stipulated that expropriated banks had to be privatized immediately after a successful stabilization and the government abstained from getting involved in further rescue operations of non-financial companies. And indeed the government of Christian Democrats and Liberals under Angela Merkel that was in office after 2009 tried to return to less interventionist policies by bringing down the budget deficit and some – even though very moderate – tax cuts.

When it comes to explaining the German government's response to the crisis, the immense magnitude of the problems clearly plays an enormously important role. In the face of a systemic banking crisis and the deepest recession in post-war history, not doing anything obviously was not an option. It is extremely interesting, however, that the government only responded when the problems were apparent in the German economy and could not be denied any more. Thus, even though the crisis on the financial markets had begun already in 2007, neither the minister of finance nor the chancellor saw the necessity of a policy response – even after the collapse of Lehman Brothers. It was only the severe difficulties of Hypo Real Estate a few days later that led the government to think of a more comprehensive strategy in response to the financial crisis. Similarly, the government was very reluctant to devise a stimulus package and was only convinced of its necessity after the forecasts of GDP decline became increasingly gloomy.

More importantly, however, even in the face of a systemic banking crisis and a GDP decline of 5 per cent, programmatic differences between the coalition partners had not disappeared and even became manifest in government programmes. For example, elements of the bank rescue package of 2008 have been criticized in the literature as somewhat contradictory (see Enderlein, 2010). Contrary to other countries, ailing banks were not obliged to accept capital injections (which would have implied a partial nationalization) but those that did were punished by a strict regulation of salaries, bonuses and dividends. Some authors believe that this has kept banks from using the rescue package. This incoherence of the bank rescue package is the result of the diverging programmatic positions of the coalition partners of Christian Democrats and Social Democrats. The Social Democrats did not want to spend an immense amount of public money to save banks without holding to account the managers who were responsible for the problems of their institutions. This meant that some kind of punishment had to be introduced for those banks that needed help from the state. Therefore, the salaries of managers of banks obtaining help were capped and bonuses were strictly regulated. On the other hand, the Christian Democrats refused all policy options that would imply (partial) nationalizations. This meant that banks could not be obliged to make use of capital injections. In the end, these conflicting positions led to the ineffective combination of a voluntary scheme with penalties for participating banks.

Similar differences could also be observed with regard to potential interventions to rescue ailing non-financial companies (see Zohlnhöfer, 2011). Most Christian Democrats were reluctant to save those companies. The Christian Democratic minister of economic affairs even publicly opposed his own government's rescue plans for car manufacturer Opel and suggested the company should file for insolvency. In contrast, many Social Democratic politicians including party leader Franz Müntefering and chancellor candidate Frank-Walter Steinmeier argued that not only Opel, but also other companies of the real economy should be rescued with public money. In the end, the SPD got its way at least to some extent regarding Opel as the government offered federal loans of up to €4.5 billion to the company that planned to acquire Opel. This involvement did not come about for reasons beyond the control of the government. In all other cases, the government completely abstained from intervening in the end.

Back to normal? The economic policy reforms of the Christian–Liberal government since 2009

The coalition of Christian Democrats and Liberals under Chancellor Angela Merkel that came to power after the 2009 Bundestag election did not engage in large-scale economic reforms. As both parties had campaigned for far-reaching liberal reforms in the 2005 campaign (the result of which did not allow for the formation of a coalition of CDU/CSU and FDP), some observers had expected the parties to come back to their earlier ideas and adopt them once the coalition had become possible four years later. This was not the case, as can be seen from the reforms the Merkel II government adopted in the areas in which it had proposed the most far-reaching reforms in 2005: taxes and health care (see Moog and Raffelhüschen, 2011; Pressel, 2012: 197–210; Sturm, 2012: 267–71; Zohlnhöfer, forthcoming). While in the early 2000s both the CDU/CSU and FDP had advocated a (further) structural reform with the aim of simplifying the tax system, the changes that the government actually was able to agree on hardly went further than correcting for bracket-creep, that is for the effects of inflation on the tax system. And even these limited tax cuts were mostly blocked by the SPD-dominated Bundesrat. Similarly, although the government's health care reform fixed the contributions of employers and employees to the health insurance fund at 7.3 and 8.2 per cent of gross wages respectively (which essentially means that future increases in health care costs will have to be paid for by the insured exclusively via surcharges levied by their health insurance funds), the reform did not introduce a flat-rate contribution for everyone along the lines of the Christian Democrats' proposal of 2005, let alone the ideas put forward by the FDP. As of autumn 2013, no health fund has levied a surcharge, so the policy has not yet yielded any real effect on the insured.

So why were the parties that formed the government in 2009 unable or unwilling to adopt reforms they had advocated only a few years earlier? There are a number of interrelated reasons for this.

To begin with, the euro crisis dominated the agenda to an extent that did not leave much room for other reform initiatives. It is uncontroversial that the capacities and political resources of central governments to process large-scale reforms are limited in all political systems (Jones and

Baumgartner, 2012). In the case of the Merkel II government these processing capacities were completely absorbed by the euro crisis during most of the parliamentary term, so only a very small number of domestic reform projects could be processed. For a number of reasons, economic policy reforms were not among these projects as the government decided to invest its remaining political resources in other projects like the phasing-out of nuclear energy or the introduction of a new benefit for families that do not put their one- to three-year-old children into day care (*Betreuungsgeld*).

The first reason is that a number of important economic policy reforms had already been adopted by previous governments. This meant that further reforms seemed less necessary, particularly given that the economy was recovering surprisingly fast from the crisis and that unemployment had been falling almost continuously since 2009. So there was no pressure for the coalition to carry out more ambitious reforms. What is more, the Christian Democrats in particular had learnt the 'lesson of 2005' and were anxious not to upset the voters with a liberal economic policy agenda again. This led to serious conflicts between the FDP, who were pressing for more liberal reforms, and the Christian Democrats, who were keen not to adopt reforms that could be criticized as unfair. The Bavarian CSU, for example, in particular vehemently fought against the idea of per capita contributions to health care funds that were unrelated to income.

Finally, given the multi-billion euro rescue packages for the banks and the real economy adopted in 2008/09 and the enormous sums involved in the diverse euro rescue packages that the government had to push through the *Bundestag* after 2009, money was particularly scarce. The coalition agreement stipulated that all policies the coalition partners had agreed on were conditional upon financial feasibility (Saalfeld, 2010: 96). The minister of finance, Wolfgang Schäuble, used this clause and his considerable veto power to block many projects that would have meant revenue losses or increasing expenditure, among them the health care and the tax reforms. Regarding health care, decoupling contributions from income, as the FDP preferred, would have necessitated substantial funds to subsidize people that were unable to pay their contributions. As these subsidies would have had to be financed by the federal government, Schäuble blocked them (Pressel, 2012: 205). A fundamental tax reform would also have led to falling revenues and was thus out of the question for the finance minister, too. As a revenue-neutral tax reform is extremely difficult to adopt politically, because those people losing cannot be compensated, the coalition, particularly the Christian Democrats, lost interest in the project. So in the end, the coalition abstained from more far-reaching reforms until the end of the parliamentary term.

Conclusion

While Germany was seen as the 'sick man of the euro' at the turn of the century as unemployment was high, growth was slow and governments of different partisan complexions seemed unable to adopt the necessary reforms, today it is something like a 'teacher's pet' – a country with comparatively low unemployment and a decreasing budget deficit. Many observers argue that this is to a substantial degree the result of structural reforms, particularly structural labour market reforms, that were accompanied by a business tax reform and significant reforms of most welfare programmes (OECD, 2012a). These reforms have – according to many observers – even helped the German economy to cope comparatively well with the worst economic crisis in post-war history. Indeed, unemployment is lower in the autumn of 2013 than it was before the crisis, and German sovereign bonds are still among 'the most sought-after fixed interest securities in the world', as they had been prior to the crisis (Leaman, 2010: 24) – in stark contrast to many other countries of the eurozone. Therefore, the German government demands similar reforms of those countries that are currently in a much weaker economic position.

But why was the German political system plagued by a reform logjam ten years ago? And how did it become possible to break the gridlock? It is indeed difficult to get far-reaching economic policy reforms adopted in Germany, and that was the reason for the delay of the necessary economic policy reforms. First, there are many veto players whose agreement is required for a change of the status quo. The most important of these is the second chamber of parliament that is more often than not controlled by the opposition. Second, there used to exist substantial political differences between the relevant parties with regard to economic policy. This meant that the opposition either prevented the adoption of certain reforms via the second chamber of parliament or that it revoked the reforms after a change of government. Third, the fierce electoral competition in Germany makes reforms very risky for any government, particularly as an important election at the *Land* level is almost always forthcoming. Finally, the large parties, particularly the SPD, suffered from low internal cohesion which made comprehensive reforms even more difficult.

That significant reforms finally became possible between 2003 and 2007 was essentially thanks to special circumstances. As the lack of reforms endangered the government's re-election, Chancellor Schröder had to circumvent the traditionalist faction of the Social Democratic Party and commit the SPD to a rather ambitious reform programme. As the opposition was happy to get the reforms adopted (as otherwise it would have needed to adopted them itself next time in office), party competition was partially suspended and veto players, particularly the second chamber of parliament, became much less relevant. Similarly, the rather successful response to the financial crisis was due to the fact that the problems were so large that not doing anything clearly was not an option. As both large parties were in government together they shared an interest in solving the crisis together. Even though programmatic differences remained and in part shaped the German response to the crisis, electoral competition did not play an overriding role and most veto points were absorbed. Since 2009, German economic policy-making seems to be back to normal. As the domestic economy was going well, unemployment was falling and tax revenues rising, the government has not introduced any significant reforms.

Thus, for the time being, it can be concluded that Germany has weathered the storms of the recent crises comparatively well. Politics played its part in that outcome but other factors like monetary policy and the development of wages clearly were important too (Reisenbichler and Morgan, 2012). As successful as these reforms may have been in boosting German competitiveness and improving the country's overall economic situation, they may also have aggravated the problems of the eurozone because strong German competitiveness drove the current account deficits of the euro periphery still deeper into the red and thus triggered the euro crisis. Therefore, the success of the economic policy reforms of the first decade of the twenty-first century created new problems, not only for the Southern European countries but also for Germany itself as the country which will have to shoulder the largest financial burden of any euro bailout.

It is difficult to predict how the euro crisis will develop and which effects this most recent crisis will have on the German economy. It is pretty safe to guess that government finances will be strained severely as the crisis continues, almost irrespective of whether Greece or other countries from the euro periphery remain in the euro or not. But it might also be the case that the crisis will have a substantial negative effect on the banking system and the real economy. If this were the case, the government's capacity to respond to the crisis would probably be smaller this time around as public finances are much more strained than in 2008/09. Therefore, the most important economic policy issue for the incoming government is certainly to find a lasting solution to the euro crisis.

Chapter 9

Germany and the European Union

WILLIAM E. PATERSON

Germany's European vocation was a constant in its European policy from the early days of the Federal Republic. This policy was associated with a 'reflexive multilateralism' (a fixed preference for supranational methods) and a reluctance to base policy explicitly on national interest discourse. In exercising its European vocation of 'more Europe' as the default position, the Federal Republic operated through the Franco–German relationship. This policy had brought Germany great prosperity and was a key facilitator of German unity. In recent years the 2004 eastern enlargement of the EU and France's weakening economic position has eroded the traction of the Franco–German relationship. Generational change has greatly modified the instinctive affinity of the political elite with the EU. The key game changer however has been the onset of the crisis in the eurozone, a crisis which has propelled Germany as the principal creditor into the leadership position in the eurozone and placed great strains on the EU founding myth that in some sense all the member states are equal.

The European context

The eastern enlargement of the EU to include the Czech Republic, Hungary, Poland, Slovakia and Slovenia (Malta and the Baltic States also joined) brought with it new opportunities and new challenges for Germany. The expansion eastwards allowed German industry to outsource a great deal of the productive process to lower wage economies – a huge benefit to German industry. On the other hand expansion was seen as a grave competitive challenge by a number of German actors, especially those with interests close to the enlargement border. These interests greatly strengthened the protectionist impulse of the German *Länder*. At a more macro-level enlargement challenged the acquis of the EU, especially the Common Agricultural Policy (CAP). This change to a

166

certain extent threw France and Germany onto the defensive, and the relationship in some areas especially the defence of the CAP now functioned as a brake rather than as a motor of the EU (see Chirac–Schröder accord on agriculture of September 2002). Enlargement altered Germany's geographical position to the centre of the new Europe. Together with its growing economic strength this has added to the perception of the country both internally and externally as Europe's central power rather than the Brussels oriented poster boy of European integration associated with the European Vocation.

Externally eastern enlargement and the declining effectiveness of the Franco–German relationship has given Germany a more powerful but also more exposed position which has weakened the automatic pro-European reflex. Internally domestic politics has reflected a more contentious environment for European policy.

From reflexive multilateralism to reluctant hegemon

German European policy has been based on a European vocation and a reflexive multilateralism associated with a leadership avoidance reflex. Both of these principles came under extreme pressure in the second Merkel Government. In the following sections the degree to which these pillars of German European policy have crumbled will be more closely analysed and the implications for the future of German European policy and the future of the EU will be reviewed.

Reflexive multilateralism

The restricted range of choices open to the Federal Republic at its inception and its lack of full sovereignty meant that policy choices once made were characterized by constancy – and Germany's European vocation was one of these central constancies. The motives underpinning this vocation were brilliantly summarized by Michael Stuermer (Stuermer and Neal, 1996: 513) as being 'to eat well, to sleep well and never, never to be alone'. Eating well involved lifting the discriminatory trade provision which had been imposed on West Germany after the Second World War. In order to do this an area of cooperation had to exist alongside an arena of competition without which the discriminatory provisions would never have been lifted and Germany's quickly emerging role as export champion/extraordinary trader (Hager, 1980) would have been perceived as a threat. 'To sleep well', given the immediate past, entailed adopting a future oriented Europeanized identity. 'Never, never to be alone' reflected a fear that other states would never accept a German *Alleingang* (solo position). The solution was the Franco–German relationship where France would be the senior partner politically (Germany was the cart to the French horse as de Gaulle unkindly put it), flanked by an embrace of supranational institutions (reflexive multilateralism).

Perhaps the most influential theoretical explanation of Germany's European vocation and its persistence over a long period was given by Peter Katzenstein (1997: 33) who stressed the depth of Germany's Europeanized identity and the degree of congruence between German institutions and those of the EU:

> Although distinctive, the institutional practices that mark the European polity resemble Germany's on this score. The system of governance in the European polity is based on what one might call 'associated sovereignty', pooled competencies in overlapping domains of power and interest, which is characteristic also of Germany's 'semi sovereign' state.

Katzenstein concluded that this congruence would ensure the persistence of Germany's European vocation:

> Because the European polity offers a familiar political stage, it is highly improbable that German political elites will any time soon turn their back on European institutions that have served German interests so well at home and abroad. (Ibid.: 48)

His views were strengthened by the experience of the first post-unity government. Helmut Kohl together with François Mitterrand pressed for deeper integration together with the uploading of German preferences which would help shape the regional milieu (Bulmer et al., 2000).

Germany's shrinking European vocation

Having reached an apogee under the Kohl chancellorship, Germany's European vocation was subject to a continuing process of erosion under his successors (Paterson, 2010). This process was first visible in the Schröder chancellorship. Jeffery and Paterson (2004: 63) used the metaphor of 'shifting tectonic plates' to describe this change:

> To us the tectonic plates of German and EU politics appear to be shifting, opening up a critical juncture for change. Our hypothesis is that at this critical juncture the virtuous circle embedding Germany in a congenial environment of German–EU congruence is beginning to break down forcing reconsideration of the values which had underpinned German European policy through to the 1990s.

This metaphor captures the long-term nature of the process, with the changes not initially visible above the surface, but with the long-term prospect of an earthquake.

Tremors but not (yet) an earthquake

Cumulatively the resource crunch, enlargement to the east, identity and generational change had begun to shift the tectonic plates; but it is the eurozone crisis which has exposed the new quality in Germany's place in the EU. Peter Katzenstein and others argued that a European Germany was one which best suited the country's interests and aspirations, not least because of the congruence between its semi-sovereign domestic institutions and the 'associated sovereignty' of the EU. The impact of the eurozone crisis has been to disturb the equilibrium between these two levels. In the central area of the eurozone we are now observing not so much a European Germany but a forced congruence, a German Europe.

A normalized Germany

In seeking to locate Germany's departure from the Katzenstein 'tamed power' position two main approaches have been employed. In Katzenstein's depiction of Germany as a 'tamed power', German 'soft power' was exercised through multilateral institutions in which the country was a classic coalition builder. He also stressed the manner in which Germany treated small states with kid gloves: together the two elements made up the European vocation. The shrinking of this vocation has led to visible changes. Germany is no longer reflexively multilateralist and within multilateral institutions the traditional 'leadership avoidance reflex' is no longer in evidence. It is very striking in the handling of the eurozone crisis just how much bilateral negotiation has taken place and the strain that has been imposed on relations with Germany's southern partners. Small states are no longer given the same attention. France and Germany allowed themselves a latitude in breaching the Stability and Growth Pact in 2002/03, which has not been accorded to small states – and Chancellor Merkel's adoption of the Union Method (an emphasis on interstate rather than supranational methods) in her Bruges Speech of November 2010 clearly downgraded the former emphasis on multilateral institutions in favour of the large member states.

'Normalization' entered the discourse through the writings of Hans Peter Schwarz (Schwarz, 1994). His argument was that in the post-unity situation a fully sovereign Germany should pursue a post-classical policy analogous to France and Britain. Within Europe, Germany would be the central power by virtue of its greater power resources, and a process of European and German normalization would place the country in the position of central balancer. While Schwarz's arguments rest on geopolitics those of Gunther Hellmann and his collaborators are based on close observation of policy decisions in the area of asylum and defence which led them to conclude that we were witnessing a departure from Germany's European poster-boy role which had been replaced by 'de-Europeanization by default' (Hellmann, 2006). Bulmer and Paterson (2010) have sought to confront a central difficulty in the use of the term 'normalization' which reflects its lack of theoretical underpinning – that of the yardstick to be used in defining 'normality'. In their article they took it to mean a new readiness to use 'hard bargaining' as a mechanism for projecting German European policy in the EU. As Thomas De Maizière, then Minister in the Chancellor's Office, famously put it: 'for our European friends, they need to come to terms with the fact that Germany is going to act just as other countries do in Brussels' (*Financial Times*, 25 May 2011: 10).

Germany as a reluctant hegemon

The normalization thesis suggests that Germany has made a deliberate choice to down play, though not wholly abandon, multilateralism. The reluctant hegemon thesis by contrast argues that this is not a position which Germany has actively sought; indeed it would be more accurate to describe elite and popular attitudes as characterized by ambivalence and reservation. I coined the term (Paterson, 2011; see also *The Economist*, 15 June 2013) to describe a situation where Germany had emerged as a 'reluctant hegemon' as a result of the eurozone crisis where its ever strengthening economy and principal creditor status placed it in the driving seat in relation to setting the rules in the zone. This core argument was flanked by the increasingly asymmetric nature of the Franco–German relationship and a new readiness by other member states to accept solo German leadership.

The reluctant hegemon position has been embraced very reluctantly. Germany wishes to set the rules in the eurozone without accepting the obligations of a hegemon. Blyth and Matthijs (2011) point out that Germany has failed to provide any of the five public goods identified by Charles Kindleberger as necessary to describe a state as a hegemonic stabilizer – and the increased role of domestic politics and the parapublic institutions will greatly constrain the exercise of hegemonic power by Germany (Bulmer and Paterson, 2013). This reluctance also reflects the pervasive influence of the dominant German economic doctrine of ordoliberalism whose advocates as supporters of a free market economy fear that support for the debtor countries would create moral hazard and free them from the urgent need to reform their economies in the ultra-competitive direction prescribed by ordoliberalism (Funk, 2014). Without the provision of public goods, however, the danger is that resentment against Germany could build up to a dangerous level in the southern countries (*Financial Times*, 2013).

Merkel's European policy

On becoming chancellor, Angela Merkel had limited experience of EU policy at the highest level. She had some experience of EU negotiations as environment minister for a period under Helmut Kohl but sectoral negotiations which involve more junior players are quite different from guiding overall policy. European policy was an area which did not come naturally to her. Her personal history as an East German Protestant excluded the natural Europeanism of all previous Christian Democratic chancellors. Structurally the foreign minister normally enjoys an advantage in the first years of government as he or she has all the expert resources of the Foreign Ministry at his or her command, whilst each new chancellor has to pick a foreign policy team. This balance of advantage was very apparent in the Red/Green government where Joschka Fischer's prominence in the first one slipped away in the second. To add to his anticipated advantage Foreign Minister Steinmeier had also brought in Reinhard Silberberg, perhaps the top Eurocrat in the German government to the Foreign Ministry.

Somewhat surprisingly it all turned out very differently and Chancellor Merkel completely dominated European policy. There are a number of explanations for this unexpected development. Perhaps most importantly she came to power at a point when the other European leaders were about to change, a situation which offered her the chance to become the pre-eminent European leader – an opportunity that she seized with great sure-footedness. She was also greatly aided by the European agenda which not only contained the German presidency of the EU but encompassed an unusual proportion of summit meetings, including that of the G8. Here her appointment of Christoph Heusgen, formerly Javier Solana's chief of staff, as her chief foreign policy adviser brought someone with a deep knowledge of the other players. The key explanation however resides in the chancellor's formidable qualities. Her outstanding intellect was well known but what had not been anticipated was the degree to which she applied it to foreign affairs. Her fellow negotiators have remarked not only on her detailed knowledge but the fact that she had worked out a line of resolution in advance. Here the experience of coalition government probably helps.

Chancellor Merkel was greatly aided in her first government by the discipline that her coalition associate brought to the partnership and the absence of a recession. Helmut Schmidt in a conversation with me claimed that the demands on a chancellor's diary left him free to devote only 10 per cent of his time to foreign affairs (conversation with the author, 5 November 2008). However, in Schmidt's case, he was struggling with a very fractious coalition and unrest in the SPD and his main task was to revive the economy, a task which entailed very numerous meetings with German business and labour interests. In Chancellor Merkel's case the recession broke late on in her first government, leaving her freer to concentrate on European policy. Had she won the 2005 election more convincingly, she would have pushed on with the reform programme which characterized her electoral campaign. But this would have embroiled her in endless negotiations.

The fractiousness of the new CDU/CSU/FDP coalition after the September 2009 election and the feeling that the Lisbon Treaty represented all that could be achieved institutionally was reflected in a drift in German European policy and a loss of focus by Chancellor Merkel at the beginning of her second government. Like Chancellor Helmut Schmidt her strengths lie in problem solving rather than establishing new agendas. This agenda duly appeared in the form of dealing with the eurozone crisis. A collapse of the eurozone would have threatened Germany's core political and economic strategies, but committing too many resources to it would have resulted in political nemesis at the next election.

The German presidency of 2007

The German presidency of the EU in 2007 (the presidency chairs all the European Councils) was dominated by the need to salvage the European Constitutional Treaty which had set out to rationalize the European treaties. President Chirac had retired and Prime Minister Blair was on the brink of retirement, leaving Chancellor Merkel as the uncontested leading figure on the European scene. Treaty negotiations are normally handled by the Foreign Ministry, and the process had been started by the immediate past foreign minister, Joschka Fischer. On this occasion Merkel took complete charge and approached the issue in a notably bold manner. Whereas Germany was traditionally very skilful at placing itself at the centre of constitutive bargains (Bulmer, 1997) in tandem with France, and waiting until the issue was 'ready for decision' (*entscheidungsreif*), Merkel took a maximalist position in favour of the constitutional treaty as a starting point rather than burying it as a number of member states – including the United Kingdom, the Czech Republic and to a lesser degree France and the Netherlands – would have preferred. The taking up of a strong position at the beginning of negotiations and then arguing strongly for it is a presidency style more British than conventionally German. Given the failure of referenda in France and the Netherlands, two key original member states, strong reservations in a number of states and the fact that the French elections were to take place late in the presidency cycle, this was a fairly exposed position to take.

The negotiations were then conducted in a highly centralized manner from the Chancellor's Office (Phinnemore, 2013). In a letter to other governmental leaders Merkel suggested that member governments proceed by discussion of focal points for which each government should appoint two special representatives and that governmental leaders and the chancellor deal directly with each other. This process was flanked by the Berlin Declaration in March 2007 on the fiftieth anniversary of the Treaty of Rome which set out the agreed values of European integration. The detailed negotiations for the new Treaty were agreed at the Brussels Summit of June 2007 which paved the way for the Intergovernmental Conference and then the final agreement on the Treaty text at the informal European Council in Lisbon also in June 2007. The outstanding feature of these negotiations was that other member states looked to Chancellor Merkel rather than the Franco–German duo for leadership. This was a significant change, but Merkel in using her leadership capital to salvage the Lisbon Treaty had remained true to the European vocation.

The changing parameters of domestic politics

The changing external environment and the impact of German Unity go some way to explaining the shrinking of Germany's European vocation, but, in Germany as elsewhere, a growing resistance to further European integration has arisen. The deeper that European integration penetrated into national systems so the more likely there was to be a reaction. From the 1960s onwards there had been a political and societal consensus in Germany in favour of integration. As this started to burrow into the nooks and crannies of the German economy and politics a process of politicization gathered pace.

Generational change

Germany's European vocation was framed by two founding chancellors. Konrad Adenauer, the founding chancellor of the Bonn Republic, and Helmut Kohl, the founding chancellor of the Berlin Republic, were both visionary Europeans who constructed the politics of their time around these visions, even when, as in the case of adoption of the euro, Chancellor Kohl did not have the support of public opinion behind him. The story of the last decade is the partial unravelling of this European tapestry.

Germany's Europeanized identity reflected the historical experience in the Third Reich of post-war German politicians. Konrad Adenauer had been an opponent of Nazism and his worst fears were confirmed by his experience of the Third Reich. Helmut Kohl was the last chancellor to experience the Third Reich directly, albeit as a schoolboy and in an anti-aircraft battalion (*Flakhelfer*), and the shaming experience of the last years of the Reich formed the starting point of his political vision. Gerhard Schröder (born 1944) grew up in post-war Germany. By the time he became chancellor the sharp edges of historical memory had softened and the discourse underwent a marked shift:

> My generation and those following are Europeans because we want to be, not because we have to be ... Germany standing up for its national interests will be just as natural as France and Britain standing up for theirs. (*Financial Times*, 11 November 1998, p. 6)

Schröder's Europeanism was no longer guided by the impulse to repair history. It was a more rational, less emotionally based, Europeanism, a *Vernunfteuropaer* (European by reason), rather than the European credo of Kohl. The shift of discourse was not all encompassing and Joschka Fischer continued to profess the traditional Europeanism of Kohl and his predecessors.

Angela Merkel was not only born at a different time but was brought up in a different country, East Germany. Whereas Helmut Kohl and all earlier chancellors were reacting against the Third Reich, her defining experience was of a communist dictatorship. A Kohl speech would very often invoke his origins in a border area of Germany and the excitement of breaking down these borders post-war; whilst a Merkel speech refers to growing up in East Germany and places freedom at its centre. Having a different socialization from her Western contemporaries has meant that Europeanism has not come naturally to her and she has had to learn to speak 'European'. Like Helmut Schmidt she finds 'visions' alien and is happiest problem solving. This served her very well in her first government where the salvage of the Lisbon Treaty occurred at governmental level. She was aware, however, that this did not address the problem of public opinion and had initially talked of a refounding (*Neubegruendung*) of the EU which would close the gap between public and elite sentiments, mercilessly exposed in the Dutch and French referenda disasters. Little more was heard of that aim in her first government.

In the eurozone crisis she has concentrated primarily on playing to the understandable caution of German electors. This strategy has worked in terms of her personal popularity but at the expense of further softening support for Europe both internally and externally, which would be a problem were Germany ever called on to raise large resources to support the euro. Even at present the softening of support in German public opinion carries risks for the survival of the eurozone, a point trenchantly made by Douglas Webber (2013: 19):

> As domestic political constellations in many member states have become much more inimical towards the EU, German engagement and support is indispensable to the durability of the euro, the EU and European Integration and there is a very significant risk that this support will wane, and no longer be able to support the European project in the future.

Tracking German public opinion also carries the risk of always being behind the curve. Insulated from the euro crisis, public opinion takes a more relaxed or even over-relaxed view of the crisis, and the danger in taking it as a guiding star is that it may result in Chancellor Merkel acting too late.

Public opinion

This increasing politicization was first evident in public opinion. While the shift in elite discourse was gradual and was normally accompanied by a rhetoric of continuity designed to reassure Germany's neighbours, the trend in German mass opinion is much clearer and unidirectional. Mass support for European integration has steadily declined since the conclusion of the Maastricht Treaties (Dalton and Eichenberg, 2007). The abolition of the Deutschmark and entry into the eurozone strengthened this trend in popular opinion. This secular decline was reinforced by the consequences of unification. Pro-Europeanism had no historic roots in Eastern Germany, and while there was a short-lived enthusiasm for the EU immediately after German Unity among East Germans it quickly eroded when the EU failed to live up to hopes that it would provide some social protection to post-unity changes. In more recent years the strength of the post-communist Party of Democratic Socialism (PDS, now Die Linke), who alone among German parties have pursued a consistently eurosceptic line, has further weakened support for European integration in Eastern Germany. The result is that Germany is hardly contested as the dominant identity narrative in the Eastern *Länder*, given the failure of a European identity to take root (Weidenfeld, 2010: 200).

Writing in 2005 I drew attention to the implications of the tension between elite and mass opinion:

> Elite and mass opinion continue to diverge but the prevailing elite consensus and the relatively low salience of European issues has allowed continued elite autonomy. The question is for how long? (Paterson, 2005: 282)

This question was to be answered in the eurozone crisis where Chancellor Merkel has taken enormous care to track successfully German public opinion rather than to place herself at the centre of winning coalitions of European leaders in the traditional German manner.

Parapublic institutions

In his seminal work 'Politics and Policy in West Germany: The Growth of a Semisovereign State', Katzenstein (1987) analysed the taming and decentralization of political power in the Federal Republic. One key element of this 'taming' was the role of two key parapublic institutions: the Federal Constitutional Court (FCC) (*Bundesverfassungs-gericht*) and the *Bundesbank*.

The Federal Constitutional Court

'The red robed judges in Karlsruhe have become assertive protectors of German sovereignty' (*The Economist*, 15 June 2013). The lawless and arbitrary character of the Third Reich engendered a very strong commitment to the rule of law in the Federal Republic which was reflected in the wide powers given to the FCC. The Basic Law allows wide recourse to the Court and it is an opportunity which citizens, parties and groups have been keen to take advantage of. As guardian of the Basic Law the FCC has profited from the growing attachment to it. The FCC is a very self-confident body which enjoys widespread public support. It takes its role as guardian of the Basic Law very seriously and over time this has led it on occasion to resist the juridical claims of the European Court of Justice (ECJ). A pattern of rivalry with the ECJ developed quite early on, as became clear in the Solange Decision of the FCC in 1974, which attempted to move the ECJ to adopt its own fundamental rights protection (Davies, 2012). On 12 October 1993 the FCC in a widely noted judgment on the conformity of the Maastricht Treaty with the German Basic Law insisted on its right as defender of the Basic Law to rule on the balance of competences between the EU and German institutions. This claim was based on the argument that as there is no European demos there could be no European superstate and so legitimacy must necessarily reside with the existing *Volk* (people) represented by the Federal Republic.

Whereas the Maastricht judgment caused some consternation in the ECJ and certainly influenced the European policy of the federal government (Harnisch, 2001) it did not become a major element of public debate in Germany. The Lisbon judgment of 2009 was to have a much greater impact on discourse about Europe. Its tone, which could be described as eurosceptic, now resonated with a changed public and press opinion. Carl Otto Lenz, a senior German eurolawyer, pointed out that the judgment used the term 'sovereignty' 33 times despite it not being mentioned in the Basic Law which the FCC exists to defend (Proissl, 2010). It also identified five reserved areas where it saw no scope for further transfer to the EU. The FCC has, since the Maastricht judgment, insisted on the *Bundestag* being actively involved in key EU decisions – and the ruling created a number of new control powers for the *Bundestag*, the effect of which was to create a new domestic opportunity structure for a more politicized European debate in the *Bundestag*. The publicity surrounding the judgment further encouraged the recourse to constitutional challenge. It has also instilled even greater caution on the part of the federal government. It is not the usual practice of the FCC to rule on a policy that the federal government has assented to as unconstitutional, but rather to set out the conditions which would make policy in that area compatible. In that sense the FCC has moved from 'veto player' to co-shaper of German European policy – the direction it prefers is limitation of further integration.

The Bundesbank

Reflecting Germany's twentieth-century history and the trauma of mega-inflation in 1923 an instinctive commitment to 'sound money' was reflected in the strong powers and high standing of the *Bundesbank*, the German central bank. As Jacques Delors once quipped, 'not all Germans believe in God but they all believe in the *Bundesbank*'. While the Bundesbank reigned supreme, the commitment to sound money was inviolable. The situation of *Bundesbank* supremacy, also in relation to other European economies, was one which French governments found especially irksome. So great was its influence that David Marsh (1992) referred to 'The *Bundesbank*: The Bank that Ruled Europe'. The creation of the European Central Bank (ECB) potentially brought the principle of 'sound money' into conflict with the European vocation principle (van Esch, 2012). After a long period when the 'sound money' argument was in the ascendant German Unity turned the argument in favour of the European vocation (ibid.: 44). The reservations of the *Bundesbank* were to some extent alleviated by siting the ECB in Frankfurt and adopting a constitution modelled on the *Bundesbank*. At that point the policy community supporting the European vocation (the chancellor, the Foreign Ministry and German industry) was much stronger than the *Bundesbank*, which had been in the view of some relegated to the Frankfurt Branch of the ECB (Marsh, 2013: 81). The balance of forces has altered visibly over the intervening period. On the European side the chancellor is not prepared to defy German public opinion in the way that Chancellor Kohl did over the creation of the eurozone. The Foreign Ministry, the key advocate of European integration, has lost in influence, and under the present incumbent is now 'missing in action' and less European than in the past; it has been replaced in importance by the Finance Ministry.

The establishment of the ECB had been expected by many to marginalize the *Bundesbank* in terms of European policy, but the acute policy dilemmas and the threat to sound money posed by the eurozone crisis has brought it back as a central player. Axel Weber, the president of the *Bundesbank*, backed by Chancellor Merkel and widely expected to succeed Jean-Claude Trichet, withdrew from the race in February 2011 on the issue of the ECB's purchase of the debts of troubled eurozone governments. This resignation was followed in September 2011 by the resignation of Juergen Stark, the chief economist of the ECB who entertained similar objections. Stark was replaced on the ECB's executive board by Joerg Asmussen, the permanent secretary at the Finance Ministry. Jens Weidmann, who had been Chancellor Merkel's adviser, became the new president of the *Bundesbank*. Weidmann quickly emerged as an articulate defender of *Bundesbank* orthodoxy. In his position as president and member of the Council of the ECB, Weidmann has put himself at the head of those who support sound money and ordoliberalism, a liberal German economic philosophy which emphasizes the need for the state to ensure the principal role of the free market. Ordoliberalism also has a narrow view of the role of central banks which in the view of its adherents should be independent and concentrate on pursuing monetary policies with the aim of ensuring monetary stability, while governments should restrict themselves to setting the frameworks for competition and functioning markets. Whereas the support for the European vocation principle is waning, support for sound money ideas remains hugely strong in German public opinion. It is also the dominant view among German academic economists and receives strong support from the *Frankfurter Allgemeine Zeitung*. Moreover, while the Foreign Ministry is losing support, the Finance Ministry, where support for sound money is concentrated, becomes ever more central.

The political parties

The CDU/CSU has been a pro-European party from the origins of the Federal Republic. After initially privileging the pursuit of German Unity over west European integration the SPD moved to accepting European integration in the mid-1950s (Paterson, 1974); the FDP followed in the next decade. For the next 40 years there was a solid pro-European consensus in the established parties. This was very visible during the debates about entry into the eurozone where support from political parties remained solid, despite an adverse public opinion. In their early years of *Bundestag* representation the Greens opposed some aspects of German European policy, but since the advent of Joschka Fischer as foreign minister they have been strong supporters of integration. The PDS (Party of Democratic Socialism), the successor party to the SED (East German Communist Party), has been a continual critic of the EU – and this tradition has been continued by *Die Linke*, the successor to the PDS.

Although the consensus appeared unchanged by 2009 it was to some extent 'hollowed out'. In the 2009 election European integration played a smaller role than in any election since 1949. As the crisis developed reactions differed within the coalition. The FDP came out strongly against eurobonds (the chancellor and the finance minister were not keen, but neither did they rule out their introduction). The FDP's attempt to instrumentalize euroscepticism in the Berlin Land Election was a dismal failure and its vote fell from 7.6 per cent in 2006 to 1.8 per cent in September 2011. The CSU, the Bavarian partner of the CDU, has always been more populist, and with an election coming up in 2013 it has struck a critical tone at times. As Chancellor Merkel was faced with mobilizing support for bailout measures in the *Bundestag* she was persuaded by Peter Altmaier, then the chief whip and a noted European, that it was necessary to strengthen the European element – and the party programme in 2011 reflected this. Chancellor Merkel's position was made easier by the attitude of the opposition. In May 2010 the opposition SPD failed to support the coalition in the *Bundestag* by not voting for the legislation that would provide €750 million for the Greek bailout. Since then the opposition has taken a more generous line, though with the approach of the German election they took a tough line on the Cyprus bailout.

Until now Germany has lacked a eurosceptic party, but the unpopularity of the eurozone has led to the creation of a new party, the *Alternative Für Deutschland*, committed to the withdrawal of Germany from the eurozone. They polled 4.7 per cent in the 2013 federal election, a very creditable performance for a new party and which is likely to do even better in the 2014 European elections.

German political parties, while remaining broadly pro-European, are much more sensitive to public opinion than in the past and have moved from an unconditional support of the EU to a much more conditional one, and it remains to be seen how they would respond if Germany were called on to disburse huge resources.

Changing bilateral relations

The West Germany that was created in 1949 only became fully sovereign in 1990. Its principal city, Berlin, then had a quite different status as it lay over a hundred miles behind the Iron Curtain in the German Democratic Republic. The key long-term aims of the Federal Republic were to overcome German division and to regain full sovereignty, whilst the immediate aims were protection against the Soviet threat and economic prosperity. The fulfilment of these aims required close alliances. Security was overwhelmingly dependent on the United States, with the United Kingdom playing a junior role. Prosperity and the creation of Europe meant that France was the indispensable partner in the EU.

The Franco–German relationship

The founding contract of European integration was the European Coal and Steel Community where the French government proposed that Germany be allowed to recover economic power in a multilateral context under French political leadership. In the last decade the relationship has become increasingly asymmetric as the French economy had headed downwards, culminating in the loss of its AAA credit status. The eurozone has exposed fairly fundamental divisions between the austerity-centred policy of Germany and French policy which aims at growth. There is also a fundamental divide between the German embrace of globalization and France's continued mercantilist and protectionist stance – the pair resemble the couple described by David Calleo (1978: 207): 'like ageing sopranos they refuse to retire. Their technique remains impressive even if their voices have faded.' The brutal logic of the sovereign debt crisis, pitting the interests of the creditor nations against those of the debtor nations, was always going to test the Franco–German relationship. Normally Germany aggregates the interests of the Northern States on one side with France and the southern states on the other side. In the eurozone crisis interests were too polarized to craft an overarching agreement. The EU is now more complicated, with Poland playing an important role; France under Sarkozy was reluctant to place itself at the head of a southern alliance which would be perceived as a coalition of losers.

Initially too the legitimacy of a Franco–German rule-setting leadership claim was impaired by breaches of the Stability Pact in 2001–03. As Lebow (2003: 126) has pointed out, those who seek to impose rules on a system are advised to abide by them: 'Athens had to act in accord with the principles and values it espoused'.

A key strength of the Franco–German relationship is its institutionalized character; but this is very ill adapted to the sort of speedy crisis management needed to respond to the financial markets. Even when they do come to an agreement it is invariably oversold, with implementation then being delayed by the necessarily time-consuming ratification procedures. The structural drag inherent in such a relationship might have been transcended if there had been a 'dynamic duo' at the helm of France and Germany who were focused on economics. Helmut Schmidt has said that he would immediately have telephoned Giscard d'Estaing and developed a strategic plan (*Baseler Zeitung*, 29 May 2010). Such a relationship depends on a very high level of mutual trust and confidence which has been in very short supply. The reduction of the permissive consensus at the mass and institutional level (the FCC and *Bundesbank*) has also shrunk the degree of executive autonomy the federal government now enjoys in this area. The failure to craft a credible agreement pushes up the cost of settlement. So far the confidence of the bond markets has been maintained, but these things can change.

It was hoped that contrasting French and German approaches to the economy had been smoothed over in the construction of the eurozone, but the reverse has been the case. German supply-side reforms in the Agenda 2010, which lowered wages and prices, slowed down consumption and increased hyper-export orientation, are seen elsewhere as 'beggar my neighbour policies'. German reaction to criticism is simply to recommend the same policies to other member states, including and perhaps now especially France. It has been possible to accommodate the French demand for economic governance in a mild version, but the German insistence on a doctrinal interpretation of sound money principles has been more damaging.

The Merkel government has shown an unswerving commitment to austerity, a policy which has brought it into continual conflict with France and a limited agreement with the United Kingdom. This conflict has accelerated since the election of President François Hollande. Keen to close this front in the run-up to the German election, Chancellor Merkel made some concessions to France at the bilateral meeting on 30 May 2013 (*Bundesregierung*, *Pressemitteilung* (Federal Government Press release), 30 May 2013), but this did not alter the fundamentals. France must undertake substantial reforms and improve its economic performance if the Franco–German relationship is to recover its centrality. Germany is now the indispensable partner for all other member states.

The rise and rise of Poland

As the Franco–German relationship reduces in weight and intensity the relationship with Poland grows in intensity. In Chancellor Merkel's first government she was confronted with Jaroslav Kaczynski, the president of Poland, who pursued a particularly intransigent line against Germany and vastly overplayed his hand at the Berlin Conference of June 2009. His successor Donald Tusk completely reversed the policy and has pursued a concept which can best be described as a strategic European partnership with Germany. This not only seeks an active cooperation with Germany but urges the country to take up a greater leadership role in the eurozone and to welcome Poland as a key decision-maker (Handl and Paterson, 2013). This point was well made by the Polish Foreign Minister Radoslaw Sikorski: 'I fear Germany's power less than I do its inactivity' (Sikorski, 2011). A partnership with Poland would offer Germany a number of advantages. Poland would act as a counterweight to the statist France and, unlike the United Kingdom with whom it shares anti-statist views, would be keen to play a major and positive role in the EU. It has also been one of the few economic anchors throughout the various crises. Poland is also seen as a leader by other East European states and is thus a valuable ally to Germany. France used to play that role vis-à-vis the southern states; but the difference in agendas is now very great.

Relations with the USA and the UK

In both European and foreign policy Chancellor Merkel's task was to repair some of the damage inflicted by Chancellor Schröder's Iraq policy. This involved a rebuilding of relations with the USA, a task which she accomplished skilfully. Although Schröder caused huge short-term damage his policy of not supporting the USA in the Iraq crisis was an important step in the emancipation of the Federal Republic from total dependence on the USA.

In European policy the need was to lessen the hyper-dependence on France occasioned by alienation from the USA and the UK in the Iraq crisis. This proved to be easier in the UK case as Chancellor Merkel already enjoyed excellent relations with Prime Minister Blair who had felt betrayed by the Chirac/Schröder agreement on agriculture after he had supported Schröder in the immediately preceding election when Chirac had supported Edmund Stoiber. Blair, guided by the UK Embassy in Berlin, expected a clear victory for Merkel's reform agenda in the 2005 election and a subsequent alignment with the UK. Both parts of this judgement were flawed at the time; an absolute majority was always unlikely and a very close alignment with UK policy was never a possibility. Longer term it looks more accurate. There is a choice to be made between a 'social Europe' which seeks to protect the status quo and a more liberal vision which assumes that long-term employment will be better created by adjusting to globalization. In her first term Chancellor Merkel did not make that choice but in her second term she has come out unequivocally in favour of the more liberal position externally. In an important speech on 14 August 2013 she placed all the emphasis on competitiveness and adopted a position close to that of the current UK government (*Deutsche Wirtschafts Nachrichten*, 14 August 2013).

This was a theme which also appeared in her standard speech for the 2013 election campaign. Chancellor Merkel played a very constructive role at the late 2005 summit meeting in Brussels in relation to the vexed issue of the UK rebate and freed the UK from a wholly defensive position. Deleveraging the extreme dependence on France was much aided by the retirement of Chirac and the advent of Nicolas Sarkozy who was less hostile to the Anglo-Saxon powers than Chirac. The advent of President Hollande in France has moved the UK and Germany closer, as they share a policy preference for austerity which distanced them from France. Prime Minister Cameron who enjoys good personal relations with Angela Merkel (they tweet each other) hopes that she will be the key to a successful renegotiation of the UK position in the EU. Whilst Merkel is very committed to trying to keep the UK in the EU the scale of UK demands may be too much for her to accommodate.

Managing the euro crisis

Chancellor Merkel has consistently given priority to retaining power in Berlin, and this has meant a policy of extreme caution. Central to this strategy was a calculation of what the German electorate would tolerate. In his study on Angela Merkel, Stefan Kornelius (2013a: 213–68) describes how in 2011 Nikolaus Meyer-Landrut, the head of the European section in the Chancellor's Office, plotted European policy along two axes on a sheet of A4 paper: successful policies and policy failures along one axis and EU-level policies and nationally-based policies on the other. The failures that led to the euro crisis were located where control had remained at the national level, so either the EU had to be federalized or a new parallel architecture of rules binding nation states would have to be built. Judging the first to be politically unattainable (she had just completed the rescue of the Lisbon Treaty negotiations), Merkel went for the second gradualist option.

A crucial, though less often talked about, reason for caution was that the large exposure of the German banks in the Mediterranean and Ireland was potentially destabilizing. A Greek default, which might have been expected on the basis of the 'no bailout' rule and which was supposed to govern the eurozone, was seen as too damaging for German banks. A bailout of Greece was ruled out by the fact that the federal government had created a stabilization fund to bail out the German banks domestically in 2008 and repetition was judged politically unwise. Merkel was further constrained by the force of German public opinion which always had the potential in theory though rarely in practice to affect adversely the result of one of the frequent *Land* elections. She was further constrained by the prospect of an adverse ruling by the FCC which is very insistent on the fiscal sovereignty of the Bundestag.

The first policy response which came in May 2010 laid the balance of pain on Greece. In return for adopting a policy of fiscal rectitude, wage reduction and measures to improve competitiveness in the EU, the ECB, the IMF and individual member state contributors created a rescue package worth €110 billion over three years. Josef Ackermann of Deutsche Bank had been a principal adviser on the deal to Chancellor Merkel and it was as favourable to the heavily exposed German banks as it was unfavourable to Greece. The immediate effect was to deepen the crisis and to seal the fate of the Greek and later the Italian governments.

The federal government was severely shaken by the swift and comprehensive collapse of the May 2010 agreement and there has been an increase in the sums available to debtor countries; but it was the ECB under Mario Draghi – through his 2012 commitment to do whatever was necessary to preserve the euro as a stable currency and making support available to the debtor countries through 'outright monetary transactions' (the buying up of secondary bonds of debtor nations) in September 2012 – that stabilized the situation. Germany pushed forward its rule-based agenda for the eurozone which culminated in the European Fiscal Compact agreed in December 2011 by all the member states with the exception of the Czech Republic and the UK. Each member state was now to be responsible to the European level for the robustness and transparency of their public finances. There would also be a competitiveness pact entailing wage restraint, benefit cutbacks and later retirement. Considerable controversy surrounds the issue of how these objectives are to be met and whether a new treaty with attendant risks of veto and referenda is necessary.

Viewed from the 'office-seeking' perspective, Chancellor Merkel has handled the eurozone crisis brilliantly. In terms of dealing with the crisis more broadly the key issues are timing and volume of aid. On the one hand the office-seeking perspective, the veto-playing role of the German parapublic institutions, a German preoccupation with moral hazard if they acted too precipitately and let the debtor countries off the hook, and the exposure of the German banks combined to ensure that the federal government acted too slowly. On the other hand German electors would not agree to support the debtor countries unless they were convinced that the federal government was cautious with their money. The aid promised by the government has largely been in the form of guarantees. Not only is the volume not large enough but 'bigging it up' in summit communiqués has led to what David Marsh refers to as 'Merkel's law of perpetual disappointment' (Bulmer and Paterson, 2013: 1395). This effect results from the overblown nature of summit communiqués which is then further watered down by post hoc intervention by German parapublic institutions. A greater contribution was made by Mario Draghi and the ECB, though it is clear that some degree of collusion must have taken place between Draghi and the Chancellor given the size of Germany's stake.

Conclusion

Sir William Harcourt (1863) wrote that 'we are asked to go we know not whither, in order to do we know not what'. Under Chancellor Merkel Germany has emerged as unquestionably the leading state in the EU, though this position does not extend to the foreign and security policy field. Recently Charles Grant, the Director of the Centre for European Reform in a conference in Bratislava went further and talked of 'Greater Germany' (*Die Welt*, 8 July 2013), and it is easy to see what he means in terms of Germany's economic relations with Poland, the Czech Republic and Slovakia – countries which are effectively part of the German supply chain – and the close policy alignment in the eurozone crisis with Austria, Finland and Slovakia. And yet the potential challenges to Germany's new position are also obvious. Acting as a very reluctant hegemon and setting the rules in the eurozone without accepting the obligations of a hegemon (as already discussed) risks imposing too great a strain on the eurozone and provoking an implosion. Ana Palacio, the Spanish politician, described this narrow view of hegemony as 'smelling like a hegemon and dressing like an accountant' (*Financial Times*, 11 April 2011). Withdrawing from the eurozone, given its probable currency effects, would be toxic to German exports and its role as an 'extraordinary trader' (Hager, 1980) and makes this an unlikely option. The question then remains: what price would Germany pay to keep the eurozone intact? Despite occasional rhetorical flourishes about doing what it takes, no effort has been made to prepare the German public for that eventuality, and it remains unknowable at this stage. Chancellor Merkel and the federal government hope that it will not come to that and by 'muddling through' they will get over this wide patch of thin ice.

In the meantime Merkel has kept almost all her options open. Given that the SPD and the Greens scarcely diverged from her European policy, she came under very little pressure to clarify her position during the 2013 federal election. The only new commitment she announced was that Germany would not support the creation of eurobonds. Up until now the door was not totally closed on eurobonds, but it is now clear that this is a 'no fly zone'. The grand coalition has taken over the positions of the previous government with a slight change in relation to Turkey. German EU negotiations in relation to Turkey will now be handled by Foreign Minister Frank Walter Steinmeier (SPD). The SPD are in favour of Turkish membership but this is not something that Foreign Minister Steinmeier will be able to deliver

Peter Katzenstein's congruence thesis argued that German institutions which had grown up alongside the EU were strengthened by participation and that the familiarity of these institutions would encourage a continued European vocation. There has instead been a push back by German parapublic institutions (the FCC and *Bundesbank*), and the pattern is now one of rivalry between on the one hand the FCC and the ECJ and on the other hand the *Bundesbank* and the ECB, rather than congruence between 'associated sovereignty' and 'pooled competencies'. Chancellor Merkel's endorsement of the union method which relies on large member states entails abandoning 'reflexive multilateralism' and generous treatment of small member states. The new congruence is not that of a European Germany but one in which Germany's rule-setting aspirations have created a German Europe in the eurozone.

The institutions of the Federal Republic were shaped by an imperative not to repeat the hegemonial drive that had laid Europe to waste and ruined Germany in the Nazi era, but to emphasize the decentralization and limitation of power. It is not at all clear that the semi-sovereign pluralist institutions or German public opinion are fitted to play a new central role. There has been a perennial discussion in the Federal Republic as to whether a new European Ministry, either as an independent entity or as part of a reinforced Chancellor's Office, should be created to supersede the current parcelling out of responsibilities for European policy amongst a number of ministries. This division reflected Germany's multilateral policy style and close alliance with France. Coordination of European policy classically occurred late in the process; it was sometimes referred to as 'post hoc coordination'. This had the advantage that Germany could place itself at the centre of emerging constitutive bargains, though the variation in positions sometimes held by the different ministries till late on in the process could lead to confusion in other member states. This is not a situation which can be contemplated if Germany is playing a leading role. Germany's new central role entails strengthening its strategic capacity and centralizing the European policy-making machinery.

One of the oldest debates in German politics is between those who assert that foreign policy shapes the institutional structure (*Primat der Aussenpolitik*) and those like Eckart Kehr, who in his seminal Berlin dissertation (Kehr, 1927) argued for the *Primat der Innenpolitik*, a phrase that has remained identified with his name. In the Federal Republic institutions have reflected the primacy of their foreign policy setting. This is most obviously the case in relation to the role of the German armed forces in NATO, though it is also true of the European policy-making machinery. We are now moving to a phase where German domestic politics will increasingly shape these institutions just at the point when Germany is playing the central role. Interesting times lie ahead.

Chapter 10

Germany and the Euro

ANDREAS BUSCH

The introduction of the common currency – the euro – in initially 11 member states of the EU was the biggest single step of supranational integration since the beginning of that process in the 1950s. While there were big hopes about the positive economic and political consequences of that step (ranging from reduced transaction costs and increased economic growth to benefits for European identity and a weightier role in global economic politics), sceptical voices could also be heard warning of reduced flexibility for national economic policy – especially in the cases of asymmetric shocks – and the dangers of a single monetary policy that might not be appropriate for the diverging needs of member states.

More than a decade after the euro was introduced – and in particular after the crisis within the eurozone in the years since 2010 – it has become clear that the success of the project is seriously in danger if no solution to the ongoing debt crisis of several eurozone member states can be found. It is now also evident that the consequences of the introduction of the common currency have been substantial for the states concerned, but that these consequences vary a lot depending on the country and time period taken into consideration. For the case of Germany, the chapter will explain in greater detail the mix of advantageous and disadvantageous effects that the introduction of the euro has brought.

The chapter begins with a brief discussion of the rationale and history of European monetary integration and then discusses the somewhat ambiguous relationship Germany has had with the common currency from its inception through negotiations to its eventual introduction, taking both international and domestic factors into account. The positive and negative economic consequences of the euro for Germany are then outlined, arguing that the latter outweighed the former over roughly the first five years of the new currency's lifetime, while since about 2005 the benefits have clearly won the upper hand in Germany. How Germany positioned itself during the crisis in the eurozone since 2010 will be the focus of the last part of the chapter.

Monetary integration in Europe: a brief primer

Giving up a sovereign currency and opting to join a common currency is a big decision for any country to take. The reasons many European countries had for this is essential background knowledge for understanding the topics discussed in this chapter. Some key economic and historical facts and motives that played a role in the creation of the euro are then outlined.

The roots of the common currency project date back at least until the early 1970s. Under the leadership of the then Luxembourg prime minister and minister of finance, Pierre Werner, a report was produced and presented in October 1970 which recommended the introduction of a common European currency. The plan suggested three stages and a schedule for its introduction. But the breakdown of the system of fixed exchange rates – better known as the system of Bretton Woods – in 1973 initially prevented the implementation of these plans. The shift from fixed to flexible exchange rates proved a sea change in global economic policy.

Contrary to expectations, this led to massively increased volatility (rather than more stability) between national currencies, which manifested itself in wildly fluctuating exchange rates, in turn impeding trade relations. In the years after 1973, an increased desire to achieve currency stability manifested itself within Europe. The main reason for this was the close economic interdependence between the member states of the European Community (as the EU was then called). Jointly (as the EU or the EC) these states have a degree of economic openness – measured as the sum of imports and exports as a percentage of GDP – that is roughly comparable to that of other big economic areas such as the United States or Japan; taken individually (as single states), however, they show a much higher degree of economic openness. This high degree results from the very close trade relations between the member states which has been historically one of the core goals of European economic integration. Strong fluctuations in the exchange rates between the national currencies were therefore detrimental to trade relations and had a negative economic impact.

In 1979, at the initiative of German Chancellor Helmut Schmidt and French President Valéry Giscard d'Estaing, the European Monetary System (EMS) was introduced. This had the twofold aim of limiting exchange-rate volatility and exerting a disciplinary effect on economic policy by creating incentives that would let governments strive to avoid devaluation of their currency. A change in the dominant conception about the goals that economic policy was to achieve (from Keynesianism towards monetarism) added further to making disinflation a priority in the participating countries – and the result was an increase in macroeconomic discipline. The Keynesian idea of a significant and politically exploitable trade-off between unemployment and inflation (the 'Phillips curve') was given up in favour of a concept that saw low inflation as a precondition for economic growth and improved competitiveness. The EMS provided a mechanism to cope with the political and economic costs inherent in this new approach by allowing policy-makers to shift the blame for necessary adjustments to an international regime and thus avoid electoral punishment.

Even though there were occasional crises in the system (e.g. in 1992/93, see Busch, 1994) which prompted the temporary (and in some cases permanent) withdrawal of some member countries from the system, the substantial 'conversion to macroeconomic discipline' (Sandholtz, 1993) promoted by the EMS led to renewed debates about the introduction of a common European currency. These discussions eventually resulted in the calling of several intergovernmental conferences at the European level from which the concept of a common currency emerged – after laborious and highly complex negotiations which were due to the different preferences both between and within the participating nation states. Giving up their national currencies and handing over monetary policy to a supranational institution (the European Central Bank – ECB) was a massive step in terms of national sovereignty.

Initially 11 member states of the eurozone undertook this big and irreversible step towards further political and economic integration. They expected positive consequences to flow from this in two regards: first, for European citizens to increase their identification with the EU; second, for positive economic effects which would follow from increased efficiency and reduced transaction costs, such as a positive contribution to economic growth in all member states of the eurozone.

Germany and the euro

As Europe's biggest economy, the Federal Republic of Germany played a central role in these negotiations. The *Deutschmark* had established itself as the de facto anchor currency in Europe in the years after 1973 and particularly after the installation of the EMS in 1979. This was mainly due to the monetary policy pursued by the *Bundesbank* which focused above all on the goal of price stability. The German rate of inflation had consistently been one of the lowest in Europe, and the *Deutschmark* in international markets was considered a safe haven currency in terms of stability (Busch, 1994).

Why should Germany give up that dominant position, drop its successful currency and entrust its smoothly running economy to the uncertain prospect of a new currency, run at the supranational level? Looking at it from that perspective, it is quickly evident that for the Federal Republic to make that step was no easy task; and as the negotiations demonstrated, it required a number of concessions from Germany's European partners.

Conflicts about the common currency

As stated, interests regarding a common currency to replace the *Deutschmark* diverged. The federal government pushed for deeper European integration and was willing to use monetary integration as a tool to achieve that end. Foreign Minister Genscher pursued that strategy in the aftermath of the Single European Act, and he was supported by Chancellor Kohl. Both were willing to give up the *Deutschmark* if required. Kohl used the European summit in Hanover in June 1988 to establish a committee under Commission President Jacques Delors that was to study possible ways to EMU. Support for further integration on the German side also came from German industry which was keen to create more stable conditions for its export markets in Europe. In terms of economic theory, this was a position that expected European economic integration to be actively enhanced by a common currency, using it thus as an instrument in that process.

But there were also powerful opponents, or at least sceptics, with regard to the goal of further monetary integration. The most important of them was the country's powerful central bank, the Bundesbank, which was largely independent in its conduct of affairs, but afraid that it might lose its influence (and maybe even its existence) if the currency that it produced and regulated were to dissolve into a common European currency. Scepticism and often outright hostility towards the goal of monetary integration was also pronounced by many academic econo-mists in Germany. Their argument was that the potential member states for a common currency were still much too different in their economic structures for a monetary union to succeed. But a single currency, they argued, could only be successful once substantial further economic convergence had taken place.

Negotiations in the Intergovernmental Conferences that officially opened in Rome in December 1990 were highly complex and took consid-erable time (Dyson and Featherstone, 1999). For the German govern-ment, the collapse of the Berlin Wall and German unification were further motives to proceed speedily with European integration in order to assure its European partners of Germany's ongoing commitment to that process. This made it even more difficult for the *Bundesbank* to voice its opposi-tion – in spite of its independence, it could not openly contradict the federal government in international negotiations and thus chose – using its economic expertise – to put forward demands that an eventual solution would have to meet. Among them was the acceptance of price stability as the overriding goal in monetary policy as well as the safeguarding of the central bank's independence.

Support for the concept of a strongly independent central bank eventually emerged from the discussions and was enshrined in the text of the Maastricht Treaty. Its Article 105 states that the primary objective of the ECB is 'to maintain price stability. Without prejudice to the objective of price stability, the ESCB shall support the general economic policies in the Community with a view to contributing to the achievement of the objectives of the Community as laid down in Article 2.' And Article 107 declared that 'neither the ECB, nor a national central bank, nor any member of their decision-making bodies shall seek or take instructions from Community institutions or bodies, from any government of a Member State or from any other body'. The concrete regulations concerning the appointment and dismissal regulations for members of the Governing Council of the ECB were designed to provide the underpinnings for that independence by giving them long terms in office (eight years) but which were not renewable so as to avoid behaviour designed to win a second term.

These rules were even harsher in terms of securing council members' independence than those of the *Bundesbank* had been (where terms could be renewed). But they were undoubtedly inspired by the construction of the German central bank which served as a blueprint for much of the institutional set-up, not least because a combination of two levels (that of the central institution plus that of the constituent countries' central banks) was necessary, as in the German federal system. Situating the new ECB (and its precursor, the European Monetary Institute) in Frankfurt was a move intended to reassure Germans that nothing really would change. To them the message was that the new ECB was really the *Bundesbank*, but transplanted onto the European level and taking care officially of tasks that it had previously fulfilled unofficially, namely running Europe's monetary policy. Nothing had changed, so there was nothing to fear – the euro really was the Deutschmark in disguise.

But the planned new currency was not very popular in Germany. Opinion polls showed that – compared to other EU countries – Germans were far more sceptical of replacing their existing national currency with a new European one (see Figure 10.1), a position that changed little as the date of the planned introduction drew nearer. While not quite on the level of opposition found among the British population, Germans found little support for their scepticism among the established political parties.

Figure 10.1 *Support for the single currency in Germany and the EU*

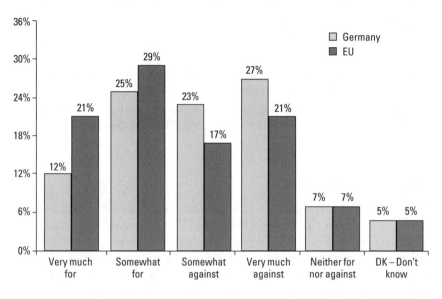

Source: European Commission (1998).

The government of Chancellor Kohl supported currency union for reasons of both economic and foreign policy – it was keen to send a clear signal of Germany's future commitment to European integration after German unification. Traditionally in favour of integration, all parties in the *Bundestag* supported the goal of a single currency. But at the level of the *Länder*, some politicians experimented with (sometimes coded) positions opposing currency union; they had, however, little electoral success. In 1992, the leader of the Baden-Württemberg SPD, Dieter Spöri, for example argued that the introduction of the common currency was too early and would endanger German jobs, because only a few countries would qualify while the others would devalue. In 1998, the then SPD Chancellor Candidate Gerhard Schröder called the euro an 'ailing preterm delivery' (*'kränkelnde Frühgeburt'*). And in 1994, former FDP politician Manfred Brunner tried to focus opposition to the new currency by founding a party called the Federation of Free Citizens (*Bund freier Bürger*), which, however, only polled 1.1 per cent at the European Parliament election and 0.2 per cent at the 1998 *Bundestag* election. Other small right-wing populist parties such as Initiative Pro D-Mark had a similar fate. The scepticism present in opinion polls, to sum it up, did not translate into political mobilization, and since the Federal Constitutional Court also did not stop the project in its 1993 ruling on the Maastricht Treaty, the new currency became a fact in 1999.

The German experience with the euro since 1999

What were the consequences for Germany of dropping its own successful currency, the *Deutschmark*, and introducing the new supranational euro? This question is of central importance, yet there is no simple answer to it. Rather, as will become evident in the following, the introduction of the new currency has had a variety of effects on the German economy. In addition, the overall effect has varied over time: while initially the disadvantages were dominant, in the years since 2005 the positive effects have prevailed.

Negative consequences

Support for the introduction of the euro had been almost uniform among political forces in the Federal Republic. The expected positive consequences, however, initially did not materialize. In the years between 1999 (when the euro was introduced as virtual money, with notes and coins only following in 2002) and 2005, Germany's economy was characterized by persistent and high unemployment and a performance, in terms of economic growth, that was consistently below that of the other eurozone countries – often more than 1 percentage point (see Table 10.1).

The bad economic performance profile that characterized Germany early in the first decade of the century was to some extent caused by disadvantageous effects that the introduction of the common currency had. These disadvantages were primarily indirect and often worked through effects on other member states of the eurozone. Above all two channels played a role: the loss of relative advantages that Germany had enjoyed in the level of interest rates; and a disadvantage due to the real interest rate effect under a single monetary policy. Let us consider both in turn.

Germany, as the European country with the lowest rate of inflation and hence the most stable exchange rate, had always enjoyed a particularly low level of interest rates compared with that of other European countries. This was an advantage since German firms could obtain money in financial markets at a cheaper rate. That advantage, however, began to dwindle during the 1990s in line with rising expectations about the introduction of the common currency. The (first expected, then realized) creation of the currency union plus the constitution of the ECB focusing on price stability meant that other states would be able to import the credibility of monetary policy regarding future low inflation that had so far only been enjoyed by Germany. This meant that interest rates for government bonds of EMU member states began to close in on those issued by Germany as the interest rate advantage of the German capital market began to disappear (see Figure 10.2).

Table 10.1 *Annual economic growth rates, 1999–2013 (%)*

	1999	2000	2001	2002	2003	2004	2005	2006	2007	2008	2009	2010	2011	2012	2013
Eurozone without Germany	4.2	4.6	2.1	1.7	1.2	2.8	2.7	3.7	4.0	0.9	−4.3	1.4	1.2	−0.7	−0.8
Germany	2.0	3.2	1.2	0.0	−0.2	1.2	0.7	3.7	3.3	1.1	−5.1	4.2	3.0	0.7	0.4

Source: Author's calculations; Eurostat database (© European Union 1995–2014).

Figure 10.2 *Comparison of interest rates on ten-year government bonds, 1993–2012*

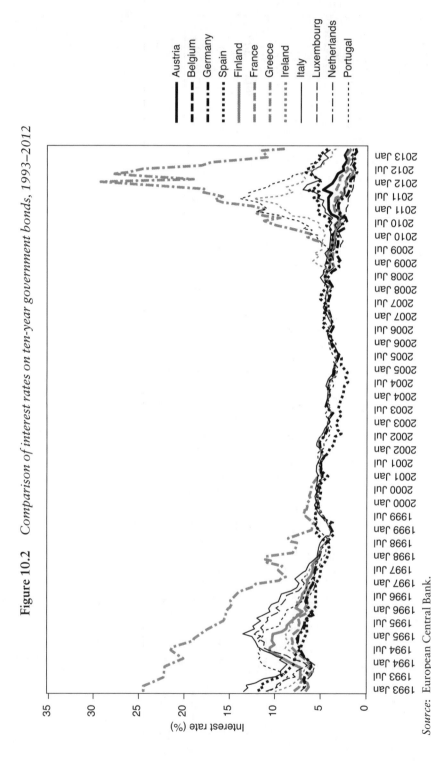

Source: European Central Bank.

Lower interest rates created an expansionary effect that was the stronger, the bigger the initial difference over the German level of interest rates had been. All countries enjoyed that effect – except the Federal Republic – and this had to have a negative effect on comparative economic growth; so German growth rates started to lag behind those of most other EMU countries.

A further effect working in a similar direction resulted from the fact that monetary policy in a currency area can only set a single level of interest; yet inflation rates between member states of the eurozone may differ considerably in spite of all attempts to achieve convergence. In economic analysis, this is acknowledged in discussions about 'optimum currency areas'. National rates of inflation can vary even though all EMU countries have the same currency. But the ECB cannot take specific national circumstances into consideration: its task is to steer the best monetary policy course for the whole of the eurozone. The more national rates of inflation differ, the more likely it is that ECB policy will be less than optimal for some countries, because it is either too expansionary or too restrictive for them. But the central bank can only determine the nominal interest rate; the effective real rate of interest is dependent on the rate of inflation in a given country, which – as we have seen above – may vary.

Particularly at the beginning of the common currency, rates of inflation differed considerably across countries in the eurozone, and this resulted in substantial differences in real interest rates. Countries enjoying already relatively robust rates of economic growth usually displayed a higher rate of inflation than Germany which traditionally enjoyed a culture of price stability (Busch, 1995). The result was somewhat paradoxical: real interest rates were *lower* in those countries of the eurozone which had *higher* rates of inflation (and were thus actually in need of a more restrictive monetary policy); and they were relatively *higher* in countries enjoying a *lower* rate of inflation – which needed a more expansionary monetary policy to stimulate their weak economic growth performance (as in Germany). Table 10.2 illustrates this effect for the year 2000 for selected

Table 10.2   *Real interest rates and inflation rates in comparison, 2000 (%)*

	Germany	*France*	*Ireland*	*Spain*
Rate of inflation	1.4	1.8	5.3	3.5
Real interest rate	1.35	0.95	–2.55	–0.75

Sources: Author's calculations; IMF *World Economic Outlook* database.

countries. It demonstrates that Germany, with lagging growth, had the highest real rate of interest, while rapidly expanding Ireland and Spain (with their high rates of inflation) even enjoyed negative real interest rates.

Positive consequences

The dismal economic growth performance, as well as consistently rising rates of unemployment, over a number of years led to soul-searching and long debates in Germany about an insufficient economic performance profile and possible ways out of the performance trap. A flood of publications appeared bemoaning the apparently inevitable 'decline' of Germany, and it probably contributed as much to the pervasive feeling of hopelessness as did the negative performance indicators themselves. Germans felt miserable about the 'backlog of reforms', about an allegedly excessive wage level and the lack of competitiveness in global markets (Sinn, 2003).

It is hard to see how the situation back then – which some likened to a collective national depression – could manifest the motivation to try to change things. Yet the SPD–Green government under Chancellor Schröder, after it had unexpectedly won the Bundestag election of 2002, initiated substantial political reforms in the areas of labour market policy and social security systems. This 'Agenda 2010' more or less confirmed that the government had failed in its initial strategy to form an 'Alliance for Jobs, Innovation, and Justice' – the cooperation of the government with trade unions and employers – to combat unemployment and encourage growth, and that it now had to pursue an alternative strategy with a focus on increasing flexibility in the labour markets (Busch, 2009).

These reforms were (and remain) politically highly contentious, but – through interaction with Germany's traditional tendency towards price stability, achieved through the institutional characteristics of the system of collective bargaining which help contain inflation by keeping wage rises moderate under conditions of low economic growth – they contributed to an improvement of economic development and a recurrence of economic growth. From about 2005 onwards, the effects that the common European currency had on the German economy began to shift, and the euro started to turn into an economic advantage for Germany. Germany had managed – contrary to its more quickly growing Eurozone partners – to keep unit labour costs largely stable; many of the other countries, however, had seen wages rise quickly during their economic upswing, and far surpass increases in productivity. Unit labour costs had risen steeply as a consequence, as can be seen in Figure 10.3.

Differences in unit labour cost development mean differences in economic competitiveness, and the German economy thus began to profit

Figure 10.3 *Unit labour costs in comparison, 1999–2013*

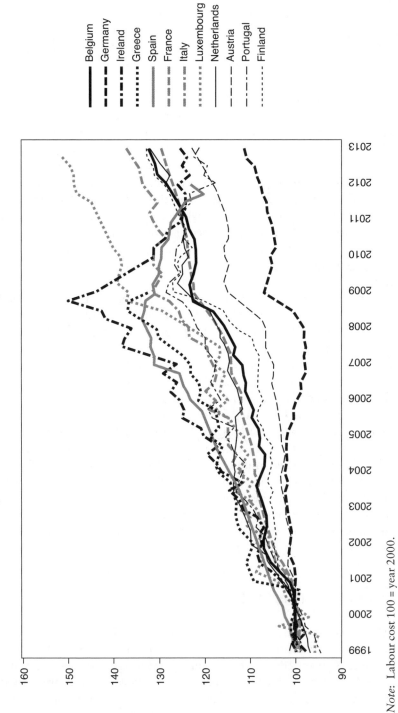

Note: Labour cost 100 = year 2000.

Source: Eurostat.

from its improvement in competitiveness. This first resulted in rising exports, but from the middle of the decade onwards also in substantially increasing rates of growth of GDP.

The common currency which had produced on balance more negative effects for Germany in the early years now turned into a benefit for the country's economy. This worked above all through two mechanisms. First, the common currency denied other eurozone countries the option of compensating for their shrunken competitiveness by devaluing their currency (a devaluation reduces the price of domestic goods in foreign currency and thus increases sales). In the past, devaluation had often been a solution that in particular had been pursued by Southern European countries to cope with problems of a mismatch between wage development and productivity development. But this option was no longer available – correcting a negative competitive development was now only possible through either cutting wages or substantially increasing productivity. The comparative advantages Germany enjoyed in the area of unit labour costs stability could no longer be neutralized through unilateral action.

The second way in which the common currency in recent years has turned out to be a clear advantage for the Federal Republic, and thus a clear plus over the *Deutschmark*, has to do with uncertainty. In the past, investors seeking safety for their money tended to flee into the currency perceived as the most stable one in Europe, namely the *Deutschmark*. In the early 1990s, for example, the *Deutschmark* with its comparatively high stability had been chosen as a 'safe haven' by international investors seeking to preserve the value of their capital. That inflow of capital then resulted in an increasing exchange rate of the *Deutschmark* which in turn made German goods more expensive abroad, leading to reduced sales and resulting in declining economic growth and loss of employment. With the creation of the euro (and the demise of the *Deutschmark*), that option was no longer available. In the crisis that began in 2007, Germany therefore enjoyed (*ceteris paribus*) higher growth and lower unemployment than would have been the case without the common currency – a clear advantage.

The euro crisis after 2010

Partly as a consequence of the financial markets crisis of 2007/08 and the ensuing 'great recession', the eurozone was plunged into grave problems in the years after 2010. At the time of writing, this crisis is not yet resolved, and no definitive assessment is therefore possible. In this section, however, the origins and manifestations of the crisis as well as the reactions to it (with a special emphasis on the German position) will be described and analysed.

On the tenth anniversary of the euro's introduction, in early 2009, there had been a lot of praise regarding the currency's performance (e.g. European Commission, 2008b; Verdun, 2010). The new currency was well established, it had held its value against the US dollar, and inflation performance had been excellent. The economic downturn that had followed the financial markets crisis had been weathered well, and the fact that the eurozone was no 'optimal currency area' in economic terms – of which much had been made by the sceptics in the 1990s – had seemed to matter little.

But not long after, a crisis seemed to throw the success of the whole project into doubt. In November 2009, the new Greek government under Prime Minister Papandreou had revised the deficit statistics of their predecessors and discovered that the deficit was expected to be 12.7 per cent in 2009, more than double the previous estimate (Zahariadis, 2013). Since the country's national debt was already substantial (around 110 per cent of GDP), a crisis of confidence ensued as investors doubted whether the country would be able to service and pay back its debts and feared that the situation had become unsustainable. This in turn led to a massive rise in borrowing costs in international bond markets for the Greek government – which further tightened the situation for a country in acute need of rolling over its debt. Quickly the interest rates required were double those for Germany, and rising further. Over the next five years, Greece would need US$240 billion to pay for interest and principal (Marsh, 2011: 248).

As Greece faced a default on its debts, its partners were put into a difficult situation. The Maastricht Treaty which established EMU contained an explicit 'no bailout' clause which ruled out direct financial help for the budget of any member state in the monetary union. Under the leadership of Chancellor Merkel and President Sarkozy, Greece's European partners therefore initially expressed political support, but insisted that the country had to reduce its deficit to become creditworthy again. When the markets displayed serious signs of uncertainty in early May 2010, however, EU finance ministers agreed on a rescue package of up to €80 billion in loans in a crisis meeting – after the Greek parliament, amid heavy protests and strikes, had passed a package of cuts amounting to 11 per cent of GDP over four years. Had there not been this reaction, it was feared that other economically and fiscally weak eurozone countries (like Portugal, Ireland and perhaps even Spain and Italy) might come under speculative attack in the financial markets; furthermore, debates about Greece eventually leaving the eurozone had prompted doubts about the currency union's future viability that could have negative consequences for all member states.

Feverish activity on the financial markets ensued in spite of these decisions. Its most visible consequence was the reversal of a trend that had characterized the process towards monetary union from the mid-1990s onwards, namely the convergence of interest rates. The 'spreads' (differences in interest rates) that markets demanded to hold government debt of different EMU member states were now rising for the first time in 15 years, and they did so most steeply for the countries hit hardest by the crisis, such as Greece, Portugal and Ireland (see Figure 10.2). Only a week after the decision about the aid package for Greece, over a hectic weekend, EU leaders agreed to combine fiscal and monetary policy measures on an unprecedented scale to stabilize the situation. Afraid that a Greek insolvency could cause turmoil similar to that of Lehman Brothers in 2008, the EU put forward €750 billion in loan guarantees while the ECB announced a bond buying programme of both government and private assets in an attempt to provide markets with liquidity. The European Financial Stability Facility (EFSF), as it came to be known, was an attempt to defuse the crisis and was a considerable step towards acknowledging a common responsibility for the fate of the common currency (Ludlow, 2010).

EMU member states were now paying the price for the decision not to complement monetary union with sufficiently stable rules for fiscal convergence or integration. The Stability and Growth Pact had proved toothless – between 1999 and 2009, the frequent breaches of the deficit criterion by member states such as Greece and Italy, but also France, Germany and Portugal, had had no serious consequences. The attempt, however, to make those rules more restrictive in an acute crisis amounted to an attempt to rebuild a ship in the open sea.

The principle of the EFSF deal (loan guarantees only in exchange for structural reforms; tighter formal rules for EU and/or EMU member states) became the role model for several rounds of crisis negotiations that ensued over the following months and years. The temporary EFSF was replaced by the permanent European Stability Mechanism (ESM) in 2011; the 'Pact for the euro' contained measures to increase member states' competitiveness; and the 'European Fiscal Compact' drastically tightened the fiscal rules for national budgets (including a mandatory embedding of these rules in national statutory or constitutional law), introduced automatic sanctions, and empowered the Commission to set targets for individual countries.

Economic conditions in many countries were dire: unemployment had risen steeply, growth was absent or negative, and the macroeconomic imbalances within the eurozone that had built up over the previous decade now lay bare. With all eyes set on the eurozone as a whole, nobody had cared much about trade imbalances between member states. But it was now clear that they were significant: many countries north of the Alps had persistent substantial current account surpluses, while many of those south of the Alps had equally persistent deficits. An expansion of domestic demand, fuelled by capital inflows (and the credit boom during the first decade of the common currency), had considerably damaged the Southern countries' competitiveness; and when the capital flows stopped after the onset of the financial markets crisis, much economic activity stopped (Gros, 2012).

The eurozone was thus split into two groups – the haves and the have-nots – turning the economic crisis into a political balancing act with substantial consequences for the EU. As the measures demanded by the IMF and the EU (in return for loan guarantees and emergency liquidity for banks from the ECB) began to bite, controversy and political protest flared up across Europe. Protesters in Greece, Portugal and Spain complained about the austerity imposed by a dominating North, while citizens in countries like Germany, the Netherlands and Finland feared for their money and saw Southerners as ungrateful recipients of their solidarity. It became clear that the technocratic approach to solving the crisis (through tightened rules, increased consultation, 'six-pack' legislation, the introduction of a 'macroeconomic imbalance procedure', visitations by the 'troika', etc.) did not easily coexist with the dynamics of electoral contest in the crisis countries, where parties were tempted to increase their electoral chances by promising to renegotiate the results of ongoing consultations, thus casting doubts on the validity of the results even before they were achieved. Also, as national governments were the ones to sign the loan guarantees, they became the dominant players in the handling of the crisis, sidelining EU institutions like the Commission.

Analysing the German response

As the biggest EU economy, Germany was a crucial player in the discussions about the handling and resolution of the crisis. No longer the 'sick man of Europe' it had been a decade earlier – since 2006, German economic growth routinely met or surpassed that of the eurozone as a whole, see Table 10.1 – the Federal Republic eventually guaranteed more than €200 billion which (at the time of writing) have been used as loans to Greece, Ireland and Portugal.

But Chancellor Merkel's handling of the crisis has also received a lot of criticism, both abroad (where likenesses of her were adorned with swastikas and Hitler moustaches, indicating a continuity between Nazi occupation and German financial dominance today) and at home (where considerable disquiet and the emergence of an anti-Euro party were the most visible signs of protest). In this section we will therefore analyse the reasons for the German government's behaviour in the euro crisis.

The German perspective on the causes of the crisis, most notably in Greece, was influenced by its own position. Germany had handled the 'great recession' well and it was clear from the beginning that the country would have to play a major role in the resolution of the crisis. Given the obvious problems of mismanagement, corruption and fiscal profligacy in Greece (Zahariadis, 2013), German political discourse quickly settled on excessive spending as the root cause. When other countries (like Ireland and Spain) also got into trouble, the fact that they did so for quite different reasons (the state bailout of an oversized banking sector in the case of Ireland, and the collapse of an excessive construction sector in the case of Spain) was conveniently ignored by the German political class. A one-size-fits-all solution was advocated, namely a reduction in public spending and a cutting of deficits. The fact that in German, the words for 'debt' and 'guilt' are the same (*Schuld*) has often been remarked upon, because it gave the discussions moral overtones. Under the German concept, the burden of adjustment would mainly fall on the deficit countries, and differences between them ignored.

Focusing on cutting deficits fitted well with two other important facts, namely the dominance of ordoliberal economic thinking and the interpretation of Germany's own recent experiences. Contrary to many other Western countries, Keynesian economic thinking – with its emphasis on the short term and an active role for state-sponsored reflation during a recession – had never been really influential in Germany except for a brief period between the mid-1960s and the mid-1970s (Allen, 1989). Instead, the emphasis was on the medium to long term and the significance of the right incentives for economic behaviour to be set by well-ordered institutions (Nicholls, 2000). For most Germans, the period of painful reforms in the labour market and the social security system that the country had undergone in the early years of the new century (Agenda 2010) were proof of the correctness of these assumptions. If Germans had managed to extricate themselves from years of economic depression through painful reforms (which included low rises in real wages and a stagnation in living standards for a decade), surely others could follow in the same way. Chancellor Merkel summarized this approach before the Bundestag in her declaration of government on 19 May 2010 after the EFSF decision:

> Too many uncompetitive members of the eurozone have lived beyond their means and have thus found the way into the debt trap. This is the real cause of the problem. Therefore we have to tackle the root of the problem. At my suggestion, on 7 May 2010 the heads of states and

governments have committed themselves to speed up within the stability pact the consolidation of their respective budgets. (Merkel, 2010)

This approach met heavy criticism from many sides. Only a week later, on 26 May 2010, the *New York Times*, in an editorial entitled 'Germany vs Europe', accused the German government of responding irresponsibly to the economic malaise:

> Instead of committing to more spending, Germany is now preparing a multiyear program of deep spending cuts. Given its troubled history, we can understand its fear of deficit spending and inflation. But right now more German austerity will likely cripple Europe's nascent recovery and Germany's own prosperity.

Criticism was also put forward by political scientists arguing that the rescue efforts for the euro were ill-suited to correct the economic imbalances within EMU while threatening to cause a crisis of democratic legitimacy (Scharpf, 2011). And economists have pointed out that – both in the UK and the eurozone – in retrospect one has to say that 'austerity has failed' (Wolf, 2013). At least for the eurozone, the argument goes, this need not have happened, as Germany enjoyed windfall profits from the crisis (in the shape of very low interest rates payable on German public debt) that the country could have shared with those under pressure (ibid.).

To understand why Chancellor Merkel chose such a demanding position one has to take into account the domestic restrictions she faced to find support for any rescue packages she would commit to in return for structural adjustment ('solidity for solidarity', as it was put). Given the nature of Germany's 'semi-sovereign state' (Green and Paterson, 2005b), a number of countervailing forces had to be taken into account:

- The *Bundesbank* had immediately formally registered its opposition to the bond buying programme when the ECB announced it as part of the EFSF. This had no practical consequences, since the *Bundesbank* operates as part of the ECB and is bound by its decisions; but it did register in German public discourse. The Bundesbank also continued to support (through speeches of their board members and publications) the position that structural reforms in the weaker countries were the best way to attain a macroeconomic rebalancing. In February 2011, *Bundesbank* President Axel Weber announced his resignation, to be followed in September by ECB chief economist and board member Jürgen Stark. Even if it was not formally stated, it was clear that both men saw the ECB decision as a watershed that amounted to state funding through monetary policy, which had been ruled out in the Maastricht Treaty. While both through their with-drawal further weakened the orthodox position in the central bank's decision-making bodies, they encouraged dissenters in the Bundestag to voice their criticisms openly. Weber's successor, Jens Weidmann, who had been Merkel's chief economic adviser, seamlessly continued the Bundesbank's traditional position by arguing (in a speech at Chatham House on 28 March 2012) that 'the risks of consolidation are consequently being exaggerated' (Weidmann, 2012).

- In Chancellor Merkel's coalition questions emerged about the money Germany (as the biggest contributor) would have to put forward. In December 2011, a ballot of FDP members which had been initiated by opponents of the European rescue programmes was only very narrowly defeated by the leadership. While an overall majority in parliament was never in question due to the Social Democrats' and the Greens' support for the measures – in line with their traditionally pro-European position – the coalition repeatedly had to make substantial efforts to ensure a parliamentary majority, which was politically important for the chancellor.

- Outside parliament there were attempts to harness the clear public discontent with the measures taken and direct it into support for a new political party. In February 2013, *Alternative für Deutschland* (AfD) was formed with the core political programme of an 'orderly dissolution of the euro currency area'. Among the initiators were a number of academic economists, though no prominent dissenters from existing parties. Organizing the new party as well as agreeing on the remainder of the party's political programme proved difficult. At the general election on 22 September, the party at 4.7 per cent of the vote missed the 5 per cent hurdle required for entry to the *Bundestag*, but only narrowly.

- A last obstacle that influenced the chancellor's strategy in the euro crisis was fear of the Federal Constitutional Court. EMU and all steps towards further European integration had been challenged before the Karlsruhe court, and any measures for crisis resolution that would include German public money were sure to end up there as well. Demands for temporary orders (by a strange coalition of dissenting CSU MP Gauweiler, the association for 'More Democracy' and the Left Party) to stop the entering into force of the ESM and the Fiscal Pact were denied by the Court in July 2012. On 7 February 2014, the Court – while making clear its doubts whether the ECB had remained within its mandate in its September 2012 decision to enter into 'outright monetary transactions' of a potentially unlimited volume – decided to refer the case to the European Court of Justice for a prelim-inary ruling. This is a first, and it will delay the eventual decision for some time. If the FCC were to declare parts of the ESM as unconstitutional, this could throw a major spanner into the rescue works of EMU.

The above can also explain why Chancellor Merkel comprehensively ruled out eurobonds at an early stage, although many different variations of such bonds can be imagined (with varying degrees of common debt guarantee between EMU member states) along with several clearly positive consequences that the establishment of a large and deep common market in European government bonds would bring. As the CDU put it in its 2013 general election manifesto, the introduction of eurobonds 'would mean introducing a European debt union in which German tax payers would have to assume almost unlimited guarantees for the debts of other countries. That we oppose' (CDU/CSU, 2013: 9). This, the document goes on, would forfeit the 'quid pro quo' principle and would undermine incentives for EMU member states to undertake 'uncomfortable reform efforts'. The FDP, too, was opposed to communalizing liabilities for past debts and emphasized the importance of further structural reforms. The SPD, however, indicated in its programme that, after agreement on the fiscal pact and other European-level control mechanisms pushing towards national budgetary discipline had been reached, 'the issue of common liability must no longer be taboo' (SPD, 2013: 105). It also pointed out that a European-level debt resolution fund of all EMU member states 'could be an instrument against financial speculation'. The Greens were even more open, demanding a European Pact for Debt Redemption and the transformation of the ESM into a European Monetary Fund as well as the introduction of eurobonds in the future, while also pointing out the necessity of budgetary consolidation (Bündnis 90/Die Grünen, 2013: 57).

To conclude the assessment of Germany's role in the euro crisis so far, one has to say that the picture looks more differentiated than the widespread perception of Angela Merkel as the dominant player would have it. Germany at an early stage (in spring 2010) managed to push the European-level crisis response in its preferred direction, insisting on clear conditions and structural reforms in exchange for limited financial help. Later measures, like the Pact for the Euro, the ESM and the Fiscal Pact, built on that decision and followed substantially on the path initially chosen. But the unquestioned dominance of Germany in this respect needs two qualifications. First, agreeing to intervene 'if the financial stability of the euro area as a whole was at stake was in and of itself a major break with both the letter and the spirit of the Treaty' (Ludlow, 2010: 49) – so that policy constituted a U-turn and certainly was not Germany's first preference, which hence questions its dominance. Second, German domination was limited to the fiscal policy dimension of the crisis response – on the monetary policy dimension several key decisions (such as those to engage in government bond purchases) went against German preferences. Of course one can speculate as to what extent the orthodox position taken by the once almighty *Bundesbank* really coincided with the preferences of Chancellor Merkel – or whether this was part of a game of playing to the gallery. Surely Axel Weber's withdrawal was ultimately a fortunate move – it is as difficult to imagine Germany dropping support for him as ECB president as it is certain that debates with him at the central bank's helm would have made decisions and a functioning division of labour between fiscal and monetary policy far more difficult than was the case under Mario Draghi.

Conclusion

The introduction of the euro has been a supremely important step in the history of all EMU member states, and for none more so than Germany. Having reflexively opted for pro-European and multilateral policy options in the past, Germany was among the political forces pushing for a common currency in the 1980s. Even if there were clearly divergent preferences within the country and little excitement in its population to give up the treasured *Deutschmark* (the symbol of the country's re-emergence and economic success in the decades after the Second World War), economic and political interests ultimately weighed in favour of adopting a common currency. All attempts to mobilize political support against this had failed in the 1990s.

Germany had managed to extract substantial concessions in the design of the EMU and especially its institutions in exchange for its willingness to give up the *Deutschmark*. The currency established itself well in global markets, and was welcomed by many as a challenger to the US dollar. Even the biggest crisis for economic policy since the 1930s, the financial markets crisis of 2007–09 that turned into a global great recession, was handled well by the eurozone, as assessments on the occasion of the currency's first decade declared (European Commission, 2008b). But already in these assessments there were premonitions that the divergence of the fiscal stance among member countries would need to be corrected. It then became very evident with the crisis in the eurozone that developed after 2009 that the institutional mechanisms governing EMU had substantial shortcomings and had to be fundamentally reformed.

As the economically dominant country, Germany had to play a key role in the resolution of this crisis. In an echo of past reflexive multilateralism, German politicians across the spectrum emphasized that the answer to the crisis had to lie in more – not less – integration, in 'more Europe' (as

Finance Minister Schäuble put it in an article in *Welt am Sonntag* on 2 October 2011). If sometimes through gritted teeth, the political class thus reacted with continuity and support for past decisions. Given the 'sunk costs' of European integration this is not really surprising. But Germany, having been aptly described as a 'reluctant hegemon' (Paterson, 2011), could not provide a resolution and was criticized for that. At the same time, the country was also criticized for dominating the austerity policies that were (as some saw it) causing economic depression in Greece and elsewhere. While the broader context for Germany's European policy is described in Chapter 9, in the perspective covered here the absence of European-level tools at the beginning of the crisis and the specific domestic obstacles faced by Chancellor Merkel have been emphasized to explain developments.

Within Germany, insecurity about the future of the euro and disenchantment with the common currency was evident during the crisis. Opinion polls repeatedly demonstrated this: in September 2011, for example, according to Politbarometer (*Forschungsgruppe Wahlen*, 2011) only 19 per cent supported the extension of the German contribution to the EFFS from €123 billion to €211 billion, while 75 per cent opposed it – across all parties. And only 46 per cent at that point thought that overall the euro was advantageous for Germany, while 50 per cent thought the single currency overall disadvantageous. The higher the educational achievement of individuals, however, the higher the perception of advantage: among those with *Abitur* and university education, euro supporters continued to have a clear majority. Yet all this doubt had little political effect. Although 2013 saw a general election campaign, the euro did not feature prominently in it. The parties in the *Bundestag* had overwhelmingly supported the rescue strategy of the chancellor and the EU; but none of them saw a debate about it as an election winner, and so none had much of an interest in pushing it. The AfD's failure to make it into the *Bundestag* proved that strategy right for the established parties.

As this volume goes to press, the new grand coalition that is the result of the general election of 2013 is still largely untested. Although the CDU/CSU won decisively and Chancellor Merkel is in her third term in office, this means that a policy shift to the left of the previous government will take place – one of the paradoxes of an election outcome which saw the demise of the FDP after almost 65 years in the Bundestag. In terms of future policy on the euro, this opens up some room for manoeuvre, as both potential coalition partners are more open about innovations regarding fiscal policy and eurobonds, as described above. The CDU, in which Angela Merkel is presently at the apogee of her power, would doubtlessly stomach another of her policy U-turns were she to decide that was necessary. However, this is unlikely to affect central areas of her previous policy stance. But compromises regarding the speed of budget consolidation, the amount of financial support put forward or even a cautious version of common bond issues are more likely now that she no longer has a coalition partner who is threatened by eurosceptic leanings of its membership and electorate (as the FDP was). On banking union (at least as far as a common resolution mechanism is concerned) a softening of the present German stance seems possible, especially since the legal arguments put forward so far against a common resolution fund are weak.

Today, it is difficult to assess whether EMU member states will succeed in fixing the initial faults that have bedevilled the eurozone in recent years, or whether 'a heinous inversion of good but poorly implemented intentions' (Marsh, 2011: 265) will lead EMU to fail. If it were to, the outcome would certainly be regarded as catastrophic by most German policy-makers. They will therefore likely do their utmost to avoid it.

Chapter 11

Foreign and Security Policy

ALISTER MISKIMMON

The last ten years have witnessed significant changes in the international system with the rise of new powers, the impact in Iraq and Afghanistan of the response to the 9/11 terrorist attacks on the USA, the so-called 'Arab Spring', and gradual changes in how defence is organized in Europe and beyond. Yet Germany has displayed a remarkable degree of continuity in foreign and security policy in response to new international pressures. The beginning of Gerhard Schröder's time as chancellor was marked by Germany's involvement in Operation Allied Force (OAF) in 1999 and German leadership in international efforts to bring an end to the Kosovo crisis (Miskimmon, 2009b). Germany's involvement in OAF did not set a trend for its greater involvement in military crisis management. As Schröder's time in office progressed he became more cautious in foreign policy and openly opposed George W. Bush's decision to invade Iraq, making it part of his re-election campaign in 2002. German foreign policy is now confronted with an array of challenges which have demanded a response from the country's foreign policy-makers. Whereas the immediate post-Cold War period was dominated by the need to stabilize Europe, the challenges facing contemporary German foreign and security policy are increasingly more global in character. The country's military involvement in Afghanistan has been a source of contention both internally and with its NATO allies. The Arab Spring and Germany's decision to reject involvement in the military operation to enforce a no-fly zone in Libya in 2011 highlighted differences with its traditional allies, France, the UK and the USA. Changes in the international system with the rise of new powers such as China, India and Brazil have altered the international context in which German foreign policy operates. Each of these developments must also be understood within the pressures of the legacy of the global financial crisis and the pressures Germany faces within the eurozone.

Germany in the EU and NATO

Berlin's foreign and security policy has been characterized by continued caution in developing its capabilities in military crisis management despite a conditional acceptance of the need for a greater involvement in the EU, NATO and UN operations. However, Germany's decision to abstain on UN Security Council Resolution 1973 on enforcing the no-fly zone over Libya demonstrated that German strategic culture remains resistant to change. The innovations contained within the EU's Lisbon Treaty of 2009 have not resulted in a reinvigoration of EU foreign and security policy and evidence suggests that Germany's commitment to building a Common Foreign and Security Policy (CFSP) has been luke-warm. Increasingly multilateral commitments are viewed as raising many challenges for German policy-makers as well as serving as a means to address the problems Germany and its allies face. Germany has played an often ambivalent role within the CFSP and NATO, though at times it has been very proactive in attempting to forge closer cooperation within the former and attempting to demonstrate its strong credentials as a leading player in the latter. However, as recent experience with Libya has demonstrated, Germany has been challenged by the development of new EU and NATO capabilities, and been reluctant for its contribution to military crisis management to outstrip what it is comfortable with domestically.

Despite this, the question of which way Germany would turn after unification has largely been answered (Garton Ash, 1994; Rummel, 1996). Germany has eschewed a 'special path' by recommitting itself to the institutions it relied on during the Cold War to achieve unification. Yet, membership of the EU and NATO has thrown up significant challenges for German foreign and security policy, which has witnessed a gradually growing self-assertion of the country's interests and preferences. Now that many of the challenges of unification have been addressed, questions about the nature of German influence within the EU have become more visible as the challenges of European integration have become more profound. Germany's reputation for being a leading player in the EU and the development of the CFSP has come into question, with a growing preference for small group cooperation and intergovernmental solutions to policy challenges becoming more prevalent (Hellmann et al., 2005). Nevertheless, Germany's size and economic clout, alongside its export-driven economy, means that it has a keen interest in a stable international environment, which lies at the heart of its national and multinational diplomacy.

The CFSP, which emerged in the Maastricht Treaty, has been a means for both Germany and the EU to transition from focusing on stabilizing Europe through NATO after the Cold War to a more global EU engagement. The CFSP has been an important forum for the emergence of German foreign policy following unification within a multilateral framework which is acceptable to its European partners. For Germany, the regional security situation is perhaps more settled than it has been for some time. Whilst its power in the EU is once more a focus of attention due to the eurozone crisis, within the limited scope of the CFSP Germany has played an increasingly leading role in operationalizing the Common Security and Defence Policy and become more adept at shaping its development. Former German Foreign Minister Guido Westerwelle's proposal in 2012 for the creation of a European army suggested a continued German preference for closer European cooperation, but this remains a far-off aspiration, rather than a reality (Future of Europe Group, 2012). In terms of status, in an area of high diplomacy such as the Iran nuclear issue, Germany has been a key player in the EU-3, playing a major role in a matter of great international importance, alongside the nuclear powers of France and the UK.

Despite this, Germany's role within the CFSP and NATO has its limitations. The country cannot currently commit to building the CFSP due to increasing domestic fiscal pressures at home and in the EU as witnessed in the eurozone crisis. Greater efforts to develop common capabilities are not at this stage a viable option. There is a great reluctance to cede further sovereignty in security and defence due to reservations which remain in German defence policy. Westerwelle's call for a European army were not received warmly by Angela Merkel. In the run-up to the 2013 German federal elections, when Angela Merkel was asked if the *Bundeswehr* would ever be integrated into a European army, she replied:

> What we have is a parliamentary army. The requirement for parliamentary approval not only endows our decisions with stability, but also demands different decision-making processes from those of other European countries ... Limited financial resources are a further reason why we need to do a lot more on a shared basis in the military arena. We need to mesh NATO and the European Security and Defence Policy far better, and bring about a genuine division of tasks over equipment issues. But this isn't going to be easy, as the various countries' defence equipment industries are of course in competition with each other. (BBC Monitoring Service, 2013)

Clearly for Merkel a European army would compromise Germany's parliamentary control over military deployment and jeopardize the country's military industrial sector. Its defence budget has significantly declined since the immediate post-Cold War period and shows no sign of increasing in the near future. Closer cooperation within CFSP has not been a priority for Angela Merkel and international crises such as Libya in 2011 and Syria in 2013 lay bare the continued reluctance to undertake military crisis management operations alongside its EU and NATO partners and allies. Fundamental differences between states over policy and national security and defence capabilities complicate cooperation in the EU and NATO.

Despite attempts to reform the armed forces, maintaining a broad spectrum of *Bundeswehr* capabilities has been placed above pressure from allies to push for a more expeditionary and interoperable army (Federal Ministry of Defence, 2006). Most fundamentally perhaps is the fact that foreign policy decisions appear to be increasingly made for domestic political reasons, rather than grounded in foreign policy strategy (Frankenberger and Maull, 2011). Nevertheless, the period 2003–13 has witnessed a significant consensus on the guiding principles of foreign and security policy in German domestic politics. The Red–Green government of 1998–2005, the grand coalition of 2005–09 and the CDU/CSU–FDP government of 2009–13 maintained a preference for Euro-Atlantic cooperation based on firm multilateral commitments and civilian-based solutions aimed at deterring crises, rather than military crisis management (Hyde-Price, 1996; Harnisch, 2010). As Gerhard Schröder stated:

> Germany's responsibility and role in international politics have increased steadily in recent years. Our country undertakes increasing contributions to international peace operations and in the fight against international terrorism, in civilian and military arenas. This is positively welcomed by the international community. We carry our responsibility within the framework of our capabilities and in close agreement with our partners and allies. (Interview with Gerhard Schröder, cited in von Bredow, 2006: 23)

This broad consensus in German domestic politics has largely resulted in continuity in its foreign and security policy over the past ten years, despite some changes in emphasis and a growing confidence within Berlin to diverge from its allies (Harnisch, 2010).

Germany's changing security environment

The EU, NATO and the UN are the main multilateral settings for German foreign and security policy. The EU has become a more important pillar since the emergence of the CFSP in 1993. In the 1980s Karl Kaiser and John Roper's emphasis on a European strategic triangle of France, Germany and the UK was central to understanding security in Europe and in particular the complexities of West Germany's ability to balance its European and transatlantic interests. This strategic triangle remains central to understanding developments in European security today. Changes in German foreign policy since unification raise the question of whether German governments are fundamentally changing their approach to crisis management or following traditional tenets of foreign policy. There has been a cautious shift to greater military interventionism due to experiences in Afghanistan, Africa and the Balkans (Schwegmann, 2011). The CFSP and NATO have been central fora in which Germany gained experience in crisis management within a multilateral framework (see *Bundesministerium der Verteidigung*, 2010). The country has also become a more assertive player in the EU due to the eurozone crisis, less willing to pick up the tab without demands to ensure cohesiveness (Bulmer and Paterson, 2010). We have also witnessed a loosening of the exclusivity of the transatlantic alliance to open up economic and political channels to emerging powers, notably China (Kornelius, 2013b: 189–98). These developments suggest that Germany is cautiously following a new course in foreign policy. Despite these changes, there has not been a radical reframing of its foreign policy narrative. We have witnessed attempts to update the foreign policy narrative without a wholesale rejection of many of the central ideas of post-1945 foreign policy.

Discussions on German power focused not on how much the country had, but how reluctant it has been to wield its power unilaterally. Peter Katzenstein's classic definition of West Germany as a semi-sovereign state highlighted the internal and external limitations on its power during the Cold War. This apparent forsaking of power, to paraphrase John Duffield (1998; 1999), ensured that West Germany developed from the wreckage of the Second World War to become the world's leading export economy and eventually, in 1990, to achieve unification without a shot being fired. Understanding (West) German power has therefore occupied a number of scholars.

The country has been described as a 'civilian power' (Maull, 2006) and a 'tamed power' (Katzenstein, 1997) and has often been viewed as the antithesis of a realist power, despite predictions that after 1990 it would throw off the shackles of the Cold War and pursue a more normal, unilateral and national interest driven agenda (Mearsheimer, 1990; Layne, 1993). Its commitment to multilateralism and institutionalized cooperation was strategic and based on the centrality of the norms of institutionalized multilateralism and military non-aggression, which became internalized and developed into the central pillars of its foreign policy narrative (Berger, 1996; Banchoff, 1999; Bach, 1999). In strategic terms multilateralism was a means to reintegrate into the international system after the Second World War and cast off the legacy of 1933–45; it also served as an important vehicle to project the country's narrative. A central pillar of Germany's emergence as a leading player in Europe and to a lesser degree on the global stage was a consistent and enduring narrative which has displayed remarkable continuity, even in times of systemic change at the end of the Cold War. Legro argues that crises in international affairs cause ideas to be reassessed, especially in instances when key ideas embodied in a state lose legitimacy and need replacing (Legro, 2005). However, the seismic shifts of the end of the Cold War appear to contradict this argument within Germany. Rather than putting its foreign policy narrative under stress, Germany's post-Cold War narrative enabled it to cope with the end of the Cold War through the reinforcement of (West) Germany's central foreign policy tenets.

The symbolism of Franco–German rapprochement has been central for German chancellors (Krotz and Schild, 2013). Strong Franco–German relations were vital for the emergence of the EU. Bonn and Paris assumed a form of cooperative hegemony over the European integration process – shaping the ideational basis of European integration as well as the required hard negotiations and power plays (Pedersen, 2002). Germany's foreign policy narrative is an important issue to study as it allows the analyst to examine its shifts and continuities since 1949. According to Sperling (2010: 171):

> The entrenched meta-narrative of Germany's post-war role in the transatlantic relationship focused on Germany's economic capacity and role as a joint manager of the Euro-Atlantic if not global economy. That narrative with significant caveats, was carried over into the post-unification period, but was transformed into the spectre of a dominant, if not hegemonic Germany in Europe and the emergence of Germany as the central European player in American foreign policy calculations in the transatlantic area and beyond. The centrality of Germany for Europe and the United States was uncontested and remains incontestable for many.

Traditionally it has been viewed that France and the UK have shaped security policy in Europe – the St Malo agreement of 1998 is a recent example. However, a test of Germany's emerging role in the CFSP might be to ask to what extent it is reactive or proactive in shaping policy. Arguably France and the UK still remain the prime shapers, setting the agenda for major developments. Yet, Germany has left its mark. It has made great strides in coming to terms with going 'out of area' – overall in the period 2003–07 Germany contributed 13.33 per cent of personnel to European Security and Defence Policy (ESDP) missions in which it participated (Harnisch and Wolf, 2010). Germany is perhaps the very model of a post-

Westphalian power; in that sense channelling its foreign and security policy through the EU is a less complicated issue than for the UK, for example, which has a reluctant approach to institutionalizing foreign policy cooperation within the EU.

The question of whether the CFSP is a counter-balance to NATO and a means for the EU to go it alone has less resonance under the Obama administration than under George W. Bush. France's more active role within NATO also changed the dynamic of security cooperation away from an overt sense of institutional competition. In a recent article Felix Berenskoetter and Bastian Giegerich argue that focusing on ontological security is the best way to understand Germany's post-Cold War strategic adjustment to develop the Common Security and Defence Policy (CSDP) instead of relying on NATO. They argue that:

> (1) states gain ontological security by investing in international institutions to negotiate and pursue ideas of order with friends; (2) deep and enduring dissonance between friends signifies a process of estrangement and poses a threat to ontological security; and (3) if states cannot restore resonance with the old friend – institution configuration, they choose a strategy of emancipation by investing in an alternative. (Berenskoetter and Giegerich, 2010: 407)

In their article Berenskoetter and Giegerich aim to highlight the conditionality associated with Germany's commitment to multilateralism. If multilateral commitments jar with Germany's foreign policy narrative, the likelihood is that the country will, they argue, reconsider institutional cooperation. This they assert lies behind Germany's development of the CSDP as a response to dissonance with the USA over security and defence policy since the end of the Cold War (Szabo, 2004). Instead of adapting to the demands of NATO membership, Germany has become estranged from US foreign policy and pursued one of emancipation within the CSDP, which is a closer fit to its 'civilian power' foreign policy narrative. This way Germany has been able to demonstrate continuity in its foreign policy since unification and therefore successive governments have retained overall public acceptance of their foreign policy choices. Rather than being a victim of circumstance, pushed and pulled by the international system, Germany has made its choice of pursing the CSDP over NATO.

Instead of seeking emancipation, Germany still continues to hedge its interests through a policy of interlocking institutions. Committing to the CSDP at the expense of its role in NATO would come with significant risks to its foreign policy. The continued heterogeneity of security and defence policies of EU member states, coupled with the continued close attachment of many of them to NATO, means that Germany must continue to exert influence in both the EU and NATO, despite the challenges which present themselves. A strategy of adaptation to the emerging role of NATO coupled with a clear attempt to influence NATO's trajectory could see Germany emerge as a more proactive player in European security. Rather than seeing it as a sign of German emancipation, the CFSP represents a safety mechanism for when US power and influence pressures the country's foreign policy too much. German foreign policy has neither fully committed to building a CFSP as an alternative to NATO, nor detached from being an active player in the transatlantic alliance.

In addition to this, there are a number of developments which may challenge Germany's involvement in the CFSP in the coming years. First, despite their differences on the eurozone crisis, closer British–French cooperation signalled by their security and defence agreement of November 2010 will affect Germany's role within the CFSP, reinforcing London and Paris as the key shapers of substantive policy developments (Prime Minister's Office, 2010; Gomis, 2011; Jones, 2011). The scarcity of resources to devote to building national and European defence capabilities might restrict projects within the EU and a reconcentration on NATO to avoid duplication.

Germany's role within Afghanistan has remained controversial through Merkel's first two periods. This reached a high point when Federal President Horst Köhler resigned in May 2010 due to criticism he received over comments he made about Germany's interests in deploying the *Bundeswehr* in Afghanistan. Köhler argued:

> A country of our size, with its focus on exports and thus reliance on foreign trade, must be aware that ... military deployments are necessary in an emergency to protect our interests – for example when it comes to trade routes, for example when it comes to preventing regional instabilities that could negatively influence our trade, jobs and incomes. (*Spiegel Online*, 2010)

The comments sparked debate within the media by suggesting that economic interests lay behind the reason for deploying the German armed forces in Afghanistan. The fact that the federal president left office as a result indicates the wider sensitivities in German society over military operations conducted by the *Bundeswehr*.

The deployment of troops in Afghanistan under the remit of NATO's International Security Assistance Force (ISAF) operation also raised questions concerning its future role in German foreign and security policy. Germany's involvement in Afghanistan raised a number of difficult questions for Schröder and Merkel. Merkel and her governments have sought to avoid the depiction of the *Bundeswehr*'s involvement in Afghanistan as being on a war footing. She has sought to describe the involvement as a stabilization mission. However, events have complicated her ability to convince voters that the *Bundeswehr* has not been involved in aggressive military activities. The Kunduz Affair, in which a German colonel – Georg Klein – ordered a US airstrike on what he considered to be a Taliban position, but which resulted in the deaths of approximately 100 Afghan civilians, sparked a heated debate over the *Bundeswehr*'s role in ISAF. The government also sought to limit the *Bundeswehr*'s exposure to some of the worst fighting and limited its deployment to the north of the country, causing resentment among NATO allies deployed in the more unstable south. These limitations are a lingering source of tension in debates over NATO's future development. Defence Minister zu Guttenberg's efforts to open a debate on Germany's role were cut short due to his resignation over the plagiarized doctoral dissertation (von Bredow, 2011).

NATO's development will have a major impact on German foreign and security policy because of how central the Atlantic Alliance is for German defence. If NATO continues to set the agenda on the strategic direction of European security, Germany may find NATO's increasingly global remit difficult to adapt to. Frühling and Schreer have pointed to the potential for NATO to emerge as a counterbalance to power shifts in Asia. They state that:

> NATO as a whole must pay greater attention to power shifts in the Asia–Pacific and the implications for the Alliance ... Any additional demands on US defence efforts in the Pacific would thus reinforce ... US demands for better transatlantic burden-sharing. Finally, major conflict in the Asia–Pacific ... would immediately raise the question of possible European participation – in much the same way as events in Afghanistan did so in 2001, in a previously unthinkable manner ... The rise of China reinforces the need for transatlantic allies to discuss the geographic scope of NATO operations, the geographic priorities of European military engagement and the respective global security roles of NATO and the EU. This debate has to occur before urgent crises demand immediate and improvised responses. (Frühling and Schreer, 2009: 102)

Such a development would certainly put Germany on the back foot and further highlight the demands of NATO membership, over benefits, and place limitations on the development of CSDP. These issues were not fully addressed in debates to decide on the new NATO Strategic Concept of 2010 which gives Germany some time to adjust to such dynamics.

Nonetheless, the development of CFSP will rely on close cooperation between the EU and NATO. In an address to the NATO summit in November 2010, the President of the European Union Council, Hermann van Rompuy (2010), concluded his speech with the following words:

> The ability of our two organisations to shape our future security environment would be enormous if they worked together ... It is time to break down the remaining walls between them.

Frustrations have been evident within NATO and the EU concerning the two organization's apparent difficulties to forge closer ties (de Hoop Scheffer, 2007). In one of his last major speeches as Secretary of Defense, Robert Gates (2011) called for more European engagement. He argued that:

> it is not too late for Europe to get its defense institutions and security relationships on track. But it will take leadership from political leaders and policy makers on this continent. It cannot be coaxed, demanded or imposed from across the Atlantic.

These frustrations often take the form of the USA and NATO's criticisms of the EU's sporadic development as a security and defence actor since the 1990s (Kagan, 2003). Criticisms stress the EU's failure to take threats and new realities of international affairs seriously, which contributes to an ever-growing gap in capabilities between European allies and the USA. Under such circumstances the alliance risks becoming a redundant institution, which would signal the end of the USA's interest in Europe and in maintaining a transatlantic community (Walt, 2010). Others predict that without the American pacifying influence, Europe will once again descend into the kinds of nationalism-driven power struggles which have defined previous centuries (Kupchan, 2010). This is further exacerbated by the EU's reluctance to outline a collective global ambition, which will ensure it remains a peripheral player concerning the big issues of the world (Toje, 2010). Attempts to build security and defence capabilities in the EU since the end of the Cold War have at best been viewed with ambivalence by successive US administrations: too many false dawns in European defence cooperation has left them understandably cautious. As a leading member of the EU, Germany must play a major part in developing any future European defence capabilities.

The global financial crisis has taken centre stage in transatlantic relations in recent years. Yet, defence, like trade, is central to EU–USA relations. It remains to be seen whether, despite the challenges of austerity, EU states can work together not only to preserve current capabilities through closer cooperation, but to build meaningful capabilities together that can contribute to the defence of the EU. The Ghent Initiative on 'pooling and sharing' has so far delivered limited results (Berlin and Stockholm, 2010). Merkel's reluctance to consider substantially increasing collective defence is as much a question of economics as it is a preference for retaining national control over security and defence policy (BBC Monitoring Service, 2013).

Libya and Germany's commitment to multilateral crisis management

Germany's struggle to reconcile competing demands of playing a larger role in military crisis management – whilst not fully casting off the lessons of the past – figures strongly in the narrative of its foreign policy-makers. German politicians stress that the country is a dependable and predictable partner for its allies and a positive contributor to international peace. More recently, in a major foreign policy speech in October 2010, Foreign Minister Guido Westerwelle (2010) outlined the core aspects of German foreign policy, stating:

> German foreign policy is based on the continuity of the previous decades. It is dependable and predictable, orientated by our values and interests and it is a motor for political openness and economic development. German foreign policy stands for equality and fair reconciliation of interests.

The pressure from the fallout of the eurozone crisis, coupled with the challenges to reduce the national debt and spending, will only exacerbate the political and economic pressures on Germany, resulting in less room for manoeuvre and greater incentives for assertive behaviour in the EU in the face of domestic political challenges (Miskimmon et al., 2009). The irony of the foreign policy narrative is that whilst it continues to be defined by continuity the world is changing very fast – and Berlin is not keeping up.

There has been a noticeable loss of momentum in the CFSP since the coming into force of the Lisbon Treaty (Menon, 2011). Emil Kirchner and James Sperling (2010) argue that the leading EU states of France, Germany and the UK view multilateral cooperation within the EU as being contingent on national interests. The tenor of cooperation is often that of pragmatism, rather than a sustained effort to Europeanize foreign and security policy (Giegerich, 2006; Miskimmon, 2007; Gross, 2009; Irondelle and Besancenot, 2010). There are clear limits to the extent to which Germany has committed to a Europeanization of security and defence policy (Miskimmon and Paterson, 2003; Miskimmon, 2007). Its behaviour in the CFSP displays a position more comfortable with bilateral/multiple bilateral cooperation, such as in the German–Swedish 'pooling and sharing' initiative, than with a CFSP involving all 28 member states. There is reluctance in Berlin to commit further to crisis management involvement, with a preference for the role of defence coordinator of the EU whilst France and the UK lead expeditionary missions (Ministry of Foreign Affairs and Defence Ministry, 2011).

At the European level it is clear that in the foreseeable future that defence will not be an area of investment, despite the dire warnings from several scholars about the implications of under-investment (Giegerich, 2010; Mölling and Brune, 2011). One way in which Germany has sought to deal with falling defence budgets has been to carry out several defence reforms since the turn of the century. Whereas the von Weizsäcker report of 2000 was aimed at charting the way to developing a *Bundeswehr* for new international tasks, the recent Weise Commission was focused overwhelmingly on reducing financial commitments rather than strategic necessity (von Weizsäcker, 2000). The Weise Commission has resulted in a lowering of the level of ambition for international deployments and demonstrates the continued challenges the *Bundeswehr* faces in interoperability with its main allies in NATO and the EU (Dyson, 2011). Failure to resource properly its security and defence policy could over time limit Germany's influence in the CFSP (Miskimmon, 2009a).

Germany's failure to reform its armed forces in a fundamental fashion presents limitations on its ability to play a leading role in the CFSP. Difficulties in interoperability are exacerbated by the continued policy differences evident in the CSFP. The EU demonstrates that in the absence of a collective position it becomes cumbersome and often unable to act. The latest example of this was the 2011 issue of the no-fly zone in Libya. France and the UK's support of United Nations Resolution 1973, alongside the USA, signalled a degree of transatlantic unity. However, Germany's decision to abstain on the resolution, alongside Russia and China, made a collective EU position more difficult to achieve. It highlighted the continued divergence on military crisis management of the EU's 'Big Three'. This divergence complicates any assumptions that the EU can present a united foreign policy to the world (Wagnsson, 2010). In light of this, Charles Grant argues for the necessity of building a defence core around the UK and France in order for the EU's CSDP not to become irrelevant (Grant, 2011).

The case of Libya is an interesting one as it highlights Germany's divergent position on military intervention from France, the UK and the USA. Germany's decision to abstain on UN Resolution 1973, which sought to enforce a no-fly zone over Libya, was explained by Foreign Minister Westerwelle who stressed that a political solution was the only viable means to achieve peace:

> I warn against having a discussion in Europe about a military intervention every time there is injustice in north Africa or in Arabia ... I am convinced that there can only be a political solution in Libya ... At the end of the day it is important that we clearly stand by the democrats ... But it is also clear that we cannot threaten military action against every country in north Africa where there is injustice. (*European Voice*, 2011)

Westerwelle expressed the concern that:

> If we had voted yes, Germany would have come under severe pressure as the largest European member of NATO to participate militarily. We would no longer be debating whether we send soldiers to Libya. Rather we would be dealing with the question: how many soldiers do we send? (*Frankfurter Rundschau*, 2011)

German foreign policy-makers remain reluctant to give the impression that the country's greater involvement in crisis management in the last decade has signalled a change in foreign policy towards an unquestioning acceptance of obligations of military crisis management (Miskimmon, 2012). Germany's approach to military deployments remains on a case-by-case basis.

Germany has found it increasingly difficult to maintain a reserved approach to crisis management operations, largely down to its involvement in building the CFSP. Despite working to build capabilities, it has remained highly cautious, most notably in the Iraq war in 2003 and in NATO's operations in Libya in 2011 (Dettke, 2009). The country's decision to abstain on Libya in 2011 suggests that building the CFSP is not a priority and that a focus on territorial defence, rather than expeditionary warfare, is Berlin's main preference (Ministry of Foreign Affairs and Defence Ministry, 2011). The challenges of presenting such a position are significant. Most clearly, however, is the appearance that foreign policy decisions have been linked to domestic electoral calculations, rather than longer-term policy objectives. Examples of Schröder's decision to oppose the Iraq war as a means to help his re-election and Merkel/Westerwelle's calculations in regional elections in Germany in regard to UN Resolution 1973 signal such a trend.

President Obama's concern to make NATO the central institution for organizing the military operation suggested that the US president is keen to engage the European allies more (Gordon, 2010a; 2010b). Calls for an 'era of engagement' for Europe's introverted military actors presents an uncomfortable situation in which Washington's call for greater cooperation will be very difficult to refuse. Europeans' ability to say no to the USA under George W. Bush, leading to a more selective US policy of multilateralism, is no longer a viable response to the Obama administration, which has made a clear point of raising expectations of the contribution of European allies to crisis management. US expectations that allies need to contribute more to enforce collective decisions are therefore becoming more characteristic of EU–NATO relations (*Financial Times*, 2011). However, due to these high expectations, Germany's abstention ensured that instead of EU–NATO cooperation on the issue of Libya, states fell back on tried and trusted NATO cooperation. Unrest in north Africa and the Middle East should focus the attention of EU member states and drive a collective response to the challenges. Significant flows of displaced people from the instability in north Africa is having a noticeable effect on EU members – Italy in particular – leading to some states wishing to reconsider their commitment to the Schengen agreement on open borders. Yet, differing views on events has ensured that Baroness Ashton has been sidelined and that national differences have defined the EU position, rather than a sustained effort to engage with the issues. The failure to work through the new institutions of the CFSP introduced by the Lisbon Treaty reinforced the intergovernmental preference that Berlin and other EU states continue to have.

Germany on the global stage

Germany presents something of a paradox in foreign and security policy. Berlin is increasingly seen as displaying aspects of hegemonic leadership in Europe (Crawford, 2007; Paterson, 2011; Beck, 2013). However, transferring this regional influence to the global level is complicated as Berlin lacks many of the trappings of emerging great powers such as a large military, nuclear weapons and a permanent seat on the United Nations' Security Council – most importantly, there is no political will within Berlin or the rest of the country for a more activist security and defence policy. Germany remains influential, however, owing to its geo-economic reach (Kundnani, 2011) and its ability to influence through non-military means (Maull, 1992). In order to continue to influence, Germany will need to respond. The emerging powers of the BRICS (Brazil, Russia, India, China and South Africa) present a range of powerful new voices within the globalized world who serve both as important markets for German goods and potential economic competitors (Le Gloannec, 2001).

Germany's foreign and security policy has grown in scope since unification as the challenges facing Berlin have become more global. The country's involvement in the EU-3 negotiations with Teheran, alongside the USA, Russia and China, over the Iranian nuclear programme have put it at centre stage of global non-proliferation diplomacy (Müller, 2006; Harnisch, 2007; Hanau Santini, 2010). Iran's nuclear programme was a major aspect of the Red–Green government's foreign policy agenda. Former Foreign Minister Joschka Fischer's concern to prevent Teheran acquiring nuclear weapons was very clear. In a newspaper comment shortly after leaving office, he declared:

> The Iran crisis is moving fast in an alarming direction. There can no longer be any reasonable doubt that Iran's ambition is to obtain nuclear weapons capability. At the heart of the issue lies the Iranian regime's aspiration to become a hegemonic Islamic and regional power and thereby position itself at eye level with the world's most powerful nations. It is precisely this ambition that sets Iran apart from North Korea: Whereas North Korea seeks nuclear weapons capability to entrench its own isolation, Iran is aiming for regional dominance and more. (Fischer, 2006)

Despite their concern, Schröder and Fischer sought to limit moves towards using military force against Iran to enforce cooperation. Chancellor Merkel has continued to support the work of the EU-3 and the coordination of efforts by the EU's High Representative for Foreign Affairs and Security Policy, Baroness Ashton.

Germany has also sought to play an increasing role in Middle East diplomacy. In his biography of the German chancellor, Stefan Kornelius (2013b: 157–79) outlines Angela Merkel's deep interest in German–Israeli relations. However, Germany's lack of a permanent seat on the United Nations Security Council limits its impact on matters of global politics. Its ability to compensate for this through sustained diplomatic activity via the EU, NATO, the UN and other multilateral institutions has been key to its international influence.

Conclusion

Foreign and security policy did not play a major role in the 2013 *Bundestagswahl*. Forefront in the election was the government's handling of the eurozone crisis. The major foreign policy issue which emerged was the issue of the extent to which German authorities had cooperated in sharing secret intelligence material with the National Security Agency of the US. Chancellor Merkel's room for manoeuvre in foreign policy is unlikely to increase. Multilateralism remains a defining feature of German foreign and security policy and there is no sense that, even with a change in government coalition, the direction of this will change. The crisis in Ukraine in 2014 highlights the continued need for close cooperation among EU and NATO members for the stability of Europe. However, there is considerable evidence to suggest that politicians will continue to remain cautious about the deployment of the *Bundeswehr* for combat operations. Growing self-confidence has been a consistent theme in Gunther Hellmann's work which claims that Germany feels more able to say no to the demands of its partners as its relative strength has grown. The discourse of policy-makers suggests this to be the case. The country, paradoxically, feels itself under pressure due to the eurozone crisis and the significant challenges it faces in controlling its own debt. As the implications of the crisis have become clearer we have witnessed Germany's lowering expectations for the CFSP in this period of austerity. Rather than pursuing greater Europeanization, the country has not sought to avoid a radical approach to develop common defence capabilities in the face of reduced budgets, preferring to seek national or bilateral solutions to the challenges it faces (Harnisch and Schieder, 2006). Realist assumptions of relative power advantages in Europe suggest that Germany's unwillingness to invest in defence is a strategic calculation (Simon, 2010; Kundnani, 2011). Germany sees no advantage in defence where others provide for it, as it allows it to concentrate on its trading strength as a leading export economy.

In the midst of the crisis in the eurozone and the failure to achieve unity on the Libya crisis, Germany has stepped back from developing collective security, ensuring that the CFSP will not be a growth area of EU policy for some time to come. The country increasingly finds foreign policy cooperation with 28 member states to be unwieldy, hence its preference for small group cooperation, such as the Swedish–German Ghent Initiative or the recent revival of the Weimar Triangle with France and Poland. Former Foreign Minister Guido Westerwelle's call alongside ten other EU members for a European army fits this mould of cooperation. However, Germany's foreign policy narrative has remained consistent, even if the connection between words and actions of foreign policy-makers has not. The country will continue to be an important international actor seeking to limit its involvement in the use of military force and in pursuing efforts to increase the scope of global governance. It will continue to seek influence over multilateral decision-making, stressing its economic strengths and its singular approach to power in the twenty-first century as hallmarks of its global engagement.

Chapter 12

Welfare State Reform and Social Policy

MARTIN SEELEIB-KAISER

During the 1990s and early 2000s Germany was perceived by many observers to be the 'sick man of Europe'. Slow economic growth and high unemployment were said to be the result of an overregulated and too generous welfare state. Subsequent reforms of the unemployment and old-age social insurance schemes emphasized a greater degree of private provision and self-reliance. For some observers the reforms were crucial for the turnaround in labour market and overall economic performance since 2005. Critics, however, highlight the social costs associated with these reforms that have led to processes of recommodification, i.e. the significant increase in low-paid and other atypical forms of employment as well as income inequality. Furthermore, employment-oriented family policies have been significantly expanded, as they are understood to be a social investment into the future of the German economy. As the duration of the economic crisis was relatively brief in Germany, the economy weathered the storms of the great recession of 2008 quite well without having to resort to policies of welfare state retrenchment. After giving a brief historical overview, this chapter will explore key recent welfare state reforms and their political drivers.

Historical overview

The German welfare state has a long tradition dating back to Imperial Germany and its Chancellor Otto von Bismarck. Historically it heavily relied on social insurance and earnings-related benefits, as the organizing principles of social protection for workers, and the concept of subsidiarity with regard to social services. Within the comparative literature the German welfare state has been characterized as a conservative one or a model of the strong male-breadwinner state (Esping-Andersen, 1990; Lewis, 1992).

Important elements of continuity have characterized welfare state development from Bismarck to the unified Germany. For example, attempts during the immediate post-Second World War period to introduce a more universal approach, based on the principle of social citizenship, along the lines of the British Beveridge Plan, failed due to opposition by organized interests (Hockerts, 2011: 43–70). Major reform steps in this period were the 1957 pension reform and the 1969 Labour Promotion Law. The 1957 reform had as its leitmotif the public guarantee of the achieved living standard during old age, based on a consensus among the political elite that pensioners should not have to rely on means-tested social assistance after years of work. As a consequence of the reform and subsequent policies the net replacement rate for the standard pensioner reached 70 per cent during the mid-1970s. A core aim of the 1969 labour market policy reform was to abolish 'substandard' employment. This was to be achieved by the introduction of active labour market policy, largely focusing on further education and training, as well as the definition of 'suitable work'. This latter was defined in such a way that an unemployed worker did not have to accept a job which either paid less or was in a different occupational field to his or her previous job. A wage replacement rate of 68 per cent of previous net earnings was introduced to ensure the achieved living standard. Thus social protection for workers was achieved by provisions of occupational status protection and generous income maintenance. The non-working poor, who did not qualify for the social insurance schemes, had to rely on means-tested social assistance. The differentiation between workers and the poor can be characterized as an institutional dualism (Leibfried and Tennstedt, 1985). Nevertheless, it has to be acknowledged that during Germany's 'economic miracle' unemployment was very low, averaging 0.7 per cent between 1964 and 1973 (Bleses and Seeleib-Kaiser, 2004: 19–22), and the poverty rate declined significantly over the years, reaching a low level of 5.3 per cent (poverty defined as less than 50 per cent of median income) of the population in 1981, the same level achieved by social-democratic Sweden. A key indicator for measuring inequality is the Gini coefficient, according to which 0 marks perfect equality and 1 marks maximum inequality. By 1981 Germany had a Gini coefficient of 0.244, one of the lowest in the OECD world (LIS, 2013).

After the end of the Cold War, and as a core element of the German unification process, the West German welfare state was largely extended to the former East Germany (Ritter, 2007). After having been identified as *Modell Deutschland* by observers in the early 1980s (Markovits, 1982), Germany had to cope with severe socio-economic challenges in the wake of unification, including historically unprecedented and rising unemployment rates, reaching more than 12 per cent in the West and almost 20 per cent in the former East Germany in the mid-1990s, as well as seemingly ever-increasing social insurance contributions, which reached a level of more than 40 per cent of gross wages in the late 1990s. The growing social insurance contributions were said to undermine the competitiveness of the country as a place to do business in a globalized world. As a result, significant labour market and pension reforms were perceived as a necessity (Seeleib-Kaiser, 2001).

However, Germany was said to be largely incapable of reform due to political gridlock (Kitschelt and Streeck, 2003), leading to the characterization of it as the 'sick man of the euro' (*The Economist*, 1999). It was argued that path dependence would make reform of the earnings and contribution-related pension system especially difficult, if not impossible (Myles and Pierson, 2001); matters were said to be further complicated by the large number of 'veto players' (Tsebelis, 2002) within the German political system. Despite the various characterizations highlighting the incapacity to reform, the German political economy underwent significant reforms, including paradigmatic changes of the statutory unemployment and pension schemes and the expansion of employment-oriented family policies (Bleses and Seeleib-Kaiser, 2004; Streeck, 2009a). According to *The Economist* (2012) Germany once again became *Modell Deutschland*, evidenced in comparatively low and declining unemployment rates since 2005 and the relatively quick return to economic growth after the sharp and deep recession of 2008/09. The comparatively good economic performance is said to be largely a result of welfare state reforms, especially labour market regulations and unemployment insurance.

Pension and labour market reforms

Recent pension and labour market reforms have reversed the road to 'quasi universalism' (Leisering, 2009) that Germany had embarked on and reinforced the institutionalized dual structure of the welfare state, differentiating between social protection insiders and outsiders. Social protection insiders can be defined as individuals, usually workers in standard employment relationships (labour market insiders), covered either through comprehensive statutory social protection *or* by statutory entitlements, complemented or supplemented by private/occupational social protection to a level that maintains living standards. Outsiders are defined as the (working) poor that would have to rely on modest (largely means-tested) public provision, primarily intended to ameliorate poverty (Seeleib-Kaiser et al., 2012). Since welfare entitlements are mostly linked to labour market status in one way or another, there tends to be a clear correlation between labour market insiders/outsiders on the one hand and social protection insiders/outsiders on the other hand. Overall, social protection for pensioners and the long-term unemployed has converged towards a more liberal model of welfare, such as is mainly found in the USA and the UK.

Until the late 1990s, the German statutory old-age insurance scheme witnessed only incremental and modest reforms, the most important of which was the reversal of early retirement policies that were used to smooth structural economic adjustment processes since the 1970s (Ebbinghaus, 2006). Nevertheless, the principle of guaranteeing the achieved living standard during old age, the leitmotif of social protection since the pension reforms of 1957, was not fundamentally questioned until the reforms following the turn of the twenty-first century, when the statutory old-age social insurance system underwent significant change. The recent reforms enacted since 2001 included major reductions in the net-replacement rate, from about 70 to 52 per cent, and a partial privatization (Leisering, 2011), which in effect put an end to the guiding principle of guaranteeing the achieved living standard for pensioners. By 2037 an average worker will have to have contributed 37 years to the statutory pension scheme to be entitled to a pension above the poverty threshold. Future pensioners will only be able to enjoy an old-age income with an approximate replacement rate level of 70 per cent, if they are covered by additional occupational or private arrangements (Schmähl, 2007; Hockerts, 2011: 294–324). Although overall occupational pension coverage has increased in all sectors after the pension reform of 2001, coverage is very uneven between the industrial sectors (see Table 12.1).

The implementation of the 2001 pension reform will lead to a 'layering' (Thelen, 2002) of the various schemes within the old-age system for the average worker, due to the growing importance of occupational and private pensions. However, as the occupational pension coverage is very uneven, we are very likely to witness an increase in social protection outsiderness. The depth of future social protection dualism can be estimated by analysing prospective replacement rates derived from public and occupational pensions for current workers. Based on OECD simulations, the average worker in Germany with an occupational pension scheme will have an overall pension replacement rate that is 22.6 percentage points higher than the replacement rate for a worker who has only been covered by the statutory pension scheme. Table 12.2 provides a comparison of pension replacement rates in Germany and the US. According to the German pension expert Schmähl (2007) the comprehensive pension reform will very likely once again lead to an increase in pensioner poverty.

Table 12.1   *Percentage of employees in the German private sector covered by occupational pension plans by industry, 2001–11*

Industry	2001	2005	2011
Manufacturing			
Production/intermediate goods	43*	73*	63
Mining, quarrying and energy	63	71	61
Construction	22	37	43
Services			
Financial intermediation	76	89	84
Wholesale/retail and repair	27	47	48
Real estate/business services	16*	28*	40
Hospitality and food services	10	26	26
Total private sector coverage	38	52	50

* Data not fully comparable with subsequent years due to reclassification of sector definition in 2008.

Sources: *TNS Infratest Sozialforschung* (2008: 42; 2012: 40).

Table 12.2   *Net pension replacement rates (%)*

	Replacement rate of public system (average worker)	Combined replacement rate of public and voluntary occupational pensions (average worker)
Germany	56.0	78.6
United States	47.3	93.9

Source: OECD (2011).

With regard to labour market reforms and social protection for unemployed workers we can also identify a process of dualization, leading to a convergence of the German model towards a more liberal approach. Despite more incremental reforms, the degree of income protection, as well as occupational status maintenance, significantly declined with labour market reforms enacted and implemented since the late 1990s. The most prominent of these were the so-called Hartz reforms, which reduced the maximum duration of unemployment insurance from 32 to 24 months, with the regular benefit being limited to 12 months. Furthermore, the reforms integrated the former earnings-related and means-tested unemployment assistance with the social assistance programme for the unemployed. Whilst short-term unemployed workers continue to receive an earnings-related benefit at 60/67 per cent of their previous net income, even after the implementation of the reforms, long-term unemployed workers with an unemployment spell of more than 12 months are only entitled to a means-tested transfer at the level of social assistance; for them any job offer is deemed suitable (Seeleib-Kaiser and Fleckenstein, 2007).

As a result of implicit and explicit disentitlement since the early 1990s a smaller percentage of unemployed workers in Germany receive regular unemployment insurance benefits than is the case in the US. The various reforms since the 1990s have clearly contributed to a deepening and widening of the dualistic structure of the German unemployment compensation scheme (Seeleib-Kaiser et al., 2012; for a critical perspective on the concept of dualism, see Clasen and Goerne, 2011). Nevertheless, a key difference to the US continues to be that in Germany the long-term unemployed are still entitled to means-tested benefits without any time limit, whilst the same people in America are either not entitled to any federal cash benefits or only to extremely low and time-limited benefits.

To mitigate the effects of unemployment for labour market insiders the US government regularly extends the maximum duration of unemployment insurance benefits during times of economic crisis, which leads to higher rates of benefit recipients among the unemployed during recessions (see Figure 12.1). Germany does not extend or liberalize the criteria for the receipt of unemployment insurance benefits in an economic crisis, but makes use of the so-called short-time work allowance scheme to mitigate the impact of the recession for insiders.

The short-time work allowance is basically a time-limited state subsidy to support workers with reduced working hours, due to a cyclical decline in demand, and thereby to avoid layoffs. For a company to be eligible to register its workers for the scheme it must have witnessed an inevitable and temporary reduction of hours worked (leading to a minimum reduction of 10 per cent in wages) as well as exhausted internal labour market adjustment measures (such as using up vacation entitlements and credits within working time accounts). If all requirements are fulfilled workers receive a short-time work allowance of 60 per cent (67 per cent if they have children) of the lost net wage due to the reduction in hours. In other words, if the reduction of hours is 100 per cent the worker receives the same level of benefit as an unemployed worker. Usually short-time work allowances are paid for a maximum of six months. During the deep economic crisis of 2009 and 2010, the German government expanded the duration of benefit receipt to 24 months, i.e. the short-time work allowance was available for 12 months longer than the regular unem-

Figure 12.1 *Percentage of unemployed receiving unemployment insurance benefits, 1971–2009*

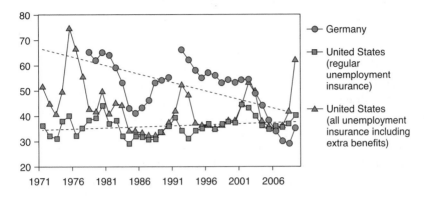

Source: Seeleib-Kaiser et al. (2012).

ployment insurance benefit. At its peak 1.14 million workers were protected from unemployment through the scheme. However, once the economy was growing again, the number of eligible workers decreased rapidly (see *Bundesagentur für Arbeit*, 2013). Most of the workers receiving the benefit were employed in the manufacturing sector (see Eichhorst and Marx, 2009b; Crimmann and Wießner, 2009).

Finally, it is worth emphasizing that for labour market insiders the various reforms of the unemployment insurance scheme have had only a modest impact on their social protection, as they are more likely to benefit from the short-time work allowance scheme or, if unemployed, are more likely to witness only a relatively short spell of unemployment.

Family policy reforms

Family policies have seen a more or less continued expansion since the late 1980s. The most important reforms in the 1980s and 1990s included: the introduction of parental leave with a maximum duration of three years, the introduction of childcare credits into the statutory pension scheme, the entitlement to days off from work to care for dependent sick children, and the introduction of an entitlement to publicly provided or subsidized childcare for children from three to six years of age. Nevertheless, the overwhelming structure of family policy continued to be biased towards transfers, including child allowance payments and joint taxation, supporting a somewhat modified male-breadwinner model.

Although the reforms of the 1990s, especially those introduced by the Red–Green coalition government, had already opened up a pathway towards more employment-oriented family policies, these policies reached their preliminary climax during the grand coalition government. These reforms included: the introduction of an earnings-related and gender-neutral parental leave benefit (capped at a maximum of €1,800 per month) for the duration of 12 months (with an additional two 'partner' months for the father) and a massive expansion of childcare provision for children between the ages of one and three. Since August 2013, every child above the age of one is entitled to a place in publicly provided or subsidized childcare. According to government data the percentage of children between the ages of one and three in day care has increased from 17.8 (2008) to 27.6 per cent (2012) (BMAS, 2013: xiii). The introduction of the two main family policy reforms has marked a clear departure from the previous policy path (Fleckenstein et al., 2011) and can be interpreted as a move towards a more Scandinavian approach in family policy.

Socio-economic outcomes

Whilst the changes in labour market regulations and social protection for the unemployed are very likely to have contributed to an overall increase in the employment rate[1] and a decline in the rate of long-term unemployment,[2] they have at the same time facilitated an increase in 'atypical' work, including (involuntary) part-time employment, temporary or fixed-term contracts, agency work and low-wage work. The proportion of workers with 'atypical' jobs, or in other words the size of the precariat, has increased from 20 to 25 per cent of the workforce in the first decade of the twenty-first century (BMAS, 2013: xxv). The incidence of low pay, defined as the share in total dependent employment of workers earning less than two-thirds of median earnings, has also significantly increased since the mid-1990s (see Table 12.3). Overall, we can characterize these developments as clear indications of significant recommodification processes within the labour market. Hence, it is not surprising that these developments have fuelled a political debate about the success of the labour market reforms and the overall assessment of economic performance (Kirbach, 2013).

---

1. The overall employment rate has increased from 72.9 (2007) to 76.3 per cent (2011), with significant increases in the employment rate among older workers (aged 55-64) from 51.3 to 59.9 per cent (BMAS, 2013: 482).
2. The rate of the long-term unemployed among the unemployed declined from 56 per cent in 2007 to 48 per cent in 2011 (BMAS, 2013: 481).

Table 12.3 *Incidence of low pay (%)*

	1996	2000	2006	2008	2009	2010
Germany	13.6	15.9	17.5	21.5	20.2	20.5
US	25.1	24.7	24.2	24.5	24.8	25.3

Source: OECD Employment Outlook (2008, 2010, 2011, 2012).

Table 12.4 *Poverty rates (post-tax and transfer)*

	Less than 40 per cent of the current median income				Less than 60 per cent of the current median income			
	mid-80s	mid-90s	mid-2000s	late 2000s	mid-80s	mid-90s	mid-200s	late 2000s
Germany	2.6	3.6	3.7	4.2	12.0	12.7	14.7	14.8
United States	11.8	11.8	11.3	11.3	23.8	23.7	23.7	24.4

Source: OECD (2012b).

The economic and labour market changes associated with increasing deindustrialization and the various policy reforms have not been without consequences for the overall income distribution, as Germany has seen a significant increase of inequality and poverty since the 1990s. Since 1997 the Gini coefficient has increased from 0.26 to 0.29, whilst in the US it increased from 0.36 to 0.38 (2010) (OECD, 2013). Whereas poverty remained at a very high level in the US during this period, extreme poverty (less than 40 per cent of the median income) and people living at risk of poverty (less than 60 per cent of the median income) increased significantly in Germany (see Table 12.4).

Drivers of change

Within the comparative welfare state literature, power resources and partisanship have been identified as key variables determining social policy outputs and outcomes (Korpi, 1983; Esping-Andersen, 1990; Huber and Stephens, 2001; Brady, 2009). However, the key social policy reforms during the past decade have not seemed to follow these theoretical propositions, as a Social-Democrat led government significantly retrenched the statutory unemployment and old-age insurance schemes and a Christian-Democratic minister within a grand coalition government enacted major family policy reforms. In this section I will argue that socio-economic challenges unsettled previous policy approaches and preferences, and that ideational change among the dominant political actors and political leadership have played a key role in determining new policy solutions (Bleses and Seeleib-Kaiser, 2004; Stiller, 2010).

In the 1990s, the process of German unification placed enormous stress on the welfare state, as it was primarily funded through social insurance contributions. This funding mechanism coupled with unprecedented high unemployment rates in the former East Germany triggered significant increases in social insurance contributions and gross wage costs. These increased costs contributed to fear among employers and politicians that Germany could be losing out in the global economic competition, should social insurance costs not be brought under control. The ensuing competitiveness debate dominated the domestic political discourse and roughly lasted from 1993 to the early 2000s. Although Social Democrats and Greens initially were very sceptical about the argument advanced by employers and the then Christian-Democratic–Liberal coalition government, whereby globalization made social policy retrenchment a necessity, they eventually accepted that social insurance contribution had to be stabilized, if not reduced. The debates on globalization were strategically interwoven with arguments emphasizing the need for more personal responsibility, private provision and market reliance. These interpretative patterns guided much of the labour market and pension reforms of the late 1990s and early 2000s (Seeleib-Kaiser, 2001). Whilst globalization 'mandated' a reduction in social insurance contributions and can thus be characterized as a 'causal belief' (Goldstein and Keohane, 1993) or as an idea used as a weapon (Blyth, 2001), supporting families and providing them with more choice constituted a new dominant interpretative pattern shared by the mainstream political parties (Bleses and Seeleib-Kaiser, 2004).

Highlighting the importance of ideational change in explaining social policy change is not to negate that the processes of deindustrialization, globalization, an ageing society and the huge challenges associated with German unification played a causal role. Clearly these were important processes that impacted on the economic and financial underpinnings of the existing social policy arrangements. For instance, increased deindustrialization, with a declining proportion of the workforce requiring specific skills, and an increasing female labour force participation, especially among those with high general skills, undermined the functional underpinnings of the welfare state, whereby the predominance of workers with specific skills required a comprehensive and generous unemployment insurance scheme – as emphasized by the influential Varieties of Capitalism approach (Hall and Soskice, 2001) – and childcare services could be neglected, as these were to be provided by the non-working mother (Fleckenstein et al., 2011). In addition, an ageing society and very low fertility rates from the 1970s will inevitably lead to a significant population decline without immigration on a massive scale (*Deutscher Bundestag*, 2002). Partially to mitigate the effects of demographic change experts proposed a greater role for funded private pension schemes (World Bank, 1994; Marschallek, 2004) and a more employment-oriented family policy approach, which it is hoped will contribute to higher fertility rates, higher female labour force participation and improved human capital formation among children (Ristau, 2005; BMFSFJ, 2006; cf. Esping-Andersen, 2009).

Furthermore, ideational change does not automatically precipitate *comprehensive* policy changes, but often requires either triggering events or policy entrepreneurs or leadership to enact reforms effectively. Within the domain of pension reform the financial services sector played an important role in organizing media campaigns to promote the partial privatization of the statutory old-age insurance scheme (Hockerts, 2011). The Social-Democratic chancellor of the first Red–Green coalition government, Gerhard Schröder, chose the union leader and Social Democrat Walter Riester for the post of Minister for Labour and Social Affairs. He was an 'ideal' choice for the post, as he was convinced that the statutory pension system needed to be reformed, whilst at the same time he could be 'trusted' by the union movement. In order to keep the pressure on pension reform, the Red–Green government *suspended* for a limited time period the implementation of the previous Christian–Democratic–Liberal coalition government's pension reform, which had been highly criticized and opposed by the opposition of the Social Democrats. Minister Riester was able to use effectively the pressure created by the time-limited suspension to build a political coalition for comprehensive pension reform, which partially privatized the statutory old-age insurance (Stiller, 2010).

A major political scandal at the Federal Employment Office surrounding statistical reporting created a political opportunity to advance a comprehensive unemployment insurance reform. The Red–Green government appointed Peter Hartz, HR executive at the automotive company Volkswagen, as the chair of the commission to reform the administration and governance of the Federal Employment Office. The report of the commission was published shortly before the 2002 federal election and included, in addition to proposals to reform the governance of the service, proposals to reform the unemployment compensation scheme, both of which were inspired by the reforms of the British Job

Centres and unemployment insurance system (Fleckenstein, 2011; 2013). In the election campaign Chancellor Schröder promised to enact the reform package if re-elected. The political leadership of Wolfgang Clement, the 'Superminister' for Economics and Labour in the second Red–Green coalition government, was crucial in pushing the policy through the political process against significant opposition from parts of the labour movement (Stiller, 2010). In this context it must be emphasized that the main unions and their representatives acted as implicit 'consenters' (Korpi, 2006), as they did not stage mass protests. This is not to say that unions and their representatives have the same or similar policy preferences regarding the retrenchment of social protection arrangements for social and labour market outsiders, as some of the literature might suggest. Clearly, the employers and their organizations can be identified as the 'protagonists' pushing for policy change in unemployment and old-age insurance (Seeleib-Kaiser et al., 2011). However, as opposed to other countries, 'political strikes' are unconstitutional in Germany, which further limits the strategic options of unions in an already severely restricted option space. Despite the success in getting the reform passed, Chancellor Schröder called for an early election in 2005. Should the call for early elections have been devised as a strategic vote-seeking instrument to provide more legitimacy to his reform agenda, this strategy failed, as Schröder lost to his challenger from the Christian-Democratic Party, Angela Merkel.

Within the domain of family policy a new interpretative pattern had emerged during the 1980s and 1990s, whereby families needed more support. Core to the interpretative pattern was the concept of parental 'choice', which included an expansion of measures to improve the reconciliation of family and work (Bleses and Seeleib-Kaiser, 2004). During the first Red–Green coalition government the importance of this policy domain was underestimated. Moreover, the government focused on a law to improve gender equality, which it failed to enact due to the strong opposition by employers and the employers' organizations. The newly appointed Family Minister Renate Schmidt of the second Red–Green coalition had 'learned' from these experiences and aimed at creating 'alliances for families' that included not only NGOs and unions, but also, and more crucially, employers. For Schmidt an employment-oriented family policy was core for sustainable economic development. Together with employers and employers' associations the minister pushed for significant reforms of parental leave and an expansion of childcare provisions. However, core reform proposals were scheduled to be enacted only after the 2005 elections.

As the Red–Green coalition government lost the 2005 elections and a new grand coalition government was formed, Schmidt's Christian-

Democratic successor in the post of family minister, Ursula von der Leyen, accelerated the speed of reform, which eventually led to the introduction of an earnings-related parental leave benefit and an entitlement to public or publicly subsidized childcare for all children over one. Von der Leyen used ideational leadership and 'brute' political force effectively to push through these reforms against opposition from the conservative wing within the Christian-Democratic Party, its Bavarian sister party and parts of the Catholic Church. Von der Leyen argued that a reformed family policy would have a positive impact on fertility, improve human capital formation through early childhood education and provide mothers with more and better opportunities to re-enter the workforce after a short parental leave. Modernizing the Christian-Democratic Party's family policy was a strategic element effectively used by von der Leyen and Chancellor Merkel to improve electoral support among female voters in urban areas. Crucial for successfully overcoming the various forces of intraparty opposition, however, was the support by employers' associations – who became promoters of employment-oriented family policy reforms (Fleckenstein and Seeleib-Kaiser, 2011) – and the opposition parties (Seeleib-Kaiser, 2010).

Broadly speaking both welfare state parties, i.e. the SPD and the CDU, agreed that social policy reform was inevitable. Whilst the SPD had converged towards a position of more limited state intervention in the domains of unemployment and old-age insurance, the Christian Democrats had moved towards supporting a more employment-oriented family policy. During the 2013 election, the main social policy cleavages between the political parties were in the domains of minimum wage legislation and improved minimum pensions for retirees with a long employment history.

With the increase in low-wage employment the Social Democrats began to demand the introduction of a minimum wage. In contrast to the United States and a number of European countries, such as Britain and France, Germany does not have a uniform statutory minimum wage, as historically wage negotiations were defined to be the sole remit of the social partners, i.e. unions and employer associations. Nevertheless, demands for minimum wages have emerged since the late 2000s and have been included in a number of sectoral collective bargaining agreements for various industrial sectors. Whereas the SPD demands a national minimum wage of €8.50 per hour (SPD, 2011), the Christian Democrats initially opposed minimum wage legislation, though they did promise to introduce some form of regional minimum wages after the 2013 federal elections (Tagesspiegel, 2013). Furthermore, both parties have identified the issue of future pensioner poverty and have developed various proposals to address the issue, without, however, questioning the overall design of the previous pension reforms, including the overall reduction of the replacement rate and partial privatization (Handelsblatt, 2013).

Conclusion

At the beginning of the twenty-first century we have witnessed comprehensive reforms of the German welfare state. Key principles of post-World War Two welfare state arrangements, such as occupational status protection and providing income maintenance at a level that protects the achieved living standard for the unemployed and pensioners, increasingly only apply to core labour market insiders, thereby once again reinforcing the institutional dualism historically inherent in the design of the welfare state. In both policy domains Germany has converged towards a more liberal approach to welfare, usually associated with policies in Britain and the United States, though it should not be characterized as a liberal welfare model, as the country has made significant progress in reorienting its family policies towards a more employment-oriented approach, increasingly along the lines found in social-democratic Scandinavia. These two processes can be characterized as a dual transformation of the German welfare state (Bleses and Seeleib-Kaiser, 2004; Fleckenstein et al., 2011).

The politics behind these reforms did not follow mainstream political science theories. Power resources and partisanship would not have predicted that a government led by the Social Democrats would significantly retrench unemployment and old-age insurance. Conversely, significant family policy reforms towards a more employment-oriented approach championed by a Christian-Democratic minister would have seemed rather unlikely. Moreover, institutional approaches, highlighting path dependence and the many veto players within the German political system, had also suggested a rather stable policy environment. I have argued that the economic challenges, largely a consequence of German unification and deindustrialization, have unsettled the previous policy environment. The concomitant uncertainty created the necessary space to develop new 'causal beliefs' (Goldstein and Keohane, 1993) and use 'ideas as weapons' (Blyth, 2001) to develop blueprints and interpretative patterns to legitimate subsequent policy change.

Chapter 13

Energy and Climate Protection Policy

STEPHEN PADGETT

Energy policy is conventionally understood in terms of the pursuit of three objectives:

- *Energy security* involves managing the supply of primary energy from domestic and external sources, maintaining the reliability of the energy infrastructure, and ensuring that energy companies are able to meet demand.
- *Economic efficiency* requires that energy prices should be affordable to both industrial and domestic consumers.
- *Sustainability* means using energy in a way that does not prejudice the well-being of future generations either by depleting limited resources or by damaging the environment.

These objectives are not always mutually compatible, and energy policy involves a complex 'trilemma' of trade-offs between them. Scientific evidence about the potentially catastrophic effects of greenhouse gas (GHG) emissions on the world's climate has led to the emergence of a new 'energy paradigm' in which sustainability is paramount. Fossil fuels are the biggest source of the carbon dioxide emissions that contribute most to global GHGs, so protecting the climate entails a shift from fossil fuels to renewable, low-carbon sources of energy.

Germany is at the forefront of this new energy paradigm. For two decades it has been amongst the world leaders in climate protection policy. Angela Merkel sees climate change as 'the biggest challenge of the 21st century' and has assumed a leadership role in international and European negotiations to reduce GHG emissions. Germany has set increasingly ambitious targets for reducing its own emissions, introducing a range of policy instruments to achieve them. Yet whilst it has made significant progress towards these targets, its performance has not always met its own high aspirations, and it remains one of the world's largest emitters. The principal reason for this is a carbon-intensive energy mix, which – despite the aggressive promotion of renewable energy – remains heavily dominated by fossil fuels.

Recent policy initiatives (BMU, 2007; BMWi/BMU, 2010) have raised the bar for climate protection, setting course for a massive *Energiewende* (energy transformation) that aims to make Germany one of the greenest economies in the world by 2020. Taking the renewables revolution to the next level, however, entails a radical redesign of the energy system and a huge investment in infrastructure and new technology. The decision following the Fukushima nuclear catastrophe in 2011 to accelerate the exit from nuclear power will deprive Germany of a significant low-carbon energy source, adding further urgency to the energy challenge. The project is almost as large in scale as reunification, involving complex coordination between stakeholders: the energy utilities, infrastructure operators, investors and consumers.

How well equipped is the German government for steering the *Energiewende*? Conventional perspectives on German policy-making raise some doubts. They emphasize the fragmentation of the policy-making framework, with decisions parcelled out between different ministries, between the government in Berlin and the *Länder*, and between public and private actors (Katzenstein, 1987; Green and Paterson, 2005a). Fragmentation creates opportunities for 'veto players' to influence policy in defence of their own interests. Often unable to define policy without the consent of societal actors, government is thus reliant on their voluntary agreement. This style of policy-making is generally geared to gradual, incremental innovation rather than the sort of rapid transformation involved in the *Energiewende*.

I begin by evaluating Germany's performance in reducing carbon dioxide emissions, cutting energy consumption and making the energy economy less carbon intensive. I go on to examine the context of energy policy-making in terms of public opinion, party politics, government and organized interests. The third part of the chapter looks at German policies in relation to the three components of the energy paradigm: the security of supply, sustainability and affordability. Finally I evaluate the government's management of structural change, asking whether Germany can realize the *Energiewende* in spite of the fragmentation of the policy environment.

Climate protection and energy: trends and targets

As can be seen from Table 13.1 Germany is amongst the international leaders in reducing carbon dioxide emissions. Between 1990 and 2011,

Table 13.1   *Carbon dioxide emissions, 1990–2011 (billion tonnes)*

	1990	2000	2011	Change (%) 1990–2011	Change (%) 2000–11
Germany	1.08	0.87	0.81	–20.6	–6.9
EU15	3.33	3.33	3.02	– 9.3	–9.3
EU27	4.32	4.06	3.79	–12.3	–6.7
UK	0.59	0.55	0.47	–20.3	–14.5
USA	4.99	5.87	5.42	8.6	–7.7

Source: Compiled by the author from data in PBL Netherlands / JRC European Commission 2012.

emissions fell by 21 per cent compared with a cut of 12 per cent across the EU27, and a 9 per cent *increase* in the USA. Most of this progress, however, came in the 1990s when emissions fell by almost 15 per cent. In part this reflects the fact that it was an early adopter of climate protection policies and so reaped the emissions bonus earlier than other countries. However, it also reflects the 'wall-fall' effect of German reunification: the collapse of heavy industry in the east and the decommissioning of carbon intensive coal-fired power stations. It has been estimated that around 60 per cent of the reduction in carbon dioxide emissions can be attributed to the 'lucky-strike' (in climate protection terms) of deindustrialization in the east (Schleich et al., 2001). Without this bonus in the 2000s, emissions fell by a much more modest 7 per cent, on a par with the EU27, and behind the UK and USA where climate protection measures were adopted later.

The energy sector has proved stubbornly resistant to emissions reduction and can be seen as the Achilles heel of climate protection policy. The sector reduced carbon dioxide emissions by 19 per cent over the period 1990–2009 compared with a 35 per cent abatement in manufacturing industry. A large part of the reduction in both cases can be attributed to the 'wall-fall' effect. After that, emissions fell by just 2.5 per cent in 2000–09, and by 2009 the sector was responsible for 45 per cent of Germany's emissions compared to about 39 per cent across the EU as a whole (European Commission, 2010b).

The most fundamental way of reducing energy-related carbon dioxide emissions is to consume less energy. Consumption, however, is subject to structural determinants like the size of the population, economic growth and the size of energy intensive manufacturing sectors relative to service sectors. As shown in Table 13.2, Germany's performance in reducing energy consumption is relatively impressive. Despite a significant increase in economic activity between 1990 and 2010, consumption fell by around

Table 13.2   *Gross energy consumption, 1990–2010*
(million tonnes oil equivalent)

	1990	2000	2010	Change (%) 1990–2010	Change (%) 2000–10
Germany	358	344	336	–6.1	–2.3
EU27	1,662	1,725	1,759	5.8	2.0
UK	211	232	213	0.9	–8.2

Source: Compiled by the author from data in European Commission, 2010b; 2012.

6 per cent, whilst consumption elsewhere in Europe continued to grow. Germany, we may conclude, has succeeded in decoupling energy consumption from economic growth.

This is reflected in a decline in the energy intensity of the economy – energy consumed per unit of gross domestic product (GDP). Despite the relatively large size of its manufacturing sector, energy intensity lies significantly below the EU average. It declined significantly between 1990 and 2010, although once again much of this may be attributed to the 'wall-fall' effect: the decline in energy intensity in the 1990s slowed down considerably after 2000.

Germany's weak point from a climate protection point of view lies not in the energy intensity of the economy, but in its carbon intensity (carbon dioxide emissions per unit of energy produced). As shown in Table 13.3, carbon intensity was exceptionally high in 1990 by international comparison. Despite abatement between 1990 and 2009, it remained significantly above the EU average. This reflects a carbon-intensive energy mix in which fossil fuels continue to play a large part.

Carbon intensity in electricity generation is particularly high. As can be seen from Table 13.4, fossil fuels still made up almost 60 per cent of the

Table 13.3   *Carbon intensity, 1990–2010 (tonnes CO_2/tonnes oil equivalent)*

	1990	2000	2010	Change (%) 1990–2010	Change (%) 2000–10
Germany	2.95	2.66	2.51	–15.0	–5.6
EU27	2.75	2.52	2.38	–13.5	–5.5
UK	2.89	2.53	2.50	–13.5	–1.2

Source: Compiled by the author from data in European Commission, 2010b; 2012.

Table 13.4   *Electricity generation by fuel type, 1995–2010 (%)*

	1995	2000	2005	2010
Oil	2	1	2	2
Coal	54	51	48	42
Gas	9	10	13	15
Nuclear	28	9	26	22
Renewables	6	7	11	18

Source: Compiled by the author from data in European Commission, 2010b; 2012.

energy mix in 2010. Germany has traditionally been a coal country, and this remains by far the biggest source of electricity generation (42 per cent compared to 25 per cent across the EU27). The other main sources of electricity generation in 2010 were nuclear energy (22 per cent), renewables (18 per cent) and natural gas (15 per cent). Renewable electricity generation has expanded at a remarkable pace, tripling between 1995 and 2010. Provisional figures suggest that renewable energies may have provided 25 per cent of German electricity in 2012. Some of this increase, however, has merely offset the decline in (low carbon) nuclear energy, which reduced the impact of the renewables revolution on the carbon intensity of the electricity sector.

Germany's *Energiewende* entails a fundamental reorientation of the energy economy, geared to achieving large-scale progressive abatements in GHG emissions through far-reaching changes in energy consumption and production. The headline target is to reduce these emissions by 40 per cent by 2020 and by 80 per cent by 2050 (based on 1990 levels). This is to be achieved in two main ways: first, by reducing primary energy consumption; second, by increasing the share of renewables in the energy mix (see Table 13. 5).

How realistic are these targets? Based on recent performance, the 2020 targets for expanding renewable energies are comfortably within sight. Targets for reducing energy consumption, on the other hand, are more remote. Given that consumption fell by only just over 2 per cent in the decade 2000–10, a 20 per cent reduction in 2008–20 appears unlikely. And if Germany falls short of this target, it will not be able to realize the headline GHG emissions reduction target. By 2011 it was only about halfway there, and in 2012 emissions actually *increased* by 1.6 per cent. To realize the objectives of the *Energiewende*, Germany will therefore have to raise its game quite significantly. In the remainder of this chapter I will assess whether it will be able to do so.

Table 13.5   *Climate change and energy targets*

	2020	2030	2040	2050
Greenhouse gas emissions (% change from 1990)	−40	−55	−70	−80
Primary energy consumption (reduction from 2008)	−20		−50	
Share of renewables in energy consumption (%)	18	30	45	60
Share of renewables in electricity generation (%)	35	50	65	80

Source: Compiled by the author from data in BMU / BMWi (2010).

Policy context

Public policy in a particular country is strongly shaped by the institutional context, and in general German institutions are favourable to a progressive climate protection policy (Weidner and Metz, 2008: 356–7; Weidner and Eberlein, 2009: 321; Hatch, 2010: 141). Public opinion is overwhelmingly supportive, and the prominence of the Greens means that any party that loses touch with public opinion is punished at the polls. On the other hand, the governance of climate protection and energy is highly fragmented across different ministries, militating against 'joined-up' policy. It is also subject to the conflicting lobbying efforts of environmental groups, the renewable energy lobby, conventional energy utilities and energy intensive industry.

Public opinion

Public opinion reflects a powerful discourse dating back to the antinuclear movements of the 1970s (see Rüdig, 2003). In the 1980s attention turned to the emotive issue of *Waldsterben* (forest death), allegedly caused by the effects of industrial emissions. Whilst this debate was characterized by conflicting scientific opinion, it sensitized Germans to the effects of man-made emissions on the earth's atmosphere. By the early 2000s there was a general consensus that climate change was a real problem, caused by the combustion of fossil fuels, and that industrial countries bore responsibility for initiating abatement measures (Weidner and Metz, 2008: 362–3).

Germans are significantly more concerned about climate change than citizens in other European countries. In 2007, 69 per cent identified the issue as one of their five main environmental concerns, as against 57 per cent across the EU27, whilst 28 per cent identified it as their main environmental concern, compared to 19 per cent across the EU27. Moreover, Germans claim to have modified their behaviour accordingly, with 63 per cent claiming to have reduced their energy consumption for environmental reasons as against 47 per cent in the EU27 (European Commission, 2008a).

Germans are also more opposed to nuclear power than their European neighbours: 52 per cent are in favour of reducing reliance on nuclear energy sources, compared to 34 per cent across the EU27 (European Commission, 2010c). Public opinion is more divided, however, about the conditions and timescale for a nuclear exit. A Forsa poll in 2008 found that 61 per cent of Germans supported an exit only on condition that alternative energy sources were sufficiently developed, compared to 34 per cent advocating an unconditional exit. It also found that whilst there was a relative majority of 47 per cent in favour of a rapid nuclear exit, a significant minority of 31 per cent were in favour of allowing existing nuclear plants a longer duration. In addition, 17 per cent were opposed to a nuclear exit (Falter, 2008).

The party politics of climate protection and energy policy

Public support for climate protection is reflected in a consensus amongst the political parties. Yet whilst there is no fundamental opposition to the principle of climate protection policy, there are significant conflicts between parties over the timescale for implementation, the appropriateness of policy instruments, the distribution of costs and the economic consequences (Weidner and Eberlein, 2009: 321). Similarly, whilst there is broad agreement over the goals of energy policy (security of supply, sustainability and affordability) there are conflicts over emphasis and balance between these objectives.

'Ownership' of the environmental and climate protection policy-space belongs to the Greens. '*Atomkraft – nein danke*' was the slogan around which they grew up, and it continues to be their signature policy. The Greens have also fought for ambitious climate protection targets and tough regulatory instruments to achieve them. In energy policy, they advocate the aggressive promotion of renewables, aiming to generate 100 per cent of electricity from these sources by 2030. They put particular emphasis on solar energy, seen by many others as the least cost-effective of the renewables. Having achieved their goal of phasing out nuclear power, they have turned their attention to blocking new coal-fired power plants. Whilst accepting the need for affordable energy, they challenge the perception that renewables are more expensive than conventional energy

sources, arguing that the renewables industry is a major source of employment and technological innovation, contributing to the 'ecological
modernization of the economy'.

Since the 1980s the CDU/CSU and SPD have sought to challenge the
Greens' 'ownership' of environmental and anti-nuclear issues by 'green-
ing' their own policies. The CDU/CSU has been closely allied to the big
energy companies and energy intensive industry. Under Merkel, however,
the party has responded to public opinion by embracing climate protection and the promotion of renewable energies, although it also emphasizes affordability and cost containment. CDU support for renewables,
along with Merkel's decision in 2011 to speed up the nuclear exit, fractured relations with the conventional energy industry. It also created
tensions in relations with the junior coalition partner, the FDP, which is
ideologically opposed to subsidies for renewable (especially solar) energy.

The SPD has a foot in both the renewable and conventional energy
camps. Its power base is North Rhine-Westphalia, which hosts two of the
big four utilities (Eon and RWE), as well as energy intensive industries and
coal. Consequently it has close ties with these interests and seeks to ring-
fence them from the effects of climate protection policy. At the same time,
however, it also has an influential climate protection faction with close
links to the renewable energy sector. It seeks to reconcile its energy and
climate change positions by advocating the construction of modern
'clean' coal-fired power plants as a medium-term bridge to a longer-term
renewable energy future. Whilst supporting the principle of the
Energiewende, it has sought to tap into concerns about energy prices by
making affordability a theme in its 2013 election campaign.

Government and organized interests

Climate protection and energy policy responsibilities are dispersed widely
across government ministries and agencies. Unusually, Germany does not
have an energy ministry. Primary responsibility used to belong to the
Federal Ministry of Economics and Technology (BMWi), a traditional
ally of the big conventional energy companies and the energy intensive
industry (Hatch, 2010: 144). The increasing importance of climate
protection in energy policy, however, was reflected in the transfer of
responsibility for renewable energies to the Federal Ministry for the
Environment, Nature Conservation and Nuclear Safety (BMU) during
the Red–Green coalition. In 2006 it was given further responsibility for
energy efficiency, and its resources were expanded with the creation of
specialist sub-directorates for 'energy and environment' and 'climate
change' (Duffield, 2009: 4286). Thereafter, the two ministries shared
energy policy responsibilities, with an underlying tension between the

BMU's climate protection perspective and the BMWi's emphasis on protecting German industry from measures that might prejudice its international competitiveness. This trend was reversed, however, by the incoming CDU–SPD government in 2013 in which energy was annexed to economics in a new Federal Ministry for Economics and Energy, signaling a reorientation of energy policy back to economic imperatives. Other energy policy responsibilities are exercised by the Federal Ministry for Education and Research (for innovation in new energy management technologies), the Federal Ministry for Transport, Building and Urban Development (for planning authorization) and the Federal Ministry for Food, Agriculture and Consumer Protection (for biofuels), whilst the Federal Network Agency is responsible for the regulation of the electricity grid.

The BMU has been the focal point for Germany's extensive climate protection lobby: the specialist research institutions and NGOs with the ability to exert influence (Weidner and Metz, 2008: 360). Energy policy lobbying has until recently been dominated by big conventional energy utilities like Eon and RWE, energy intensive companies like the chemicals giant BASF, and the Bundesverband der deutschen Industrie (Confederation of German Industry). Renewable energy, however, constitutes an increasingly powerful lobby. Employing some 370,000 people and attracting huge investment (€26.6 billion in 2010) the sector is exceptionally well organized, with industry groups like the *Bundesverband WindEnergie* (the Federal Association for Wind Energy), the *Bundesverband Solarwirtschaft* (the Federal Association for the solar economy) and the umbrella organization the *Bundesverband Erneuerbare Energie* (the Federal Association for Renewable Energy). After the Fukushima nuclear catastrophe, the renewables lobby became the dominant force in energy policy (Buchan, 2012: 15; Bosman, 2012: 16), although its influence may now wane with the takeover of energy by the economics ministry.

Energy security

Energy security is the forgotten theme in German energy policy. This neglect is somewhat surprising given the country's lack of indigenous energy endowments and its heavy dependence on imports. Dependence is particularly pronounced in oil (96 per cent) and natural gas (82 per cent), with around 40 per cent of its gas imports coming from Russia. Yet it has not historically regarded security of supply as a critical issue. Energy was seen as a 'normal commodity', subject to market forces, and security of supply was left primarily to economic actors under the broad oversight of the BMWi.

Security of supply was one of the organizing titles in the three energy summits convened by Chancellor Merkel in 2006–07. Thereafter, however, it was rapidly overshadowed by her climate protection agenda (Duffield, 2009: 4286–7), and its eclipse became more pronounced under the Christian–Liberal government (2009–13). The Energy Concept programme of 2010 identified 'the diversification of energy sources' as a central element in energy policy, but devoted less than 200 words (of a 30-page document) to the issue and was non-committal in outlining measures.

The mainstay of energy security is a strategic partnership with Russia – Germany's main supplier of oil and natural gas. The partnership dates back to the 1970s when it was an integral part of a policy of détente with the Soviet Union. Its foundations lie in a dense web of commercial relationships between the dominant German gas companies (Eon Ruhrgas and BASF Wintershall) and Russia's state controlled energy giant Gazprom (Westphal, 2008: 95–6). Relations were strengthened in the early 2000s by the construction of a new natural gas pipeline – Nord Stream – between Russia and Germany. This project was fostered by a close political relationship between President Putin and Chancellor Schröder, who subsequently assumed the chairmanship of the Nord Stream shareholders' board. Commercial and political ties offset the risks usually associated with heavy dependence on a single source of imported energy. Russia has been regarded as a reliable source of supply and the relationship construed in terms of mutual interdependence.

This perspective has become less persuasive as dependence on Russian gas has spiralled over the last decade (Dolata-Kreutzkamp, 2008: 667; Duffield, 2009: 4285). At the same time confidence in Gazprom has been shaken by its disputes with the Ukraine in 2006 and 2009, which disrupted supplies to Europe. Moreover, since Putin's return to the presidency, German–Russian relations have cooled over his human rights record, and Merkel's relationship with the president is distinctly frosty.

A more far-reaching cause for concern is the threat of a global energy crunch – particularly in natural gas – stemming from a steep rise in demand from developing Asian economies. The global race for resources has led policy-makers to think about security in terms of 'energy foreign policy'. Frank-Walter Steinmeier, foreign minister in the grand coalition (2005–09), identified it as one of the three most pressing challenges of global security (Dolata-Kreutzkamp, 2008: 668). The reinvention of energy security in foreign policy terms is mirrored in the increased prominence of the foreign office in energy policy. Its main goals are: first, to persuade energy producer and transit countries to sign up to the Energy Charter Treaty (an international legal framework for cross-border energy cooperation); second, to promote the international dissemination of renewables, thereby reducing global demand for fossil fuels; and third, to promote the international integration of emissions trading in order to create a level playing field for German industry in global competition.

On the domestic front, Germany seeks to reap the benefits of its sustainable energy agenda in terms of security of supply. Curbing domestic demand through energy savings and efficiency can be expected to ease pressure on supply, whilst expanding renewable energies reduces reliance on imported fossil fuels. However, these expectations are hedged around with uncertainties over whether Germany will meet its targets for reducing energy consumption and expanding renewables. The exit from nuclear power also raises new questions about the country's capacity to meet its demand for electricity. The BMWi noted that, following the decommissioning of eight nuclear power plants in 2011, 'secure capacity' was only just sufficient to meet 'peak demand'. New-build capacity (mainly in coal-fired power plants) due to come on-stream shortly means that security of supply will become less of a concern by 2015, but it will become increasingly critical towards 2022 as more nuclear capacity is decommissioned (BMWi, 2012: 23–4).

One way of easing security of supply concerns would be for Germany to exploit its resources of shale gas. Estimates of the reserves vary, but they could be as high as 2,300 billion cubic metres – enough to satisfy natural gas consumption for over ten years. Extraction involves a technology of fracturing rock with a high-pressure mix of water, sand and chemicals to unlock the gas. Widely practised in North America, 'fracking' carries potential environmental risks of groundwater contamination and increasing seismic activity. Some European countries – notably France – have banned the technology. Germany, however, faces a dilemma: shale gas offers an answer to its security of supply concerns, but the environmental risks make it politically controversial. Merkel's Christian–Liberal coalition sidestepped the issue ahead of the 2013 election. The new government recognizes the potential of shale gas, and rejects Green calls for an outright ban on fracking. Responsibility for licensing gas extraction rests with the *Länder*, however, and the government lacks the political will to take the lead by establishing a clear regulatory framework for the industry. In the absence of such, legal uncertainty discourages companies from making the investment required to get the gas out of the ground, and the contribution that shale gas will make to Germany's energy security remains uncertain. The government itself was divided, with Environment Minister Peter Altmaier urging caution and Economics Minister Philipp Rösler emphasizing the economic opportunities. Initially, the government was reluctant to establish a framework of regulatory rules ahead of the 2013 election. But whilst keeping the door open to the industry, the legal uncertainty discouraged companies from making the investment needed to get the gas out of the ground. So in early 2013 the government drafted legislation defining the conditions under which shale gas extraction will be permitted. Legislation, however, is subject to the opposition's block-ade in the Bundesrat, and the contribution that shale gas will make to Germany's energy security remains uncertain.

Sustainability

Sustainability has been the dominant theme in the German energy para-digm since the late 1980s, when scientific evidence of the effects of GHGs on climate entered the political arena (Weidner and Metz, 2008: 360). The main objective has been to reduce carbon dioxide emissions resulting from the combustion of fossil fuels. Policies are designed to reduce consumption through energy savings and efficiency, and to shift the energy mix from fossil fuels towards renewables. The defining programmes of recent policy are the Integrated Energy and Climate Protection Programme (BMU, 2007) and the Energy Concept for an Environmentally Sound, Reliable and Affordable Energy Supply (BMWi/BMU, 2010). The main instruments are the eco-tax, the EU emis-sions trading scheme and the promotion of renewable energy through the 'feed-in tariff' system. Germany has also decided that the risks associated with nuclear energy are unjustifiable and is committed to closing the industry, although the timescale for closure has been contested.

The eco-tax

Taxation can be a powerful market-based instrument of energy and climate protection policy with the potential to create economic incentives for energy savings and efficiency. Germany's energy tax regime reflects its climate protection commitments, but it is also marked by efforts to safe-guard the international competitiveness of energy intensive industry. The current regime can be traced back to the eco-tax reform enacted by the Red–Green government in 1999, which included a hike in existing taxes on petrol, natural gas and mineral oils, and a new levy on electricity (Rüdig, 2003: 259–61; Weidner and Metz, 2008: 364–5). The idea had been around for a decade, but was opposed by business and industry on the grounds that it would undermine Germany's international competi-tiveness. Chancellor Kohl had supported the principle of the eco-tax, but had backed down in return for a voluntary undertaking by industry asso-ciations to reduce carbon dioxide emissions. Pushed by the Greens,

Schröder went ahead with the tax, but made concessions to industrial interests which have compromised its effectiveness.

The effectiveness of the eco-tax suffers from two main flaws. First, energy intensive industry enjoys reduced rates of taxation. Second, the tax fails to discriminate between fossil fuels and low-carbon energy, so, whilst it creates incentives to reduce overall consumption, it fails to target the most carbon-intensive energy sources. Indeed coal is exempted from the tax altogether. Thus the overall impact of the eco-tax has been a modest reduction of around 2–3 per cent in carbon dioxide emissions between 2003 and 2010, mostly derived from the transport sector, with minimal reductions in energy related emissions (Klein, 2012: 16).

The EU Emissions Trading Scheme (ETS)

The ETS was the EU's flagship instrument of climate protection, designed to enable it to meet its GHG reduction obligations under the Kyoto protocol. Businesses in industrial and energy sectors are allocated allowances or permits for emissions within overall limits set by member states and the European Commission. Permits can be traded in a market, which sets a price on carbon, designed to act as a constraint on emissions. The effectiveness of the scheme, however, has been compromised by the over-allocation of permits, depressing the market price of carbon to the point where it has ceased to provide any incentive for companies to reduce emissions.

As Europe's largest economy and its biggest GHG emitter, Germany has a key role in the ETS. But it has an uneasy relationship with the scheme, and has not exerted the sort of leadership that might have been expected from a climate protection champion (Wettestad, 2011: 98). The BMWi in particular has been very wary of the effect of carbon pricing on the competitiveness of industry. It has therefore been over-generous in the allocation of allowances and has resisted calls to auction permits, preferring to allocate them freely. Germany's implementation of the ETS has been described as 'sobering and disappointing', resulting in a 'bureaucratic system ... heavily biased in favour of ... utility and other industry interests' (Ziesing, 2009: 344). Its lack of leadership was shown up particularly starkly in 2013 by its inability to break an EU deadlock over a proposal to suspend the allocation of permits in order to revive a moribund carbon market. With the CDU–FDP coalition divided, and chancellor Merkel unwilling to risk conflict in the run-up to the election, ETS reform was delayed until 2014.

Promoting renewable energy sources

The aggressive promotion of renewable energy has been the most successful of Germany's climate protection policies (Lauber and Mez, 2006;

Oschmann, 2010). The main driver is the 'feed-in tariff', designed to encourage investment in renewable energy technologies. Producers of renewable energy get a set price for their output, based on the costs of production. Solar power, for instance, is more expensive than wind power, so it attracts a higher tariff. The instrument dates from the 1991 Electricity Feed-In Act, which was replaced under the Red–Green coalition in 2000 by the more expansive Renewable Energy Sources Act. This act established a schedule of enhanced feed-in tariffs that were fixed for 20 years, thereby reducing the uncertainty that had held back investment in the 1990s. It also gave renewable electricity preferential access to the grid and imposed an obligation on utilities to purchase all the renewable power that was offered to them. The feed-in tariff system is 'broadly well-designed' (Klein, 2012) and it has been very successful in promoting renewables. Overall the share of renewables in electricity generation increased almost threefold in the decade from 2000, and by 2011 it accounted for over 20 per cent. Wind energy is the leader, increasing six-fold since 2000, and contributing 40 per cent of renewable electricity generation in 2011, ahead of biomass/biogas (30 per cent), hydroelectricity (15 per cent) and solar power (15 per cent).

The next step in the renewables revolution presents formidable structural, technological and financial challenges. The electricity system reflects the historic structure of the industry, which is highly centralized, with a few big utilities operating large-scale fossil fuel or nuclear power plants in close proximity to the urban industrial centres of consumption. Renewable electricity generation by contrast is based on a large number of small-scale wind farms and solar installations. Incorporating these into the electricity grid places a major strain on network capacity, especially since most wind power is located in north-east Germany, far from the centres of consumption in the south-west. The BMWi estimates that overcoming bottlenecks in the grid requires the construction or upgrade of 8,200 km of power lines over the next ten years at an estimated cost of €20 billion, though the project has yet to gain momentum (BMWi, 2012).

Most of Germany's wind energy is currently onshore, and transforming it from a niche market to a mainstream source of electricity entails harnessing offshore wind. Offshore wind installations are expected to generate the equivalent of ten nuclear power plants by 2020. Planning applications have been lodged for over 120 installations, but only six were under construction in 2013, all behind schedule. Projects are stalled by delays in the technically challenging business of connecting deep-water installations (some over 150 km offshore) to the mainland grid – at an overall cost of some €15 billion.

The investment needed to adapt the electricity grid for the energy mix envisaged in the *Energiewende* has stagnated. Government legislation –

the Network Development Act (2009) and the Network Expansion Acceleration Act (2011) – was designed to facilitate expansion by streamlining the regulatory and planning regimes. Ultimately, though, responsibility lies with the four companies that own the grid (three of which are non-German), but they lack the requisite financial muscle. So serious is the threat to the *Energiewende* from network investment failure that a member of Merkel's Cabinet called in 2013 for the public ownership of the grid, long advocated by the SPD and Greens, but strongly opposed by the FDP (*Der Spiegel*, 14 January 2013).

A second problem stems from the inherently intermittent character of renewable energy. The output of wind and solar power varies with weather conditions and is difficult to balance with fluctuating demand. There are two approaches to solving this problem: storing electricity to even out supply, and changing the patterns of consumption through 'smart metering' (Römer et al., 2012). The technologies of storage and smart metering, however, are in their infancy and do not offer an immediate solution to the problem. So even though the volume of renewable energy continues to increase, it requires back-up from conventional sources – coal and gas plants operated by the big utilities – to provide flexible fill-in power during periods of low wind or solar output. But because the Renewable Energy Act gives wind and solar power priority dispatch on the transmission network, the utilities cannot be sure how much back-up capacity will be purchased or at what price. This uncertainty discourages them from investing in the new power stations needed to avert an 'energy crunch' as nuclear plants are closed towards the end of the decade (*Spiegel Online*, 29 August 2012). The government has considered legislation to compel the companies to do so, but this would lead to a legal battle with the industry and would almost certainly fail in the courts. Another option would be to guarantee the companies a price for back-up power; but the incalculable cost of such an undertaking is likely to be prohibitive.

The closure of the nuclear industry

Nuclear power is the most politically sensitive issue in German energy policy. It also lies at the intersection of the three energy policy objectives outlined at the start of this chapter. Delivering a large slice of Germany's power generation, nuclear energy plays a key role in security of supply. Once the massive start-up costs have been absorbed, it produces relatively affordable power. At the same time, it offers a non-carbon energy source. But the potential dangers of catastrophic accidents, and the risks associated with the transportation and storage of nuclear waste, mean that its sustainability is questionable.

Germany is not the only country to have taken the decision to exit from nuclear power, but it is the only major manufacturing economy to have done so, and the stakes are therefore higher. Nuclear exit entails large-scale system change, so the timescale of the transition is critical. The initial decision was taken by the Red–Green coalition (1998–2005). The Greens' participation in the government was conditional on Chancellor Schröder's commitment to shut down the nuclear industry. Some Greens would have preferred a rapid closure, but the party leadership accepted Schröder's strategy of seeking a consensual agreement with the industry. After bitter and protracted wrangling, the two sides agreed a timetable that would see the last nuclear power plants closing in the early 2020s (see Rüdig, 2003: 261–3).

The return of a centre-right government in 2009 provided an opportunity for revisiting the decision, particularly as it coincided with a world-wide renaissance in nuclear power and a new emphasis on economic stability in the wake of the global financial crisis. On the other hand, a majority of Germans continued to support a nuclear exit, mobilized by a revivified anti-nuclear movement. The CDU/CSU was divided over how far to extend the phase-out. Merkel herself was faced with a dilemma, having established a reputation in 2007 as a 'green' chancellor, but having also pledged in 2008 to protect German jobs and investment. The industry itself was desperate to reprieve nuclear assets that would collectively generate an estimated €10 billion for each additional year of life. It was also in a hurry because some plants were fast approaching their closure date under the 2001 agreement. In a balancing act that typifies her style, Merkel came to terms with the industry in autumn 2010. Older plants would be granted eight-year extensions, newer ones an additional 14 years. In return the industry agreed to a nuclear fuel tax worth an annual €2.3 billion and payments into a renewable energy fund expected to amount to some €15 billion.

This agreement unravelled dramatically six months later with the Fukushima catastrophe in March 2011. Merkel responded to an outburst of anti-nuclear protest with a rapid volte-face, immediately suspending the operation of the seven oldest nuclear plants (and one that was already off-grid for safety reasons) and imposing a three-month moratorium on future plans, pending the report of the hastily convened Ethics Commission for a Safe Energy Supply. Widely perceived as a cynical manoeuvre in the run-up to state elections, the move failed to prevent the Greens (already flying high in the polls following the 2010 decision) from increasing their vote by 10–12 per cent and winning the state premiership in Baden-Württemberg. When the Ethics Commission concluded that the risks associated with nuclear energy were unjustifiable (Ethics Commission, 2011), the government proceeded with legislation closing the eight suspended plants and phasing out the remaining ones by 2022. The move precipitated a furious reaction from the four utilities operating the nuclear plants. They initiated legal actions for damages arising from the closure of their plants, which they claimed was unconstitutional. Actions are currently winding their way through the courts and are not expected to be resolved until 2015.

Economic efficiency/affordability

Economic efficiency and affordability has been described as 'the most constant goal of post-war German energy policy' (Duffield and Westphal, 2011: 171). Manufacturing industry is central to the economy, and it needs affordable energy to remain internationally competitive. Successive energy programmes reiterate the imperative of an economically viable energy supply (BMU, 2007; BMWi/BMU, 2010). Yet German energy prices are amongst the highest in Europe: domestic electricity was 37 per cent higher than the EU average in 2011; and industrial consumers paid 11 per cent more than their European counterparts for electricity and 32 per cent more for natural gas (Eurostat, 2012). The explanation for high prices lies in the oligopolistic structure of the electricity and natural gas industries and the consequent lack of competition. Powerful 'national champion' energy utilities are seen as essential in managing relations with foreign companies like Gazprom on which Germany relies for much its energy (Westphal, 2008: 101). Governments have therefore sought to protect the big utilities from competition, resisting global trends towards the liberalization of energy sectors, and giving only half-hearted support to EU attempts to open up European markets (Duffield and Westphal, 2011: 177–83).

Electricity prices are also loaded with the costs of supporting renewable energy. The feed-in tariff for renewable electricity is higher than the market price, and the difference is passed on to the consumer in the form of a renewables surcharge. The steep rise in the volume of renewable electricity since 2000 has been reflected in progressive increases in the surcharge. The overall annual cost (calculated by multiplying the difference between the feed-in tariff and the market price by the volume of renewable electricity) reached €13.2 billion in 2010 (Klein, 2012). Feed-in tariffs are guaranteed for 20 years and cannot be altered retrospectively, so the only way to reduce costs is to reduce the tariff for new projects. Since 2009, the government has made annual cuts in the tariff for solar power (the least cost-effective renewable energy source). The strength of the solar energy lobby, however, means that tariff reductions are politically difficult to achieve, and the tariff remains uneconomically high.

German industry has been able to live with high energy costs, partly because it competes internationally on the basis of quality rather than price, partly because it has kept energy costs down by improving energy efficiency, thereby reducing consumption and cutting costs. However, it has also been cushioned from the effects of high underlying prices by a wide range of tax concessions and exemptions (Umweltbundesamt, 2010). Manufacturing industry and agriculture pay only 60 per cent of the standard rate of energy and eco-taxes, and the most energy intensive companies benefit from additional concessions that can bring their energy tax bill close to zero. These concessions were initially intended to expire in 2012, but they were renewed until 2022 with the proviso that companies have to show annual energy efficiency savings of 1.3 per cent. Energy intensive industry also benefits from concessions in relation to the renewables surcharge. Whilst these 'electricity guzzlers' account for 18 per cent of overall consumption, they bear a mere 0.3 per cent of the cost burden (*Spiegel Online*, 29 August 2012). The exemption of some 1,700 such companies from the renewables surcharge is currently under investigation by the European Commission as a form of state aid. Anticipating the outcome, the government plans to reduce subsidies to renewable energy although this will not begin until 2015.

The energy sector itself is virtually exempt from energy and eco-taxes, and the coal industry benefits from a range of additional subsidies without which it could not have survived. The nuclear industry is also extensively subsidized through state support for research, decommissioning of nuclear plants and insurance guarantees. Overall, the Umweltbundesamt (Federal Environment Agency) estimates that energy tax concessions to industry, along with subsidies to the energy sector, amount to €11.6 billion annually, most of which supports fossil fuels. Tax concessions and subsidies for fossil fuel energy sit uneasily with Germany's commitment to sustainability.

Tax concessions also have the effect of loading energy costs onto domestic consumers. The renewables surcharge on household electricity bills increased from 1.2 cents per unit to 3.5 cents in 2009, and despite Merkel's commitment in 2011 to freeze the surcharge, it was increased again to 5.5 cents in 2013. It now adds over 10 per cent (around €185) to the average household electricity bill (Klein, 2012: 22). Although most consumers regard this as an acceptable price for a sustainable energy future, the uneven distribution of the renewables surcharge between industry and households risks undermining public support for the *Energiewende*.

Managing the Energiewende

Can Germany succeed in meeting its GHG emissions reduction targets whilst phasing out nuclear energy and maintaining the security and affordability of its energy supply? The answer depends in large part on the capacity of government to manage structural change and to contain the associated costs – and on the commitment of private economy actors. Early indications are not promising. The government's steering capacity is compromised by the syndrome of institutional pluralism outlined at the start of this chapter. In the absence of an energy ministry, the main responsibilities are parcelled out between ministries, and the division of labour is not conducive to 'joined-up' policy-making. For instance, whilst the BMU is responsible for expanding renewable energy, responsibility for upgrading the electricity grid to deliver it to consumers is in the hands of the BMWi. The lack of progress in resolving the bottlenecks that are holding back the *Energiewende* has been blamed on the lack of overall coordination.

Turf conflicts were compounded by policy tensions between ministers and coalition parties over the spiralling costs of support for renewable energy – especially for solar energy. Cost-conscious Economics Minister Philipp Rösler (FDP) pressed for a major overhaul of the Renewable Energy Sources Act to limit feed-in tariffs. Environment Minister Norbert Röttgen (CDU) adopted a less radical approach of piecemeal cuts in the tariff. The simmering row between the two cost Röttgen his job in 2012. His successor, Peter Altmaier, attempted to tackle the issue in 2013, proposing a two-year cap on the renewable surcharge, the partial suspension of the feed-in tariff, and an 'energy solidarity tax' on renewable energy profits. In the face of a backlash from the renewables industry, however, he was overruled by Chancellor Merkel. Under the challenge from the EU, however, it seems certain that the CDU–SPD government will rein back subsidies to renewable energies, thus slowing the pace of the *Energiewende*.

The success of the *Energiewende* also depends on the commitment of the private energy economy. Energy and climate change policy has often involved voluntary agreement on the part of industry and the energy sector to cooperate with the government in pursuit of its objectives. Underlying this consensual approach was a 'cosy' relationship between government, the big energy utilities and industrial power consumers. Merkel's volte-face on nuclear phase-out has fractured this relationship. The utilities are now involved in a legal war with the government. The Confederation of German Industry, once a key broker in relations between government and the energy sector, is split between winners and losers from the nuclear phase-out. And the electricity grid is now owned by non-German companies with less obligation to comply with government policy.

Conclusion

Since the wall-fall effect of the early 1990s, Germany's progress in reducing carbon dioxide emissions has been steady but unspectacular. Climate protection policy has succeeded in decoupling energy consumption from economic growth by encouraging energy savings and efficiency. But the carbon intensity of the energy economy remains stubbornly high. In part this reflects the gradual phase-out of (low-carbon) nuclear power, which has offset the effects of a rapid increase in renewable energies – the major success story of German climate protection policy. However, it also stems from the exemptions or concessions granted to the energy sector and energy intensive industries under the eco- and energy-tax regimes, which have weakened incentives to reduce the carbon intensity of the economy. Tax concessions reflect conflicts between the objectives of sustainability and affordability, which are embedded in the structure of policy-making. Whilst the BMU has been a forceful advocate of sustainability, the BMWi has prioritized affordable energy in the interests of Germany's international competitiveness. For a decade the BMU has been in the ascendancy, but there are now indications that the trend is reversing.

Accelerating the shift from fossil fuels to renewables whilst exiting from nuclear energy involves large-scale structural change in the energy sector, testing the steering capacity of government. The lack of coordination between the expansion of renewable electricity and the development of the power grid is a stark example of this. The distribution of energy policy competences across government ministries defies coordination and contributes to a sense that the project is out of control. Attempts to manage costs encountered coalition and lobby group differences, notably between the FDP's ideological aversion to renewables subsidies and the resistance of the renewables lobby to their curtailment. Above all, Merkel's rallying call to stakeholders to invest in the *Energiewende* as a 'collective national project' cut little ice with an energy industry still reeling from her volte-face over the phase-out of nuclear power.

Whilst Merkel's new grand coalition government remains committed to the *Energiewende*, it is also agreed on the need to make the transition to a renewable energy future more affordable. This was already evident in the 2013 election, in which energy policy debate focused on electricity prices, the cost of supporting renewables, and the distribution of those costs. The new government programme includes an immediate amendment to the Renewable Energy Act to reduce the feed-in tariff for new onshore wind power. There are also longer-term plans to make renewable electricity producers more market oriented and less reliant on the renewables surcharge. The critical question is how this will impact on Germany's ability to replace the capacity of nuclear plants due to close by the end of the decade, whilst simultaneously meeting its targets for reducing the carbon emission of the energy sector.

Leading the way towards low-carbon, low-risk energy promises Germany a sustainable energy future. Expanding renewable energy increases the diversity of energy supply, and could boost security of supply by reducing dependence on Russian gas. Costs may in the long term be offset by the technological and competitive advantage accruing to the domestic renewable energy industry. At the same time, however, the disruptive affects of the *Energiewende* entail risks to security of supply over the next decade. There is a very real possibility that the project may stall over costs and that Germany may fail to realize its emissions reductions targets by 2020. Its fate will ultimately depend on the assertion of policy leadership on the part of Chancellor Merkel and the dynamics of her new government.

Chapter 14

Citizenship, Migration and Cultural Pluralism

SIMON GREEN

German immigration and citizenship policy is characterized by a striking paradox. On the one hand, Germany is one of the primary destinations for immigration in the developed world. It has by far the largest absolute number of non-nationals in the EU living within its territory, and more citizens from outside the EU (so-called third country nationals), who are principally affected by immigration regulations, than any other EU member state. This non-national population is moreover very well settled: in 2010, almost two-fifths had been resident in the country for at least 20 years.

On the other hand, until relatively recently, official government policy was that Germany was 'not a country of immigration' (*Deutschland ist kein Einwanderungsland*) (Joppke, 1999: 62–99; Green, 2004; Messina, 2007: 124–34) and did not seek to increase its population through immigration in the way that countries such as the United States had done. In consequence, Germany's legislative framework in this field was, until 1990, surprisingly meagre for a country which had received such large numbers of immigrants. In addition, the country's definition of citizenship was highly restrictive, with significant barriers to naturalization.

This mismatch between high levels of de facto immigration and a historically low level of policy regulation has meant that the policy domain has been defined by an underlying tension, with the policy framework lagging behind the social reality of immigration on the ground. Yet at the same time, immigration is not static but evolves over time, thereby creating a significant challenge for policy-makers. Other European countries face a similar challenge, but it is particularly acute in Germany, both because of the range of policy issues to be resolved and the levels of immigration it has experienced. Especially since 1998, German policy-makers have attempted to meet this challenge by matching the policy framework to the reality of immigration as well as the changing needs and priorities of the German economy. In this chapter I explain these shifts in the policy and politics of immigration, focusing on the reassessment of labour migration and the quest for integration and citizenship. I go on to discuss the related issues of ethnic Germans, asylum and family reunification, before concluding with a reflection on the future trajectory of this policy domain. First, though, we need to understand the historical context, and it is here that the chapter begins.

Historical background

Immigration in post-war Germany has taken two main forms. First, ethnic German migrants from eastern Europe and the Soviet Union were given the right to immigrate to and settle in West Germany, and over 4.5 million persons have done so since 1950. Second, labour migrants (so-called 'guestworkers' or *Gastarbeiter*) were recruited by West German companies from southern Europe and the Mediterranean between 1955 and 1973. Thereafter, they were followed by their dependants and, after 1980, growing numbers of asylum seekers. By 1989, some 4.8 million persons without German nationality (*Ausländer*), comprising 7.7 per cent of the total population, lived in West Germany (Marshall, 1992; Herbert, 2001; Green, 2003).

Immigration increased strongly with German unification. Between 1989 and 1993, over 1.4 million ethnic Germans arrived in the country; in addition, over 1.2 million asylum applications were lodged between 1990 and 1993, with over 438,000 in 1992 alone. Since the mid-1990s, the number of non-nationals (which excludes ethnic Germans) has held broadly steady, notwithstanding a recent sharp increase in 2011 and 2012 (see Table 14.1).

Despite this steady stream of immigration, the official policy of the federal government until 1998, regardless of its party political composition, was that Germany was 'not a country of immigration'. While such an interpretation might conceivably have made sense when viewed on its own terms, it could scarcely be reconciled with the reality in Germany's cities, where up to 30 per cent of the population did not hold a German passport. But it was complicated further by the fact that ethnic German migrants from eastern Europe and what was then the Soviet Union were considered German citizens, and were thus excluded from this goal altogether (Brubaker, 1992).

However, since unification, a substantial number of policy developments have taken place. Already in January 1991, a new Foreigners' Law (*Ausländergesetz*) came into force, replacing the previous version which dated back to 1965, when immigration to Germany was still in its infancy. In 1992, in a major cross-party compromise, two key sources of

Table 14.1   *Non-national population of Germany, 1990–2012*

Year	Non-national population
1990	5,342,500
1991	5,882,300
1992	6,495,800
1993	6,878,100
1994	6,990,500
1995	7,173,900
1996	7,314,000
1997	7,365,800
1998	7,319,600
1999	7,343,600
2000	7,296,800
2001	7,318,600
2002	7,335,600
2003	7,334,800
2004*	6,717,100
2005*	6,755,800
2006*	6,751,000
2007*	6,744,900
2008*	6,727,600
2009*	6,694,800
2010*	6,753,600
2011*	6,930,900
2012*	7,213,700

* In 2004, the data in this register was revised and corrected; as a result, the figures from this year onwards are not comparable with previous years.
Source: *Ausländerzentralregister* data, listed in *Statistisches Bundesamt* (2013: 15).

immigration were limited (Green, 2003: 234–6). On the one hand, Germany's constitutional right to asylum was restricted in an attempt to stem the very high numbers of applications which were being lodged in the country. On the other hand, the deal included the limitation of ethnic German migration to those born before 1993. Together, these restrictions have helped to reduce both forms of migration substantially (see Figure 14.1). Indeed, by 2012, the number of ethnic Germans (*Spätaussiedler*) had fallen to effectively negligible levels.

The pace of policy reform quickened markedly following the 1998 federal election, which saw the CDU/CSU–FDP government under Helmut Kohl replaced by an SPD–Green coalition under the chancellorship of Gerhard Schröder. One of the new government's first priorities was to liberalize the citizenship law, which remarkably had not been updated in its essence since 1913. This attempt was only partially successful, with the government's proposal to introduce dual citizenship proving to be especially controversial. Nonetheless, a compromise was found and

Figure 14.1   *Asylum seekers and ethnic German migration, 1991–2012*

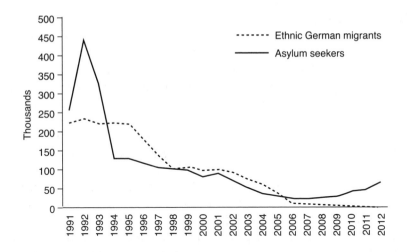

Source: Figure constructed from data contained in *Bundesamt für Migration und Flüchtlinge* (2013a: 11; 2013b: 52).

the new law took effect on 1 January 2000 (Howard, 2008). In 2000, the government also introduced a temporary programme for the recruitment of IT specialists (the so-called 'Green Card' programme), although this was only partially successful.

However, it was the 2005 Immigration Law (*Zuwanderungsgesetz*) which arguably sealed the transformation of the policy management of this sector. As well as being the first law of its kind in Germany's history, it introduced the possibility, however limited, for the recruitment of permanent high-skilled migration for the first time since 1973. It also radically simplified the residence status of non-nationals and introduced Dutch-style integration courses, as well as a number of other changes (to be discussed below) which have impacted on all aspects of immigration policy (Green et al., 2012: 131). Following the return of the CDU/CSU to government after the 2005 federal election, in a grand coalition with the SPD under Angela Merkel, the focus has shifted again, away from large-scale major policy reforms to an evolution in the way the debate over immigration has been framed.

The reassessment of labour migration

The first major change to have taken place over the past ten years is the return of labour migration to the political agenda. In turn, this has been linked to two broader societal developments, namely demographic change and skills shortages.

First, far-reaching change to the size of (West) Germany's population has been looming ever since the total fertility rate of women fell within ten years from about 2.5 children per woman in 1965 to 1.4 children per woman in 1975 – a level far below the rate of 2.2 which is required for a population to replace itself without recourse to migration. Moreover, this level has remained largely constant ever since the 1970s, including after unification. This already significant trend has been compounded by increasing life expectancy, which has increased steadily to reach around 80 today. The combined effect of these two dynamics will be for Germany both to shrink and age: by 2060, its population is projected to decline from currently 80 million to 65 million, with the share of the population aged 65 or more rising from one-fifth in 2009 to over one-third in the next 50 years (*Statistisches Bundesamt*, 2009).

Clearly, this development has not crept up on policy-makers or on the public; in fact, the impact of demographic change has been debated since the mid-1970s. Nor is Germany alone in experiencing such a development: on the contrary, several other European countries, notably Spain and the Baltic states, have even lower fertility rates than Germany. Nonetheless, as the EU's most populous member state, the impact of such change is particularly keenly felt. There is also a growing sense of urgency, as the projections show that the decline in Germany's overall population will begin to accelerate in earnest after 2020. The results of the 2011 census, which found that the total population was 1.5 million, or 2 per cent, lower than previously calculated, has only reinforced that concern.

Inevitably, the demographic challenge affects a significant number of areas of public policy, including welfare, family policy and even the decision to suspend conscription to the *Bundeswehr* (Green et al., 2012: 122). In recognition of this fact, the federal government in 2012 published its first integrated demographic strategy (*Bundesministerium des Innern*, 2012). But the demographic challenge also clearly has implications for migration policy, as new labour migration is one obvious option for counteracting such population trends. In fact, two key policy commissions on immigration which reported in 2001, one (the so-called Süssmuth Commission) convened by the federal government, the other (the so-called Müller Commission) convened by the opposition CDU, recognized that immigration had at least some role to play in addressing the demographic shortages that were likely to develop.

Germany's need for new migration is further accentuated by a growing awareness of shortages in key sectors, both high skilled and low skilled. Already, seasonal labour migration in agriculture has been possible since unification, and sustained lobbying by industry over IT shortages underpinned the SPD–Green government's Green Card programme of 2000. But until 2010, such pressures were masked first by the sluggish growth of the economy until 2006, and then by the impact of the financial crisis. However, Germany emerged from its deep recession in 2009 unexpectedly quickly, and with its economy highly competitive, so the political perception of skills and labour shortages have become particularly acute. In consequence, the political emphasis has shifted very much onto the need to recruit skilled labour from outside the EU, rather than prevent it. That already represents a remarkable degree of progress in the country's policy in this field.

And yet, the federal government has taken only tepid steps to open access to its labour market. A Canadian-style points-based system for entry was not part of the political compromise for the 2005 *Zuwanderungsgesetz*, and instead a relatively high annual salary level was set as a prerequisite for a residence permit. This has only gradually been reduced, most recently in the context of the EU-wide 'Blue Card' to around €45,000 annually. In consequence, the take-up of the available routes for high-skilled migrants from outside the EU has been so low as to border on the negligible (Green, 2013a: 339). The SPD–Green government also imposed a seven-year transition period on the free movement of labour from the new central and eastern European EU member states who joined in 2004; and the CDU/CSU–SPD grand coalition imposed the same on Bulgaria and Romania when they joined the EU in 2007. On the other hand, the recognition of foreign qualifications was eased in 2012, and the federal government has relaxed the restrictions on non-EU students at German universities staying on to work after their degree programmes ended.

While such policy innovations have prompted the OECD (2013: 15) to declare Germany as among the countries 'with the fewest restrictions on labour migration for highly skilled occupations', its net migration flows since unification underline the scale of the challenge the country faces. Figure 14.2 shows that the overall level of net migration has fallen substantially from its peak of 782,000 in 1992, and then quite steadily after 2001; indeed, in 2008 and 2009 the country even experienced net emigration, with more people leaving the country than arriving. The reason for this lies in the combination of declining immigration and a steady level of emigration, not only by people from immigrant communities, notably Turks, but also by Germans (Green, 2013a). Often, those emigrating have been highly educated, including university researchers and doctors who have sought new opportunities in countries such as the UK, the US, Canada and Australia. Both in its size and composition by nationality, this development represents a significant turnaround from the situation before unification, and even in the period up to 2000.

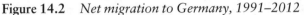

Figure 14.2   *Net migration to Germany, 1991–2012*

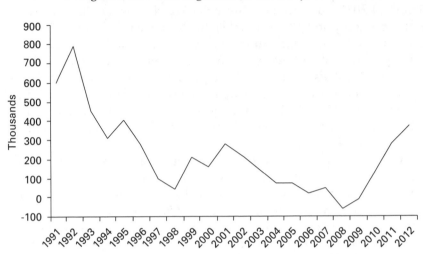

Source: *Statistisches Bundesamt*, available at https://www.destatis.de/DE/ZahlenFakten/
Indikatoren/LangeReihen/Bevoelkerung/lrbev07.html, accessed 10 December 2013.

Certainly, Germany's strong economic position coming out of the global recession has helped to attract the highest levels of immigration for 20 years, principally from the new eastern member states of the EU. Even so, the longer-term perspective is one of relatively low levels of net migration, which will moreover exacerbate Germany's demographic development. More broadly, the low levels of residence permits granted to high-skilled non-EU citizens indicate that Germany may find it more difficult than it thinks to compete directly with countries such as the United States and Canada for the world's 'brightest and best'.

The quest for integration and citizenship

The second key area where approaches and policy have evolved over the past decade is integration and citizenship. In this respect too, (West) Germany's starting position was traditionally defined by the aspiration towards a non-immigration country, which dictated that the regularization of residence status, and especially access to citizenship, were considered the exception rather than the rule. In turn, this exclusive approach had its roots in a historical conception of German nationality as an ethno-cultural construct (Brubaker, 1992). This conception underpinned the 1913 Imperial Citizenship Law (*Reichs- und Staatsangehörigkeitsgesetz*), which, as noted above, remained in force until 2000. This law also stipulated that citizenship at birth could only be acquired through descent (*jus sanguinis*) and not through birth within Germany (*jus soli*), the method of ascription traditionally employed by both the UK and France.

In practice, this meant that policy in this area was traditionally extremely restrictive. The 1965 *Ausländergesetz* assumed that immigrants would not generally be granted permanent residence status, and it took a landmark ruling of the Federal Constitutional Court in 1978 to change this practice (see Joppke, 1999: 73). The result was that considerable numbers of non-nationals spent years, if not decades, living in West Germany on nothing more than a temporary residence permit.

In the area of citizenship, West Germany was arguably even more exclusive. Again drawing on the mantra of the 'non-immigration country', the 1977 Guidelines on Naturalisation (*Einbürgerungsrichtlinien*) specified the acquisition of citizenship as an exceptional act and made this subject to long periods of residence, high fees and the requirement for applicants to obtain release from their former citizenship – a lengthy, time-consuming and often expensive process. In consequence, the numbers of naturalized immigrants during the 1970s and 1980s, at around 15,000 per annum or 0.3 per cent of the non-national population, was insignificantly low. When combined with an exclusive reliance on *jus sanguinis* for the ascription of citizenship at birth, this resulted in families where the children and grandchildren of the first-generation migrants from the 1950s and 1960s were born and raised in Germany, yet remained non-nationals throughout their lives.

Both approaches chimed closely with the way in which the process and aims of integration were conceived of in West Germany. Germany's legacy of National Socialism dictated that no migrant could be expected, let alone required, to become German, either culturally or legally. A French assimilationist tradition thus never took hold in Germany. Yet at the same time, if a non-national did wish to become German, the ethnocultural basis of German citizenship meant that the bar for membership was set so high that few were prepared to make the considerable effort to leap over it.

Just as in the area of labour migration, unification was to prove a critical juncture for integration and citizenship, marking the beginning of a gradual process of liberalization. Thus, the 1991 *Ausländergesetz* created legal entitlements both to permanent residence permits and, after 1993, to a 'simplified' naturalization process for long-term resident non-nationals. The 2000 reform of citizenship proved particularly important, by introducing *jus soli* for the first time in German history, and increasing the number of cases where dual citizenship was tolerated to around one in two. In doing so, the law constituted a decisive departure from the ethnocultural orientation of the 1913 law (Palmowski, 2008). At the same time, the law also took a first step towards the more assertive approach to citizenship which has since become widespread in Europe, requiring applicants to show language skills, loyalty to the constitution and, after 2007, to pass a naturalization test (Joppke, 2010).

The 2005 *Zuwanderungsgesetz* further simplified the categories of residence status and thereby contributed to a major improvement in the share of non-nationals with permanent residence permits (*Beauftragte der Bundesregierung*, 2011: 25–31). In addition, by introducing integration courses, it also reinforced the trend towards a more explicit formulation of the degree of assimilation which was expected of immigrants. Lastly, in 2006, Germany also enacted its first anti-discrimination legislation by way of implementing two EU directives from 2000.

But over and above the legislative dimension, a number of formal and informal structures have been established in this domain since 2005 (Green, 2013a). First, at the federal level, migration and integration has since 2005 been located within the domain of the Federal Chancellery, where the Commissioner for Migration and Integration, Maria Böhmer, holds the rank of *Staatsministerin*. The upgrading of this role has been mirrored at sub-national level, where several *Länder* have incorporated integration into their ministerial portfolios (see *Beauftragte der Bundesregierung*, 2012: 36 for the full list). Second, Ms Böhmer was the driving force behind the establishment of a national 'integration summit' (*Integrationsgipfel*), with a resulting action plan (*Nationaler Integrationsplan*). In parallel, the then Federal Interior Minister Wolfgang Schäuble in 2006 instituted a dialogue with Islamic organizations (*Deutsche Islam Konferenz*). While the composition and outcomes of both bodies have not been without controversy (Musch, 2012), their very existence already signifies a greater degree of political acceptance of Germany's migrant communities.

Perhaps the single most significant change, though, has been that of the terminologies employed in Germany. Traditionally, the distinction was between the legal status of German citizens and non-nationals (*Ausländer*). However, the combination of growing numbers of non-nationals who were born in Germany, combined with the historical legacy of ethnic German immigration in the 1980s and 1990s, who all obtained German nationality without further requirements, rendered this distinction increasingly redundant. Instead, in 2005 the *Statistisches Bundesamt* developed a new category of 'migrant background' (*Migrationshintergrund*) to capture this changed situation (Palmowski, 2008).

Although the definition of this status is rather broader than 'foreign born', and therefore not comparable to the discourse in other European countries or even the US and Canada, this new taxonomy has transformed Germany's perspective on migration by defining it beyond the simple question of what passport a person holds. But the use of this status also provided a different perspective on the cumulative scale of migration, by finding that around 20 per cent of the population, or 16 million persons, has a *Migrationshintergrund*. In doing so, the term also recognizes the impact of migration beyond the major urban areas, as most medium-sized towns and cities in Germany have sizeable populations of a migrant background. Furthermore, the term highlights how this status varies by generation. Thus, around 30 per cent of families with minor children, and almost 50 per cent of children in major cities with over 500,000 inhabitants, have a *Migrationshintergrund*. In one fell swoop, therefore, migration has been recast as an issue which cuts across the German population as a whole, and not as something which affects only those without a German passport – something which of course also changes the perspective of political parties.

In German society too, things are changing. On a prosaic level, Germany's football team is now as much of a melting pot as France's legendary 1998 World Cup winning squad was. Persons of migrant background are beginning to make more of an impact in the media. In politics too, things are changing, albeit from a very low base (see Donovan, 2007; Bird et al., 2011). At the *Land* level, the first instances of immigrant ministers have occurred, and not only from the parties of the centre-left: one of the first ministers of Turkish origin was in the CDU government of Lower Saxony. Indeed, it was there that a CDU politician with the distinctly ungermanic name of David McAllister became Minister-President in 2010. McAllister was the son of a Scottish soldier serving in West Germany and a German mother; he was thus the first leader of a German *Land* to hold dual citizenship. At federal level, the party leader of the Greens since 2008, Cem Özdemir, is of Turkish origin; and the leader of the FDP from 2011–13, Philipp Rösler, was born in Vietnam but adopted by German parents. In the 2013 federal elections, the proportion of members of the Bundestag with *Migrationshintergrund* doubled from 3.4 to 5.9 per cent, as did the number of parliamentarians of Turkish background; in addition, 2013 also saw the election of the first two Germans of African origin to the Bundestag (Mediendienst Integration, 2013).

Overall, the gradual 'opening' of German society, which was already identified in *Developments in German Politics 3* (Green, 2003), has undoubtedly continued. That is not to say that this process has been straightforward, nor has it been unchallenged. The diversification of the German political class is proceeding only at a snail's pace. Most notably, the deficits in the socio-economic profile of either non-nationals or those with *Migrationshintergrund* compared to that of German citizens remain firmly entrenched. Despite some areas of absolute and relative improvement, often linked to the improving economic situation, migrants are still generally twice as likely to be unemployed or have no qualifications at all, as well as having poorer levels of housing and lower salaries (*Beauftragte der Bundesregierung*, 2011).

Figure 14.3　*Naturalizations in Germany, 1991–2012*

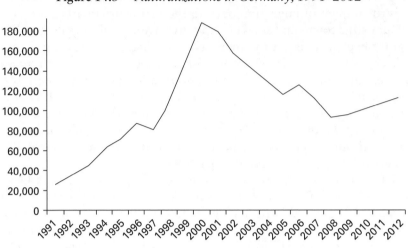

Note:　Figures exclude naturalizations of ethnic Germans.

Source:　Figure constructed from data contained in *Statistisches Bundesamt* (2013: 15).

A second area of concern is the trend in the acquisition of citizenship. Figure 14.3 illustrates this trend over time, and shows clearly how the liberalizations of the 1990s generated a growing number of naturalizations by non-nationals. Remarkably though, the 2000 Citizenship Law has had the opposite effect from what was initially expected: far from producing an ever-increasing number of naturalizations, these fell back sharply until 2008 before staging a slight recovery. Yet they still remain far below their peak in 1999. There are several reasons for this, but the most obvious explanation is Germany's continued insistence that applicants should seek release from their former citizenship (Green, 2012). In fact, and as noted above, dual citizenship is ultimately tolerated in around half of all naturalizations, but often only after applicants can show that they have spent several years attempting to be released by their former home country. Put differently, were Germany to accept dual citizenships as a rule, instead of only as an exception, the number of naturalizations would undoubtedly be higher. However, on this specific question, the CDU/CSU has remained particularly intransigent.

This matters because only citizenship ascribes absolute security of entry to and residence in Germany. It also matters because of voting rights: in large cities such as Frankfurt and Stuttgart, between 20 and 30 per cent of the population are non-nationals, which thus excludes them from voting at regional and national elections, even if EU citizens can at least vote at local and European elections. But in large urban areas there is a persistent challenge of democratic legitimacy, which consultative bodies for non-nationals (the *Ausländerbeiräte*) at municipal, state and federal levels can do little to mitigate.

Furthermore, the introduction of *jus soli* in the 2000 Citizenship Law, while in itself a landmark reform, came with a sting in the tail: under the law, the beneficiaries of this provision, who by virtue of its combination with *jus sanguinis* became dual nationals, are required to choose between their inherited parents' citizenship and their German citizenship by the age of 23. The first such cases started to occur in 2013, and the constitutionality of this particular provision is certain to be challenged in the courts over the coming years.

Beyond the formal legal and policy framework, Germany has over the past decade also witnessed an increasingly polarized debate over the implications and indeed desirability of its growing and visible diversity. This has taken several forms. For example, in 2003 the issue of Islamic headscarves came to the fore, albeit in a quite different way to the situation in France, when a female teacher went to court over the right to wear one at school (Joppke, 2009). The case went all the way to the Constitutional Court, which in the final analysis passed this back to *Länder* governments to legislate on (von Blumenthal, 2009). Meanwhile, in 2005, a book by the Turkish-German writer Necla Kelek caused considerable controversy when it maintained that forced marriages were a commonplace in the Turkish community (Kelek, 2005).

Most infamously, in 2010 the former Berlin Finance Senator and SPD member Thilo Sarrazin published a polemic against immigration with the title *Deutschland schafft sich ab* (Sarrazin, 2010). Although his arguments in several places constituted little more than a crude form of genetically based racism, they struck an undoubted chord with the population: the book sold some 1.5 million copies and its author fast became a minor celebrity and regular guest on talkshows. The main parties struggled to find the right response both to him and to his arguments: the SPD attempted, unsuccessfully, to expel Sarrazin, while Chancellor Merkel both criticized Sarrazin and made a widely noted speech in October 2010 declaring that multiculturalism had utterly failed. In fact, this statement was not nearly as radical as it seems: Germany never practised formal multiculturalism in the Canadian mould, and few mainstream politicians had ever claimed this to be the case.

The Sarrazin furore fed into a wider debate on the role and status Islam should have in modern Germany, a debate which has not fallen neatly within party lines. For instance, in early October 2010, just two weeks before Merkel's own foray into the issue, the then Federal

President, Christian Wulff (CDU), used his speech to mark the twentieth anniversary of unification to declare that Islam was a part of Germany, a statement which would have been unthinkable just ten years earlier. However, this was followed in early 2011 by the newly appointed Federal Interior Minister, Hans-Peter Friedrich (CSU), who took the opportunity of his first appearance at the *Deutsche Islam Konferenz* in 2011 to declare precisely the opposite.

A more worrying dimension of the societal response to migration has been the steady increase in politically motivated extreme right-wing crime since unification. Among violent crime from this group, it is particularly the new *Länder* in the east who are affected, with much higher per capita rates of offences committed than the western half of the country. The most disturbing example of this by some distance was the revelation in 2011 that a neo-Nazi terrorist cell, which called itself *National-sozialistischer Untergrund* (NSU), conducted a wave of murders, bomb attacks and bank robberies throughout Germany over a period of more than a decade, claiming ten lives, mostly those of immigrants. In fact, the NSU's campaign only came to an end when, following a botched bank robbery in 2011, two of its three members committed suicide and the third, the only female in the group, handed herself in at a police station.

Subsequently, it transpired that the members of the NSU had at various different junctures been on the radar of both the police and domestic security services; however, these had failed to make the relevant connections, instead blaming immigrant criminal gang wars for the murders. A cross-party investigative committee of the *Bundestag* (*Untersuchungs-ausschuss*) also found that the security services had attempted to cover up their failings. The committee's final report in 2013 concluded that German law enforcement had suffered a historic failure in its duty to combat extreme right-wing groups.

Even so, such developments must be seen in context (Braunthal, 2009). Extreme right-wing political parties have failed to make any significant impact in Germany, quite in contrast to countries such as France. In 2013, the main such party, the *Nationaldemokratische Partei Deutschlands* (NPD) was represented in just 2 out of 16 *Länder* parliaments, and scored only 1.3 per cent at the 2013 federal elections. Its financial situation was desolate and the established parties have considered a renewed case before the Federal Constitutional Court to have the party banned altogether. The NPD's prospects for a breakthrough at federal level therefore remain distant. More broadly, immigration has rarely been an issue at election time, and was almost completely absent from the 2013 federal election, despite Germany receiving the highest levels of immigration for decades.

Ethnic Germans, asylum and family reunification

In parallel with the two dominant issues of the last decade – labour migration and integration and citizenship – three other main sources of migration need to be mentioned: ethnic Germans, asylum and family reunification. As Figure 14.1 shows, the number of ethnic Germans coming to Germany not only dropped sharply after the mid-1990s, but has now fallen to minimal levels: in 2012, there were just 1,800 new arrivals, 98 per cent of which came from the countries of the former Soviet Union. A key reason for this is not only the restrictions introduced in 1993 (Green, 2003: 236), but also the requirement after 1996 for primary applicants to demonstrate proficiency in the German language. In 2005, as part of the *Zuwanderungsgesetz*, this was also extended to dependants, who typically made up three-quarters of the arrivals under this heading. While pass rates for the language test were initially high at around 70 per cent, they have since dropped off and are now well below 50 per cent. Under the current rules, it is therefore highly unlikely that this source of immigration will again attain the prominence it had 20 years ago.

Figure 14.1 also illustrates how the number of asylum seekers fell sharply after the constitutional amendment of 1993, and continued to drop until 2007. Indeed, from the turn of the millennium, Germany lost its long-held status as the primary destination for asylum seekers in Europe, first to the UK and later to countries such as France and Sweden. From 2008, however, numbers have begun to increase once more, reaching over 60,000 in 2012. Given that Germany is probably the single most important immigration country in Europe, thereby exerting considerable 'pull', that upturn cannot be entirely surprising; it also reflects the existence of conflicts in Syria, Iraq and Afghanistan. At the same time, Germany's recognition practice remains quite restrictive, even though recognition of persecution on the grounds of gender as well as by non-state agents was introduced in the 2005 *Zuwanderungsgesetz*. Between 2010 and 2012, only around 15 per cent of decisions each year resulted in the granting of refugee status; over half were rejections on substantive grounds, while over 20 per cent were rejections on formal grounds (*Bundesamt für Migration und Flüchtlinge*, 2013a: 45). In parallel, and like many other countries, Germany has sought to increase the number of failed asylum seekers deported back to their countries of origin (Ellermann, 2009).

A third long-standing issue in immigration to Germany has been the conditions under which spouses and their children (so-called secondary migrants) can join a primary migrant. Already in late 1981, this issue had exploded onto the political agenda, and specifically the question of the maximum age for children to join their parents in Germany (Joppke,

1999: 75–85). At the time, a compromise was found around the age of 16 years, but the issue, and notably attempts to reduce this age limit to six, has periodically reappeared. In particular, the formulation and content of the EU's family reunification directive in 2003 was largely determined by Germany's internal debate over whether the maximum age for children should be kept at 16, or reduced to 12 (Menz, 2011: 443–9). Under the 2005 *Zuwanderungsgesetz*, this age limit was finally brought into line with most other EU member states at 18. In 2007, pre-entry integration requirements, notably German language skills, were introduced, in part as a direct response to the debate over forced marriages triggered by Necla Kelek. Nonetheless, with over 50,000 visas for this purpose granted every year, family reunification has in fact been the main source of legal non-EU immigration to Germany over the past decade.

Lastly, Germany's relationship with the EU in this area has continued to evolve, from being an enthusiastic supporter of integration in this area in the early 1990s to taking an increasingly differentiated perspective, reflecting the more nuanced approach Germany has adopted to European integration more generally (Bulmer and Paterson, 2010). While the country has supported further integration in the area of asylum, it was cautious about the prospects of EU-wide access to labour markets. In Justice and Home Affairs, Germany therefore has adopted the so-called 'venue shopping' approach to policy-making (Bulmer, 2011). Perhaps most of all, partly in response to fears about migration, it imposed a seven-year transition period for the introduction of the free movement of labour from the new central and east European member-states of the EU. This expired in 2011, and since then Germany's booming economy has exerted a strong pull on such countries: Poland, Romania, Hungary and Bulgaria were the top four countries for net migration to Germany in 2012 (Bundesamt für Migration und Flüchtlinge, 2013a: 70).

Conclusion

The aim of this chapter has been to sketch out the main contours of the issues and debates surrounding migration in Germany over the course of the past decade. There can be no doubt that in terms of the legal framework and the way that the debate has been structured, notably the terminological change from *Ausländer* to *Migrationshintergrund*, Germany has come a very long way during this period (Green, 2013a). In effect, the 'opening' identified in the previous volume in this series has continued, both externally (through the return of labour migration) and internally (through a more nuanced approach to integration and citizenship). The cumulative extent of change over this period becomes even more apparent when compared with the almost glacial pace of change during previous decades, and especially prior to unification.

With hindsight, the change of government after the 1998 election was absolutely crucial in moving the debate on. The SPD–Green government between 1998 and 2005 passed both the reform of citizenship and the 2005 *Zuwanderungsgesetz* – both pieces of legislation that redefined the policy aims and instruments in this field. Crucially, the CDU/CSU then also used its time in opposition to review some of its own positions, notably its totemic opposition to the notion that Germany was 'not a country of immigration'. When it returned to government in 2005, it therefore broadly continued the direction of travel already begun by Chancellor Schröder's government.

But this chapter has also highlighted some of the challenges Germany faces. In particular, the country is not nearly as attractive a migration destination as it once was. This goes both for humanitarian and ethnic German migration, where the restrictions from the early 1990s onwards served to achieve a sustained decline in numbers, including that for high-skilled labour migration. In fact, the long-term decline in Germany's net migration figures until 2009 was not least due to high levels of emigration, including highly qualified Germans and non-nationals leaving the country to seek opportunities elsewhere.

In turn, this highlights the unsurprising link between levels of migration and the state of the economy. During the first half of the past decade, Germany's economy struggled with an indifferent performance, meaning that opportunities even for the indigenous population were not always there. By contrast, the sharp upturn in net migration after 2009 is surely linked to the country's strong economic growth. This is also likely to help account for the increase in asylum seekers in that same period. This is not because asylum seekers to Germany are somehow intrinsically 'bogus', but rather a reflection of the fact that they want to be able to build up new lives – something which is obviously easier in a country with a growing economy.

Meanwhile, this chapter has shown that the relationship between Germany and 'its' migrants, and in particular the single largest national group of Turkish citizens, has not always been easy. Although riots of the kind experienced in the *banlieues* of Paris in 2005 have not occurred in Germany, there has long been a sense of unease among policy-makers and voters more generally over the impact of the increasing ethnic and cultural diversity which today characterizes most larger towns and cities in western Germany (although not in eastern Germany, with the notable exception of Berlin). The full range of this complex relationship obviously lies beyond the reach of this chapter, although it can broadly be reduced to different ideas about how integration should function in practice. Thus, for many Germans, immigrants and non-nationals should make greater efforts to adapt to German society, as evidenced by their comparatively poor performance in education and the labour market. By contrast, migrant communities, increasing numbers of whose members have by now acquired German citizenship, highlight what they perceive as the unwillingness of German society to adapt to their presence, including the everyday instances of racism and discrimination which characterize most western European countries with a history of migration.

In consequence, a number of tensions remain at the heart of migration and integration to Germany. On the one hand, the federal government has sought to make it easier to recruit high-skilled migrants from outside the EU, but on the other hand it has insisted on the full seven-year transition periods for the free movement of labour from the new eastern member-states of the EU. In integration, liberalizations in residence status and a raised institutional profile have been matched by an increase in assimilatory requirements, as well as by a persistent refusal to allow dual citizenships as a rule. And while the distinction between 'insiders' and 'outsiders' in Germany may no longer revolve solely around nationality, a new boundary has emerged around Islam and its associated cultural practices, as the Sarrazin debate clearly illustrates. Perhaps most of all, Germany knows that it will almost certainly need more migration over the coming decades for demographic reasons, but selling that proposition to the electorate is very much easier said than done.

Yet at the same time, it is also clear that Germany needs to open itself more to other cultures and identities. The proportion of the population with *Migrationshintergrund* is only likely to increase, and while German cities may still be some way from the 'superdiversity' of places like London, the likelihood is that they will move in this direction over the coming 30 or 40 years. What this means is that an acceptance of a greater degree of cultural pluralism will necessarily be required in Germany – a process that will incidentally surely also involve at least some of the items from the multiculturalist toolbox, in particular in education and in the representation of diversity publicly. That agenda contains no shortage of political conflict, and in consequence this domain is certain to remain at the core of German politics for the foreseeable future.

Guide to Further Reading

Chapter 1   Government at the Centre

German coalition politics has been analysed by Miller (2011), Saalfeld (2003b) and Rudzio (2005). Busse and Hofmann (2010) offer a detailed account of the Chancellery and the formal and informal working practices within the Federal government. The edited volumes by Bröchler and Blumenthal (2011) and Korte and Grunden (2013) analyse different aspects of the working of government. The website of the Federal Government *http://www.bundesregierung.de/* presents all formal aspects of the government, the Chancellor and the ministries.

Chapter 2   The Reform of German Federalism

The public hearings conducted as part of the Federal reform commission's deliberations have been published by the *Deutscher Bundestag* und *Bundesrat* (2010), and offer excellent insights into the key lines of conflict and negotiation points which were significant in determining the scope of the reforms themselves. The *Bundesrat* website links to the main files from the federal reform commission – http://www.bundesrat.de/cln_350/nn_8344/DE/br-dbt/foedref/foedref-node.html?__nnn=true. The debates over the reform process are presented clearly and comprehensively in the excellent work by Scharpf (2009). Scharpf's work also offers an analysis of both the reform dynamics and the potential for future reform of German federalism. Further insights into the reforms and their broader significance for German politics are set out clearly in the comprehensive volume edited by Moore and Jacoby (2010). A number of interesting works offer early assessments of the impact of the reforms available. Hildebrandt and Wolf's collection (2008) considers continuity and change across a number of the policy fields affected.

Chapter 3   Partisan Dealignment and Voting Choice

Baker and his colleagues (1981) provide a comprehensive overview of the evolution of public opinion and voting behavior from the early 1950s to the late 1970s; Anderson and Zelle (1998) and Dalton (2013) update this research. The German language literature on public opinion and voting behaviour is exceptionally rich and sophisticated. For an introduction to this research see Klein et al. (2000) and the edited volumes prepared by Gabriel et al. (2009), and Schmitt-Beck (2012). Finally, a series of books tracks the actions of the parties and the voters through the recent Bundestag elections: 2005 (Langenbacher, 2007; Clemens and Saalfeld, 2008); and 2009 (Wessels et al., 2013; Langenbacher, 2010; Rohrschneider, 2012).

Chapter 4   Parties and the Party System

Much of the recent literature on German political parties in English language is published in academic journals, especially *German Politics*, *West European Politics* and the *European Journal of Political Research*. For a comprehensive comparative survey of political parties in modern democracies, including Germany, Dalton and Wattenberg's (2000) collection is still extremely useful. Lees (2005) provides a comparative analysis of the main parties. Recent monographs on individual parties in English are rare. They include Hough et al. (2007) on the Left Party and a special issue of *German Politics* (2013, vol. 22, issues 1–2) on the Christian Democrats. The literature in German language is extremely rich. Decker and Neu's handbook (2013) provides comprehensive, up-to-date yet concise information on more than 100 parties and includes many further bibliographic references with an emphasis on the German literature.

Chapter 5   Political Leadership

There is no obvious successor to the classic study on the German executive territory and executive leadership by Johnson (1983). The volume by Padgett (1993) offers valuable assessments of the chancellorship from Adenauer to Kohl. The study by Helms (2005a) puts the evolving patterns of executive leadership in the Federal Republic in comparative perspective. A special issue of *German Politics* (vol. 20, issue 3, 2011) adds useful evaluations of the Merkel chancellorship looked at through a gender lens. The German-language literature on the subject is considerably richer: arguably the most comprehensive studies on executive organization and leadership are those by Helms (2005b), Korte and Fröhlich (2009), and Gast (2011). Most other recent contributions develop a more specific focus, such as for example on chancellor/media relations (Rosumek, 2007) or the Chancellor's Office (Busse and Hofmann, 2010). Offering detailed biographical information on all chancellors and federal ministers since 1949, the two volumes by Kempf and Merz (2001; 2008) mark a unique resource.

Chapter 6   The Politics of Social Protest

Various authors provide an overview on the development of a broad range of social movements from the 1950s until 2007 in a comprehensive handbook edited by Roth and Rucht (2008). Walter and his collaborators (2013) have studied contemporary protest groups in the domains of public infrastructure and urban planning, energy, education, nuclear power, regulation of the finance sector (the Occupy movement), euroscepticism, critique of established party politics, and regulation of the internet. The quarterly *Forschungsjournal Soziale Bewegungen* offers numerous articles on specific protest groups and campaigns, mostly with a focus on contemporary Germany, written by social scientists or political practitioners. Roth (2011), taking a clear stance in favour of more democracy and citizen participation, discusses the respective efforts and gives numerous empirical illustrations. Similarly, Leggewie (2011) calls for a 'new democracy' and promotes a new societal contract. Apart from these partly descriptive, partly also partisan books, several authors, most of them with a journalistic rather than scientific background, have published popular work on contemporary protest in Germany (e.g., Kessler, 2013). To some extent, they also advise activists on how to organize protest campaigns, usually referring to recent examples of failure and success.

Chapter 7   The German Model in Transition

Streeck (2009a) has a comprehensive treatment of the changes of the German model over the last three decades. An earlier assessment of the question 'What is German capitalism and can it survive?' can be found in Streeck (1995). More nuanced discussions on institutional changes in the German model are Hall and Thelen (2009) and Hassel (2012). The classic earlier books on the varieties of market economies are provided by Albert (1993) and Shonfield (1965). Explanations on the historical developments of German capitalism in contrast to more liberal market economies are Iversen and Soskice (2009), Yamamura and Streeck (2001) and Thelen (2004). The most prominent and promising theoretical explanation of institutional differences of political economies and their effects remains the edited volume by Hall and Soskice (2001).

Chapter 8   Economic Policy

Streeck (2009a) is a good example of the literature about Germany as the sick man of the Euro while Reisenbichler and Morgan (2012) provide an explanation for the good German economic performance after the financial crisis. Hassel and Schiller (2010) give a comprehensive overview of the most important reform project of the period of observation, the Hartz reforms, while

Zohlnhöfer (2011) discusses the response to the financial crisis in some detail. More detailed accounts of individual reforms and the related policy-making processes can be found in the edited volumes by Egle and Zohlnhöfer (2007; 2010) and Saalfeld and Zohlnhöfer (forthcoming). Moreover, the Council of Economic Advisers produces annual reports that provide an overview and a critical discussion of current economic policies. These reports can be downloaded without charge from the internet (http://www.sachverstaendigenrat-wirtschaft.de).

Chapter 9   Germany and the European Union

Chancellor Merkel is at the centre of German and European policy-making. Kornelius (2013) is a must read for anyone who wishes to understand the Chancellor's European policy. Although losing in traction the Franco–German relationship remains a vital element of German EU policy and is brilliantly analysed in Krotz and Schild (2012). A key feature of German EU policy is the influence of parapublic institutions. On the Federal Constitutional Court the key text is Davies (2012). Marsh has written frequently on the *Bundesbank* and his latest volume (2013) is a brilliant guide to the politics of the eurozone crisis.

Chapter 10   Germany and the Euro

Still unparalleled as an account of the negotiations leading up to EMU – and as a guide to bargains between the differing interests of the participants – is the voluminous study by Dyson and Featherstone (1999). The developments since the launch of the euro are best described in the study by David Marsh (2011). From an economic point of view, Bordo and Jonung (1999) provide an early assessment that political institutions ultimately determine the fate of monetary union. Enderlein and Verdun (2009) assess EMU before the sovereign debt crisis crowded out all other perspectives. Peter Hall (2012) provides a comprehensive analysis of that crisis. Heisenberg (2005) discusses the balance of economic and political interests in Germany's decision to create EMU. The German Council of Economic Advisers provides a detailed explanation of its analysis of and recommendations for solving the eurozone crisis in its annual report 2011/12 (SVB, 2011).

Chapter 11   Foreign and Security Policy

There are a number of books which provide good surveys of the development of German security and defence policy. These include Haftendorn (2006), and Schmidt et al. (2007). Kornelius (2013) is an excellent insight in to how Chancellor Merkel views international issues.

Chapter 12 Welfare State Reform and Social Policy

For an introduction to social policy in Germany see Hockerts (2011) on the historical development of the welfare state since 1945, and Ritter (2007) on the challenges and costs of German unification for social policy. Esping-Andersen (1990) constitutes the classic reading for anyone interested in comparative social policy research. Employing an ideational framework Bleses and Seeleib-Kaiser (2004) provide a comprehensive analysis of welfare state reform at the turn of the century, whilst Fleckenstein (2011) provides a constructivist institutional study of the unemployment insurance reforms of 2004, and Stiller (2010) focuses on the dimension of ideational leadership and social policy change. Streeck (2009a) places the recent welfare reforms in the context of the broader political economy.

Chapter 13 Energy and Climate Protection Policy

A definitive conceptual account of the new energy paradigm can be found in Helm (2007), although the empirical part of the book focuses on the UK. There is no convenient overview of German energy policy, but see Duffield (2009) for energy security, Lauber and Mez (2006) and Oschmann (2010) on renewable energy policy, Duffield and Westphal (2011) on German and EU energy policy, and Westphal (2008) on German–Russian energy relations. The best English-language evaluation of Germany's *Energiewende* is Buchan (2012). On climate change policy, Weidner and Metz (2008) and Weidner and Eberlein (2009) provide excellent overviews, whilst Klein (2012) gives a valuable critical evaluation of policies and their impact.

Chapter 14 Citizenship, Migration and Cultural Pluralism

A concise introduction to the issues of immigration and citizenship in Germany is given in Chapter 6 of Green et al. (2012). More detailed discussion can be found in Klusmeyer and Papademetriou (2009) and Green (2004), while Messina (2007) provides a comparative overview of the politics of migration in Europe which draws heavily on the German case. A number of sectoral studies of Germany in a comparative context can also be recommended, notably Menz (2008), Joppke (2010) and Gibney (2004). For a useful website see Federal Office for Migration and Refugees (also available in English) – there is also a newsletter on migration policy (in German) – http://www.bpb.de/gesellschaft/migration/dossier-migration/56804/newsletter.

Bibliography

Adelberger, K. (2001) 'Federalism and Its Discontents: Fiscal and Legislative Power-Sharing in Germany, 1948–99', *Regional & Federal Studies*, 11(2): 43–68.

Albert, M. (1993) *Capitalism vs. Capitalism: How America's Obsession with Individual Achievement and Short-Term Profit Has Led it to the Brink of Collapse*, New York: Four Walls Eight Windows.

Alexander, R. (2013) 'Ronald Pofalla – Merkels Buhmann für alles Übel', www.welt.de/politik/deutschland/article116512507/Ronald-Pofalla-Merkels- Buhmann-fuer-alles-Uebel.html, accessed 17 June 2013.

Allen, C. S. (1989) 'The Underdevelopment of Keynesianism in the Federal Republic of Germany', in P. A. Hall (ed.), *The Political Power of Economic Ideas: Keynesianism across Nations*, Princeton, NJ: Princeton University Press: 263–89.

Anderson, C. and Zelle, C. (1998) *Stability and Change in German Elections: How Electorates Merge, Converge, or Collide*, Westport, CT: Praeger.

Arnim, H. H. von (1980) *Ämterpatronage durch politische Parteien*, Wiesbaden: Karl-Bräuer-Institut.

Bach, J. P. G. (1999) *Between Sovereignty and Integration: German Foreign Policy and National Identity After 1989*, New York: St Martin's Press.

Baethge, M., Solga, H., Wieck, M. and Petsch, C. (2007) *Berufsbildung im Umbruch: Signale eines überfälligen Aufbruchs*, Berlin: Friedrich-Ebert-Stiftung.

Baker, K., Dalton, R. and Hildebrandt, K. (1981) *Germany Transformed*, Cambridge: Harvard University Press.

Banchoff, T. (1999) 'German Identity and European Integration', *European Journal of International Relations*, 5(3): 259–89.

Bannas, G. (2011a) 'Angela Merkel's Berater: Das einblättrige Kleeblatt', www.faz.net/aktuell/politik/inland/angela-merkels-berater-das-einblaet-trige- kleeblatt-1591398.html, accessed 17 June 2013.

Bannas, G. (2011b) 'Regierung unter Druck', FAZ, 6 July.

Bannas, G. (2012) 'Das starke, schwache Parlament', FAZ, 20 July.

Banse, F. and Habermann, F. (2012) 'Vom Ende der Globalisierungsbewegung – und dem was kommt. Ein Rück- und Ausblick', *Forschungsjournal Soziale Bewegungen*, 25(1): 51–60.

Batt, H. (2008) 'Weder stark noch schwach – aber nicht groß: Die Große Koalition und ihre Reformpolitik', in J. Tenscher and H. Batt (eds), *100 Tage Schonfrist. Bundespolitik und Landtagswahlen im Schatten der Großen Koalition*, Wiesbaden: VS Verlag für Sozialwissenschaften: 215–46.

BBC Monitoring Service (2013) 'German Chancellor warns EU to focus on global effectiveness', translation of interview with Angela Merkel in *Der Spiegel*, 2 June 2013, pp. 29–31, www.lexisnexis.com.

Beauftragte der Bundesregierung für Migration, Flüchtlinge und Integration (2011) *Zweiter Integrationsindikatorenbericht*, Berlin: Beauftragte der Bundesregierung.

Beauftragte der Bundesregierung für Migration, Flüchtlinge und Integration (2012) *Bericht der Beauftragten der Bundesregierung für Migration, Flüchtlinge und Integration über die Lage der Ausländerinnen und Ausländer in Deutschland*, Berlin: Beauftragte der Bundesregierung.

Beck, U. (2013) *German Europe*, Cambridge: Polity.

Behnke, N. and Benz, A. (2009) 'The Politics of Constitutional Change between Reform and Evolution', *Publius: The Journal of Federalism*, 39(2): 213–40.

Benoit, K. and Laver, M. (2006) *Party Policy in Modern Democracies*, London: Routledge.

Benz, A. (2008) 'From Joint Decision Traps to Over-regulated Federalism: Adverse Effects of a Successful Constitutional Reform', *German Politics*, 17(4): 440–56.

Berenskoetter, F. and Giegerich, B. (2010) 'From NATO to ESDP: A Social Constructivist Analysis of German Strategic Adjustment after the End of the Cold War', *Security Studies*, 19: 407–52.

Berger, T. U. (1996) 'Norms, Identity, and National Security in Germany and Japan', in P. J. Katzenstein (ed.), *The Culture of National Security: Norms and Identity in World Politics*, New York: Columbia University Press: 317–56.

Berlin and Stockholm (2010) 'Pooling and Sharing Food For Thought Paper', November, www.europarl.europa.eu/meetdocs/2009_2014/documents/sede/dv/sede260511deseinitiative_/sede260511deseinitiative_en.pdf.

Beyme, K. von (1997) *Der Gesetzgeber. Der Bundestag als Entscheidungszentrum*, Opladen: Westdeutscher Verlag.

Bird, K., Saalfeld, T. and Wüst, A. (eds) (2011) *The Political Representation of Immigrants and Minorities: Voters, Parties and Parliaments in Liberal Democracies*, London: Routledge/ECPR.

Blancke, S. and Schmid, J. (2003) 'Bilanz der Bundesregierung Schröder in der Arbeitsmarktpolitik 1998–2002: Ansätze zu einer doppelten Wende', in C. Egle, T. Ostheim and R. Zohlnhöfer (eds) *Das rot-grüne Projekt. Eine Bilanz der Regierung Schröder 1998–2002*, Wiesbaden: Westdeutscher Verlag: 215–38.

Bleses, P. and Seeleib-Kaiser, M. (2004) *The Dual Transformation of the German Welfare State*, Basingstoke: Palgrave Macmillan.

Blühdorn, I. (2009a) 'Option Grün: Alliance 90/The Greens at the Dawn of New Opportunities?', *Politics and Society*, 27(2): 45–62.

Blühdorn, I. (2009b) 'Reinventing Green Politics: On the Strategic Repositioning of the German Green Party', *German Politics*, 18(1): 39–54.

Blumenthal, J. von (2009) *Das Kopftuch in der Landesgesetzgebung. Governance im Bundesstaat zwischen Unitarisierung und Föderalisierung*, Baden-Baden: Nomos.

Blyth, M. (2001) 'The Transformation of the Swedish Model: Economic

Ideas, Distributional Conflict, and Institutional Change', *World Politics*, 54: 1–26.

Blyth, M. and Matthijs, M. (2011) 'Why only Germany can Fix the Euro: Reading Kindleberger in Berlin', *Foreign Affairs*, www.foreignaffairs.com/articles/136685/mattias-matthijs-and-mark-blyth/why-only-Germany-can-fix-the euro, accessed 30 May 2013.

BMAS (2013) *Lebenslagen in Deutschland. Der vierte Armuts- und Reichtumsbericht der Bundesregierung*, Berlin: BMAS, www.bmas.de/SharedDocs/Downloads/DE/PDF-Publikationen-DinA4/a334-4-armuts-reichtumsbericht-2013.pdf?__blob=publicationFile, accessed 14 August 2013.

BMFSFJ (2006) *Familie zwischen Flexibilität und Verlässlichkeit. Perspektiven für eine lebenslaufbezogene Familienpolitik. Siebter Familienbericht*, Berlin: Deutscher Bundestag, www.bmfsfj.de/doku/Publikationen/familienbericht/download/familienbericht_gesamt.pdf, accessed 14 August 2014.

BMU (2007) *Eckpunkte für ein integriertes Energie- und Klimaprogramm*, Berlin, www.bmu.de/en/topics/climate-energy/, accessed 13 February 2013.

BMWi/BMU (2010) *An Energy Concept for an Environmentally Sensitive, Reliable and Affordable Energy Supply*, Berlin, www.bmu.de, accessed 13 February 2013.

BMWi (2012) *Monitoring-Bericht zur Versorgungssicherheit im Bereich der leitungsgebundenen Versorgung mit Elektrizität*, Berlin, www.bmwi.de, accessed 22 March 2013.

Bodegan, C., Brehmer, W. and Herzog-Stein, A. (2009) *Betriebliche Beschäftigungssicherung in der Krise*, Düsseldorf: Eine Kurzauswertung der WSI-Betriebsrätebefragung.

Bogumil, J. and Jann, W. (2009) *Verwaltung und Verwaltungswissenschaft in Deutschland*, Wiesbaden: VS Verlag für Sozialwissenschaften.

Bonoli, G. (2010) 'The political economy of active labor-market policy', *Politics & Society*, 38(4): 435–57.

Bordo, M. D. and Jonung, L. (1999) *The Future of EMU: What Does the History of Monetary Unions Tell Us?*, Cambridge, MA: National Bureau of Economic Research (Working Paper, 7365).

Bosman, R. (2012) 'Germany's Energiewende: Redefining the Rules of the Energy Game', Briefing Paper, Clingendael International Energy Programme.

Brady, D. (2009) *Rich Democracies, Poor People: How Politics Explain Poverty*, New York: Oxford University Press.

Bräuninger, T. and Debus, M. (2009) 'Legislative Agenda-setting in Parliamentary Democracies', *European Journal of Political Research*, 48: 804–39.

Bräuninger, T. and Debus, M. (2012) *Parteienwettbewerb in den deutschen Bundesländern*, Wiesbaden: Springer VS Verlag für Sozialwissenschaften.

Braunthal, G. (2003) 'The SPD, the welfare state, and Agenda 2010', *German Politics and Society*, 21(4): 1–29.

Braunthal, G. (2009) *Right-Wing Extremism in Contemporary Germany*, London: Palgrave Macmillan.

Brettschneider, F. (2001) 'Candidate-Voting: Die Bedeutung von Spitzenkandidaten für das Wählerverhalten in Deutschland, Großbritannien und den USA von 1960 bis 1998', in H. Klingemann and M. Kaase (eds), *Wahlen und Wähler. Analysen aus Anlass der Bundestagswahl 1998*, Opladen, Wiesbaden: Westdeutscher Verlag.

Brettschneider, F. and Schuster, W. (2013) *Stuttgart 21. Ein Großprojekt zwischen Protest und Akzeptanz*, Wiesbaden: Springer VS Verlag für Sozialwissenschaften.

Brettschneider, F., Nildermayer, O. and Wessels, B. (eds) (2009) *Die Bundestagswahl 2005: Analysen des Wahlkampfes und der Wahlergebnisse*, Wiesbaden: Verlag für Sozialwissenschaften.

Bröchler, S. and Blumenthal, J. (eds) (2011) *Regierungskanzleien im politischen Prozess*, Wiesbaden: VS Verlag für Sozialwissenschaften.

Broughton, D. (2000) 'The First Six Länder Elections of 1999: Initial Electoral Consequences and Political Fallout of the Neue Mitte in Action', *German Politics*, 9(2): 51–70.

Brubaker, R. (1992) *Citizenship and Nationhood in France and Germany*, Cambridge, MA: Harvard University Press.

Buchan, D. (2012) '*The Energiewende: Germany's Gamble*', Working Paper SP 26, Oxford: Oxford Institute for Energy Studies.

Bulmer, S. (1997) 'Shaping the Rules? The Constitutive Politics of the European Union and German Power', in P. Katzenstein (ed.), *Tamed Power: Germany in Europe*, Ithaca: Cornell: 47–79.

Bulmer, S. (2011) 'Shop till you drop? The German executive as venue-shopper in Justice and Home Affairs?', in P. Bendel et al. (eds), *The Europeanization of Control: Venues and Outcomes of EU Justice and Home Affairs Cooperation*, Berlin: Lit.

Bulmer S. and Paterson, W. E. (2010) 'Germany and the European Union: From "Tamed Power" to Normalized Power?', *International Affairs*, 86(5): 1051–73.

Bulmer, S. and Paterson, W. E. (2013) 'Germany as the EU's Reluctant Hegemon: Of Economic Strength and Political Constraints', *Journal of European Public Policy,* 20(10): 1387–405.

Bulmer, S., Jeffrey, C. and Paterson, W. E. (2000) *Germany's European Diplomacy: Shaping the Regional Milieu*, Manchester: Manchester University Press.

Bundesagentur für Arbeit (2013) http://statistik.arbeitsagentur.de/nn_32018/SiteGlobals/Forms/Rubrikensuche/Rubrikensuche_Form.html?view=processForm&resourceId=210368&input_=&pageLocale=de&topicId=255298&year_month=aktuell&year_month.GROUP=1&search=Suchen, accessed 10 December 2013.

Bundesamt für Migration und Flüchtlinge (2013a) *Das Bundesamt in Zahlen 2012*, Nürnberg: *Bundesamt für Migration und Flüchtlinge*.

Bundesamt für Migration und Flüchtlinge (2013b) *Migrationsbericht 2011*, Nürnberg: *Bundesamt für Migration und Flüchtlinge*.

Bundesministerium des Innern (2012) *Jedes Alter zählt. Demografiestrategie der Bundesregierung*, Berlin: *Bundesministerium des Innern*.

Bundesministerium der Verteidigung (2010) Einsatzzahlen: Die Stärke der deutschen Einsatzkontingente, available at http://www.bundeswehr. de/portal/a/bwde/!ut/p/c4/04_SB8K8xLLM9MSSzPy8xBz9CP3I5EyrpH K9pPKUVL3UzLzixNSSKiirpKoqMSMnNU-_INtREQD2RLYK/, accessed 6 December 2013.

Bündnis 90/Die Grünen (2013) *Zeit für den Grünen Wandel. Bundestagswahlprogramm 2013 von Bündnis 90 / Die Grünen*, Berlin.

Burkhart, S. (2005) 'Parteipolitikverflechtung. Über den Einfluss der Bundespolitik auf Landtagswahlentscheidungen von 1976–2000', *Politische Vierteljahresschrift*, 46(1): 14–38.

Burkhart, S. (2009) 'Reforming Federalism in Germany: Incremental Changes instead of the Big Deal', *Publius: The Journal of Federalism*, 39(2): 341–65.

Burns, J. M. (1978) *Leadership*, New York: Harper.

Busch, A. (1994) 'The Crisis in the EMS', *Government & Opposition*, 29(1): 80–96.

Busch, A. (1995) *Preisstabilitätspolitik. Politik und Inflationsraten im internationalen Vergleich*, Opladen: Leske + Budrich.

Busch, A. (2005) 'Globalisation and National Varieties of Capitalism: The Contested Viability of the "German Model"', *German Politics*, 14(2): 125–39.

Busch, A. (2009) 'Schröder's Agenda 2010: From "Plan B" to Lasting Legacy?', in A. Miskimmon, W. E. Paterson and J. Sloan (eds), *Germany's Gathering Crisis: The 2005 Federal Election and the Grand Coalition*, New York: Palgrave Macmillan: 64–79.

Busemeyer, M. R. and Thelen, K. (2012) 'Institutional change in German vocational training: From collectivism towards segmentalism' in M. R. Busemeyer and C. Trampusch (eds), *The Comparative Political Economy of Collective Skill Systems*, Oxford: Oxford University Press: 68–100.

Busse, V. (2006) 'Organisation der Bundesregierung und Organisationsentscheidungen der Bundeskanzler in ihrer historischen Entwicklung und im Spannungsfeld zwischen Exekutive und Legislative', *Der Staat: Zeitschrift für Staatslehre und Verfassungsgeschichte, deutsches und europäisches öffentliches Recht*, 45(2): 245–68.

Busse, Volker and Hofmann, Hans (2010) *Bundeskanzleramt und Bundesregierung: Aufgaben – Organisation – Arbeitsweise*, 5th edn, Heidelberg: C.F. Müller.

Calleo, D. (1978) *The German Problem Reconsidered: Germany and the World Order: 1870 To the Present*, Cambridge: Cambridge University Press.

Carlin, W. and Soskice, D. (2008) 'German economic performance: disentangling the role of supply-side reforms, macroeconomic policy and coordinated economy institutions', *Socio-Economic Review*, 7(1): 67–99.

CDU/CSU (2013) *Gemeinsam erfolgreich für Deutschland. Regierungsprogramm 2013–2017*, Berlin: CDU-Bundesgeschäftsstelle.

Chandler, W. E. (2010) 'European Leadership in Transition: Angela Merkel and Nicolas Sarkozy', in S. Bulmer, C. Jeffery and S. Padgett (eds), *Rethinking Germany and Europe*, Basingstoke: Palgrave Macmillan: 154–70.

Clasen, J. and Goerne, A. (2011) 'Exit Bismarck, enter dualism? Assessing contemporary German labour market policy', *Journal of Social Policy*, 40(4): 795–810.

Clegg, D. (2007) 'Continental Drift: On Unemployment Policy Change in Bismarckian Welfare States', *Social Policy and Administration*, 40(6): 597–617.

Clemens, C. (1994) 'The Chancellor as Manager: Helmut Kohl, the CDU and Governance in Germany', *West European Politics*, 17(4): 28–51.

Clemens, C. (1998) 'Party Management as a Leadership Resource: Kohl and the CDU/CSU', *German Politics*, 7(1): 76–100.

Clemens, C. (2010) 'The Chancellor and Her Party', in S. Bulmer, C. Jeffery and S. Padgett (eds), *Rethinking Germany and Europe*, Basingstoke: Palgrave Macmillan: 25–41.

Clemens, C. (2011) 'Explaining Merkel's Autonomy in the Grand Coalition: Personalisation or Party Organisation?', *German Politics*, 20(4): 469–85.

Clemens, C. (2013) 'Beyond Christian Democracy? Welfare State Politics and Policy in a Changing CDU', *German Politics*, 22(1–2): 191–211.

Clemens, C. and Saalfeld, T. (eds) (2008) *The German Election of 2005: Voters, Parties and Grand Coalition Politics*, London: Routledge.

Coffé, H. and Plassa, R. (2010) 'Party Policy Position of Die Linke: A Continuation of the PDS?', *Party Politics*, 16(6): 721–35.

Crawford, B. (2007) *Power and German Foreign Policy: Embedded Hegemony in Europe*, Basingstoke: Palgrave Macmillan.

Crimmann, A. and Wießner, F. (2009) 'Verschnaufpause dank Kurzarbeit', *IAB-Kurzbericht*, 14.

Culpepper, P. (2011) *Quiet Politics and Business Power: Corporate Control in Europe and Japan*, Cambridge: Cambridge University Press.

Czada, R. (1995) 'Der Kampf um die Finanzierung der deutschen Einheit', in G. Lehmbruch (ed), *Einigung und Zerfall. Deutschland und Europa nach dem Ende des Ost-West-Konflikts*, Opladen: Leske + Budrich: 73–102.

Dalton, R. (2012a) 'Apartisans and the Changing German Electorate', *Electoral Studies*, 31: 35–45.

Dalton, R. (2013) *Citizen Politics: Public Opinion and Political Parties in Advanced Industrial Democracies*, 6th edn, New York: Chatham House Publishers.

Dalton, R. (2014) 'Interpreting Partisan Dealignment in Germany', *German Politics*, forthcoming: available at Taylor Francis Online at http://www.tandfonline.com/doi/full/10.1080/09644008.2013.85304#.UytNi4WjM5c.

Dalton, R. and Eichenberg, R. (2007) 'Post Maastricht Blues: The Transformation of Citizen Support for European Integration', *Acta Politica*, 42: 121–52.

Dalton, R. J. and Wattenberg, M. P. (eds) (2000) *Parties without Partisans: Political Change in Advanced Industrial Democracies*, Oxford: Oxford University Press.

Dalton, R. and Weldon, S. (2005) 'Public Images of Political Parties: A Necessary Evil?', *West European Politics*, 28: 931–51.

Davidson-Schmich, Louise K. (2011) 'Gender, Intersectionality, and the Executive Branch: The Case of Angela Merkel', *German Politics*, 20(3): 325–41.

Davies, B. (2012) *Resisting the European Court of Justice: West Germany's Confrontation with European Law, 1949–1979*, Cambridge: Cambridge University Press.

Debus, M. and Müller, J. (2013) 'The Programmatic Development of CDU and CSU since Reunification: Incentives and Constraints for Changing Policy Positions in the German Multi-Level System', *German Politics*, 22(1–2): 151–71.

Decker, F. and Miliopoulos, L. (2009) 'From a Five to a Six-Party System? Prospects of the Right-wing Extremist NPD', *Politics and Society*, 27(2): 92–107.

Decker, F. and Neu, V. (eds) (2013) *Handbuch der Deutschen Parteien*, 2nd edn, Wiesbaden: Springer VS Verlag für Sozialwissenschaften.

Deeg, R. (2005) 'The Comeback of Modell Deutschland? The New German Political Economy in the EU', *German Politics*, 14(3): 332–53.

Delius, M., Koß, M. and Stecker, C. (2013) 'Ich erkenne also Fraktionsdisziplin grundsätzlich auch an... – Innerfraktioneller Dissens in der SPD-Fraktion der Großen Koalition 2005–2009', *Zeitschrift für Parlamentsfragen*, 44(3): 546–66.

Derlien, H.-U. (1996) 'Zur Logik und Politik des Ressortzuschnitts', *Verwaltungsarchiv*, 87: 548–80.

Der Spiegel (2013) 'Kosmische Katastrophe', no. 3, 14 January.

Dettke, D. (2009) *Germany Says No: The Iraq War and the Future of German Foreign and Security Policy*, Washington, DC: Woodrow Wilson Centre Press.

Deutscher Bundestag (2002) *Schlussbericht der Enquete Kommission Demographischer Wandel*, BT-Drs 14/8800, Berlin: Deutscher Bundestag, http://dip21.bundestag.de/dip21/btd/14/088/1408800.pdf, accessed 14 August 2013.

Deutscher Bundestag (2003) 'Einsetzung einer gemeinsamen Kommission von Bundestag und Bundesrat zur Modernisierung der bundesstaatlichen Ordnung', *Drucksache* 15/1685, 14 October.

Deutscher Bundestag und Bundesrat (2010) *Die Gemeinsame Kommission von Bundestag und Bundesrat zur Modernisierung der Bund-Länder-Finanzbeziehungen, Die Beratungen und ihre Ergebnisse*, Berlin: Deutscher Bundestag/Bundesrat: available at https://www.btg.bestell service.de/pdf/20457000.pdf.

Döhler, M., Fleischer, J. and Hunstedt, T. (2007) *Government Reform as Institutional Politics: Varieties and Policy Patterns from a Comparative Perspective*, Potsdam: Lehrstuhl für Politikwissenschaft, Verwaltung und Organisation.

Dolata-Kreuztkamp, P. (2008) 'Canada-Germany-EU: Energy Security and Climate Change', *International Journal*, 63: 665–85.

Donovan, B. (2007) 'Minority Representation in Germany', *German Politics*, 16(4): 455–80.

Döring, H. and Hönnige, C. (2006) 'Vote of Confidence Procedure and Gesetzgebungsnotstand: Two Toothless German Tigers of Governmental Agenda Control', *German Politics*, 15(1): 1–26.

Duffield, J. S. (1998) *World Power Forsaken: Political Culture, International Institutions, and German Security Policy After Unification*, Stanford: Stanford University Press.

Duffield, J. S. (1999) 'Political Culture and State Behavior: Why Germany Confounds Neorealism', *International Organization*, 34: 765–803.

Duffield, J. S. (2009) 'Germany and Energy Security in the 2000s: Rise and Fall of a Policy Issue?', *Energy Policy*, 37: 4284–92.

Duffield, J. S. and Westphal, K. (2011) 'Germany and EU Energy Policy: Conflicted Champion of Integration?', in V. L. Birchfield and J. S. Duffield (eds), *Towards a Common European Union Energy Policy: Problems, Progress and Prospects*, Basingstoke and New York: Palgrave Macmillan: 169–86.

Dümig, K. (2010) 'Ruhe nach und vor dem Sturm: Die Arbeitsmarkt- und Beschäftigungspolitik der Großen Koalition', in C. Egle and R. Zohlnhöfer (eds), *Die zweite Große Koalition. Eine Bilanz der Regierung Merkel, 2005–2009*, Wiesbaden: VS Verlag für Sozialwissenschaften: 279–301.

Dunleavy, P. and Rhodes, R. A. W. (1990) 'Core Executive Studies in Britain', *Public Administration*, 68(1): 3–28.

Dyson, K. and Featherstone, K. (1999) *The Road to Maastricht: Negotiating Economic and Monetary Union*, Oxford: Oxford University Press.

Dyson, K. and Goetz, K. H. (eds) (2003) *Germany, Europe and the Politics of Constraint*, Oxford: Oxford University Press.

Dyson, T. (2011) '"Condemned forever to becoming and never to being"? The Weise Commission and German Military Isomorphism', *German Politics*, 20(4): 545–67.

Ebbinghaus, B. (2006) *Reforming Early Retirement in Europe, Japan and the USA*, Oxford: Oxford University Press.

Ebinger, F. and Jochheim, L. (2009) 'Wessen loyale Diener? Wie die Große Koalition die deutsche Ministerialbürokratie veränderte', *dms – der moderne staat – Zeitschrift für Public Policy, Recht und Management*, 2: 327–45.

Economist, The (1999) 'The sick man of the euro', 3 June, www.economist.com/node/209559, accessed 30 August 2013.

Economist, The (2012) 'Modell Deutschland über alles', 12 April, www.economist.com/node/21552579, accessed 14 August 2013.

Economist, The (2013) 'Europe's reluctant hegemon: special report on Germany', 15 June.

Egle, C. (2009a) 'No Escape from the Long-term Crisis? The Social Democrats' Failure to Devise a Promising Political Strategy', *Politics and Society*, 27(2): 9–27.

Egle, C. (2009b) *Reformpolitik in Deutschland und Frankreich. Wirtschafts-und Sozialpolitik bürgerlicher und sozialdemokratischer Regierungen*, Wiesbaden: VS Verlag für Sozialwissenschaften.

Egle, C. (2010) 'Im Schatten der Linkspartei. Die Entwicklung des Parteienwettbewerbs während der 16. Legislaturperiode', in C. Egle and R. Zohlnhöfer (eds), *Die zweite Große Koalition. Eine Bilanz der Regierung Merkel, 2005–2009*, Wiesbaden: VS Verlag für Sozialwissenschaften: 99–122.

Egle, C. and Zohlnhöfer, R. (eds) (2007) *Ende des rot-grünen Projektes. Eine Bilanz der Regierung Schröder 2002–2005*, Wiesbaden: VS Verlag für Sozialwissenschaften.

Egle, C. and Zohlnhöfer, R. (eds) (2010) *Die zweite Große Koalition. Eine Bilanz der Regierung Merkel, 2005–2009*, Wiesbaden: VS Verlag für Sozialwissenschaften.

Eichhorst, W. and Marx, P. (2009a) 'Reforming German Labour Market Institutions: A Dual Path to Flexibility', IZA Discussion Paper 4100, Bonn: Forschungsinstitut zur Zukunft der Arbeit.

Eichhorst, W. and Marx, P. (2009b) 'Kurzarbeit: Sinnvoller Konjunktur-puffer oder verlängertes Arbeitslosengeld?', *IZA Standpunkte 5*, Bonn: Institute for the Study of Labor.

Elff, M., and Roßteutscher, S. (2011) 'Stability or Decline? Class, Religion and the Vote in Germany', *German Politics*, 20: 107–27.

Elgie, R. (2011) *Semi-Presidentialism: Sub-types and Democratic Performance*, Oxford: Oxford University Press.

Ellermann, A. (2009) *States against Migrants: Deportation in Germany and the United States*, Cambridge: Cambridge University Press.

Enderlein, H. (2010) 'Finanzkrise und große Koalition: Eine Bewertung des Krisenmanagements der Bundesregierung', in C. Egle and R. Zohlnhöfer (eds), *Die zweite Große Koalition. Eine Bilanz der Regierung Merkel, 2005–2009*, Wiesbaden: VS Verlag für Sozialwissenschaften: 234–53.

Enderlein, H. and Verdun, A. (2009) 'EMU's Teenage Challenge: What Have We Learned and Can We Predict from Political Science?', *Journal of European Public Policy*, 16(4): 490–507.

Epstein, L. (1979) *Political Parties in Western Democracies*, New Brunswick, NJ: Transaction Publishers.

Esping-Andersen, G. (1990) *The Three Worlds of Welfare Capitalism*, Cambridge: Polity Press.

Esping-Andersen, G. (2009) *The Incomplete Revolution*, Cambridge: Polity Press.

Estevez-Abe, M. et al. (2001) 'Social Protection and the Formation of Skills: A Reinterpretation of the Welfare State', in P. A. Hall and D. Soskice (eds), *Varieties of Capitalism: The Institutional Foundations of Comparative Advantage*, Oxford: Oxford University Press.

Ethics Commission for a Safe Energy Supply (2011) 'Germany's energy transition: A collective project for the future', Berlin, www.bundesregierung.de/Content/DE/_Anlagen/2011/05/2011-05-30-abschlussbericht-ethikkommission_en.pdf, accessed 15 March 2013.

European Commission (1998) *Eurobarometer*, Public Opinion in the European Union, Report Number 48, Brussels: Directorate-General X.

European Commission (2008a) *Attitudes of European Citizens towards the Environment*, Special Eurobarometer 295, Brussels.

European Commission (2008b) *EMU@10. Successes and Challenges after 10 Years of Economic and Monetary Union*, Luxembourg: Office for Official Publications of the European Communities.

European Commission (2010a) *Employment in Europe 2010*, Brussels: European Commission.

European Commission (2010b) *EU Energy and Transport in Figures 2010: Statistical Pocketbook*, http://ec.europa.eu/energy/publications/doc/2010 _energy_transport_figures.pdf, accessed 11 February 2013.

European Commission (2010c) *Europeans and Nuclear Safety*, Special Eurobarometer 324, Brussels.

European Commission (2012) *European Energy in Figures: Statistical Pocketbook 2012*, http://ec.europa.eu/energy/publications/doc/2012_ energy_figures.pdf, accessed 11 February 2013.

European Council (2013) *Council Recommendation on Germany's 2013 National Reform Programme and Delivering a Council Opinion on Germany's Stability Programme for 2012–2017.*

European Voice (2011) 'French German Libya Rift Deepens', 25 March, www.europeanvoice.com/article/2011/march/french-german-libya-rift-deepens/70661.aspx?bPrint=1, accessed 4 August 2011.

Eurostat (2012) *Energy Price Statistics 2012*, http://epp.eurostat.ec.europa. eu/statistics_explained/index.php/Energy_price_statistics#Further_Euros tat_information, accessed 13 March 2013.

Faas, T. (2010) 'The German Federal Election of 2009: Sprouting Coalitions, Drooping Social Democrats', *West European Politics*, 33(4): 894–903.

Falter, J. (2008) 'Public Opinion on Nuclear Energy in Germany', in J. Lesourne (ed.), *L'Énergie Nucléaire et les Opinions Publiques Européennes, Gouvernance Européenne et Géopolitique de l'Énergie*, vol. 2, Paris: IFRI: 31–44.

Federal Constitutional Court (2012) Press release no. 42/2012, 19 June.

Federal Ministry of Defence (2006) *White Paper on German Security Policy and the Future of the Bundeswehr*, www.bmvg.de/portal/a/bmvg/sicher-heitspolitik/angebote/dokumente/weissbuch.

Feist, U. and Hoffmann, H.-J. (1999) 'Die Bundestagswahl 1998: Wahl des Wechsels', *Zeitschrift für Parlamentsfragen*, 30(2): 215–51.

Feld, L. and Baskaran, T. (2009) 'Federalism Commission II – Recent Reforms of Federal-Länder Financial Relationships in Germany', Forum of Federations, Working Paper, www.forumfed.org/en/pubs/2009-10-26-feld.pdf.

Financial Times (2011) 'Foreign Policy: A Reticent America', 23 March, www.ft.com/.

Financial Times (2013) 'Austerity fuels Spanish irritation with Germany', 24 June.

Fischer, J. (2006) 'Iran: Last exit for Diplomacy', *Wall Street Journal*, 29 May.

Fleckenstein, T. (2008) 'Restructuring welfare for the unemployed: the Hartz legislation in Germany', *Journal of European Social Policy*, 18(2): 177–88.

Fleckenstein, T. (2011) *Institutions, Ideas and Learning in Welfare State Change: Labour Market Reforms in Germany*, Basingstoke: Palgrave Macmillan.

Fleckenstein, T. (2013) 'Learning to depart from a policy path: institutional change and the reform of German labour market policy', *Government and Opposition*, 48(1): 55–79.

Fleckenstein, T. and Seeleib-Kaiser, M. (2011) 'Business, skills and the welfare state: the political economy of employment-oriented family policies in Britain and Germany', *Journal of European Social Policy*, 21(2): 136–49.

Fleckenstein, T. , Saunders, A. and Seeleib-Kaiser, M. (2011) 'The Dual Transformation of Social Protection and Human Capital: Comparing Britain and Germany', *Comparative Political Studies*, 44(12): 1622–50.

Fleischer, J. (2010) 'A Dual Centre? Executive Politics under the Second Grand Coalition in Germany', *German Politics*, 19(3): 353–68.

Fleischer, J. (2011a) 'Das Primat der Richtlinienkompetenz im politischen Prozess', in M. Florack and T. Grunden (eds), *Regierungszentralen*, VS Verlag für Sozialwissenschaften: 201–23.

Fleischer, J. (2011b) 'Steering From the German Center: More Policy Coordination and Less Policy Initiatives', in C. Dahlström et al. (eds), *Steering From the Center: Strengthening Political Control in Western Democracies*, Toronto: Toronto University Press: 54–79.

Fleischer, J. and Parrado, S. (2010) 'Power Distribution in Ambiguous Times: The Effects of the Financial Crisis on Executive Decision-Making in Germany and Spain', *Der Moderne Staat*, 3(2): 361–76.

Fleischer, J. and Seyfried, M. (2013) 'Drawing from the bargaining pool: Determinants of ministerial selection in Germany', *Party Politics, online first*.

Fleischhauer, J. et al. (2012) 'Unter Wölfen', *Der Spiegel*, 21 May: 18–26.

Forschungsgruppe Wahlen (2011) *Politbarometer*, September I Issue (http://www.forschungsgruppe.de/Umfragen/Politbarometer/Archiv/Poli tbarometer_2011/September_I/).

Forschungsgruppe Wahlen (2013a) 'Sowohl-als-auch: Die Bundestagswahl vom 18. September 2005', in F. Brettschneider et al. (eds), *Die Bundestagswahl 2005: Analysen des Wahlkampfes und der Wahlergebnisse*, Wiesbaden: Verlag für Sozialwissenschaften.

Forschungsgruppe Wahlen (2013b) *Bundestagswahl 22. September 2013*, Mannheim: Kurzbericht (www.forschungsgruppe.de/Wahlen/ Wahlanalysen/Newsl_BTW_2013.pdf).

Frankenberger, K.-D. and Maull, H. W. (2011) 'Gimme a Break', *Foreign Policy in Focus* 494, 24 March, www.deutsche-aussenpolitik.de.

Frankfurter Rundschau (2011) 'Wir sind nicht isoliert', interview with Guido Westerwelle, 14 April, www.fr-online.de/politik/-wir-sind-nicht-isoliert-/-/1472596/8341026/-/index.html, accessed 4 August 2011.

Freitag, M. and Vatter, A. (2008) (eds) *Die Demokratien der deutschen Bundesländer: Politische Institutionen im Vergleich*, Opladen: Barbara Budrich.

Fromme, F. K. (1969) *Das Grundgesetz und die Lehren von Weimar*, Berlin: Duncker & Humblot.

Frühling, S. and Schreer, B. (2009) 'NATO's New Strategic Concept and US Commitments in the Asia-Pacific', *The RUSI Journal*, 154(5): 98–103.

Fuchs, D. and Klingemann, H. (1989) 'The Left–Right schema', in M. K. Jennings and J. van Deth (eds), *Continuities in Political Action*, Berlin: de Gruyter.

Funk, L. (2014) '*The Economy in Western Europe 2014*, London: Europa Publications: 310–23.

Future of Europe Group (2012) 'Final Report of the Future of Europe Group of foreign ministers of Austria, Belgium, Denmark, France, Italy, Germany, Luxembourg, the Netherlands, Poland, Portugal and Spain', 17 September, www.auswaertiges-amt.de/cae/servlet/contentblob/626338/publicationFile/171842/120918-Abschlussbericht-Zukunftsgruppe.pdf, accessed 3 October 2013.

Gabriel, O., Wessels, B. and Falter, J. (eds) (2009) *Wahlen und Wähler: Analysen aus Anlass der Bundestagswahl 2005*, Opladen: VS Verlag für Sozialwissenschaften.

Gadinger, S., Groten, D. and Reitzenstein, A. (2013) *Der schwarz-gelbe Koalitionsvertrag und seine Umsetzung. Handreichung zu einer Bilanz der Regierungsarbeit im Bund 2009 bis 2013*, Munich: CAP.

Gammelin, C. (2013) 'Deutsche Hegemonie: Merkel, Kohl und Europe', *Süddeutsche Zeitung*, www.sueddeutsche.de/kultur/deutsche-hegemonie-merkel-kohl-und-europa-1.1661456, accessed 5 June 2013.

Ganghof, S. (2004) *Wer regiert in der Steuerpolitik?*, Frankfurt/New York: Campus.

Garton Ash, T. (1994) 'Germany's Choice', *Foreign Affairs*, 73(4): 65–81.

Gast, H. (2008) 'Bundeskanzler und Parteiführer – zwei Rollen im Konflikt? Parteiendemokratie, Parteivorsitz und politische Führung', *Zeitschrift für Parlamentsfragen*, 39(1): 42–60.

Gast, H. (2011) *Der Bundeskanzler als politischer Führer: Potenziale und Probleme deutscher Regierungschefs aus interdisziplinärer Perspektive*, Wiesbaden: VS Verlag für Sozialwissenschaften.

Gates, R. (2011) 'The Security and Defense Agenda (Future of NATO)', Delivered by Secretary of Defense Robert M. Gates, Brussels, Belgium, 10 June, www.defense.gov/speeches/speech.aspx?speechid=1581.

Gibney, M. (2004) *The Ethics and Politics of Asylum*, Cambridge: Cambridge University Press.

Giegerich, B. (2006) *European Security and Strategic Culture*, Baden-Baden: Nomos.

Giegerich, B. (2010) 'Budget Crunch: Implications for Europe Defence', *Survival*, 52: 87–98.

Giugni, M. (1998) 'Was it "Worth the Effort"? The Outcomes and

Consequences of Social Movements', *Annual Review of Sociology*, 98: 371–93.

Glaab, M. (2007) 'Die Strategie der Politik. Das Fallbeispiel Deutschland', in T. Fischer et al. (eds), *Die Strategie der Politik. Ergebnisse einer vergleichenden Studie*, Gütersloh: Verlag Bertelsmann Stiftung: 67–115.

Glaab, M. (2010) 'Political Leadership in der Großen Koalition. Führungsressourcen und -stile von Bundeskanzlerin Merkel', in C. Egle and R. Zohlnhöfer (eds), *Die Große Koalition 2005–2009*, Wiesbaden: VS Verlag für Sozialwissenschaften: 121–53.

Goetz, K. H. (1996) 'Integration Policy in a Europeanized State: Germany and the Intergovernmental Conference', *Journal of European Public Policy*, 3: 23–44.

Goetz, K. H. (1997) 'Acquiring Political Craft: Training Grounds for Top Officials in the German Core Executive', *Public Administration*, 75(4): 753–75.

Goetz, K. H. (1999) 'Senior Officials in the German Federal Administration: Institutional Change and Positional Differentiation', in E. C. Page and V. Wright (eds), *Bureaucratic Elites in Western European States: A Comparative Analysis of Top Officials*, Oxford: Oxford University Press: 147–77.

Goetz, K. H. (2007) 'German Officials and the Federal Policy Process: The Decline of Sectional Leadership', in E. C. Page (ed.), *The Changing Role of the Civil Service in Comparative Perspective*, Basingstoke: Palgrave Macmillan: 164–88.

Goetz, K. H. (2011) 'The Development and Current Features of the German Civil Service', in F. M. v.d. Meer (ed.), *Civil Service Systems in Western Europe*, 2nd edn, Cheltenham: Edward Elgar: 37–65.

Goetz, K. H. (2014) 'A Question of Time: Responsive and Responsible Democratic Politics', *West European Politics*, 38(2).

Goldstein, J. and Keohane, R. O. (1993) 'Ideas and Foreign Policy: An Analytical Framework', in J. Goldstein and R. O. Keohane (eds), *Ideas and Foreign Policy: Beliefs, Institutions, and Political Change*, Ithaca and London: Cornell University Press: 3–30.

Gomis, B. (2011) 'Franco–British Defence and Security Treaties: Entente while it last?', Royal Institute for International Affairs/Chatham House, Programme Paper: ISP PP 2001/01, March.

Gordon, P. (2010a) 'The United States and Europe: An Agenda for Engagement', Remarks at the Centre for Transatlantic Relations, Paul H. Nitze School of Advanced International Studies, Johns Hopkins University, Washington, DC, 18 October.

Gordon, P. (2010b) 'The United States and Europe: A New Era of Engagement', The C. Douglas Dillon Lecturer on European–American Relations at Chatham House, London, UK, 10 November.

Grant, C. (2011) 'Europe needs a military avant-garde', Centre for European Reform Bulletin, April/May 2011 no.77, www.cer.org.uk.

Green, S. (2003) 'Towards an Open Society? Citizenship and Immigration', in S. Padgett, W. E. Paterson and G. Smith (eds), *Developments in German Politics 3*, Basingstoke: Palgrave Macmillan.

Green, S. (2004) *The Politics of Exclusion: Institutions and Immigration Policy in Contemporary Germany*, Manchester: Manchester University Press.

Green, S. (2012) 'Much Ado About Not-Very-Much? Assessing Ten Years of German Citizenship Reform', *Citizenship Studies*, 16(2): 173–88.

Green, S. (2013a) 'Germany: A Changing Country of Immigration', *German Politics*, 22(3): 333–51.

Green, S. (2013b) 'Societal Transformation and Programmatic Change in the CDU', *German Politics*, 22(1–2): 46–63.

Green, S. and Paterson, W. E. (2005a) 'Introduction: Semisovereignty Challenged', in S. Green and W. E. Paterson (eds), *Governance in Contemporary Germany: The Semisovereign State Revisited*, Cambridge: Cambridge University Press: 1–20.

Green, S. and Paterson, W. E. (eds) (2005b) *Governance in Contemporary Germany: The Semisovereign State Revisited*, Cambridge: Cambridge University Press.

Green, S., Hough, D. and Miskimmon, A. (2012) *The Politics of the New Germany*, 2nd edn, London: Routledge.

Gros, D. (2012) *How to Deal with Macroeconomic Imbalances?*, Brussels: Centre for European Policy Studies.

Gross, E. (2009) *The Europeanization of National Foreign Policy: Continuity and Change in European Crisis Management*, Basingstoke: Palgrave Macmillan.

Grube, N. (2004) 'Unverzichtbares Korrektiv oder Ineffective Reformbremse? Wahrnehmungen föderaler Strukturen und Institutionen in Deutschland', *Jahrbuch des Föderalismus* 2004, Baden-Baden: Nomos.

Grube, N. (2009) 'Nähe und Distanz: Föderale Einstellungen der Bevölkerung in 60 Jharen Bundesrepublik Deutschland', *Jahrbuch des Föderalismus* 2009, Baden-Baden: Nomos.

Gusy, C. (1997) *Die Weimarer Reichsverfassung*, Tübingen: Mohr Siebeck.

Gusy, C. (2011) *Parlamentarische Kontrolle der Nachrichtendienste im demokratischen Rechtsstaat*, Wiesbaden: VS Verlag für Sozialwissenschaften.

Habermas, J. (2013) Merkel's European Failure: Germany Dozes on a Volcano, http://www.spiegel.de/international/germany/Juergen-habermas-merkel-needs-to conf. accessed 21 February.

Hafterdom, H. (2006) *Coming of Age: German Foreign Policy since 1945*, Oxford: Rowman and Littlefield.

Hager, W. (1980) 'Germany as an Extraordinary Trader', in W. Kohl and G. Basevi (eds), *West Germany: A European and a Global Power*, Lexington, MA: Lexington Books: 3–43.

Hall, P. A. (2012) 'The Economics and Politics of the Euro Crisis', *German Politics*, 21: 355–71.

Hall, P. A. and Soskice, D. (2001) 'An Introduction to Varieties of Capitalism', in P. A. Hall and D. Soskice (eds), *Varieties of Capitalism: The Institutional Foundations of Comparative Advantage*, Oxford: Oxford University Press: 1–68.

Hall, P. A. and Thelen, K. (2009) 'Institutional Change in Varieties of Capitalism', *Socio-Economic Review*, 7: 7–34.

Hammerstein, K. von et al. (2012) 'Merkels Alptraum', *Der Spiegel*, 27 February: 20–2.

Hanau Santini, R. (2010) 'European Union discourses and practices on the Iranian nuclear program', *European Security*, 19(3): 467–89.

Hancké, B. (2012) 'Worlds apart? Labour Unions, Wages and Monetary Integration in Continental Europe', IHS Political Science Series, no. 128, February.

Handl, V. and Paterson, W. E. (2013) 'The Continuing Relevance of Germany's Engine For CEE and the EU', *Communist and Post Communist Studies*, 46: 327–37.

Handelsblatt (2013) 'Von der Leyen klammert sich an Rentenkonzept', *Handelsblatt*, 28 January, www.handelsblatt.com/politik/deutschland/trotz-widerstands-von-der-leyen-klammert-sich-an-rentenkonzept/7696390.html, accessed 16 August 2013.

Harcourt, W. V. (1863) 'A Letter on the Perils of Intervention', in W. Harcourt, *Letters of Historicus on Some Questions of International Law*, London: Macmillan.

Harmel, R. and Janda, K. (1994) 'An Integrated Theory of Party Goals and Party Change', *Journal of Theoretical Politics*, 6: 259–87.

Harnisch, S. (2001) 'Change and Continuity in Post-unification German Foreign Policy', *German Politics*, 10: 135–60.

Harnisch, S. (2007) 'Minilateral Cooperation and Transatlantic Coalition Building: The EU3–Iran Initiative', *European Security*, 16(1): 1–27.

Harnisch, S. (2010) 'Die Große Koalition in der Außen- und Sicherheitspolitik: die Selbstbehauptung der Vetospieler', in C. Egle and R. Zohlnhöfer (eds), *Die zweite Große Koalition*, Wiesbaden: VS Verlag für Sozialwissenschaften: 503–29.

Harnisch, S. and Schieder, S. (2006) 'Germany's New European Policy: Weaker, Leaner, Meaner', in H. W. Maull (ed.), *Germany's Uncertain Power: Foreign Policy of the Berlin Republic*, Basingstoke: Palgrave Macmillan.

Harnisch, S. and Wolf, R. (2010) 'Germany: the continuity of change', in E. Kirchner and J. Sperling (eds), *National Security Cultures: Patterns of Global Governance*, New York and London: Routledge.

Hartz Commission (2002) *Moderne Dienstleistungen am Arbeitsmarkt. Bericht der Kommission*, Berlin: Federal Government.

Hassel, A. (2006) *Wage Setting, Social Pacts and the Euro: A New Role for the State*, Amsterdam: Amsterdam University Press.

Hassel, A. (2012) 'The Paradox of Liberalization: Understanding dualism and the recovery of the German political economy', *British Journal of Industrial Relations*, 41: 707–26.

Hassel, A. (forthcoming) *Transformation der Deutschland AG: Analyse der 100 größten deutschen Unternehmen von 1986–2006*, research report written for the Hans–Böckler-Stiftung.

Hassel, A. and Lütz, S. (2010) 'Does the Financial Crisis Help to Overcome the Crisis of the State? (Durch die Krise aus der Krise. Die neue Stärke des Staates)', *Der Moderne Staat*, 2: 251–71.

Hassel, A. and Rehder, B. (2001) 'Institutional Change in the German Wage Bargaining System: The Role of Big Companies', MPIfG Working Paper 01/9, December, Cologne.

Hassel, A. and Schelkle, W. (2012) 'The Policy Consensus Ruling European Political Economy: The Political Attractions of Discredited Economics', *Global Policy*: 16–27.

Hassel, A. and Schiller, C. (2010) *Der Fall Hartz IV. Wie es zur Agenda 2010 kam und wie es weiter gehen wird*, Frankfurt: Campus Verlag.

Hassel, A. and Williamson, H. (2004) *The Evolution of the German Model: How to Judge Reforms in Europe's Largest Economy*, Anglo-German Foundation.

Hatch, M. T. (2010) 'The role of Renewable Energy in German Climate Change Policy', *Renewable Energy Law and Policy Review*, 45(2): 141–51.

Häusermann, S. (2010) *The Politics of Welfare State Reform in Continental Europe: Modernization in Hard Times*, Cambridge: Cambridge University Press.

Heinz, D. (2010) 'Federal Reform II in Germany', *Perspectives on Federalism*, 2(2).

Heisenberg, D. (2005) 'Taking a Second Look at Germany's Motivation to Establish Economic and Monetary Union: A Critique of "Economic Interests" Claims', *German Politics*, 14(1): 95–109.

Hellmann, G., Baumann, R. Bösche, M., Herborth, B. and Wagner, W. (2005) 'De-Europeanization by Default? Germany's EU Policy in Defence and Asylum', *Foreign Policy Analysis*, 1: 143–64.

Hellmann, G. (ed.) (2006) *Germany's EU Policy on Asylum and Defence: De-europeanization by Default?*, Basingstoke: Palgrave Macmillan.

Helm, D. (2007) *The New Energy Paradigm*, Oxford: Oxford University Press.

Helms, L. (2005a) *Presidents, Prime Ministers and Chancellors: Executive Leadership in Western Democracies*, Basingstoke: Palgrave Macmillan.

Helms, L. (2005b) *Regierungsorganisation und politische Führung in Deutschland*, Wiesbaden: VS Verlag für Sozialwissenschaften.

Helms, L. (2006) 'The Grand Coalition: Precedents and Prospects', *German Politics and Society*, 24(1): 47–66.

Helms, L. (2011) 'Angela Merkel and the Unfulfilled Promise of Chancellor Democracy', *Current History: A Journal of Contemporary World Affairs*, 110(1): 97–102.

Helms, L. (ed.) (2012) *Comparative Political Leadership*, Basingstoke: Palgrave Macmillan.

Helms, L. (2013) 'Regierungsführung und Regierungsorganisation', in K.-R. Korte and T. Grunden (eds), *Handbuch Regierungsforschung*, Wiesbaden: Springer VS Verlag für Sozialwissenschaften: 239–46.

Henderson, A. et al (eds) (2013) *Citizenship after the Nation-State. Regionalism, Nationalism and Public Attitudes in Europe*, London: Palgrave Macmillan.

Herbert, U. (2001) *Geschichte der Ausländerpolitik in Deutschland*, München: C.H. Beck.

Herweg, N. and Zohlnhöfer, R. (2010) 'Das Verhältnis von Markt und Staat unter der Großen Koalition: Entstaatlichung in der Ruhe und Verstaatlichung während des Sturms?', C. Egle and R. Zohlnhöfer (eds), *Die zweite Große Koalition. Eine Bilanz der Regierung Merkel, 2005–2009*, Wiesbaden: VS Verlag für Sozialwissenschaften: 254–78.

Hesse, K. (1962) *Der unitarische Bundesstaat*, Karlsruhe: Müller.

Hildebrandt, A. and Wolf, F. (eds) (2008) *Die Politik der Bundesländer: Staatstätigkeit im Vergleich*, Wiesbaden: VS Verlag für Sozialwissenschaften.

Hinich, M. J. and Munger, M. C. (1997) *Analytical Politics*, Cambridge: Cambridge University Press.

Hockerts, H. G. (2011) *Der deutsche Sozialstaat. Entfaltung und Gefährdung seit 1945*, Göttingen: Vandenhoeck & Ruprecht.

Holtmann, E. (2001) *Zwischen Wettbewerbs- und Verhandlungsdemokratie: Analysen zum Regierungssystem der Bundesrepublik Deutschland*, Wiesbaden: Westdeutscher Verlag.

de Hoop Scheffer, J. (2007) 'NATO and the EU: Time for a new chapter', keynote speech by the NATO Secretary-General, Berlin, 29 January, http://eu2007.de/en/News/Speeches_Interviews/January/0120AAESVPScheffer.html, accessed 14 January 2011.

Hough, D. (2011) 'Small but Perfectly Formed? The Rise and Rise of Germany's Smaller Parties', *German Politics*, 20(1): 186–99.

Hough, D. and Koß, M. (2009) 'Populism Personified or Reinvigorated Reformers? The German Left Party in 2009 and Beyond', *Politics and Society*, 27(2): 76–91.

Hough, D. and Jeffery, C. (2003) 'Landtagswahlen: Bundestestwahlen oder Regionalwahlen', *Zeitschrift für Parlamentsfragen*, 33(1): 49–66.

Hough, D., Koß, M. and Olsen, J. (2007) *The Left Party in Contemporary German Politics*, Basingstoke: Palgrave Macmillan.

Howard, M. (2008) 'The Causes and Consequences of Germany's New Citizenship Law', *German Politics*, 17(2): 41–62.

Hrbek, R. (1986) 'Doppelte Politikverflechtung: Deutscher Förderalismus und europäische Integration. Die deutschen Länder im EG-Entscheidungsprozess', in R. Hrbek and U. Thaysen (eds), *Die Deutschen Länder und die Europäischen Gemeinschaften*, Baden-Baden: Nomos.

Huber, E. and Stephens, J. D. (2001) *Development and Crisis of the Welfare State*, Chicago/London: Chicago University Press.

Hustedt, T. and Tiessen, J. (2006) *Central Government Coordination in Denmark, Germany and Sweden: An Institutional Policy Perspective*, Potsdam: Lehrstuhl für Politikwissenschaft, Verwaltung und Organisation.

Hutter, S. and Teune, S. (2012) 'Politik auf der Straße: Deutschland Protestprofil im Wandel', *Aus Politik und Zeitgeschichte*, 62(25–26), 18 June: 5–15.

Hyde-Price, A. (1996) '"Of Dragons and Snakes": Contemporary German Security Policy', in G. Smith, W. E. Paterson and S. Padgett (eds), *Developments in German Politics 2*, London: Macmillan: 173–91.

Inglehart, R. (1997) *Modernization and Postmoderization: Cultural, Economic, and Political Change in 43 Societies*, Princeton: Princeton University Press.

Irondelle, B. and Besancenot, S. (2010) 'France: a departure from exceptionalism?', in E. Kirchner and J. Sperling (eds), *National Security Cultures: Patterns of Global Governance*, London: Routledge.

Ismayr, W. (2008) 'Gesetzgebung im politischen System Deutschlands', in W. Ismayr (ed.), *Gesetzgebung in Westeuropa. EU-Staaten und Europäische Union*, Wiesbaden: VS Verlag für Sozialwissenschaften: 383–429.

Ismayr, W. (2012) *Der Deutsche Bundestag*, Wiesbaden: Springer VS Verlag für Sozialwissenschaften.

Iversen, T. and Soskice, D. (2009) 'Dualism and Political Coalitions', Annual Meeting of the American Political Science Association (Toronto).

Jacobs, A. D. (2012) 'EU Crisis Management in Berlin: The Fall of Ministerial Walls?', *West European Politics*, 35(3): 466–90.

Jalalzai, F. (2011) 'A Critical Departure for Women Executives or More of the Same? The Powers of Chancellor Merkel', *German Politics*, 20(3): 428–48.

Jeffery, C. (1996) 'Towards a "Third Level" in Europe? The German Länder in the European Union', *Political Studies*, 44(2): 253–66.

Jeffery, C. (2002) 'Uniformity and Diversity in Policy Provision: Insights From the US, Germany and Canada', in J. Adams and P. Robinson (eds), *Devolution in Practice: Public Policy Differences Within the UK*, London: PPR: 176–97.

Jeffery, C. (2008) 'Groundhog Day: The Non-Reform of German Federalism, Again', *German Politics*, 17(4): 587–92.

Jeffery, C. and Paterson, W. E. (2004) 'Germany and European Integration: A Shifting of Tectonic Plates', in W. Streeck and H. Kitschelt (eds), *Germany Beyond the Stable State*, London: Frank Cass: 59–78.

Johnson, N. (1983) *State and Government in the Federal Republic of Germany: The Executive at Work*, 2nd edn, Oxford: Pergamon Press.

Johnston, A. (2009) 'Labour Unions, Wage Restraint and European Monetary Union: The Rise of Sectoral Divergence', Paper for the PhD Conference, 'Emerging Research in Political Economy and Public Policy', European Institute, London School of Economics, London, 11 March.

Jones, B. (2011) 'Franco–British Defence Co-operation: A new engine for European Defence?', Occasional Paper No.88, European Union Institute for Security Studies, www.iss.europa.eu/uploads/media/op88—Franco-British_military_cooperation—a_new_engine_for_European_defence.pdf, accessed 1 September 2011.

Jones, B. D. and Baumgartner, F. R. (2012) 'From There to Here: Punctuated Equilibrium to the General Punctuation Thesis to a Theory of Government Information Processing', *Policy Studies Journal*, 40(1): 1–19.

Jones, E. (2010) 'Merkel's Folly', *Survival*, 52(3): 21–38.

Joppke, C. (1999) *Immigration and the Nation-State*, Oxford: Oxford University Press.

Joppke, C. (2009) *Veil: Mirror of Identity*, Cambridge: Polity Press.

Joppke, C. (2010) *Citizenship and Immigration*, Cambridge: Polity Press.

Jun, U. (2009) 'Organisationsreformen der Mitgliederparteien ohne durchschlagenden Erfolg: Die innerparteilichen Veränderungen von CDU und SPD seit den 1990er Jahren', in U. Jun et al. (eds), *Die Zukunft der Mitgliederpartei*, Opladen: Barbara Budrich: 187–210.

Jun, U. (2011) 'Volksparteien under Pressure: Challenges and Adaptation', *German Politics*, 20(1): 200–22.

Jun, U. and Höhne, B. (eds) (2010) *Parteien als fragmentierte Organisationen: Erfolgsbedingungen und Veränderungsprozesse*, Opladen: Barbara Budrich.

Jun, U., Haas, M. and Niedermayer, O. (eds) (2008) *Parteien und Parteiensysteme in den deutschen Ländern*, Wiesbaden: VS Verlag für Sozialwissenschaften.

Jun, U. et al., (eds) (2009) *Die Zukunft der Mitgliederpartei*, Opladen: Barbara Budrich.

Kaase, M. and Klingemann, H. -D. (1994) 'The cumbersome way to partisan orientations in a "new" democracy', in M. K. Jennings and T. Mann (eds), *Elections at Home and Abroad*, Ann Arbor: University of Michigan Press.

Kagan, R. (2003) *Paradise and Power: American and Europe in the New World Order*, London: Atlantic Books.

Kaiser, A. (2007) 'Ressortübergreifende Steuerung politischer Reformprogramme. Was kann die Bundesrepublik Deutschland von anderen parlamentarischen Demokratien lernen?', in Bertelsmann Stiftung (ed.), *'Jenseits des Ressortdenkens' – Reformüberlegungen zur Institutionalisierung strategischer Regierungsführung in Deutschland*, Gütersloh: Verlag Bertelsmann Stiftung: 5–55.

Kaiser, A. and Fischer, J. (2009) 'Linkages between Parliamentary and Ministerial Careers in Germany, 1949–2008: The Bundestag as Recruitment Pool', *German Politics*, 18(2): 140–54.

Kane, J. and Patapan, H. (2012) *The Democratic Leader: How Democracy Defines, Empowers, and Limits its Leaders*, Oxford: Oxford University Press.

Karapin, R. (2007) *Protest Politics in Germany: Movements on the Left and Right Since the 1960s*, Pennsylvania Park: The Pennsylvania State University Press.

Katz, R. S and Mair, P. (1993) 'The Evolution of Party Organizations in Europe: The Three Faces of Party Organization', *American Review of Politics*, 14: 593–617.

Katz, R. S. and Mair, P. (1995) 'Changing Models of Party Organization and Party Democracy: The Emergence of the Cartel Party', *Party Politics*, 1(1): 5–28.

Katz, R. S. and Mair, P. (2002) 'The Ascendancy of the Party in Public Office: Party Organizational Change in Twentieth-Century Democracies', in R Gunther et al. (eds), *Political Parties: Old Concepts and New Challenges*, Oxford: Oxford University Press: 113–35.

Katzenstein, P. (1987) *Politics and Policy in West Germany: The Growth of a Semisovereign State*, Philadelphia: Temple University Press.

Katzenstein, P. (1997) 'United Germany in an Integrating Europe', in P. Katzenstein (ed.), *Tamed Power: Germany in Europe*, Ithaca and London: Cornell University Press.

Kehr, E. (1927) 'Schlachtflottenbau und Parteipolitik 1890–14', dissertation, Berlin.

Kelek, N. (2005) *Die Fremde Braut. Ein Bericht aus dem Innern des türkischen Lebens in Deutschland*, Köln: Kiepenheuer & Witsch.

Kempf, U. and Merz, H.-G. (eds), (2001) *Kanzler und Minister: Biographisches Lexikon der deutschen Bundesregierungen*, Wiesbaden: VS Verlag für Sozialwissenschaften.

Kempf, U. and Merz, H.-G. (eds) (2008) *Kanzler und Minister 1998–2005: Biographisches Lexikon der deutschen Bundesregierungen*, Wiesbaden: VS Verlag für Sozialwissenschaften.

Kessler, F. (2013) *Mut Bürger. Die Kunst des neuen Demonstrierens*, München: Hanser Berlin.

Key, V. O. (1964) *Politics, Parties, and Pressure Groups*, 5th edn, New York: Crowell.

King, A. (1994) 'Chief Executives in Western Europe', in I. Budge and D. McKay (eds), *Developing Democracy: Comparative Research in Honour of J. F. P. Blondel*, London: Sage: 150–63.

King, A. (2002) 'The Outsider as Political Leader: The Case of Margaret Thatcher', *British Journal of Political Science*, 32(3): 435–54.

Kirbach, R. (2013) 'und raus bist du', *Die Zeit*, 8 August: 13–15.

Kirchheimer, O. (1966) 'The Transformation of West European Party Systems', in J. LaPalombara and M. Weiner (eds), *Political Parties and Political Development*, Princeton, NJ: Princeton University Press: 177–200.

Kirchner, E. and Sperling, J. (eds) (2010) *National Security Cultures: Patterns of Global Governance*, New York: Routledge.

Kitschelt, H. and Streeck, W. (2003) 'From Stability to Stagnation: Germany at the Beginning of the Twenty-First Century', *West European Politics*, 26(4): 1–34.

Klein, C. (2012) 'Climate Change Policies in Germany: Make Ambition Pay', OECD Economics Department Working Papers No. 982, Paris: OECD Publishing, http://dx.doi.org/10.1787/5k92sn0f8dbt_en, accessed 13 March 2013.

Klein, M., Jagodzinski, W., Ohr, D. and Mochmann, E. (eds), (2000) *50 Jahre empirische Wahlforschung in Deutschland*, Opladen: Westdeutscher Verlag.

Klein, M. and von Alemann, U. (2011) 'Warum brauchen Parteien Mitglieder?', in T. Spier et al. (eds), *Parteimitglieder in Deutschland*, Wiesbaden: Springer US: 19–30.

Klingemann, H.-D. and Kaase, M. (eds), (2001) *Wahlen und Wähler: Analysen aus Anlass der Bundestagswahl 1998*, Opladen: Westdeutscher Verlag.

Klusmeyer, D. and Papademetriou, D. (2009) *Immigration Policy in the Federal Republic of Germany: Negotiating Membership and Remaking the Nation*, Oxford: Berghahn.

Knodt, M. and Kohler-Koch, B. (eds) (2000) *Deutschland zwischen Europäisierung und Selbstbehauptung*, Frankfurt am Main: Campus.

Knutsen, O. (2006) *Class Voting in Western Europe: A Comparative Longitudinal Study*, Lanham, MD: Lexington.

Kolb, F. (2007) *Protest and Opportunities: The Political Outcomes of Social Movements*, Frankfurt: Campus.

König, T., Blume.T and Luig, B. (2003) 'Policy Change without Government Change? German Gridlock after the 2002 Elections', *German Politics*, 12(2): 86–146.

König, T. and Mäder, L. (2008) 'Das Regieren jenseits des Nationalstaates und der Mythos einer 80-Prozent-Europäisierung in Deutschland', *Politische Vierteljahresschrift*, 49(3): 438–63.

Kornelius, S. (2013a) *Angela Merkel: Die Kanzlerin und ihre Welt*, Hamburg: Hoffmann and Campe.

Kornelius, S. (2013b) *Angela Merkel: The Chancellor and her World*, Richmond: Alma Books.

Korpi, W. (1983) *The Democratic Class Struggle*, London: Routledge.

Korpi, W. (2006) 'Power Resources and Employer-Centered Approaches in Explanations of Welfare States and Varieties of Capitalism: Protagonists, Consenters, and Antagonists', *World Politics*, 58(2): 167–206.

Korte, K.-R. (2000) 'Solutions for the Decision Dilemma: Political Styles of Germany's Chancellors', *German Politics*, 9(1): 1–22.

Korte, K.-R. (2010) 'Präsidentielles Zaudern: Der Regierungsstil von Angela Merkel in der Großen Koalition 2005–2009', in S. Bukow and W. Seemann (eds), *Die Große Koalition*, Wiesbaden: VS Verlag für Sozialwissenschaften: 102–19.

Korte, K-R. and Fröhlich, M. (2009) *Politik und Regieren in Deutschland*, 3rd edn, Paderborn: Schöningh/UTB.

Korte, K.-R. and Grunden, T. (2013) *Handbuch Regierungsforschung*, Wiesbaden: Springer VS Verlag für Sozialwissenschaften.

Kraushaar, W. (2012) *Der Aufruhr der Ausgebildeten. Vom Arabischen Frühling zur Occupy-Bewegung*, Hamburg: Hamburger Edition.

Kriesi, H. et al. (1995) *New Social Movements in Western Europe: A Comparative Analysis*, Minneapolis: University of Minnesota Press.

Kropp, S. (2010a) 'German Parliamentary Party Groups in Europeanised Policymaking: Awakening from the Sleep? Institutions and Heuristics as MPs' Resources', *German Politics*, 19(2): 123–47.

Kropp, S. (2010b) 'The Ubiquity and Strategic Complexity of Grand Coalition in the German Federal System', *German Politics*, 19(3): 286–311.

Krotz, U. and Schild, J. (2013) *Shaping Europe: France, Germany and Embedded Bilateralism from the Elysée Treaty to Twenty-First Century Politics*, Oxford: Oxford University Press.

Kundnani, H. (2011) 'Germany as a Geo-Economic Power', *The Washington Quarterly*, 34(3): 31–45.

Kupchan, C. (2010) 'As Nationalism rises, will the European Union fail?', *The Washington Post*, 29 August.

Kurbjuweit, D. (2010) 'Der Wutbürger', *Der Spiegel*, no. 41, 11 October: 26–7.

Kurbjuweit, D. (2011) 'Ein unterzuckertes Land: Die politische Kommunikation Angela Merkels ist ein Desaster', *Der Spiegel*, 18 July: 24–5.

Laakso, M. and Taagepera, R. (1979) 'The "Effective" Number of Parties: A Measure with Application to West Europe', *Comparative Political Studies*, 12(1): 3–27.

Langenbacher, E. (ed.) (2007) *Launching the Grand Coalition: The 2005 Bundestag Election and the Future of German Politics*, Oxford, UK: Berghahn.

Langenbacher, E. (ed.) (2010) *Between Left and Right: The 2009 Bundestag Elections and the Transformation of the German Party System*, Brooklyn, NY: Berghahn.

Langer, A. I. (2010) 'The Politicization of Private Persona: Exceptional Leaders or the New Rule? The Case of the United Kingdom and the Blair Effect', *International Journal Press/Politics*, 15(1): 60–75.

Lauber, V. and Mez, L. (2006) 'Renewable Electricity Policy in Germany 1974–2005', *Bulletin of Science, Technology and Society*, 26(2): 105–20.

Layne, C. (1993) 'The Unipolar Illusion: Why New Great Will Rise', *International Security*, Spring.

Leaman, J. (2010) 'Germany Country Report', in Bertelsmann Stiftung (ed.), *Managing the Crisis: A Comparative Assessment of Economic Governance in 14 Economies*, Gütersloh: Bertelsmann Stiftung.

Lebow, R. (2003) *The Tragic Vision of Politics: Ethics, Interests and Order*, Cambridge: Cambridge University Press.

Lees, Charles (2005) *Party Politics in Germany: A Comparative Politics Approach*, Basingstoke: Palgrave Macmillan.

Lees, C. (2006) '"We Are All Comparativists Now": Why and How Single-Country Scholarship Must Adapt and Incorporate the Comparative Politics Approach', *Comparative Political Studies*, 39(9): 1084–108.

Lees, C. (2013) 'Christian Democracy is Dead: Long Live the Union Parties: Explaining CDU/CSU Dominance within the German Party System', *German Politics*, 22(1–2): 64–81.

Leggewie, C. (2011) *Mut statt Wut. Aufbruch in eine neue Demokratie*, Hamburg: Edition.

Le Gloannec, A.-M. (2001) 'Germany's power and the weakening of states in a globalised world: deconstructing a paradox', *German Politics*, 10(1): 117–34.

Legro, J. W. (2005) *Rethinking the World: Great Power Strategies and International Order*, Ithaca: Cornell University Press.

Lehmbruch, G. (1976) *Parteienwettbewerb im Bundesstaat*, Stuttgart: W. Kohlhammer.

Lehmbruch, G. (2007) *Sequences and Timing, Institutional Complementarities, and Hegemonic Discourse Coalitions: The Growth of*

Intergovernmental Federalism and Unitary Federalism in Germany, Konstanzer Online-Publikations, http://nbn-resolving.de/urn:nbn:de: bsz:352-176452.

Lehndorff, S. (2010) 'Before the Crisis, in the Crisis, and Beyond: The Upheaval of Collective Bargaining in Germany', Duisburg-Essen, mimeo.

Leibfried, S. and Tennstedt, F. (eds) (1985) *Politik der Armut und die Spaltung des Sozialstaats*, Frankfurt/Main: Suhrkamp.

Leisering, L. (2009) 'Germany: A Centrist Welfare State at the Crossroads', in P. Alcock and G. Craig (eds), *International Social Policy*, 2nd edn, Basingstoke: Palgrave Macmillan: 148 –70.

Leisering, L. (ed.) (2011) *The New Regulatory State: Regulating Pensions in Germany and the UK*, Basingstoke: Palgrave Macmillan.

Leunig, S. (2006) *Die Regierungssysteme der deutschen Länder im Vergleich*, Opladen: Verlag Barbara Budrich.

Leonard, M. (2014), The Revenge of the German Elite', at http://blogs. reuters.com/mark-leonard/2014/02/04/the -revenge of the German elite, accessed 18 February 2014.

Lewis, J. (1992) 'Gender and the Development of Welfare Regimes', *Journal of European Social Policy*, 2(3): 159–73.

LIS (2013) *LIS Key Figures*, 13 June, www.lisdatacenter.org/data-access/key-figures/download-key-figures/, accessed 29 August.

Lösche, P. (2005) 'Politische Führung und Parteivorsitzende. Einige systematische Überlegungen', in D. Forkmann and M. Schlieben (eds), *Die Parteivorsitzenden in der Bundesrepublik Deutschland 1945–2005*, Wiesbaden, US: 349–68.

Ludlow, P. (2010) 'In the last resort: The European Council and the euro crisis, Spring 2010', Eurocomment Briefing Note, 7:7/8.

Lütjen, T. and Walter, F. (2000) 'Die präsidiale Kanzlerschaft', *Blätter für deutsche und internationale Politik*, 45(11): 1309–13.

Mair, P. (2008) 'The Challenge to Party Government', *West European Politics*, 31(1–2): 211–34.

Mair, P. and van Biezen, I. (2001) 'Party Membership in Twenty European Democracies, 1980–2000', *Party Politics*, 7: 15–21.

Manow, P. (2005) 'Die politische Kontrolle der Ministerialbürokratie des Bundes: Die Bedeutung der Landesebene', in S. Ganghof and P. Manow (eds), *Mechanismen der Politik – Strategische Interaktionen im deutschen Regierungssystem*, Frankfurt a.M.: Campus: 245–75.

Manow, P. and Burkhart, S. (2007) 'Legislative Self-Restraint under Divided Government in Germany, 1976–2002', *Legislative Studies Quarterly*, XXXII(2): 167–91.

Markovits, A. S. (ed.) (1982) *The Political Economy of West Germany: Modell Deutschland*, New York: Praeger.

Marschallek, C. (2004) 'Die "schlichte" Notwendigkeit privater Altersvorsorge', *Zeitschrift für Soziologie*, 33(4): 285–302.

Marsh, D. (1992) *The Bundesbank: The Bank that Rules Europe*, London: Heinemann.

Marsh, D. (2011) *The Euro. The Battle for the New Global Currency*, New Haven: Yale University Press.

Marsh, D. (2013) *Europe's Deadlock: How the Euro Crisis Could be Solved – and Why It Won't Happen*, New Haven and London: Yale University Press.

Marshall, B. (1992) 'German Migration Policies', in G. Smith, W. Paterson, P. Merkl and S. Padgett (eds), *Developments in German Politics*, Basingstoke: Macmillan.

Martin, L. W. and Vanberg, G. (2011) *Parliaments and Coalitions: The Role of Legislative Institutions in Multiparty Governance*, Oxford/New York: Oxford University Press.

Maull, H. W. (1992) 'Zivilmacht Bundesrepublik Deutschland. Vierzehn Thesen für eine neue deutsche Außenpolitik', *Europa-Archiv*, 47(1): 269–78.

Maull, H. W. (ed.) (2006) *Germany's Uncertain Power: Foreign Policy of the Berlin Republic*, Basingstoke: Palgrave Macmillan.

Mayhew, A., Oppermann, K. and Hough, D. (2011) 'German Foreign Policy and Leadership of the EU: "You can't always get what you want ... but you sometimes get what you need"', Working Paper No. 119, Sussex European Institute, Sussex, UK.

Mayntz, R. (1980) 'Executive Leadership in Germany: Dispersion of Power or "Kanzlerdemokratie"?', in R. Rose and E. N. Suleiman (eds), *Presidents and Prime Ministers*, Washington, DC: American Enterprise Institute: 139–70.

Mayntz, R. and Derlien, H.-U. (1989) 'Party Patronage and Politicization of the West German Administrative Elite 1970–1987: Toward Hybridization?', *Governance*, 2(3): 384–404.

Mayntz, R. and Scharpf, F. W. (1975) *Policy-Making in the German Federal Bureaucracy*, Amsterdam: Elsevier.

Mearsheimer, J. J. (1990) 'Back to the Future: Instability in Europe After the Cold War', *International Security*, 15(4): 5–56.

Mediendienst Integration (2013) 'Vielfalt im Bundestag: Mehr Abgeordnete mit Migrationshintergrund', 15 October, http://mediendienst-integration.de/artikel/mehr-abgeordnete-mit-migrationshintergrund.html, accessed 21 October 2013.

Menon, A. (2011) 'European Defence Policy from Lisbon to Libya', *Survival*, 53(3): 75–90.

Menz, G. (2008) *The Political Economy of Managed Migration: Nonstate Actors, Europeanization, and the Politics of Designing Migration Policies*, Oxford: Oxford University Press.

Menz, G. (2011) 'Stopping, Shaping and Moulding Europe: Two-Level Games, Non-state Actors and the Europeanization of Migration Policies', *Journal of Common Market Studies*, 49(2): 437–62.

Merkel, A. (2010) Government Statement: Protecting the Euro to Preserve the European Vision (http://www.bundesregierung.de/Content/DE/Bulletin/2010/05/55-1-bk-bt.html).

Merkel, W. (2003) 'Institutionen und Reformpolitik: Drei Fallstudien zur Vetospieler-Theorie', in C. Egle et al. (eds), *Das rot-grüne Projekt. Eine Bilanz der Regierung Schröder 1998–2002*, Wiesbaden: Westdeutscher Verlag: 163–90.

Messina, A. (2007) *The Logics and Politics of Post-WWII Migration to Western Europe*, Cambridge: Cambridge University Press.

Miller, B. (2011) *Der Koalitionsausschuss: Existenz, Einsatz und Effekte einer informellen Arena des Koalitionsmanagements*, Baden-Baden: Nomos.

Miller, B. and Müller, W. C. (2010) 'Managing Grand Coalitions: Germany 2005–09', *German Politics*, 19(3): 332–52.

Ministry of Foreign Affairs and Defence Ministry (2011) Confidential research interviews with author at Chancellery, Berlin, July.

Mintzel, A. and Oberreuter, H. (1992*) Parteien in der Bundesrepublik Deutschland*, 2nd edn, Bonn: Bundeszentrale für Politische Bildung.

Miskimmon, A. (2007) *Germany and the Common Foreign and Security Policy of the European Union*, Basingstoke: Palgrave.

Miskimmon, A. (2009a) 'A Crisis of Influence: German Foreign Policy since 1998', in A. Miskimmon, W. E. Paterson and J. Sloam (eds), *The Gathering Crisis: Germany under the Grand Coalition*, Basingstoke: Palgrave Macmillan.

Miskimmon, A. (2009b) 'Falling into line? Kosovo and the course of German foreign policy', *International Affairs*, 85(3): 561–73.

Miskimmon, A. (2012) 'German Foreign Policy and the Libya Crisis', *German Politics*, 21(4): 392–410.

Miskimmon, A. and Paterson, W. E. (2003) 'Foreign and Security Policy: On the Cusp Between Transformation and Accommodation', in K. Dyson and K. Goetz (eds), *Germany, Europe and the Politics of Constraint*, Oxford: Oxford University Press.

Miskimmon, A., Paterson, W. E. and Sloam, J. (eds) (2009) *Germany's Gathering Crisis: The 2005 Federal Election and the Grand Coalition*, Basingstoke: Palgrave Macmillan.

Molina, O. and Rhodes, M. (2007) 'The Political Economy of Adjustment in Mixed Market Economies: A Study of Spain and Italy', in B. Hancké et al. (eds), *Beyond Varieties of Capitalism: Conflict, Contradictions, and Complementarities in the European Economy*, New York: Oxford University Press: 223–53.

Möller, J. (2010) 'The German labor market response in the world recession: de-mystifying a miracle', *Zeitschrift für Arbeitsmarktforschung*, 42(4): 325–36.

Mölling, C. and Brune, S.-C. (2011) *The Impact of the Financial Crisis on European Defence*, European Parliament, Directorate-General for External Policies, Policy Department, Document EXPO/B/SEDE/FWC/2009-01/LOT6/11.

Moog, S. and Raffelhüschen, B. (2011) 'Ehrbarer Staat? Eine Zwischenbilanz schwarz-gelber Regierungspolitik', *Zeitschrift für Staats- und Europawissenschaft*, 9(2): 244–61.

Moore, C. and Eppler, A. (2008) 'Disentangling Double *Politikverflechtung*? The Implications of the Federal Reforms for Bund-Länder Relations on Europe', *German Politics*, 17(4): 488–508.

Moore, C. and Jacoby, W. (eds) (2010) *German Federalism in Transition: Reforms in a Consensual State*, Abingdon: Routledge.

Moore, C., Jacoby, W. and Gunlicks, A. B. (2008) 'German Federalism in Transition?', *German Politics*, 17(4): 393–407.

Mosca, L. et al. (2009) 'Communicating the European Social Forum', in D. della Porta (ed.), *Another Europe: Conceptions and Practices of Democracy in the European Social Forums*, London/New York: Routledge: 46–64.

Müller, H. (2006) 'Germany and the proliferation of weapons of mass destruction', in H. W. Maull (ed.), *Germany's Uncertain Power: Foreign Policy of the Berlin Republic*, Basingstoke: Palgrave: 49–65.

Müller, K. and Walter, F. (2004) *Graue Eminenzen der Macht: Küchenkabinette in der deutschen Kanzlerdemokratie*, Wiesbaden: VS Verlag für Sozialwissenschaften.

Müller-Rommel, F. (1997) 'Federal Republic of Germany: A System of Chancellor Government', in J. Blondel and F. Müller-Rommel (eds), *Cabinets in Western Europe*, London: Macmillan: 171–91.

Murswieck, A. (2009) 'Angela Merkel als Regierungschefin und Kanzlerkandidatin', *Aus Politik- und Zeitgeschichte*, 51: 26–32.

Musch, E. (2012) 'Consultation Structures in German Immigrant Integration Politics: The National Integration Summit and the German Islam Conference', *German Politics*, 21(1): 73–90.

Myles, J. and Pierson, P. (2001) 'The Comparative Political Economy of Pension Reform', in P. Pierson (ed.), *The New Politics of the Welfare State*, Oxford: Oxford University Press.

Neidhardt, F. and Rucht, D. (1993) 'Auf dem Weg in die "Bewegungsgesellschaft"? Über die Stabilisierbarkeit sozialer Bewegungen', *Soziale Welt*, 44(3): 305–26.

Nelles, R. and Wittrock, P. (2012) 'Merkels Bürgerinitiative: Die Ersatzpräsidentin', www.spiegel.de/politik/deutschland/merkels-buergeroffensive-die-ersatzpraesidentin-a-809558.html, accessed 19 July.

Neukirch, R. (2012) 'Draußen vor der Tür', *Der Spiegel*, 30 April: 42–4.

Nicholls, A. J. (2000) *Freedom with Responsibility: The Social Market Economy in Germany, 1918–1963*, Oxford: Clarendon Press.

Niclauss, K.-H. (1988) *Kanzlerdemokratie. Bonner Regierungspraxis von Konrad Adenauer bis Helmut Kohl*, Stuttgart: Kohlhammer.

Niclauss, K. (1999) 'Bestätigung der Kanzlerdemokratie? Kanzler und Regierungen zwischen Verfassung und politischen Konventionen', *Aus Politik und Zeitgeschichte*, 20: 27–38.

Niclauss, K. (2001) 'The Federal Government: Variations of Chancellor Dominance', in L. Helms (ed.), *Institutions and Institutional Change in the Federal Republic of Germany*, Basingstoke: Palgrave Macmillan: 65–83.

Niclauss, K. (2004) *Kanzlerdemokratie: Regierungsführung von Konrad Adenauer bis Gerhard Schröder*, 2nd edn, Paderborn: Schöningh.

Niclauss, K. (2008) 'Kiesinger und Merkel in der Großen Koalition', *Aus Politik und Zeitgeschichte*, 16: 3–10.

Niclauss, K. (2011) 'SPD-Fraktion und Reformpolitik: Wie viel Mitsteuerung war möglich bei der Vorbereitung der Agenda 2010?', *Zeitschrift für Parlamentsfragen*, 42(1): 166–85.

Niedermayer, O. (2012a) 'Parteimitgliedschaften im Jahre 2011', *Zeitschrift für Parlamentsfragen*, 43(2): 389–407.

Niedermayer, O. (2012b) *Die Piratenpartei*, Wiesbaden: Springer VS Verlag für Sozialwissenschaften.

Niedermayer, O. (2013a) 'Die Entwicklung des bundesdeutschen Parteiensystems', in F. Decker and V. Neu (eds), *Handbuch der deutschen Parteien*, Wiesbaden: Springer VS Verlag für Sozialwissenschaften: 111–32.

Niedermayer, O. (2013b) 'Parteimitglieder in Deutschland: Version 2013', Arbeitshefte aus dem Otto-Stammer-Zentrum, Nr. 20, Berlin: Freie Universität Berlin.

Norpoth, H. (1983) 'The Making of a More Partisan Electorate', *British Journal of Political Science*, 14: 53–71.

Oberhofer, J. and Sturm, R. (eds) (2010) *Koalitionsregierungen in den Ländern und Parteienwettbewerb*, München: Allitera.

Oberhofer, J., Stehlin, J. and Sturm, R. (2011) 'Citizenship im unitarischen Bundesstaat', *Politische Vierteljahresschrift*, 52(2): 163–94.

OECD (2011) 'Pension model indicators', version March 2011, www.oecd.org/els/public-pensions/oecdpensionsindicators.htm.

OECD (2012a) *OECD Economic Surveys: Germany 2012*, Paris: OECD.

OECD (2012b) OECD.statExtracts. *Income Distribution and Poverty* http://stats.oecd.org/Index.aspx?DatasetCode=POVERTY, accessed 30 November 2012.

OECD (2013), http://stats.oecd.org/index.aspx?queryid=46022, accessed 16 August 2013.

OECD (various years) *Employment Outlook*, Paris: OECD.

Ohmke-Reinicke, A. (2012) *Das große Unbehagen. Die Protestbewegung gegen 'Stuttgart 21': Aufbruch zu neuem bürgerlichen Selbstbewusstsein?*, Stuttgart: Schmetterling Verlag.

Ohr, D. (2000) 'Wird das Wählerverhalten zunehmend personalisierter, oder ist dede Wahl anders?', in M. Klein, W. Jagodzinski, D. Ohr and E. Mochmann (eds), *50 Jahre empirische Walhforschung in Deutschland*, Opladen: Westdeutscher Verlag.

Olsen, J. (2007) 'The Merger of the PDS and WASG: From Eastern regional party to national radical left party?', *German Politics*, 16(2): 205–21.

Olsen, J. (2011) 'Leadership in Grand Coalitions: Comparing Angela Merkel and Kurt Georg Kiesinger', *German Politics*, 20(3): 342–59.

Osborne, D. (1988) *Laboratories of Democracy*, Boston: Harvard Business School Press.

Oschmann, V. (2010) 'A Success Story: The German Renewable Energy Act Turns Ten', *Renewable Energy Law and Policy Review*, 45(1): 45–61.

Padgett, S. (ed.) (1993) *Adenauer to Kohl: The Development of the German Chancellorship*, London: Hurst.

Padgett, S., Paterson, W. E. and Smith, G. (2003) 'Introduction', in S. Padgett, W. E. Paterson and G. Smith (eds), *Developments in German Politics 3*, Basingstoke: Palgrave Macmillan: 1–16.

Palier, B. and Thelen, K. (2010) 'Institutionalizing Dualism:

Complementarities and Change in France and Germany', *Politics & Society*, 38(1): 119–48.

Palmowski, J. (2008) 'In search of the German nation: citizenship and the challenge of integration', *Citizenship Studies*, 12(6): 547–63.

Panebianco, A. (1988) *Political Parties: Organization and Power*, Cambridge: Cambridge University Press.

Pappi, F. U. (1984) 'The West German Party System', *West European Politics*, 7(4): 7–26.

Paris, R. (1989) 'Situative Bewegung. Moderne Protestmentalität und politisches Engagement', *Leviathan*, 17(3): 322–36.

Paterson, W. E. (1974) *The SPD and European Integration*, Lexington: Saxon House.

Paterson, W. E. (1994) 'The Chancellor and Foreign Policy', in S. Padgett (ed.), *Adenauer to Kohl: The Development of the German Chancellorship*, London: Hurst: 127–56.

Paterson, W. E. (2005) 'European Policy Making: Between Associated Sovereignty and Semi Sovereignty', in S. Green and W. E. Paterson (eds), *Governance in Contemporary Germany: The Semi Sovereign State Revisited*, Cambridge: Cambridge University Press: 261–82.

Paterson, W. E. (2008) 'Did France and Germany Lead Europe? A Retrospect', in Jack Hayward (ed.), *Leaderless Europe*, Oxford: Oxford University Press: 89–110.

Paterson, W. E. (2010) 'Does Germany Still Have a European Vocation?', *German Politics*, 19(1): 41–52.

Paterson, W. E. (2011) 'The Reluctant Hegemon? Germany Moves Centre Stage in the European Union', *JCMS: Journal of Common Market Studies*, 49(s1): 57–75.

Patton, D. F. (2013) 'The Left Party at Six: The PDS–WASG Merger in Comparative Perspective', *German Politics*, 22(3): 219–34.

PBL Netherlands Environmental Assessment Agency/Joint Research Centre European Commission (2012) *Trends in Global CO_2 Emissions: 2012 Report*, www.pbl.nl/en/publications, accessed 10 February 2013.

Pedersen, T. (2002) 'Cooperative hegemony: Power, ideas and institutions in regional integration', *Review of International Studies*, 28: 677–96.

Pehle, H. (1998) *Das Bundesministerium für Umwelt, Naturschutz und Reaktorsicherheit: Ausgegrenzt statt integriert?*, Wiesbaden: Deutscher Universitäts-Verlag.

Pergande, F. (2009) 'Auf die Finanzkraft schauen, nicht auf die Schulden', *Frankfurter Allgemeine Zeitung*, 6 March 2009.

Phinnemore, D. (2013) *The Treaty of Lisbon: Origins and Negotiations*, Basingstoke: Palgrave.

Poguntke, T. (2009) 'The German Core Executive: Ever More Power to the Chancellor?', paper prepared for delivery at the American Political Science Annual Meeting, Toronto, Canada, September 2–5.

Poguntke, T. and Webb, P. (eds) (2005a) *The Presidentialization of Politics: A Comparative Study of Modern Democracies*, Oxford: Oxford University Press.

Poguntke, T. and Webb, P. (2005b) 'The Presidentialization of Politics in Democratic Societies: A Framework for Analysis', in T. Poguntke and P. Webb (eds), *The Presidentialization of Politics: A Comparative Study of Modern Democracies*, Oxford: Oxford University Press: 1–25.

Pressel, H. (2012) *Der Gesundheitsfonds. Entstehung – Einführung – Weiterentwicklung – Folgen*, Wiesbaden: Springer VS Verlag für Sozialwissenschaften.

Prime Minister's Office (2010) 'UK–French Summit 2010: Declaration on Security and Defence Co-operation', 2 November, www.number10. gov.uk/news/uk–france-summit-2010-declaration-on-defence-and-security-co-operation/, accessed 1 September 2011.

Proissl, W. (2010) *Why Germany Fell out of Love with Europe*, Brussels: Bruegel.

Proksch, S.-O. and Slapin, J. B. (2006) 'Institutions and Coalition Formation: The German Election of 2005', *West European Politics*, 29(3): 540–59.

Rath, C. (2013) *Der Schiedsrichterstaat: Die Macht des Bundesverfassungsgerichts*, Berlin: Wagenbach.

Reisenbichler, A. and Morgan, K. J. (2012) 'From "Sick Man" to "Miracle": Explaining the Robustness of the German Labor Market During and After the Financial Crisis 2008–09', *Politics & Society*, 40(4): 549–79.

Renzsch, W. (2010) 'Kontinuitäten und Diskontinuitäten in Entscheidungsprozessen über föderale Finanzbeziehungen oder: Die ewig Unvollendete', *Perspektiven der Wirtschaftspolitik*, 11(3): 288–306.

Reutter, W. (2008) *Föderalismus, Parlamentarismus und Demokratie*, Opladen: Leske & Budrich.

Ridley, F. F. (1966) 'Chancellor Democracy as a Political Principle', *Parliamentary Affairs*, 11(4): 446–62.

Ristau, M. (2005) 'Der ökonomische Charme der Familie', *Aus Politik und Zeitgeschichte*, 23(4): 16–23.

Ritter, G. A. (2007) *Der Preis der deutschen Einheit: Die Wiedervereinigung und die Krise des Sozialstaats*, 2nd edn, Munich: C.H. Beck.

Rodden, J. (2006) 'Fiscal Discipline in Federations: Germany and the EMU', in P. Wierts et al. (eds), *Fiscal Policy Surveillance in Europe*, Basingstoke: Palgrave Macmillan: 137–60.

Rohrschneider, R. (ed.) (2012) 'Germany's Federal Election, September 2009', Symposium in *Electoral Studies*, 31.

Römer, B., Reichhart, P., Kranz, J. and Picot, A. (2012) 'The role of smart metering and decentralized electricity storage for smart grids: The importance of positive externalities', *Energy Policy*, 50: 486–95.

Rose, R. and McAllister, I. (1989) *When Voters Begin to Choose*, Beverly Hills: Sage Publications.

Roßteutscher, S. and Scherer, P. (2012) 'Links und rechts im politischen Raum eine vergleichende Analyse der ideologischen Entwicklung in Ost- und West-deutschland', in B. Wessels, H. Schoen and O. Gabriel (eds), *Wahlen und Wähler. Analysen aus Anlass der Bundestagswahl 2009*, Wiesbaden: VS Verlag für Sozialwissenschaften.

Rosumek, L. (2007) *Die Kanzler und die Medien: Acht Porträts von Adenauer bis Merkel*, Frankfurt and New York: Campus.

Roth, R. (2011) *Bürgermacht. Eine Streitschrift für mehr Partizipation*, Hamburg: Körber-Stiftung.

Roth, R. and Rucht, D. (eds) (2008) *Soziale Bewegungen in Deutschland seit 1949. Ein Handbuch*, Frankfurt: Campus.

Rowe, C. and Turner, E. (2013) 'Party Servants, Ideologues or Regional Representatives? The German Länder and the Reform of Federalism', in *West European Politics*, 36(2): 382–404.

Rüb, F. W. (2011) 'Regieren, Regierungszentrale und Regierungsstile. Konzeptionelle Überlegungen zum Regierungsprozess in einer sich beschleunigenden Welt', in S. Bröchler and J. Blumenthal (eds), *Regierungskanzleien im politischen Prozess*, Wiesbaden: VS Verlag für Sozialwissenschaften: 69–101.

Rucht, D. (ed.) (2001) *Protest in der Bundesrepublik. Strukturen und Entwicklungen*, Frankfurt: Campus.

Rucht, D. (2011) 'Social Forums as Public Stage and Infrastructure of Global Justice Movements', in J. Smith, S. Byrd, E. Reese and E. Smythe (eds), *Handbook on World Social Forum Activism*, Boulder/London: Paradigm: 11–28.

Rucht, D. (2013) 'Aufstieg und Fall der Occupy-Bewegung', in K. Sonntag (ed.), *E-Protest. Neue soziale Bewegungen und Revolutionen*, Heidelberg: Universitätsverlag: 111–35.

Rucht, D. and Teune, S. (eds) (2008) *Nur Clowns und Chaoten? Die G8-Proteste in Heiligendamm im Spiegel der Massenmedien*, Frankfurt: Campus.

Rüdig, W. (2003) 'The Environment and Nuclear Power', in S. Padgettet, W. E. Paterson and G. Smith (eds), *Developments in German Politics 3*, Basingstoke and New York: Palgrave Macmillan: 248–68.

Rudolf, R., Bischoff, R. and Leiderer, E. (2011) *Protest - Bewegung - Umbruch. Von der Stellvertreter- zur Beteiligungsdemokratie*, Hamburg: VSA.

Rudzio, W. (2005) *Informelles Regieren. Zum Koalitionsmanagement in deutschen und österreichischen Regierungen*, Wiesbaden: VS Verlag für Sozialwissenschaften.

Rummel, R. (1996) 'Germany's Role in the CFSP: "Normalität" or "Sonderweg"', in C. Hill (ed.), *The Actors in Europe's Foreign Policy*, London: Routledge.

Saalfeld, T (1997) 'Up and Down with the Extreme Right in Germany, 1949–96', *Politics*, 17(1): 1–8.

Saalfeld, T. (2003a) 'Germany: Multiple Veto Points, Informal Co-ordination, and Problems of Hidden Action', in K. Strøm et al. (eds), *Delegation and Accountability in Parliamentary Democracies*, Oxford: Oxford University Press: 347–75.

Saalfeld, T. (2003b) 'Germany: Stable Parties, Chancellor Democracy, and the Art of Informal Settlement', in W. C. Müller and K. Strøm (eds), *Coalition Governments in Western Europe*, Oxford: Oxford University Press: 33–85.

Saalfeld, T. (2005a) 'Germany: Stability and Strategy in a Mixed-Member

Proportional System', in M. Gallagher and P. Mitchell (eds), *The Politics of Electoral Systems*, Oxford: Oxford University Press: 209–28.

Saalfeld, T. (2005b) 'Political Parties', in S. Green and W. E. Paterson (eds), *Governance in Contemporary Germany: The Semisovereign State Revisited*, Cambridge: Cambridge University Press: 46–77.

Saalfeld, T. (2009) 'The German Party System Since 1998: Cooperation and Competition under Growing Uncertainty', in A. Miskimmon et al. (eds), *Germany's Gathering Crisis: The 2005 Federal Election and the Grand Coalition*, Basingstoke: Palgrave Macmillan: 80–105.

Saalfeld, T. (2010) 'Coalition Governance under Chancellor Merkel's Grand Coalition: A Comparison of the Cabinets Merkel I and Merkel II', *German Politics and Society*, 28(3): 82–102.

Saalfeld, T. (2013) 'Economic Performance, Political Institutions and Cabinet Durability in 28 European Parliamentary Democracies, 1945–2011', in W. C. Müller and H.-M. Narud (eds), *Party Governance and Party Democracy*, New York: Springer: 51–79.

Saalfeld, T. and Zohlnhöfer, R. (eds) (forthcoming) *Politik im Schatten der Krise. Eine Bilanz der Regierung Merkel 2009–2013*, Wiesbaden: Springer VS Verlag für Sozialwissenschaften.

Sandholtz, W. (1993) 'Choosing union. Monetary politics and Maastricht', *International Organization*, 47(1): 1–39.

Sarrazin, T. (2010) *Deutschland schafft sich ab*, München: Deutsche Verlags-Anstalt.

Sartori, G. (1976) *Parties and Party Systems: A Framework for Analysis*, Cambridge: Cambridge University Press.

Scharpf, F. W. (1988) 'The Joint-Decision Trap: Lessons from German Federalism and European Integration', *Public Administration*, 66(3): 239–78.

Scharpf, F. W. (2005) 'No Exit from the Joint Decision Trap? Can German Federalism Reform Itself?', EUI Working Paper Series, RSCAS No. 2005/24.

Scharpf, F. W. (2007) 'Nicht genutzte Chancen der Föderalismusreform', in C. Egle and R. Zohlnhöfer (eds), *Ende des rot-grünen Projektes. Eine Bilanz der Regierung Schröder 2002–2005*, Wiesbaden: Verlag für Sozialwissenschaften.

Scharpf, F. W. (2008) 'Community, Diversity and Autonomy: The Challenges of Reforming German Federalism', *German Politics*, 17(4): 509–21.

Scharpf, F. W. (2009) *Föderalismusreform. Kein Ausweg aus der Politikverflechtungsfalle*, Frankfurt am Main: Campus Verlag.

Scharpf, F. W. (2011) 'Monetary Union, Fiscal Crisis and the Preemption of Democracy', MPIfG Discussion Paper 11/11, www.mpifg.de/pu/mpifg_dp/dp11-11.pdf.

Scharpf, F.W. et al. (1976) *Politikverflechtung. Theorie und empirie des kooperativen föderalismus in der Bundesrepublik*, Kronberg: Scriptor.

Schild, J. (2012) 'Leadership in Hard Times: Germany, France, and the Management of the Eurozone Crisis', *German Politics and Society*, 31(1): 24–47.

Schleich, J. et al. (2001) 'Greenhouse Gas Reductions in Germany – Lucky Strike or Hard Work?', *Climate Policy*, 1: 363–80.

Schmähl, W. (2007) 'Dismantling an Earnings-Related Social Pension Scheme: Germany's New Pension Policy', *Journal of Social Policy*, 36(2): 319–40.

Schmidt, M. G. (1996) 'Germany: The Grand Coalition State', in J. M. Colomer (ed.), *Political Institutions in Europe*, London/New York: Routledge: 62–98.

Schmidt, M. G. (2008) 'Germany: The Grand Coalition State', in J. M. Colomer (ed.), *Comparative European Politics*, 3rd edn, London: Routledge: 58–93.

Schmidt, M. G. (2010) 'Die Sozialpolitik der zweiten Großen Koalition (2005 bis 2009)', in C. Egle and R. Zohlnhöfer (eds), *Die zweite Große Koalition. Eine Bilanz der Regierung Merkel, 2005–2009*, Wiesbaden: VS Verlag für Sozialwissenschaften: 302–26.

Schmidt, S., Hellmann, G. and Wolf, R. (eds) (2006) *Handbuch zur deutschen Aussenpolitik*, Wiesbaden: VS Verlag für Sozialwissenschaften.

Schmitt-Beck, R. (ed.) (2012) 'Wählen in Deutschland', Special issue of *Politische Vierteljahresschrift*, 45.

Schneider, H.-P. (2012) 'Die Föderalismusreform I auf dem Prüfstand: Ein Zwischenbericht über Teilbereiche ihrer Umsetzung', in Europäisches Zentrum für Föderalismus-Forschung Tübingen (eds), *Jahrbuch des Föderalismus*: 222–33.

Schoen. H. (2000) 'Stimmensplitting bei Bundestagswahlen: Ein Spiegelbild des Verhältnisses zwischen Bürgern und Parteien?', in M. Klein, W. Jagodzinski, D. Ohr and E. Hochmann, *50 Jahre empirische Washforschung in Deutschland*, Opladen: Westdeutscher Verlag.

Schoen, H. (2004) 'Wechselwähler in den USA, Großbritannien und der Bundesrepublik Deutschland: Politische versiert oder ignorant?', *Zeitschrift für Parlamentsfragen*, 34: 99–101.

Schröder, G. (2014) Klare Worte: Im Gespraech mit Georg Meck über Mut, Macht und unsere Zukunft, Freiburg: Herder Verlag.

Schüttemeyer, S. S. (1998) *Fraktionen im deutschen Bundestag 1949–1997. Empirische Befunde und theoretische Folgerungen*, Opladen: Leske + Budrich.

Schwarz, H.-P. (1994) *Die Zentralmacht Europas: Deutschlands Rueckkehr auf die Weltbuehne*, Berlin: Siedler Verlag.

Schwegmann, Christoph (ed.) (2011) *Bewährungsproben einer Nation: die Entsendung der Bundeswehr ins Ausland*, Berlin: Dunker & Humblot.

Seeleib-Kaiser, M. (2001) *Globalisierung und Sozialpolitik*, Frankfurt: Campus.

Seeleib-Kaiser, M. (2010) 'Socio-Economic Change, Party Competition and Intra-Party Conflict: The Family Policy of the Grand Coalition', *German Politics*, 19(3–4): 416–28.

Seeleib-Kaiser, M. and Fleckenstein, T. (2007) 'Discourse, learning and welfare state change: the case of German labour market reforms', *Social Policy & Administration*, 41(5): 427–48.

Seeleib-Kaiser, M., Saunders, A. and Naczyk, M. (2011) 'Social Protection Dualism, De-industrialization and Cost Containment', in D. Brady (ed.), *Comparing European Workers. Part B: Policies and Institutions. Research in the Sociology of Work, Vol. 22*, Bingley: Emerald: 83–118.

Seeleib-Kaiser, M. Saunders, A. and Naczyk, M. (2012) 'Shifting the Public–Private Mix: A New Dualization of Welfare?', in P. Emmenegger, S. Haüsermann, B. Palier and M. Seeleib-Kaizer (eds), *The Age of Dualization*, New York: Oxford University Press: 151–75.

Selmer, P. (2009) 'Folgen der neuen Abweichungsgesetzgebung der Länder – Abschied vom Leitbild "gleichwertige Lebensverhältnisse"?', in R. Baus et al. (eds), *Der deutsche Föderalismus 2020*, Baden-Baden: Nomos.

Shonfield, A. (1965) *Modern Capitalism: The Changing Balance of Public and Private Power*, London and Toronto: Oxford University Press.

Siefken, S. T. (2007) *Expertenkommissionen im politischen Prozess. Eine Bilanz der rot-grünen Bundesregierung 1998–2005*, Wiesbaden: VS Verlag für Sozialwissenschaften.

Sikorski, R. (2011) 'I fear Germany's power less than her inactivity', *Financial Times*, 28 November, avaailable at http//www.ft.com/cms/s/0/b753cb42-19b3-11e1-ba5d-00144feabdc0.hml//axzz2t0dy7mac, accessed 11 February 2014.

Simon, L. (2010) 'International change, national grand strategy and the future of European power: Britain, France, Germany and the evolution of the European Union common security and defence policy and NATO (2001–2009)', unpublished PhD thesis, Royal Holloway, University of London.

Sinn, H.-W. (2003) *Ist Deutschland noch zu retten?*, München: Econ.

Slapin, J. B. and Proksch, S.O. (2008) 'A Scaling Model for Estimating Time-Series Party Positions from Texts', *American Journal of Political Science*, 52(3): 705–22.

Smith, G. (1989) 'Political Leadership', in G. Smith, W. E. Paterson and P. Merkl (eds), *Developments in West German Politics*, London: Macmillan: 60–76.

Smith, G. (1991) 'The Resources of a German Chancellor', *West European Politics* 14(2): 48–61.

Smith, G. (1992) 'The "New" Party System', in G. Smith et al. (eds), *Developments in German Politics*, London: Macmillan: 77–102.

Smith, G. (1996) 'The Party System at the Crossroads', in G. Smith et al. (eds), *Developments in German Politics 2*, London: Macmillan: 55–75.

Smith, G. (2003) 'The "New Model" Party System', in S. Padgett et al. (eds), *Developments in German Politics 3*, Basingstoke: Palgrave Macmillan: 82–100.

SPD (2011) 'Den Wert der Arbeit und die Lebensqualität im Alter erhöhen', Parteitagsbeschluss, http://www.spd.de/linkableblob/21858/data/beschluss_arbeit_alterssicherung_kurz.pdf, accessed 16 August 2013.

SPD (2013) *Das Wir entscheidet. Das Regierungsprogramm 2013–2017*, Berlin: SPD-Parteivorstand.

Sperling, J. (2010) 'Gulliver's Travail: Crafting a New Transatlantic

Bargain', in S. Bulmer, C. Jeffery and S. Padgett (eds), *Rethinking Germany and Europe: Democracy and Diplomacy in a Semi-Sovereign State*, Basingstoke: Palgrave Macmillan: 171–87.

Spiegel Online (2010) 'Controversy of Afghanistan Remarks: German President Horst Köhler resigns', www.spiegel.de/international/germany/controversy-over-afghanistan-remarks-german-president-horst-koehler-resigns-a-697785.html.

Spiegel Online (2012) 'Germany Rethinks Path to Green Future', 29 August, www.spiegel.de/, accessed 11 February 2013.

Spiegel Online (2013) Angela's Agenda: A Grand Controversial Plan for Europe http;//www.spigel.de/international/germany/merkel-wants to - reform –eu –with –more –powers, accessed 21 February 2014.

Statistisches Bundesamt (2009) *Bevölkerung Deutschlands bis 2060. 12. koordinierte Bevölkerungsvorausberechnung*, Wiesbaden: *Statistisches Bundesamt*.

Statistisches Bundesamt (2013) *Bevölkerung und Erwerbstätigkeit: Einbürgerungen* (Wiesbaden: *Statistisches Bundesamt*), available via:https://www.destatis.de/DE/Publikationen/Thematisch/Bevoelkerung/MigrationIntegration/Einbuergerungen.html, accessed 8 December 2013.

Steinbrück, P. (2010) 'The Global Economy "Still Has Deep-Seated Structural Problems"', *Der Spiegel*, 14 September, www.spiegel.de/international/germany/former-german-finance-minister-peer-steinbrueck-the-global-economy-still-has-deep-seated-structural-problems-a-717248.html.

Steltemeier, R. (2009) 'On the Way Back into Government? The Free Democratic Party Gearing Up for the 2009 Elections', *Politics and Society*, 27(2): 63–75.

Stiller, S. (2010) *Ideational Leadership in German Welfare State Reform*, Amsterdam: Amsterdam University Press.

Streeck, W. (1991) 'On the Institutional Conditions of Diversified Quality Production', in E. Matzner and W. Streeck (eds), *Beyond Keynesianism: The Socio-Economics of Production and Employment*, London: Edward Elgar: 21–61.

Streeck, W. (1995) *German Capitalism: Does It Exist? Can It Survive?*, Berlin: Max-Planck-Institut für Gesellschaftsforschung Köln.

Streeck, W. (2003) 'No Longer the Century of Corporatism. Das Ende des "Bündnisses für Arbeit"', MPIfG Working Paper 03/4, Köln: MPIfG.

Streeck, W. (2009a) *Re-Forming Capitalism: Institutional Change in the German Political Economy*, Oxford: Oxford University Press.

Streeck, W. (2009b) 'Endgame? The Fiscal Crisis of the German State', in A. Miskimmon et al. (eds), *Germany's Gathering Crisis: The 2005 Federal Election and the Grand Coalition*, Basingstoke: Palgrave Macmillan: 38–63.

Streeck, W. and Hassel, A. (2003), The Crumbling Pillars of Social Partnership', in H. Kitschelt and W. Streeck (eds), *Germany Beyond the Stable State*, London: Frank Cass, 101–24.

Sturm, R. (2012) 'Eine Renaissance der Kanzlerdemokratie? Die Zwischenbilanz der Politik der christlich-liberalen Koalition', in E. Jesse and R. Sturm (eds), *'Superwahljahr' 2011 und die Folgen*, Baden-Baden: Nomos: 257–82.

Sturm, R. and Pehle, H. (2007) 'Das Bundeskanzleramt als strategische Machtzentrale', in Bertelsmann Stiftung (ed.), *'Jenseits des Ressortdenkens' – Reformüberlegungen zur Institutionalisierung strategischer Regierungsführung in Deutschland*, Gütersloh: Verlag Bertelsmann Stiftung: 56–106.

Stuermer, M. and Neal, M. (1996) 'Les conséquences de 1989, les objectifs de la politique allemande', *Politique Etrangère*, 61(3): 513–19

SVR (Sachverständigenrat zur Begutachtung der gesamtwirtschaftlichen Entwicklung) (2007) *Das Erreichte nicht verspielen. Jahresgutachten 2007/08*, Wiesbaden.

SVR (Sachverständigenrat zur Begutachtung der gesamtwirtschaftlichen Entwicklung) (2008) *Jahresgutachten 2008/09*, Deutscher Bundestag Drucksache 16/10985.

SVR (Sachverständigenrat zur Begutachtung der gesamtwirtschaftlichen Entwicklung) (2011) Verantwortung für Europe wahrnehmen. Wiesbaden: Statistisches Bundesamt (Jahresgutachten/ Sachverständigenrat zur Begutachtung der Gesamtwirtschaftlichen Entwicklung, [48].2011/12); online at http://www.sachverstaendigenratwirtschaft.de/fileadmin/ dateiablage/an2011/a11_ges.pdf.

Szabo, S. (2004) *Parting Ways: The Crisis in German-American Relations*, Washington, DC: Brookings Institution.

Tagesspiegel (2013) 'Von der Leyen: Mindestlohn nach der Bundestagswahl', *Tagesspiegel*, 12 May, www.tagesspiegel.de/politik/bundesarbeitsminis-terin-von-der-leyen-mindestlohn-nach-der-bundestagswahl/8192416. html, accessed 16 August 2013.

Thelen, K. (2002) 'How Institutions Evolve: Insights from Comparative-Historical Analysis', in J. Mahoney and D. Rueschemeyer (eds), *Comparative Historical Analysis in the Social Sciences*, New York: Cambridge University Press.

Thelen, K. (2004) *How Institutions Evolve: The Political Economy of Skills in Germany, Britain, the United States and Japan*, Cambridge: Cambridge University Press.

Tils, R. (2011) 'Strategisches Zentrum und Regierungszentrale im Kontext von Party-Government. Strategische Regierungssteuerung am Beispiel der Agenda 2010', in S. Bröchler and J. Blumenthal (eds), *Regierungskanzleien im politischen Prozess*, Wiesbaden: VS Verlag für Sozialwissenschaften: 103–31.

TNS Infratest Sozialforschung (2008) *Situation und Entwicklung der betrieblichen Altersversorgung in Privatwirtschaft und öffentlichem Dienst 2001 – 2007*, Untersuchung im Auftrag des Bundesministeriums für Arbeit und Soziales, Endbericht, München.

TNS Infratest Sozialforschung (2012) *Situation und Entwicklung der betrieblichen Altersversorgung in Privatwirtschaft und öffentlichem*

Dienst (BAV 2011), Untersuchung im Auftrag des Bundesministeriums für Arbeit und Soziales, Endbericht, München.

Toje, A. (2010) 'The European Union as a Small Power', *Journal of Common Market Studies*, 49(1): 43–60.

Töller, A. E. (2008) 'Mythen und Methoden. Zur Messung der Europäisierung der Gesetzgebung des Deutschen Bundestages jenseits des 80-Prozent-Mythos', *Zeitschrift für Parlamentsfragen*, 39(1): 3–17.

Tsebelis, G. (2002) *Veto Players: How Political Institutions Work*, Princeton: Princeton University Press.

Turner, E. (2011) *Political Parties and Public Policy in the German Länder: When Parties Matter*, Basingstoke, Palgrave Macmillan.

Turner, E. (2013) 'The CDU and Party Organisational Change', *German Politics*, 22(1–2): 114–33.

Umweltbundesamt (2010) *Environmentally Harmful Subsidies in Germany*, Dessau-Rosslau: UBA, www.umweltdaten.de/publikationen/fpdf-l/3896.pdf, accessed 23 April 2013.

van Ackeren, M. (2011) 'Keiler und Koch', www.focus.de/politik/deutschland/tid-24083/politik-keiler-und-koch_aid_672967.html, accessed 17 June.

van Esch, F. (2012) 'Why Germany wanted EMU: The Role of Helmut Kohl's Belief System and the Fall of the Berlin Wall', *German Politics*, 21(1): 34–42.

van Rompuy, H. (2010) 'Transatlantic responses to Global Insecurity', Dinner Remarks at the Brussels Forum of the German Marshall Fund, Brussels, 26 March.

Verdun, A. (2010) 'Ten years EMU: an assessment of ten critical claims', *International Journal of Economics and Business Research*, 2(1/2): 144–63.

Visser, J. (2013) *Data Base on Institutional Characteristics of Trade Unions, Wage Setting, State Intervention and Social Pacts, 1960–2011* (ICTWSS), Amsterdam Institute for Advanced Labour Studies (AIAS), University of Amsterdam.

von Bredow, W. (2006) *Die Aussenpolitik der Bundesrepublik Deutschland: Eine Einführung*, Wiesbaden: VS Verlag für Sozialwissenschaften.

von Bredow, W. (2011) 'Germany in Afghanistan: The Pitfalls of Peace-Building in National and International Perspective', *Res Militaris*, 2(1), www.resmilitaris.net/ressources/10161/21/1.pdf.

von Weizsäcker Kommission der Bundeswehr (2000) 'Gemeinsame Sicherheit und Zukunft der Bundeswehr', www.spdfraktion.de/rs_datei/0,,1663,00.pdf, accessed 4 September 2011.

Völkl, K. et al. (eds) (2008) *Wähler und Landtagswahlen in der Bundesrepublik Deutschland*, Baden-Baden: Nomos.

Wagnsson, Charlotte (2010) 'Divided power Europe: normative divergences among the EU "big three"', *Journal of European Public Policy*, 17(8): 1089–105.

Walgrave, S. and Rucht, D. (eds) (2010) *The World Says No to War: Demonstrations against the War on Iraq*, Minneapolis: University of Minnesota Press.

Walt, S. (2010) 'Is NATO irrelevant', Blog Post, *Foreign Affairs*, 24 September, http://walt.foreignpolicy.com/posts/2010/09/24/is_nato_irrelevant.

Walter, F., Marg, S., Geiges, L. and Butzloff, F. (eds) (2013) *Die neue Bürgermacht. Was motiviert die Protestbewegungen?*, Reinbek bei Hamburg: Rowohlt.

Wattenberg, M. (1996) *The Decline of American Political Parties*, 4th edn, Cambridge: Harvard University Press.

Webber, D. (2013) 'How likely is it that the European Union will disintegrate? A critical analysis of competing theoretical perspectives', *European Journal of International Relations*, available online.

Wehling, H.-G. (2006) 'Landespolitik und Länderpolitik im föderalistischen System Deutschlands', in H. Schneider and H.-G. Wehling (eds), *Landespolitik in Deutschland. Grundlagen – Strukturen – Arbeitsfelder*, Wiesbaden: Verlag für Sozialwissenschaften: 7–21.

Weidenfeld, W. (2010) 'Nationalstaat versus Europäische Integration', in M. Glaab, W. Weidenfeld and M. Weigl (eds, *Deutsche Kontraste: 1990–2010*, Frankfurt/New York: Campus Verlag: 171–205.

Weidmann, J. (2012) Rebalancing Europe. Speech given at Chatham House, 26 March 2012 (http://www.chathamhouse.org/sites/default/files/public/Meetings/Meeting%20Transcripts/280312weidmann.pdf).

Weidner, H. and Eberlein, B. (2009) 'Still Walking the Talk? German Climate Change Policy and Performance', in B. Eberlein and B. Doern (eds), *Governing the Energy Challenge: Germany and Canada in Multi-level, Regional and Global Context*, Toronto: University of Toronto Press: 314–43.

Weidner, H. and Metz, L. (2008) 'German Climate Change Policy: a Success Story with Some Flaws', *Journal of Environment and Development*, 17: 356–78.

Welsh, H. A. (2012) 'Party Formation and Dilemmas of Opportunity Structure: Freie Wähler in the German Political System', *Politics and Society*, 30(4): 1–22.

Wessels, B. (2009) 'Re-Mobilisierung, Floating oder Abwanderung? Wechselwähler 2002 und 2005 im Vergleich', in F. Brettschneider, O. Niedermayer and B. Wessels (eds), *Die Bundestagswahl 2005: Analysen des Wahlkampfes und der Wahlergebnisse*, Wiesbaden: Verlag für Sozialwissenschaften.

Wessels, B., Schoen, H. and Gabriel, O. (eds) (2013) *Wahlen und Wähler. Analysen aus Anlass der Bundestagswahl 2009*, Wiesbaden: VS Verlag für Sozialwissenschaften.

Wessels, W. (2000) *Die Öffnung des Staates*, Opladen: Leske & Budrich.

Westerwelle, G. (2010) 'Speech to the German Council on Foreign Relations', 21 October, www.auswaertiges-amt.de/DE/Infoservice/Presse/Reden/2010/101021-BM-dgap-grundsatzrede.html, accessed 4 August 2011.

Westphal, K. (2008) 'Germany and the EU-Russia Energy Dialogue', in P. Aalto (ed.), *The EU-Russia Energy Dialogue: Europe's Future Energy Security*, Aldershot and Burlington, VT: Ashgate: 93–118.

Wettestad, J. (2011) 'EU Emissions Trading: Achievements and Challenges', in V. L. Birchfield and J. S. Duffield (eds), *Towards a Common European Union Energy Policy: Problems, Progress and Prospects*, Basingstoke and New York: Palgrave Macmillan: 87–112.

Wheare, K. (1953) *Federal Government*, 3rd edn, Oxford: Oxford University Press.

Wiliarty, S. E. (2008) 'Angela Merkel's Path to Power: The Role of Internal Party Dynamics and Leadership', *German Politics*, 17(1): 81–96.

Wintermann, O., Petersen, T. and Scheller, H. (2008) 'Prospects for a Reform of German Fiscal Federalism: Differences Between Public Opinion and the Political Debate', *German Politics*, 17(4).

Wirtschaftswoche (2013) *Ausländische Investoren dominieren im Dax*, 10 May.

Wolf, M. (2013) 'How Austerity Has Failed', *The New York Review of Books*, 60(12): 20–1.

World Bank (1994) *Averting the Old-Age Crisis*, New York: Oxford University Press.

Yamamura, K. and Streeck, W. (eds) (2001) *The Origins of Nonliberal Capitalism: Germany and Japan in Comparison*, Ithaca, NY: Cornell University Press.

Yoder, J. A. (2011) 'An Intersectional Approach to Angela Merkel's Foreign Policy', *German Politics*, 20(3): 360–75.

Zahariadis, N. (2013) 'National Fiscal Profligacy and European Institutional Adolescence: The Greek Trigger to Europe's Sovereign Debt Crisis', *Government and Opposition*, 48(1): 33–54.

Ziblatt, D. (2002) 'Recasting German Federalism? The New Politics of Fiscal Decentralization in Post-Unification Germany', *Politische Vierteljahresschrift*, 43(4): 624–52.

Ziesing, H.-J. (2009) 'EU Emissions Trading', in B. Eberlein and B. Doern (eds), *Governing the Energy Challenge: Germany and Canada in Multilevel, Regional and Global Context*, Toronto: University of Toronto Press: 344–72.

Zohlnhöfer, R. (2004) 'Destination anywhere? The German Red–Green Government's Inconclusive Search for a Third Way in Economic Policy', *German Politics*, 13(1): 106–31.

Zohlnhöfer, R. (2008) 'An End to the Reform Logjam? The Reform of German Federalism and Economic Policy-Making', *German Politics*, 17(4): 457–69.

Zohlnhöfer, R. (2009) *Globalisierung der Wirtschaft und finanzpolitische Anpassungsreaktionen in Westeuropa*, Baden-Baden: Nomos.

Zohlnhöfer, R. (2010) 'New Possibilities or Permanent Gridlock? The Policies and Politics of the Grand Coalition', in S. Bolgherini and F. Grotz (eds), *Germany after the Grand Coalition 2005–2009: Governance and Politics in a Turbulent Environment*, New York: Palgrave Macmillan: 15–30.

Zohlnhöfer, R. (2011) 'Between a Rock and a Hard Place: The German Response to the Economic Crisis', *German Politics*, 20(2): 227–42.

Zohlnhöfer, R. (forthcoming) 'Eine zu spät gekommene Koalition? Die Bilanz der wirtschafts- und sozialpolitischen Reformtätigkeit der zweiten Regierung Merkel', in E. Jesse and R. Sturm (eds), *Bilanz der Bundestagswahl 2013 – Voraussetzungen, Ergebnisse, Folgen*, Baden-Baden: Nomos.

Zohlnhöfer, R. and Egle, C. (2007) 'Einleitung: Der Episode zweiter Teil – ein Überblick über die 15. Legislaturperiode', in C. Egle and R. Zohlnhöfer (eds), *Ende des rot-grünen Projektes. Eine Bilanz der Regierung Schröder 2002–2005*, Wiesbaden: VS Verlag für Sozialwissenschaften: 11–25.

Zolleis, U. and Bartz, J. (2010) 'Die CDU in der Großen Koalition – Unbestimmt erfolgreich', in C. Egle and R. Zohlnhöfer (eds), *Die zweite Große Koalition. Eine Bilanz der Regierung Merkel, 2005–2009*, Wiesbaden: VS Verlag für Sozialwissenschaften: 51–68.

Zolleis, U. and Wertheimer, C. (2013) 'Is the CSU still a Volkspartei?', *German Politics*, 22(1–2): 97–113.

Index